ALTERNATIVE PARADIGMS

The Impact of Islamic and Western *Weltanschauungs* on Political Theory

Ahmet Davutoglu

UNIVERSITY
PRESS OF
AMERICA

Lanham • New York • London

D1381690

Library of Congress Cataloging-in-Publication Data
Davutoglu, Ahmet.
Alternative paradigms : the impact of Islamic and Western
Weltanschauungs on political theory / Ahmet Davutoglu.
p.   cm.
Research "in conjunction with the writing of . . . Ph. D. dissertation at
Bogazici University, Istanbul . . . in 1990"—Acknowledgements.
Includes bibliographical references and index.
1. Islam and state.   2. Political science—Philosophy.   3. Islam—
Doctrines.   I. Title.
JC49.D37   1993   320.5'5—dc20   92–46275 CIP

ISBN 0–8191–9046–2 (cloth : alk. paper)
ISBN 0–8191–9047–0 (pbk. : alk. paper)
ISBN: 978-0-8191-9047-5

DEDICATION

To my father.

ACKNOWLEDGEMENTS

Research for this book was completed in two stages. The major portion occurred in conjunction with the writing of my Ph.D. dissertation at Bogazici University, Istanbul, which was completed in 1990. I am particularly grateful to my academic advisor, Prof. Serif Mardin, and to Prof. Ilkay Sunar, Prof. Binnaz Toprak, Prof. Ustun Erguder and Prof. Metin Heper for their encouragement throughout the process. Further research was conducted as a member of the Department of Political Science at International Islamic University, Malaysia. I owe a special debt of gratitude to the former head of the department, Prof. F. Abdalla Botchway and to Prof. Robert Manley of Seton Hall University for their assistance in getting the book published.

While I would like to thank all of the many friends who assisted me in countless ways to bring this project to completion, two deserve special mention. Throughout the book, I have attempted to employ a consistent scheme of transliteration for Arabic terms. This would have been impossible without the meticulous work of Prof. Mehmet Maksutoglu in perusing the entire manuscript. I also thank Faruq abd ul-Rafi (R. A. Nelson) for his excellent editorial work and for preparing the final manuscript for publication. Of course, I take responsibility for any errors that may remain.

Finally, I wish to record my most sincere gratitude to my family, who have been a constant source of support and understanding as I struggled to complete this project. I appreciate their many sacrifices more than I will ever be fully able to express.

TRANSLITERATION
OF ARABIC CHARACTERS

'	ء	d̲	ض
b	ب	t̤	ط
t	ت	z̤	ظ
th	ث	'a	ع
j	ج	gh	غ
ḥ	ح	f	ف
kh	خ	q	ق
d	د	k	ك
dh	ذ	l	ل
r	ر	m	م
z	ز	n	ن
s	س	h	ه
sh	ش	w	و
s̤	ص	y	ى

CONTENTS

ALTERNATIVE PARADIGMS

CHAPTER 1

INTRODUCTION

Focus of the problem

Many scholars and politicians were convinced that the existing Western style of life, thought, and political institutions could easily be adapted to Muslim societies by bringing them into line with Islamic belief systems and rules. But after some experiences they were surprised when they saw that even those intellectuals who had Western academic training remained deeply attached to Islamic belief system, doctrine, civilization, history, and culture. Therefore, a spate of books appeared in the 1980s on Islamic revivalism.[1] In many of these books, there is a feeling of grief related to the rise of these movements. The wide-spread prejudice that Islamic revivalism might become an international threat, originated from such a feeling, is the basic cause of the lack of originality, comprehensiveness, and objectivity of much of the research on Islam. Thus, Islamic studies became merely a subject of international politics in the 1980s. It should be noted that pragmatic political centers provoked this tendency among academic circles in order to benefit from this phenomenon. The pragmatic questions of how these movements affect the internal political structures of Muslim societies and of which consequences might come from these changes related to international politics became the core points of many of these research works. Hence, they produced prejudicial denominations, categorizations, and oversimplifications, which prevented a comprehensive analysis of the internal dynamics of Islamic civilization.

The categorizations of Islamic responses to Western civilizational challenge might become a methodological barrier to an understanding of the real origins of this phenomenon. Therefore, the categorizations of these responses—such as fundamentalist Islam, non-fundamentalist Islam, radical Islam, traditional Islam, and secular Islam—might lead to subjectivist generalizations (e.g., Pipe, 1983:340-41). The terms "fundamentalist" or "radical," used by orientalists to isolate from the ordinary Muslim population those groups that aim to establish an Islamic way of life with an all-inclusive socio-political system, can not explain the increasing Islamic response to Western ways of thought and life. The obscurity of these terms conceals the comprehensive character of the problem by omitting the roots of the conflicting issues.

---

[1]Esposito's editions *Islam and Development* (1980) and *Voice of Resurgent Islam* (1983), E. Mortimer's *Faith and Power* (1982), D. Pipe's *In the Path of God: Islam and Political Power* (1983), M. Ruthven's *Islam in the World* (1984), E. Sivan's *Radical Islam* (1985), and R. Dekmejian's *Islam in Revolution: Fundamentalism in the Arab World* (1985), W.M.Watt's *Islamic Fundamentalism and Modernity* (1988) might be mentioned among many others. A spate of books on the Iranian revolution should be added to this list.

Furthermore, the fact that these responses began to be spread among the most industrialized and modernized Muslim masses proves that sociological and economic analyses related to theories of modernization are also not sufficient to understand and evaluate this response. Today, nobody can claim that, after a certain stage of industrialization and modernization, Muslim masses as a whole will adopt Western styles of thought and life, due to the reality that it is more than a problem of stage. This response should be seen from the perspective of the reality that Islam is conceived as an alternative *Weltanschauung* to the Western philosophico-political tradition, rather than from the perspective of the "ideological intransigence of Islam *vis-a-vis* the Western world today" (Crone & Hinds, 1986:110), because Muslims might equally well accuse the West of "ideological intransigence."

On the other hand, some oversimplified explanations for the Islamic revival have lost their value because of the increasing Islamic revival in spite of the decline of the factors on which the explanations are based. Pipe's (1983:331) claim that Islamic revival is a temporary fact based on the oil boom is an interesting example of these arguments: "To the extent that the Islamic revival is based on the oil boom, it is a mirage. Legalist and autonomist impulses strengthened and proliferated during the 1970s in large part because some activist Muslim regimes had huge amounts of discretionary revenues and others were able to exploit oil's disruptive effects to agitate for power; but neither of these can endure for long." His analogy between Muslims in the modern age and the Jews after the destruction of the Temple in 586 B.C. is another interesting but not-descriptive interpretation related to the Islamic revival: "The legalist impulse in general and fundamentalism in particular present great difficulties to Muslims trying to modernize, but the Islamicite legacy presents no less of an impediment. Muslims need to confront the assumption of success in worldly affairs, then must try to eliminate it. The destruction of the Temple in 586 B.C. created a dilemma which parallels that of the Muslim today; what Ezekiel and second Isaiah did to disengage faith from mundane matters must be imitated by Muslims, for God's will is inscrutable to humans and misfortune may serve His intent. Islamicite expectations of nearly fourteen centuries cannot be undone instantly, but progress in this direction is essential if the *ummah* is to modernize" (1983:335). It seems that the developments in the Muslim World do not confirm Pipe's assumptions. Rather, the wide-spread Islamic revival verifies Voll's (1982:347) argument that Islamdom at the beginning of its fifteenth century (which started in November 1980) is "in the midst of major transformations in all dimensions of its experience" and "that the Islamic revival has altered the *ummah* by providing it with new temptations and new opportunities."

The aim of this book is to develop a comparative analysis between Western and Islamic political theories and images from the perspective of their philosophical and theoretical background. The fundamental argument of the book is that the conflicts and contrasts between Islamic and Western political thought originate mainly from their philosophical, methodological, and theoretical background rather than from mere institutional and historical differences. In fact, historical and institutional differences are counterparts of these philosophico-political bases and images. The questions of how and through which processes these alternative conceptions of the world affect political ideas via a set of axiological presuppositions are the crux of the book.

The interconnection between all-embracing Islamic jurisprudence (*fiqh*) and Islamic political thought related to such problems as qualifications for political rule, political institutionalization, etc., has been deeply examined. But the relationship between '*aqâ'id*, as the origin of the doctrinal antecedents, and *fiqh*, as the origin of the axiological normativeness and of the political formal structuralism, has not been considered to such a great extent. This book will concentrate more on the intellectual and doctrinal mechanisms of Muslim consciousness than on practical applications or institutional adaptations of the rules of Islamic jurisprudence.

The same method will be used for the subjects of Western political tradition. The intellectual and theoretical link between philosophical and political images will be explored through an analysis of the impact of philosophical leanings on political theories. The process of political institutionalization will be examined as the actualization of philosophical images rather than as mere historico-political fact.

Thus, the direction of the interconnected impact of Western philosophy and theology on Western political theories, together with its theoretical links, will be compared with the transcendental supremacy of the Islamic doctrinal science, '*aqâ'id*, over political thought through an all-inclusive jurisprudential scheme, *fiqh*. My focus will not be the comparison of the prescriptivist characteristics and their consequences but the sources and essences of their prescriptivism within the context of the alternative axiological presuppositions. Why their axiological presuppositions differ and how this difference effects political theories are the fundamental questions of the book. The essential relationship between normativism and prescriptivism which shapes an interesting link between axiology and politics will be discussed to specify the axiologico-political differences of these two alternative *Weltanschauungs*.

Problem of nomenclature and conceptual framework

At the center of any comparative study between Islam and Western civilization, we face a problem of nomenclature. Becker's (1916:s) argument that "Das Islamproblem wird meist als religiöses Problem gewertet, doch ist der Islam nicht nur eine Religion, sondern eine Zivilisation und ein Staatsgedanke. Ursprünglich eine semitische Religion auf Christlich-jüdischer Basis, ist der Islam als Weltanschauung im weitesten Sinne des Wortes der Erbe des Christlichen Hellenismus geworden" is a very interesting example for this problem of nomenclature. He tries to define Islam within the semantic context of the Western conceptual framework. For example *Religion* as a critical concept in this sentence does not correspond to *dîn* —which is the literal translation of religion—and its characteristics within the semantic links in the Qur'ân, since Allâh says in the Qur'ân: "This day have I perfected your religion [*dîn*] for you and completed my favor unto you, and have chosen for you as religion [*dîn*] Islam" (5:3). Such a conception of *dîn* is much more ample than *Religion*. It is not alternative to *Zivilisation* and *Staatsgedanke*, but instead embraces both. From an Islamic point of view, *Staatsgedanke* is a very natural imaginative and theoretical consequence of *dîn* , while *Zivilisation* is a cumulative material formation of it. Therefore, *dîn* is beyond Western conceptions and definitions of religion. For example Schleiermacher's definition of religion as "the feeling of absolute dependence," or Tillich's definition of religion as "the all-embracing function of man's spiritual life" (1967:15) are meaningful within the semantic environment of a certain process of conceptualization which is strictly bound to a specific set of images. Tillich's argument against Schleiermacher's successors that they located religion in the realm of feeling as one psychological function among others and his reference of spirit to "the dynamic-creative nature of man's personal and communal life" might be accepted as one of the broadest definition of religion. But even such a definition does not annul the semantic gap between *dîn* and religion. The compound expression "Muslim Church" used by some orientalists (e.g., Macdonald, 1909:39,159) is an interesting example for the reflection of this semantic gap which creates a comprehensive vagueness of meaning. Nicholson's statement (1985:182) that "Since the Muslim Church and State are essentially one, it is impossible to treat of politics apart from religion, nor can religious phenomena be understood without continual reference to political events" shows how such a semantic gap may lead to a misimagination, although the purpose of the usage of the key-concept is to picture the same phenomena.

Due to the fact that the essential issue of a semantic analysis of a key-concept is its process of gaining a conceptual meaning, we have to concentrate both on the historico-theoretical and on the semantic basis of the key-concepts. The problem of semantic fields is valid especially for some critical key-concepts, such as *'adâlah* and *sa'âdah*. Although, for example, happiness might be chosen for *sa'âdah*, it is an unsatisfactory equivalent. As Anṣârî (1963:319-20) asserts: "Literally *happiness* means a state of feeling, differing from pleasure by its suggestion of permanence, depth and serenity, whereas *sa'âdah* is a comprehensive concept, including in it happiness, prosperity, success, perfection, blessedness and beatitude. Similarly, as compared with its Greek original, which in ordinary usage meant happiness often with special reference to external prosperity, *sa'âdah* has a fullness and completeness of meaning that is not found in the original. Well-being is another possible equivalent but that too falls short of its plenitude and sublimity. *Sa'âdah* primarily means the attainment of some desirable end or good, involving happiness or pleasure as a necessary concomitant. But in the widest sense the end or good expands to embrace the whole life and becomes the ideal or the end of all the activities of the soul."

We have to clarify even some modern concepts to differentiate the corresponding imaginations of them for the historical experiences of these civilizations. For example, von Grünebaum's definition of pluralism as "the coexistence within a political, religious, cultural unit of smaller bodies, whose recognized differences from the dominant group and/or from one another will yet not exclude them" (1962a:37) might be an anchor point for the analysis of Islamic religious-cultural pluralism. But it does not necessarily imply Western socio-economic pluralism, where the coexistence occurs between several socio-economic groups which might have parts of the same political, religious, or cultural unit.

Hence, Becker's assertion is right within the Western semantic and conceptual framework; but it is meaningless within the context of the Islamic semantic set of links. This dilemma is very significant especially for a comparative analysis. Therefore, I prefer to use original concepts for the inter-theoretical analyses, while I try to develop some new concepts like "ontological proximity" and "epistemological differentiation" for the intra-theoretical analysis. *Weltanschauung* seems to me as the most available concept for such a global comparative analysis because of its vast and deep dimensions of meaning. Additionally, it embraces philosophical as well as religious tendencies. That is very significant especially for finding out the basic and common features of the pyramidal-historical continuity and horizontal consistency in Western intellectual history. On the other hand, it facilitates an underlining of the starting point of this comparative analysis. We can show this facility with the help of a comparison of two descriptions. Using the descriptions like "the incompatibility of the Western and Islamic religious trends" or "the incompatibility of the Western and Islamic philosophical trends," it is not only impossible to show the internal consistency of these trends, but also to show the comparative basis of them. From this perspective, "the incompatibility of the Western and Islamic *Weltanschauungs*" is much more descriptive for the extension of the comparison. It is also more useful for avoiding the semantic gap mentioned above.

Thus, I will try to find out the imaginative and theoretical contrasts between the Islamic belief of *tawḥīd* and Western ontological proximity as two alternative *Weltanschauungs* which specify socio-political imaginations, theories, and cultures. The most significant questions to be clarified at this stage are why have I selected ontology as the anchor issue for such a comparative analysis and why do I derive a new compound expression—"ontological proximity"—to denominate the Western paradigm. I think a new base beyond theology should be framed to explain this contrast, due to the fact that the modern Western challenge to Islam carries more than just Christian theological characteristics. Thus, the Islamic belief of *tawḥīd* does not contrast merely with the Christian Trinity; rather its consequences offer imaginative alternatives to the modern philosophical leanings. Therefore, ontology and ontological consciousness seems to be a more proper mainstay both to show the philosophico-theological continuity of the Western paradigm and to underline its paradigmatic contrasting feature compared to the Islamic principle of *tawḥīd*. I prefer to develop a new key-concept for this purpose, namely ontological proximity. The focus of chapter 2 will be to show the continual characteristics of several different forms of this specific ontological consciousness from the early ages of human history to the modern age. Fraser's following description of the ancient beliefs in early ages of human history might be accepted as a primitive form of the ontological consciousness I call ontological proximity: "By primitive peoples the supernatural agents are not regarded as greatly, if at all, superior to man, for they may be frightened and coerced by him into doing his will. At this stage of thought *the world is viewed as a great democracy; all beings in it, whether natural or supernatural, are supposed to stand on a footing of tolerable equity.* but with the growth of his knowledge man learns to realize more clearly the vastness of nature and his own littleness and feebleness in presence of it" (Fraser, 1925:91). The imaginative, intellectual, and theoretical adventure from this primitive feeling to Spinoza's pantheism and Mill's limited theism will be analyzed to underline this continual feature and its historico-cultural origins in Western civilization.

The interrelationship of ontology, epistemology, axiology, and politics might be a meaningful anchor point to understand the irreconcilability of the philosophical bases of Islamic and Western political theories, images, and cultures. As Horten signifies (1973:2), "penetration of a foreign intellectual culture is especially facilitated by absorption in the basic ideas underlying the world images of that culture." The principal difference between Islamic and Western *Weltanschauungs* is related to the contrast between the "ontologically determined epistemology" of Islam and the "epistemologically defined ontology" of the Western philosophical traditions. This difference is especially significant in understanding the axiological basis of political legitimacy and the process of justification. Even several different approaches within these *Weltanschauungs* are based on a paradigmatic unity from this perspective.

I think *tawḥīd* and ontological proximity—as two alternative paradigmatic bases—reflect two alternative ways of ontological consciousness. Such a reduction during the process of conceptualization in the sense of ontological proximity as a specific way of ontological consciousness might be accepted as a version of the Husserlian phenomenological reduction in the sense of the performance of an *epoché* (Reese, 1980:152-53) which assumes a specific relationship between *cogitationes, cogitatum*, and *cogitata*: "The stream of my *cogitationes* is immediately and apodictically given; and the world is there as a *cogitatum*, or as the corresponding object of experience. The objects of experience are not then limited to the factual world, but include all possible objects (as *cogitata*), such as ideal objects, so called impossible objects, etc. That is the gain, since this attitude is then directly useful for epistemology, logic and metaphysics" (Farber, 1967:526).

Hence, when I use ontological proximity, I intend an extensive phenomenological consciousness related to the relationship between God, nature, and man. Using Husserl's conceptions, it might be said that I aim to show the philosophico-theological continuity in Western intellectual history through the denomination of the paradigmatic base of this continuity as ontological proximity in the process of the imagination of *Selbstverständnis* (self-perception)[2] and *Lebenswelt* (the world of common experience)[3] as ontological entities. Thus, my essential purpose is to analyze the emergence and continuity of a feeling of consciousness and its relation to the perception and experience of God, ego, and nature.[4] Husserl insists that "the *Lebenswelt* does intervene in the elaboration of science; the *Lebenswelt* is given to us, and we experience ourselves as existing within it" (Gurwitsch, 1966:423). I want to extend my investigations beyond this interpretation of *Lebenswelt* which has been developed by Husserl to define historico-cultural reality of the modern Western man. Rather, I will concentrate on the imaginative relationship between Western man to the *Lebenswelt* and its origin as a specific type of *Selbstverständnis*. The continuity of the idea of the perfectibility of man[5] throughout the ages of the Western civilization might be accepted as reflecting such a *Selbstverständnis*. The fundamental assumption of my book related to this consciousness is that one of the significant elements of this *Selbstverständnis* is the ontological imagination of man related to his place in the relationship between his ego, *Lebenswelt*, and the origin of them—namely God or the identification of God to these elements in the sense of pantheism or materialism, which I interpret as two ultimate cases of ontological proximity.

Husserl's approach assigns this special mission to modern Western man. But members of every civilization have such a feeling of consciousness in the sense of *Selbstverständnis*, and perhaps the most important aspect of civilizational challenge is the challenge of these alternative *Selbstverständnises*. Therefore, modernization

---

[2] Husserl's interpretation of this concept might be found in his masterpiece *Die Krises der europäischen Wissenschaften und die transzendentale Phänomenologie* (1954:275-80).

[3] As Gruwitsch (1966:422) mentions, Husserl set up a connection between ontology and epistemology via this fundamental concept especially related to the scientific achievements of modern Western man: "Like every other cultural activity, the pursuit of scientific knowledge is carried on in the Lebenswelt. Scientific problems arise within the Lebenswelt. "

[4] In fact Husserl's purpose in developing phenomenology as a methodology is to reach a perfect perception (1901:II/8).

[5] Passmore's (1972) work *The Perfectibility of Man* provides significant accounts on the continual process of this idea of the perfectibility of man.

attempts in Muslim societies aim to change the traditional *Selbstverständnis* of Islamic civilization in the direction of the Western man's *Selbstverständnis* formulated by Husserl as the basic reason for the supremacy of the Western civilization.[6] The basic phenomenon of contrast occurs between the Muslim's *Selbstverständnis* attached to ontological presuppositions and conjectural/material *Selbstverständnis* of modernizers in an age of the supremacy of the Western civilization. Such a clash results in divided personalities in Muslim societies which might be denominated as an official/secular *taqiyyah*. Turkish society might be evaluated as a model for such an extensive clash. Grünebaum (1962:104) exemplifies this aim to form a new *Selbstverständnis* in the direction of Western images by quoting a speech from Atatürk: "We shall take science and knowledge from wherever they may be, and put them in the mind of every member of the nation. For science and for knowledge, there are no restriction and no conditions. For a nation that insists on preserving a host of traditions and beliefs that rest on no logical proof, progress is very difficult, perhaps even impossible." Mardin (1983:108-113) analyzes these attempts for the transformation of *Selbstverständnis* by analyzing the transformation of value systems and argues that the impact of Kemalist education in Turkey became superficial in the process of the transformation of the traditional values that children inherited from their families.

The fundamental difference of this clash between two *Selbstverständnis*es is that the modernizer's new self-image depends on an epistemological renovation like that mentioned in Atatürk's speech, while Islamic self-image offers a very strong ontological consciousness for which the modernizers failed to set up a substitute. The attempts for this purpose like poems written by A. Gündüz, B. Kemal, and K. Kamu in the early Republican period on the divine qualities of Atatürk became examples of political toadyism rather than a substitute for religion. Therefore after a certain dominant period of the modernizers, the ontological consciousness began to specify the everyday life of an ordinary person due to the fact that state "was not interested in elaborating a map of everyday relations" (Mardin, 1989:227).

On the other hand, Muslim scholars aimed to rebuild epistemological and methodological structures of Islamic intellectual accumulation to overcome the challenge of the epistemologically formulated *Selbstverständnis* of the Westernization-oriented elite. The spread of periodicals and books for the verification of religious truths via scientific innovations might be explained through this necessity. The origin of this clash is not a local feature of Turkish society. Rather, it is a contrast between epistemologically defined ontologies based on Western and Islamic *Selbstverständnis*es. We have to be aware of these two alternative self-perceptions to analyze the increasing tendency in Islamic revivalism.

Although ontology has been viewed as a secondary branch of modern philosophy compared to epistemology in our age, I suppose that ontological consciousness might be the most appropriate anchor point for a comparative study between Islam and West. On the other hand, as will be shown in the following chapters, it is very difficult to isolate the evolutions related to these branches. I will try in chapter 2 to prove that there is a continuity in Western philosophico-theological history as a paradigmatic feature related to transformations in the idea of God and their links to the imaginations of these ontological entities in the sense of

---

[6]Grünebaum's (1962:97-127) analysis clarifies the changes in self-perception that result from attempts at modernization and their epistemological dimension.

ontological proximity and the epistemological and axiological consequences of this consciousness.

Chapter 3 will concentrate on the Islamic paradigm of *tawḥîd* as an imagination of the ontological hierarchy and differentiation and on its consequences for Islamic epistemology and axiology, which specified Muslim's *Selbstverständnis*. At this stage, as has been mentioned, we are facing a problem of finding out the most appropriate equivalences to the Islamic concepts. Therefore, the reader should be aware of some essential differences when the most suitable equivalent concept in English is used for an Arabic concept. For example, we should not forget the essential difference between *wujûd* and *mawjûdât* in Islamic philosophico-theological tradition when we speak of ontology and ontological differences in English. Therefore, *Seinschicte* in German might be a better correspondence for *marâtib al-wujûd*. I intend this meaning when I mention ontological hierarchy or ontological differentiation. It also means the strata of reality (*Wirklichkeit*) as well as the strata of being.

In part II, which is composed of chapters 4 through 7, the impact of these alternative *Weltanschauungs* on political imaginations, cultures, and theories will be discussed. The origins of the processes of justification of state as a socio-political unity reflecting the cosmologico-ontological imaginations of these paradigms will be discussed from this perspective in chapter 4. The processes of legitimating an established political authority will be shown within the context of epistemologico-axiological consequences of these alternative approaches in chapter 5. The same methodology will be applied in chapters 6 and 7 to two very significant political phenomena, namely the alternative ways of pluralism based on the alternative interpretations of political power and socio-political unity as the basis of the universal political system.

A short concluding summary will be developed in chapter 8.

PART I

THEORETICAL INQUIRIES

CHAPTER 2

WESTERN PARADIGM: ONTOLOGICAL PROXIMITY

Ontological proximity and particularization of divinity

The fundamental characteristic of post-Renaissance Western intellectual trends is the formation of a specific "epistemologically defined ontology" through the centripetal forces of "humanized knowledge." Epistemology became the center of philosophy as a determining factor, having the role of the systematization of knowledge. The humanization of epistemology around "knowledge" whether through empiricism, or through materialism, or through logical forms after the reemergence of ancient philosophy, created a relationship of dependency between ontology and epistemology in the Western philosophical tradition. From the perspective of ontological question, Christianity formed a preparatory stage for this development. Therefore, in contrast to the common idea, the epistemologically defined ontology which emerged after the Renaissance took its sources from Christian theology. The idea of the particularization of divinity was taken from the eclectic belief-structure of *Pax Romana* and was reformed within a gnostic Christian theology. It included the Incarnation and Fatherhood of God as the legacy from the mystery religions to Christianity, the deification of Jesus within the dogma of the Trinity, and similar complex ontological problems in Christian theology. This particularization led ultimately to a proximity or identification between ontological levels of God, man, and nature.

From the perspective of this "ontological proximity" there is an essential, continual link between ancient mythology, ancient philosophy, Christian theology, and modern philosophy. The idea of the deification of man[1]—as in the imperial cult of ancient Rome, the Docetist view of the nature of Christ, or the Hindu belief in *avatars*—was based on polytheist and pantheist elements. This was maintained in the Christian ontology within a new form which facilitated the proximity of ontological levels through preventing the ideating of an ontological hierarchy as in the Islamic principle of *tanzîh*.

Feibleman's (1953:352) definition of theology as "mythologized metaphysics" is very appropriate especially for the relationship of mythology, metaphysics and theology in Ancient Greece. The doctrine based on the principles of *chronos* (time) and *adrasteia* (necessity) in the Orphic theogony of the pre-Socratic period provided the theological bases for a dyadic ontology which might be accepted as a specific particularization on the ontological level.

---

[1]Hume (1907:327) explains the psychological and ceremonial origins of the deification of man in ancient time in his *The Natural History of Religion*.

As More (1921:41) specifies, the word *theos* (God), in accordance with the genius of the Greek language, has a fluidity of meaning[2] because "it is applied quite freely by the Hellenistic Fathers, after the manner of the philosophers, to men, and, in general, is equivalent loosely to the divine quality, more specifically to the immortal, wherever it occurs." This fluidity is very evident in Plato's cosmology and ontology. Although there are several discussions related to the question of whether Platonic argumentative theism or Aristotelian empirical and logical evaluations were based on a monotheistic framework or not, it might be argued that their cosmological and ontological speculations have been influenced by pantheistic and polytheistic elements.

The understanding of ontological proximity in Plato's philosophy is based on the image of God as craftsman (or maker) and as father, the existence of gods—as an intermediary ontological category—who participated to the process of creation after a certain stage, and the possibility for human beings to be like a god. These fundamental presuppositions necessitate at least three ontological levels concerning the relationship between God and human beings, but the existence of these ontological levels does not mean an ontological hierarchy like in Islam. First of all, the vagueness and fluidity of the description of the Demiurge prevents the development of the image of God as possessing all absoluteness.[3] The Demiurge as the divine craftsman who framed the universe is not in the normal sense of the word a creator at all, e.g., he did not create the world of Ideas. Plato's conclusion that "the maker and father of the universe, it is a hard task to find, and having found him it would be impossible to declare him to all mankind" (Timaeus 28c; Cornford, 1937:22) is, in fact, a declaration of the vagueness and relativity of his *imago dei*.

Secondly, the relationship between the Demiurge and other gods is not clear in the Platonic dialogues. As both seem to possess the same divine qualities, the distinction between God and gods is rather artificial in Plato's philosophy. His classification of ontological levels (Timaeus 39E-40; Cornford,1937:117-118) is an attempt to systematize this relationship and the process of creation. The Demiurge creates only the first category, namely "the heavenly race of gods" or "gods within the heaven," which are the fixed stars, the planets, and the earth. But, at the same time, Plato was aware of the difficulties with the notion of "created gods", and so he (Timaeus 40D-E; Cornford, 1937:138) adds that "as concerning the other divinities [gods], to know and to declare their generation is too high a task for us; we must trust those who have declared it in former times: being, as they said,

---

[2]Although it has been argued that Xenophanes reached a more absolute and supreme conception of God, his image of God should not be confused with the highly concentrated monotheism of Islam. His belief that "there is one God, supreme among Gods and men, resembling neither mortals neither in body nor in mind" (MacInerny,1963:29; fragment 23) is really very close to a monotheistic approach compared with the mythologized theology of his ancestors; but the plurality of gods as intermediary ontological beings is also very evident from his definition itself. On the other hand, his theory carries significant pantheistic elements.

[3]Such a conception of God might be accepted as the correspondence of only the name al-Muṣawwir in the Islamic belief system around a very clear image of Allâh based on the ninety-nine names, each of which indicates an absoluteness.

descendants of gods, they must no doubt have had certain knowledge of their ancestors."[4]

Agnostic, polytheistic, and pantheistic characteristics have been blended in Plato's ontology with a form of mystery and mythology. Although he lays emphasis on the divinity of the visible celestial gods together with the invisible spirits in the air and in the water in *Epinomis*, like in *Timaeus*, their ontological status is not clear in the dialogues. Socrates' argument in *Cratylus* (400d; Plato;1937:I/190)—repeating Protagoras' saying—that "we know nothing about the gods, neither about the gods themselves nor about the names they may call one another by", and the speculations in the *Phaedrus* (246c; Plato; 1917:231) are agnostic evaluations to evade this vagueness on ontological status of these inferior gods.

The address (Timaeus 41A) in which the Demiurge delegates the task of making inferior living creatures is a very significant evidence not only for understanding ontological proximity, but also for the metaphysical attitude of the particularization of divinity.[5] The polytheistic characteristics of Platonic ontology basing on such a particularization of divinity has been systematized via the intermediary status of

---

[4]He uses mythological background for this explanation through arguing that human beings should trust the children of gods though they speak without probable or necessary proofs.This mythological explanation coincided with the existing cosmological imagination; f.i. as children of Earth and Heaven were born Oceanus and Tethys; and of these Porkhys and Chronos and Rhyea and all their company and of Chronos and Rhea, Zeus and Hera and all their brothers and sisters ... and of these yet offsprings" (Timaeus 40D-E; Cornford, 1937:138).

[5]"Be that as it may, when all the gods had come to birth... the author of this universe addressed them in these words: 'Gods, of gods whereof I am the maker and of works the *father* , those which are my own handiwork are indissoluble, save with my consent.... although you, having come into being, are not immortal nor indissoluble altogether, nevertheless you shall not be dissolved nor taste of death, finding my will a bond yet stronger and more sovereign than those wherewith you were bound together when you came to be. Now, therefore take heed to this that I declare to you. There are yet left mortal creatures of three kinds that have not been brought into being. If these be not born, the Heaven will be imperfect; for it will not contain all the kinds of living being, as it must if it is to be perfect and complete. But if I myself gave them birth and life,they would be equal to gods. In order, then, that mortal things may exist and these All may be truly all, turn according to your own nature to the making of living creatures, imitating my power in generating you.'"(Timaeus 40D-E; Cornford, 1937:139-40).This intermediary divine category of being in the Platonic ontology and cosmology became a problematic issue in the commentaries of the Muslim philosophers. As it will be shown in Chapter 3, Muslim philosophers tended to translate and interpret them as angels and demons to reconcile Platonic legacy with the Islamic monotheistic belief system which does not accept any intermediary divine category of being possessing the power of creation. So, Platonic ontology which became one of the sources of ontological proximity and particularization in western philosophical tradition did not create such a consequence in the Islamic philosophy.

these "inferior deities."[6] The Demiurge, as a personal "creator" and regulating power rather than an "Absolute Creator," together with the image of inferior deities who share the role of this supreme power (Statesman 273; Plato, 1937:300) shapes Platonic pantheism around the idea of the divinity of the "visible universe." "The heavenly tribe of the gods"—earth, moon, stars, and sun—are "the visible and created gods" within this divine universe. In *Phaedrus* (246d) they have been identified with Olympic gods, e.g., Zeus was the equivalent of the heaven of the fixed stars, Hestia was the earth. The divinity of the world as a blessed God (Timaeus 34B; Cornford, 1937:58) and the composition of the World Soul out of three elements—Existence, Sameness, and Difference—is not only the essence of Platonic pantheism, but it became also a significant contribution to Christian theology of the Trinity (Timaeus 34A-B; Cornford,1937:58-60). Raven (1965:236) clarifies this pantheistic element arguing that "the Demiurge represents the orderly, predictable and therefore fully intelligible element in the world order." Therefore, it might be summarized that the Demiurge, as a mythical figure, symbolizes the rational element immanent in the universe. It is very important to understand the systematization of such an *imago dei* to follow the continuity from ancient philosophy to the modern mentality of natural teleology depending on pantheistic elements. From this perspective, the similarity between Plato's and Spinoza's conceptions of Godhood gives us an interesting clue.

The possibility of becoming like a god in *Theaetetus* (176B) is another significant indication for the characteristic of the ontological proximity in Plato's ontology and ethics.That is a proximity from the level of human being rather than from the level of the gods, as mentioned above, especially in the cases of the proximity between the levels of gods and nature. The image of *homoiosis*— becoming like to God—which permeates the whole Platonic system and which was one of the problematic issues discussed in the Council of Nicea on the nature of the Son, is a fundamental continual link between mythology, theology, and philosophy. The parallelism between the images of Olympic gods in Homer, "like-God" interpretations of Plato in *Theaetetus,* the belief of *homoiosis* in early Christian theology, and Aquinas' assumption of "God-like" perfection in the *Summa contra gentiles* shows this continual link basing on the deiform perfection of the human being. The origins of the deification of "the technological man" and his ontological crisis leading to discussions of the existential value of human being might be examined within this context. This type of ontological proximity creates very significant axiological consequences related to the subject of the perfectibility of man.

The point at which Aristotelian philosophy diverges from the popular religion originated from Greek mythology might be seen in Aristotle's investigation of the existence of God. Nevertheless, Aristotelian theology shares significant common characteristics with its ancestors, especially from the perspective of ontological proximity and the particularization of divinity. First, the fluidity of the image of God continues in Aristotelian ontology and theology. There are several discussions among interpreters of Aristotle on the question of whether Aristotle aims to reach a

---

[6]"And the several parts of the universe were distributed under the rule of certain inferior deities, as is the way in some places still. There were demigods, who were the shepherds of the various species and herds of the animals" (Statesman 271-272; Plato, 1937:299).

monistic system or not.[7] But, it is very difficult to find a unique and clear concept of God in his philosophical works. The descriptions of the First Mover in *Physics* and *Metaphysics* differ to a significant extent.[8] The image of the First Mover as "perfectly unmoved, unique and eternal, at the origin of all movement found in the universe" is a common feature of both works. In the *Physics*, additionally, Aristotle defines the First Mover as immanent within the corporeal world, even though it is itself immaterial. His description of the First Mover in Physics as the soul of the first thing that is movable, which encircles all the other heavenly spheres, is a significant pantheistic element in Aristotelian ontology. Such a description as the soul of the first sphere or as the efficient cause of its movement is not consistent with the arguments in Book XII of the *Metaphysics*, where the First Mover has been described as absolutely separate from anything sensible whatsoever.

Although Aristotle's cosmological evaluations[9] ascend to an idea of God[10], the status of God and the style of relationship between God and moved things (the universe) is not clear. Therefore it is very difficult to prove that Aristotle intended to reach a concentrated monotheistic system. The unity of things is a problem of teleology in Aristotle's philosophy rather than a problem of ontology because he dealt with the problem of order, not of derivation. His comparison of God to an army commander in *Metaphysics* (Aristotle, 1941:885-86) should be evaluated from this perspective rather than as evidence for the image of an absolute-sovereign and active God.

Aristotle's fundamental division of potentiality and actuality might also be understood within this context. His philosophical inquiries related to potentialities depend on the actuality of the teleology. His question is mainly attached to the mechanism of this teleological order, rather than its origin. Therefore Aristotle's God is a part of this cosmological complexity, not an ontologically transcendent active Creator. Hence, Aristotle might be accepted as the forerunner of those modern philosophers, like Mill and James, who argue for a "limited theism" that assumes a finite God. Defining God as thinking on thinking (*noesis noeseos*) in *Metaphysics* (1074b33-35; 1941:885), Aristotle limits God's activity to contemplation in *Nicomachean Ethics* (1178b10; 1980:268), while he argues in

---

[7]The discussion between Brentano, who interprets Aristotelian philosophy from a theistic point of view, and Zeller, who rejects such an approach, is one interesting example. The details of this discussion can be found in Elser's work (1893). On the other hand, Owens (1963:445-50) strongly avers that Aristotle does not wish to reach a monistic system.

[8]Van Steenberghen (1974:556-57) summarizes this difference very well.

[9]If we analyze Aristotelian cosmological and ontological arguments, we can discover the following steps to reach an idea of the Unmoved Mover: (i) there is an eternal motion in the world, (ii) everything in motion is being moved by something actual, (iii) things in motion are either self-moved or being moved by another, (iv) the series of things being moved by another must come to an end in either a self-mover or an unmoved mover, (v) self-movers reduce to unmoved movers, and (vi) there must be an unmoved mover that is the cause of eternal motion. A detailed schematization of these cosmological evaluations can be found in Craig's work (1980:37-40).

[10]Some parts of the *Metaphysics* seem close to the comparatively clear image of God (Aristotle, 1941:886).

Politics (1325b28-30; 1941:1282) that God and universe "have no external actions over and above their own energies".

There are interesting indications of pantheistic and polytheistic elements in Aristotle's philosophy. Defining time, motion, and some heavenly bodies as eternal substances, it can be argued that he has an image of God as co-eternal with some other substances. As a very clear evidence for his understanding of ontological proximity, this limited God and co-eternal substances are on the same ontological level. His argument in *On The Heavens* (271a-33; 1941:404) that "God and Nature create nothing that has not its use" and his mention of God and universe together for some judgements, e.g., in *Politics* (1325b28-30), originates from a veiled assumption of the ontological proximity (even identification) between God and nature (or universe). On the other hand, his assumption of the plurality of "unmoved movers" in *Physics* (258b11, 259a6-13, 259b28-31, etc.) and in *Metaphysics* (I/8) might be interpreted as a polytheistic element, if we accept his conception of the "First Unmoved Mover" as God.[11] Additionally, Aristotle mentions gods in several places (e.g., Nic. Eth. 1159aII; 1980:204). Such an assumption of the plurality of unmoved movers is an intermediary ontological status, at least. Therefore it is very difficult to answer the question clearly as to whether Aristotle believed there to be one God or not. Nevertheless, we can say that his cosmological and ontological approach, together with pantheistic and polytheistic elements such as his discussions on eternity, on the plurality of unmoved movers, and on the limited activity of God, give us significant clues for a denial of the argument that Aristotle has a monotheistic philosophical framework depending on a highly concentrated ontological transcendency.

When we combine Aristotle's ontology with his empiric epistemology, we can say that Aristotle was one of the founders of the tradition of making ontology dependent on epistemology. This is the fundamental Aristotelian legacy to modern philosophy which strictly affects all spheres of thought, including political thought. The dependency of ontology on epistemology might be accepted as the philosophical foundation of the secularization of knowledge and thought, due to the fact that this dependency resulted in the mentality of "the relativity of ontology" and "the relativity of the ontological transcendency". The centrality of empiric-realistic knowledge in the Aristotelian epistemology has been used against the scholastic type of Aristotelianism depending on logical forms. This is the dilemma of the Aristotelian impact both on Christianity and on the culture of the Renaissance,[12] but from another perspective it shows the continuity of the Western philosophical and theological background.

---

[11]Aristotle uses different names for God in his works. For example, he uses "First Unmoved Mover" in *Physics* and in some parts of *Metaphysics*, but he prefers "Theos" in other parts of *Metaphysics* (I/7) and "Theoi" in *Nicomachean Ethics*.

[12]This judgement does not mean that medieval and Renaissance scholars approved Aristotelian conclusions without any reservations. As Grant (1987) shows, there are significant departures from the Aristotelian system even in its period of dominance—between the thirteenth and seventeenth centuries—especially in the fields of cosmology , astronomy, and physics.

The transformation of Christianity[13] from a Messianic religion of Semitic origin to an all-inclusive mixture of belief systems within the syncretic atmosphere of the *Pax Romana* should be understood in order to follow this continuity of the Western philosophical background from ancient culture to the modern era. As a bridge between the Graeco-Oriental culture of Alexander and Graeco-Roman culture, the *Pax Romana* was a period of fusion for several cultures, beliefs, and philosophies. The highly complex *theologia* of Christianity was formed within this syncretic geographical-cultural atmosphere.[14] The interconnected impact of the ancient Roman polytheist and paganist tradition, Greek philosophy, mystery religions (e.g., ancient Syrian and Babylonian religions and Mithraism), Teutonic culture, and Hebrew origins is posited as the basic reason for the ontological vagueness in Christian theology, in contrast to the Islamic ontological hierarchy, which is based on a comprehensively systematized monotheism.

The Greek influence on Christianity is mainly related to the theoretical and ethical aspect—especially philosophy, theology, ethics, exegesis, rhetoric, and metaphysics—whereas the Roman influence concentrated on cults, ceremonies, and institutions of organized power.[15] It should be underlined, however, that Roman era became a bridge between Greek philosophies and Christianity especially with regards to the transmission of Stoicism. Greek Stoicism under the leadership of Zeno had been manipulated in the Roman understanding of life to compromise with ancient polytheism. Therefore, Roman Stoics argued that gods could be worshipped as manifestations of Divine Reason, which is the source of Peace and Wisdom. These ideas led to the process of humanization of Roman life and law beyond its deep theoretical and intellectual impact. In particular, Seneca and the emperor Marcus Aurelius played key roles in this marriage of Stoicism and other

---

[13]Because of this transformation and because of the lack of sources for Jesus' original teachings, such theologians as A. Drews in Germany and W. B. Smith and J. M. Robertson in England denied even the historical reality of Jesus (Robertson, 1914). Bruno Bauer asserted in 1840 that Jesus was a myth, the personified form of a cult evolved in the second century from a fusion of Jewish, Greek, and Roman theologies. We have to differentiate the historical Jesus and his teachings, which can not be denied because of the reliable sources on his life (some of them written by pagan and Jewish writers), from the mystical Christ, who is only a myth of a syncretic cultural and theological atmosphere.

[14]It is very difficult to find out the original creeds, ceremonies, and rites of Jesus' teachings because of the absence of any document written during the life of Jesus. The gospels, which have been written afterwards, have some significant contradictions, which have been analyzed very deeply. Herder's work (1796; Durant, 1972:553) is especially significant on this subject. The differential characteristics of the fourth gospel and the letters of Paul give us some important clues regarding Paul's leadership in the transformation of Christianity from a Semitic cult to a complex new belief system (Durant,1972:579). The essential doctrines of institutionalized Christianity, like the notion of original sin, redemption, and grace, were formulated by Paul.

[15]Therefore Hatch (1957:127) defines Christianity as "misunderstood Platonism," while Durant (1972:611) calls Plotinus, Epictetus, and Marcus Aurelius "Christians without Christ."

Greek philosophies with Roman polytheism and paganism. Stoic philosophy affected Christian thought via this marriage.

The dualistic character of Christianity in theology, philosophy, and politics has its origins in the Stoic assumption that the world is a product of two interacting principles: the one active and determinant, the other passive and determined. One of the significant Stoic thinkers, Posidonius of Syria, became effective for the spread of the dualistic Stoic philosophy through re-emphasizing the duality of matter and spirit, and consequently of body and soul. Cicero in Rome, where Posidonius of Syria spent his later life, was influenced by this doctrine. The blending of this way of thought with the thoroughgoing dualism of Ptolemaean gnosis depending on the acknowledgement of two worlds—divine (*pleroma*) and material[16]—affected medieval cosmological and ontological speculations to a great extent. This cosmological dualism created axiological and political dualisms that survived throughout the Western civilizational tradition. These will be discussed in the following pages.

Polytheistic elements based on the particularization of divinity in ancient Roman religions[17] might be accepted as one of the sources of the ontological proximity of God and man in Christian theology. Before Christianity, the Roman religious atmosphere had a tendency towards the divinity and deification of man as man-god through the process of the personification of God. At this stage, pantheistic and polytheistic elements acted together to form an ontological proximity and identification. Christianity adapted itself to the previous religious-cultural atmosphere through the deification of Jesus and through matching the miracle works of the pagans with wonder-working saints.[18]The term "Divus" acquired its

---

[16]"The first—the original and noblest world—was the immortal realm of what he [Irenaeus] called 'the Pleroma'—'the Fullness.' This was a society of Divine Beings, or 'Eons' at whose apex stood the unknown and unknowable Ultimate—'the Abyss.' It was the divine world of which spirit was held to be a displaced native. Outside and beneath the Pleroma was the material world, which was regarded as including within itself the very principle of evil. Between these two realms, the spiritual and material, there was a connection, but a connection only indirect and tenuous. As the Gnostic saw it, the existence of the material world was the unintended product of a temporary disorder within the life of Pleroma" (Norris, 1965:76).

[17]The native religion of Rome was animistic. The adventure of the Roman native animism to the late complex polytheistic state religion might be analyzed in following stages: "(i) primitive animism and magic, (ii) the beginning of the personification of the spirits and powers of nature during the late regal period, (iii) the humanizing of these spirits following contacts with Latins, Etruscans, and Greeks during the Republic, (iv) a process completed after the Hannibalic War in the identification of Roman with corresponding Greek deities, (v) the corruption of orthodoxy as a result of the increasing skepticism ushered in by Rome's foreign wars, (vi) the revival of ancient faith under Augustus, (vii) and lastly the long decline during the empire when Caesarism, later Greek philosophies, oriental mystery cults, and Christianity held sway" (Weiss, 1959:1).

[18]Laing (1963) shows interesting indications of the survival of Roman theological elements, creeds, cults, and rites within Christianity, e.g., the idea of deity, gods of the family, serpent-worship, gods of marriage, gods of agriculture,

special connotation through the deification of emperors as it was applied to Christian saints. The transformation of Divus Ianuarius to St. Gennaro, of Divus Iosephus to St. Giuseppe and of Diva Agatha to St. Agatha are some examples for this application (Laing,1963:121). The particularization of divinity among several gods was transformed to the specialization of functions among saints in Christianity. This prevented the evolution of an image of concentrated ontological transcendency.

The native Roman idea of pandemonism and the particularization of divinities was transformed to a new eclectic faith which was originally monotheistic.[19] Some theological elements in the Old Testament (e.g., Psalms 82:1,6-8) and in Hebraic tradition facilitated the process of the imaginative internalization of the theologically pluralistic particularization of divinity. This transformation brought about two fundamental consequences, one theoretical and the other organizational. On the theoretical plane, ontological proximity and identification between the ontological levels of God and the universe was developed. Organizationally, an intermediary spiritual organization—the Catholic Church—emerged for the solution of ontological problems.[20]

The status of Jesus in Christianity is one of the anchor points of ontological proximity and identification which created its own epistemological and axiological counterparts. Additionally, the ontological characteristics of Christianity and Jesus' status show the continual process from the ancient to the mediaeval Christian eras. Pagans and members of mystery religions within the syncretic atmosphere of the *Pax Romana* believed in gods—Osiris, Attis, Dionysus—who died to redeem mankind with such titles as *Soter* (Savior) and *Eleutheriom* (Deliverer). The theological name of Jesus as Christ is originally a name given in Syrian-Greek cults to the dying and redeeming Dionysus as *Kyrios* (Lord) (Guignebert, 1927:88). The creed of the redeeming blood of Christ formulated by St. Paul has no literal justification in the Gospels. It is also very similar to the mythraic idea of the divine sacrifice (Walker, 1939:103) and to the *avatar* of Hinduism for the salvation of the human being.[21] Tillich (1963:II/93) defines the ontological status of Christ as "the Mediator" and "the Savior" who represents God to man, but his differentiation of the ontological status of Christ from that of mediator gods who appear in the history of religion at those moments in which the highest God becomes increasingly abstract and removed is not clear enough to show the ontological transcendence in Christianity, because in the following pages he argues, on the concept of

---

river spirits, the worship of the spirits of the dead, man-god, the mother of the gods, baptism of blood.

[19]There are some verses in the New Testament for the unity and omnipotence of God, e.g., Mark 12:29 and Revelation 11:17.

[20]Hume (1907, II/360) explains this practical necessity for Church thus: "The more tremendous the divinity is represented, the more tame and submissive do men become to his ministers: And the more unaccountable the measures of acceptance required by him, the more necessary does it become to abandon our natural reason, and yield to their ghostly guidance and direction."

[21]Greeks were, at that time, also familiar with the idea of Incarnation because when Paul and Barnabas performed a miracle in Lystria, the Lycaonian people cried out "the gods have come down to us in the likeness of men," and Barnabas was called Jupiter and Paul Mercurius, according to the New Testament (Acts 14:8-12).

Incarnation, that "it is preferable to speak of a divine being which has become man and to refer to the terms 'Son of God' or the 'Spiritual Man' or 'the Man from Above', as they are used in biblical language" (Tillich, 1963: II/94).

The transformation of the historical Jesus to mythical Christ as a very significant indication for ontological proximity might be seen in the transformation of the imagination of him. Although Jesus never saw a painting nor a statue, ancient statues have been adopted to Christian worship—not only in the form of statues of such saints as Helena and Sannazaro, which were taken respectively from the ancient gods Juno and Neptune, but also images of Christ himself (Laing, 1963:244). Even the name Christianity came, etymologically, from a pagan origin (Durant, 1972:582).

The adaptation of the Greek Logos of neo-Platonism and the Stoic legacy,[22] together with these factors, restructured all the basic creeds of Jesus' religion and formed a new ontological foundation. This idea of Christ created a new conception of God in Christian theology confused with the image of the Fatherhood of God which had its sources in ancient philosophies and religions. Hence, Wolfson (1956:362) calls the orthodox Christian notion of God as "a combination of Jewish monotheism and pagan polytheism." This image of the belief of the Fatherhood of God (gods) has been used as a significant tool for the justification of the political authority in ancient Egyptian and Mesopotamian traditions, although there were some differences in usage of this term.[23] The relationship of parentage of the pharaohs, Hammurabi, and Assurbanipal with gods and goddess are very indicative

---

[22]This adaptation began in the time of St. Paul, who wrote in Greek and read the Old Testament in Greek (Grant,1961:66). For example, Paul uses the mystical conception of Philo's *Book of Wisdom* in I Corinthians 1:24 for the description of Jesus.

[23]"When we refer back to Egypt, we find Pharaoh could appear as the son of any god or goddess but that he counted specifically as the child (in the literal sense) of certain deities. As far as physical existence was concerned, Pharaoh had been begotten by Amon-Re upon the queen mother. As regards his divine potency, he was Horus, the son of Hathor. As the legitimate successor to the throne (a notion with cosmic implications) he was Horus the son of Osiris and Isis, the grandson of Geb, the earth. In Mesopotamia we do not find equivalents for the unchanging, precisely defined relationship which connected Pharaoh with Amon-Re and Osiris, with Hathor, and with Isis. Only the general formula which makes it possible for Pharaoh to appear as the son of any god or goddess recurs in Mesopotamia. In both countries, moreover, we find that the king can appear as the child of a number of gods at one and the same time. Gudea calls himself the son of Ninsun, Nanshe or Baba... In Mesopotamia, as elsewhere, the terms of parentage are used in connection with the deity to express both intimacy and dependence. Hence it is possible for Hammurabi, in the preamble to his code, to call himself 'son of Sin' , 'son of Dagan' and 'brother of the god of Zamama' while in yet another text he is the son of Marduk.... [Assurbanipal] names as his mother sometimes Ninlil, sometimes Belit of Nineveh, and sometimes Ishtar of Arbela" (Frankfort, 1948:299-300). As it will be analyzed in Chapter 3, the Qur'ânic theocentric belief system denies any claim of parentage in man-God relationship.which was a fundamental characteristic of the pre-Islamic traditions.(See, the hermeneutical analysis of Sûrah al-Ikhlâṣ, p.101-7)

examples for the pre-Christian imagination. As Hyde (1946:134) underlines, the Fatherhood of God was an elementary concept expressed for the early Greeks a millennium before by Homer in the Iliad where Zeus is called "father of gods and men," and after Socrates, especially in the writings of Plato (e.g., Timaeus 28C; Cornford, 1937:22) and the Stoics, this idea of the fatherhood was embodied in the concept of God as the Creator and Director of the universe. This image of fatherhood is also very evident in the Jewish tradition (e.g., Job 38:7) together with the idea that Yahweh is father to the Jews alone. Hence, the concept of brotherhood of men and fatherhood of God as two cardinal principles of Christianity originated from Hebrew and mysterious religious[24] traditions and philosophized by Stoic influence.

The dogma of Trinity as one of the significant elements of the ontological proximity in Christian theology has imaginative and theoretical sources in pre-Christian legacy. In fact, many ancient religious and philosophical traditions have had some sort of Trinity. Therefore, the dogma of Trinity, which is not found in the Bible literally, might be accepted as a continuation of Hindu (Brahma-Shiva-Vishnu), Egyptian Hermetic (Osiris-Isis-Horus), Zoroastrian (Ahura Mazda-Spenta Mainyush-Armaiti Intelligence and Mind), Orphic Greek (Being-Life-Intellect) and neo-Platonic (Good-Intelligence-World Soul) concepts of the Trinity.[25] Theologically sophisticated interpretations of the dogma of Trinity necessitated the usage of the pre-Christian legacy. Even Greek drama has been used for some explanations (Horton, 1940:25).

Hence, the theoretical transformation towards ontological proximity is a counterpart of the adaptability of Christianity to the syncretic pre-Christian atmosphere. It has been justified by St. Paul's doctrine that Jesus was not only the Messiah of the Jews but also the Savior of the gentile world. This process of the gentilization of Christianity might be accepted as the dynamics of the process of the universalization of this belief-system. This process has been supported by St. Paul's method of training (I Corinthians 9:19-20). Rand (1928:35-36) stresses the same argument when he says that he sees something Greek in St. Paul's temperament and his method of winning his audiences.

There are some significant classical works as cornerstones for the philosophical and theological transmission from ancient to medieval ages specifying the continual process of a specific ontological color on the sphere of *Weltanschauung*. Among

---

[24]Hebrew impact was also effective through the indirect impact of interacting relationships of mysterious religions and Greek philosophy. It is very difficult to distinguish these influences. For example, it has been argued that they obtained the concept of Yahweh from the Egyptian culture and religion systematized in the period of Amenhathep IV (Larson, 1959:197). The Babylonian impact on the image of Hebrew Yahweh shows the very complex intra-belief structure of these belief-systems, because Merodach, a Babylonian god, accompanied the kings in wars and fought for the nation like Yahweh (Bogardus,1955:31). This image of partial and serviceable god is a common element of these belief-systems and a common legacy to Christianity.

[25]Tanner summarizes these several types of Trinity and argues (1973:68) that "Christianity quickly absorbed most of the mystery schools of that day because the 'Christian mysteries' were essentially the same teachings."

them *De Mundo*[26] and Albinus' *Epitome of the Teachings of Plato* are very interesting and clear examples. The unknown writer of *De Mundo* was probably a member of Stoicism because as in Stoicism, "the God of the *De Mundo* is an immanent cohesive force as well as a directing Reason. He is within the world, not outside it or above it. Nevertheless he is localized within it. The writer does not agree with the saying that 'All things are full of God'" (De Mundo 397b16; Norris, 1965:31). Albinus, an influential student of the Platonic tradition, describes the "First God" as a "divine Intelligence who is the ultimate, unchanging source of all motion and order, the apex of ingenerate existence" (Norris, 1965:35). He interprets Platonic cosmology within a new formulation defining the World Soul of the *Timaeus* as an inferior secondary deity who mediates between the First God and the world. He tries to synthesize alternative approaches arguing that although the Supreme God, unlike the God of *De Mundo*, is not a particular force within the world, neither is he a reality separable from it. These attempts facilitated the comprehensive transformation and fusion in these centuries.

The adaptability of Christianity to the pre-Christian syncretic atmosphere has been accelerated as a process of impact-response-transformation after St. Paul, by the attempts of such Christian Fathers (especially the Apologists) as Athanasius, Basil, Gregory of Naziansus, Gregory of Nyssa, Cyril of Jerusalem, Justin Martyr, Clement, Origen, Hippolytus, Irenaeus, Tertullian, Ambrose, and Augustine, although some others like Vigilantius and Faustus opposed internalization of some pagan traditions within Christianity. The impact of Platonism on Justin Martyr's and Origen's theologies, Tertullian's challenge to Latin background, and Irenaeus' approach to gnosticism are especially interesting for discovery of the challenge and continual links between the ancient legacy and the Christian reformulation of theology (Taylor, 1949:5). The discussion on the nature of the Logos is an example of the blending of philosophies and belief-systems. Justin Martyr's claim that when Plato talks about the World Soul, he is talking about the Son of God, who is the Logos, shows the origins of the sovereign ontological color as the basic dimension of the medieval mind. The consensus of Apologists on the description of the Logos (Harnack, 1961:209-211) as the visible God and their argument that Logos is not himself the world, but he is its creator and in a certain fashion its archetype, together with the sophisticated theological discussions resulted in a proximity of ontological levels via a fusion of Semitic and Greek traditions.[27] Wolfson's description (1956:vi) of the recasting of Christian beliefs in the form of a philosophy—which took place between about 100 A.D. and the Sixth Ecumenical Council in 681—as a "Christian version of Greek philosophy" is very meaningful to the clarification of this fusion.

The theological discussions after St. Augustine and councils between fourth and sixth centuries (like Nicea, Ephesus, Constantinople, Chalcedon) dogmatized these transformed Christian characteristics and strengthened the tendency towards ontological proximity, especially around the debates on the natures of Christ and Mary.

---

[26]This treatise, which was probably written in the first or second Christian century, was traditionally, though falsely, attributed to Aristotle.

[27]This fusion has its origin in the period of Hellenistic civilization, especially in the cultural centers where several ancient belief systems and philosophies were effective (Tarn, 1974:225).

The Christian notion of God around the dogma of Trinity and the Fatherhood of God, as a very significant symbol of ontological proximity, shaped all other theoretical evaluations of transformed Christianity. First, it created an *imago dei* depending on the particularization of divinity which prevented the formation of an image of absolute ontological transcendency and a differentiation of ontological levels based on ontological hierarchy such as Allâh-man-nature in Islam. Second, the vagueness of Christian ontology depending on the concept of the Trinity led to a complex epistemological problem parallel to the question of the epistemological channel between *Deus Revelatus* and man. Third, ontological and epistemological proximities became intrinsic elements in the idea of religious subjectivism and historical relativism, together with the humanization and secularization of knowledge. Fourth, as another intrinsic characteristic, axiology has potentially been differentiated from its ontological antecedents through the equalization of epistemological spheres and the application of common and objective criteria both for the principles of revelation and reason. All of these characteristics have directly and deeply affected Christian political images and theories.

Obviously these characteristics did not come into the picture spontaneously, but Christianity harbored these intrinsic elements as the nucleus of its antithesis and became a bridge from antique to modern culture. There were several attempts to balance these characteristics within a systematic framework. For example, Scotus Erigena's *On the Divisions of Nature* attempted to reconcile Platonic Ideas, Aristotelian ontological categorization, pantheistic imagination, and Christian theology.[28] St. Anselm's *Proslogion, Monologion,* and *Cur Deus homo?* formulate an ontological argument for the existence of God. St. Thomas Aquinas' *Summa Contra Gentiles* and *Summa Theologiae* synthesize reason and faith for a logical scholastic formulation of Christian complex theology. That is one of the most significant characteristics of the age of scholasticism which began with Anselm and reached its zenith with Aquinas, though there were contrasting tendencies within this period, as the disputes between Anselm and Aquinas and between Aquinas and Duns Scotus illustrate. This attempt at reconciliation between dogma and thought or between faith and reason leads Durant (1950:982) to an analogy between scholasticism and Greek tragedy whose nemesis lurked in its essence, because "the attempt to establish the faith by reason implicitly acknowledged the authority of reason."[29] The attacks and criticisms of William of Ockham, Duns Scotus, and

---

[28]Scotus Erigena divides nature into four parts: (i) nature that creates and is not created, (ii) nature that is created and creates, (iii) nature that is created and does not create, (iv) nature that neither creates nor is created. This ontological categorization resembles the Aristotelian formulation of motion, while the second category includes Platonic eternal ideas. Since God is the first and fourth category, God is to be thought of as a part of nature (pantheistic element); yet this must be in a very special sense, for Scotus Erigena thinks of God also as above nature. His principle of Logos as a channel between the one and the many and his interpretation of the Trinity are Christian elements in his theoretical system. Nicholas of Cusa borrowed Scotus Erigena's terminology for his own ontological division.

[29]His conclusion that Aristotle's philosophy was a Greek gift to Latin Christendom, a Trojan horse concealing a thousand hostile elements, supports my argument mentioned above that Christianity harbored the intrinsic elements of its antithesis and clarifies also my assumption for the ways Aristotelianism impacted

others that the faith could not be established by reason opened a new phase on the paradigmatic base of the "epistemologically defined ontology." From another perspective, scholastic attempts like the Thomistic synthesis between philosophy and theology created a new transition within the Western intellectual tradition on a re-formed paradigm that developed after the rediscovery of ancient philosophy.

The whole *Quattrocento* was a transitional period under the hegemony of the transitional figures such as Jean de Montreuil, Marsiglio of Padua, Nicholas of Cusa, and Erasmus whose fundamental aims were the rediscovery of ancient philosophy and the reconciliation and unification of these ancient classics with Christian theology. As early as 1409, Jean de Montreuil—an admirer of Francesco Petrarca, who is regarded as the earliest representative of Renaissance humanism because of his attention to Latin and Greek sources—defended Cicero and Virgil. The Florentine Academy became the most significant center for these attempts at unification. As Cassirer (1963:3) clarifies, "in such attempts of unification, the great philosophical systems lose their own distinctive features; they dissolve in the mist for a primordial Christian-philosophical revelation, as witnesses to which [Marsiglio] cites Moses and Plato, Zoroaster and Hermes Trismegistos, Orpheus and Pythagoras, Virgil and Plotinus." Hence, this process might be accepted as the beginning of the second great fusion of the basic intellectual elements of Western civilization. From our perspective, the cosmological and ontological speculations of Nicholas of Cusa are typical of this new form of the ontological proximity of God, man, and nature which aims to systematize the proximity (and union) between God and man and God and all creation, within the Christian theological framework.[30] This rediscovery of pagan sources has been justified depending on the argument of the strength of Christianity in an age of the fall of scholasticism (Burckhardt, 1981:123). Erasmus' assertion that "the study of classical antiquity assisted the rediscovery of the literal text of the Scriptures and the return of the values of the primitive Church, obscured and lost through the aridities of scholastic and the abuses and corruption which had crept into the Church" (Green, 1967) was not only another way of justification, but also a final blow against scholasticism and an implicitly opened door for Protestantism.

---

upon both on scholasticism and the Renaissance. But, additionally, I argue that it shows at the same time the continual links and paradigmatic base of these disputing tendencies within the same theoretical environment.

[30]"In Medieval thought, redemption signified above all liberation from the world, i.e., the uplifting of men above their sensible, earthly existence. But [Nicholas of Cusa] no longer recognizes such a separation between man and nature. If man as a microcosm includes the natures of all things within himself, then is redemption, his rising up to the divinity, must include the ascension of all things. Nothing is isolated, cut off, or in any way rejected; nothing falls outside this fundamental religious process of redemption. Not only man rises up to God through Christ; the universe is redeemed within man and through him. The *regnum gratiae* and the *regnum naturae* no longer stand opposed to to each other, strangers and enemies; now they are related to each other and to their common, divine goal. The union has been completed not only between God and man, but between God and all creation. The gap between them is closed; between the creative principle and the created, between God and creature, stands the spirit of humanity, humanitas, as something that once creator and created" (Cassirer, 1963:40).

The cornerstone of the "epistemologically defined ontology" is Descartes' philosophy, but the origins of the intellectual transformation should be sought within the phases of the transition from the period of scholasticism to the formation of the new philosophical elán parallel to the new scientific approach which encouraged the central place of epistemology in modern philosophy.[31] The development of nature-centered cosmology and anthropocentric epistemology accelerated the process of the formation of a new paradigm through the intrinsic ontological characteristics of Christianity and the impact of the ancient philosophies. Step by step, theocentric ontology vacated the stage for the nature-centered cosmology and anthropocentric epistemology. The heliocentric conception of the universe with the famous sequence of the new astronomy —Copernicus, Tycho Brahe, Kepler, and Galileo— ontologically pushed God and man from the center of thought to the periphery. This means a radical departure from the medieval physics depending on the assumption that man is in every sense the center of the universe and that the whole word of nature is teleologically subordinated to him. With Burrt's (1980:24) formulation "just as it was thoroughly natural for medieval thinkers to view nature as subservient to man's knowledge, purpose and destiny; so now it has become natural to view her as existing and operating in her own self-contained independence, and so far as man's ultimate relation to her is clear at all, to consider his knowledge and purpose somehow produced by her, and his destiny wholly dependent on her." But, this reality does not mean that they were consciously against Christian background and its metaphysics; e.g., Russell (1962:513) underlines that Copernicus, whose orthodoxy was sincere, protested against the view that his theory contradicted the Bible.

From our perspective, this assertion shows the continuity between phases of sequence from the ancient to modern period. Kepler's inclination to sun-worship, though being a good Protestant, which might be accepted as an opposite transformation of Christianity toward polytheistic antique culture, shows the intersecting points of these phases; that is ontological proximity or ontological identification in an ultimate sense of proximity. Bruno was a typical transitional figure for the formation of such an ontological approach based on this new scientific innovations. His conclusion that "since the universe is infinite, and there can not be two infinites, the infinite God and the infinite universe must be one" (Durant,1961:VII/624) might be accepted as a preparatory formulation of Spinoza's *Deus siva substantia siva Natura* —God or Substance or Nature. So, such an image of ultimate ontological proximity within a pantheistic interpretation and nature-centered cosmology developed side by side. This necessitated a new conception of God as one who is not an external intelligence because "it is more worthy for him to be the internal principle of motion, which is his own nature, his own soul" (Cassirer, 1951:41). Bruno became a channel between Lucretius and Leibniz with his speculation that the world is composed of minute monads as the souls of things, indivisible units of force, of life, of inchoate mind. These views might be evaluated as a systematic and scientific philosophization of ancient mythological polytheism and pantheism.

---

[31]Whitehead's (1982:3) conception of nature as "that which we observe in perception through the senses" is an evident terminological extension of this characteristic of modern philosophy.

The assumption of the divine mind in every particle of reality was consistent with the assumption of the centrality of nature in the newly developed cosmology. The new physics based on the Newtonian "world-machine" created a new image of God as a person responsible for planning, building, and setting in motion this machine. Such an image of God is very close to the Platonic Demiurge. After the Newtonian revolution, to use Brinton's differentiation,[32] deism replaced theism. As Brinton argues, this deistic interpretation proved the existence of God by two very old arguments, the argument from a first cause and the argument from design. But once this necessary God had got the world-machine running, he ceased to do anything about it. This deistic interpretation used the Newtonian world-machine for its replacement of Christian theology with a simple acceptance of one God. Such an image of God was not an alternative to Bruno's (later Spinoza's and Leibniz's) pantheistic tendencies, because it assumed, too, a specific identification of God with nature and its laws. The Newtonian system in *Principia* provided support for the theologians, especially after Bentley's Boyle lectures (1692), "by stressing the apparent unity, order and grandeur of the universe as evidences of the wisdom, power and majesty of God" (Durant, 1963:VII/546). The image of God in *Principia* (Newton, 1803:II/309-14) is perhaps literally more monotheistic than medieval complex Christian theology, but the Newtonian system harbored elements for several speculative approaches. The results of the Newtonian world-machine strengthened the tendency towards the understanding of "self-subsistent and self-adjusting nature" which became the scientific base for ontological proximity and ontological identification in the modern era. The origins of Mill's and James' limited theism should be sought within the transitional phases of this tendency.

The ontological status of man has been re-shaped within the context of this nature-centered cosmology and scientific elán. Francis Bacon's judgement in the first sentence of his *Novum Organum* that "Man, the servant and interpreter of nature, can do and understand so much only as he has observed in fact or in thought of the course of nature: beyond this he neither knows anything nor can do anything," is the most pithy expression of this status. This judgement shows, at the same time, the new epistemological dimensions in the modern era. As Berns (1978:2) clarifies, this judgement means that "man is servant of nature in so far as he can do or make nothing except by obeying the hidden chain of causes" while "man is the interpreter of nature in so far as he does not accept what he receives as if it were self-evident, but rather as being results and signs only of the hidden chain of causes." Bacon's third aphorism in *Novum Organum* indicates not only his understanding of the subordination of man to nature, but also of the contemporary dilemma related to the relationship of man and nature: "For nature is not conquered, except by being obeyed."

---

[32]"Now deism is a fairly definite and concrete belief about the universe and, save in some polemics of the time and since, is not a synonym either of atheism or of skepticism. Deism needs to be distinguished from theism, which involves a more personal God, a God not necessarily anthropomorphic, but at least in some senses immanent, capable of being prayed to; from pantheism , which has God penetrate every article of the universe; and from philosophical idealism, which talks of spirit (*Geist*) rather than God.... The deist's belief is the neatest possible reflection of Newton's orderly universe, spinning around according to law" (Brinton, 1963:119).

Descartes' imagination of nature as a complete scheme, whose principles are linked together as are the axioms and theorems of a mathematical system, declares both the centrality of the deterministic machine-like nature and the epistemological tool to conquer it. Eaton's judgement in his introductory chapter for the selections from Descartes (1927:vii) that "Descartes stands where the streams of European thought meet" is very meaningful from the perspective of the re-formed paradigm and its link to the epistemological centralism. Descartes' categorization of substances as mind, matter, and God became the basic point of departure for all philosophical and theological inclinations after him. Eaton gives us trustworthy evidence[33] for his assertion that Cartesianism harbors under a single roof the elements of at least three widely different philosophies—pantheism, materialism, and idealism—although Descartes stoutly resisted all these ways of thinking, which were later to grow out of his premises. Even Fraser's (1899) classification of the philosophical tendencies as panegoism, materialism, and pantheism carries traces of trialistic Cartesianism. Each of these inclinations creates ontological proximity, and identification in the ultimate sense, through the fusion of two Cartesian elements in the third one, rather than setting up an ontological hierarchy through the specification of the ontological and epistemological status of each element. Cartesian dualism between mind and matter as an extension of Platonic and Christian philosophy results in an imagination of "two parallel but independent worlds, that of mind and that of matter, each of which can be studied without reference to the other" (Russell, 1962:551). Such a theoretical and imaginative dualism might be evaluated as the ontological ground of the epistemological and axiological secularization in Western intellectual tradition. So, it is one of the vital elements of the historico-cultural experience of the Western civilization throughout several different phases and ages.

"Epistemologically defined ontology" as another paradigmatic characteristic of Western tradition finds its best expression with Descartes' famous formulation "*Cogito ergo sum*" in *Meditations*. His identification of the self with *res cogitans* and of *mens* as *substantia cogitans* (Beck, 1965:109) and his equation as "*Mens siva animus, siva Intellectus, siva Ratio*" are very fair statements for the dependency of ontology on epistemology. Descartes' proofs for the existence of God in the *Meditations* (two anthropological proofs in the third *Meditation* and one ontological proof in the fifth *Meditation)* and his theological interpretations give us interesting clues how "he stands where the streams of European thought meet." These proofs, especially his reasoning from the imperfection of the self to the perfection of God (Beck, 1965:169) and his analogy between geometrical perfections and God (Beck,1965:217), are typical examples for the meeting of the streams for the philosophical systematization of theological assumptions.

Spinoza's (1930:115) usage of the same analogy in *Ethic* for his pantheistic interpretation of God, e.g., in his argument that things are caused by God "in the same way as it follows from the nature of a triangle... that its three angles are equal

---

[33]"Make mind and matter coordinate aspects of God, who becomes the indwelling substance of all things, and you have the pantheism of Spinoza. Abolish the realm of thinking substance and explain thought as a function of the bodily machine, and you have the materialism of Hobbes or La Mettrie. Absorb matter into spirit, as a thought in the Divine Mind, and you have the idealism of Malebranche and Berkeley" (Eaton, 1927:xxii).

of two right angles," shows the debts of several different speculations to the Cartesian system. Collingwood (1981:105) tries to show the impact of Descartes' philosophy on Spinoza's pantheism by stating that Spinoza took the Descartes' qualification on two-substance doctrine and drew out its logical consequences. He argues that through these logical consequences "he [Spinoza] asserted that there was only one substance, God; and that since there could be no other substance neither mind nor matter was a substance created by God." Russell (1962:553) argues that Spinoza's metaphysic is a modification of Descartes' and compares the relation of Spinoza to Descartes to the relation of Plotinus to Plato. On the other hand, Wolfson (1934:I/201) shows some parallels between Descartes and Spinoza on proof for the existence of God. Spinoza's assumption of *Deus siva Natura* as the only substance is the ultimate ontological proximity or ontological identification between God and nature.

The deterministic extension of this ontological identification based on the assumption that there is no such thing as free will in the mental sphere or chance in the physical world strengthened the tendency towards nature-centered cosmology via the peripherality of God and man as ontological beings and its epistemological counterparts. Humber's conclusions in his article (1972) that Spinoza justifies the existence of substance (God) empirically, namely by perception, and that the proofs for God are attempts to show that God belongs to the category of substance and thus exists by nature are very interesting from this perspective. Spinoza's belief in the self-sufficing, lawful order of nature on ontological sphere together with his assertion that we need only the revelation afforded by the natural powers of reason operative in us because even for our understanding of God's own nature, divine revelation is wholly unnecessary, specify two significant characteristics of the Western paradigm in contrast to the Islamic paradigm, namely nature-centered ontological proximity (or identification in the ultimate sense) based on a self-sufficing nature-machine and the centrality of anthropocentric epistemology to conceive the realities of *Deus siva Natura*.

Collingwood's interpretation (1981:105) that the mainstream movement from Descartes has been directed by Spinoza, Leibniz, Newton, and Locke is completely right when we try to find out the philosophical, scientific, and theological components of this re-formed Western paradigm. Locke's epistemological contribution, which systematized the dependency of ontology on epistemology, became the crossing point between this stream and modern materialism and empiricism. Resting on the two significant assumption that there are no innate ideas and that all our knowledge springs from experience, Locke's philosophy of knowledge became the point of departure for subsequent theories and approaches—such as Hume's empiricism, James' radical empiricism, and the theory of pluralistic universe—because it made all philosophical and theological issues subject to anthropocentric epistemology.

As Schwegler (1871:184) signifies, Hume's skepticism was but a more consistent following out of Locke's empiricism. Hume's application of his modified self-consistent empiricism to theological issues leads him to the argument of the incomprehensibility of the idea of God. His refutation of the a priori (ontological) and cosmological arguments for God's existence and his assertion that the teleological argument at best proves a finite, imperfect deity might be evaluated as the systematization of the subjectivist interpretation of God and as the forerunner of the idea of relativity and conscientiousness of religion in modern Western understanding of religion which cuts the links between ontological assumptions and practical life. N. K. Smith's (1947:25) imputation that Hume has reduced the content of the concepts "God" and "religion" to a beggarly minimum is not unjust from this perspective. Hume's pragmatic approach, which is very fair in his comparison of polytheism and theism related to their advantages and disadvantages in his *The Natural History of Religions* (Hume, 1907b:II/336), shows his interpretation of religion as a subject of epistemological and axiological presuppositions rather than as an objective and inclusive ontological approach.

Hume's contribution affected the followers of limited theism. James' attempt to synthesize epistemological empiricism, axiological pragmatism, and ontological pluralism is greatly indebted to this approach. His argumentation for his preference of a deity who is a little superior to mankind instead of a deity who is infinitely superior to mankind[34] is very clear evidence for our thesis on ontological proximity as a paradigmatic component of Western philosophico-theological tradition and on the interconnection of ontological proximity, axiological pragmatism, and limited theism.

Rousseau's romanticism accelerated the inclination to the relativity and conscientiousness of ontological approaches especially in the sense of religious feelings, while Kant's three *Critiques* formed a new set of links among ontology, epistemology, and axiology in favor of the pragmatic evaluation of theism. Rousseau's understanding of natural religion and its epistemological characteristic connected directly to the individual heart,[35] as explained in the "Confession of Faith of a Savoyard Vicar" in the fourth book of *Emile*, is a very influential interpretation of religious subjectivism. Such a subjectivism has very significant axiological consequences in the direction of the peripherality of religious law. It might be also the first stimulus for the formation of a new ethical base directly connected to nature and natural religion.

Kant's new set of links among ontology, epistemology, and axiology affected almost all significant scientific, religious, philosophical, and political tendencies after him, especially in the nineteenth century. Therefore, his philosophy carries some significant characteristics of the paradigmatic components of Western

---

[34]"Where the deity is represented as infinitely superior to mankind, this belief, though altogether just, is apt, when joined with superstitious terrors, to sink the human mind into the lowest submission and abasement, and to represent the monkish virtues of mortification, penance, humility, and passive suffering, as the only qualities which are acceptable to him. But where the gods are conceived to be only a little superior to mankind, and to have been, many of them, advanced from that inferior rank,we are more at our ease in our addresses to them, and may even without profaneness, aspire sometimes to a rivalship and emulation of them. Hence, activity, spirit, courage, magnanimity, love of liberty, and all the virtues which aggrandize a people" (Hume, 1907b:II/339).

[35]"Our passions are the chief means of self-preservation; to try to destroy them is therefore as absurd as it is useless; this would be to overcome nature, to reshape God's handiwork. If God bade man annihilate the passions he has given him, God would bid him be and not be; He would contradict Himself. He has never given such a foolish commandment, there is nothing like it written on the heart of man, and what God will have a man do, He does not leave to the words of another man, He speaks Himself; His words are written in the secret heart" (Rousseau, 1948:173).

civilization. Schwegler's (1871:209) judgement that "Kant is the great restorer of philosophy, again conjoining into unity and totality the one-sided philosophical endeavours of those who proceeded him," is completely right from this point of view. His doctrine, in the *Critique of Pure Reason*, that we can know only a phenomenal world which we make in the act of knowing it, together with his general understanding of nature might be accepted as one of the metaphysical origins of the scientific elán in the nineteenth century. The most significant characteristic of this elán is its assumption of the physical universe as a vast and complicated machine obeying immutable laws, which have been substituted for the conception of God in the Newtonian world-machine as the one who stands behind the physical universe as the author of the invariable laws of nature. As Barnes (1965:III/981) underlines, "cause and effect relationship occupied much the same position among nineteenth century scientists that God, the perfect being, occupied in the perspective of Descartes." Kantian relationship of the phenomenal world and mind created a marriage of the nature-centered cosmology and anthropocentric epistemology. His statement that "the proper object of scientific knowledge is not God or men or things in themselves, but nature and that the proper method of scientific knowledge is a combination of sensation with understanding," (Collingwood, 1981:119) provided a metaphysical foundation for the scientific leanings in nineteenth century while his demolition all previous arguments for the existence of God—ontological (Kant, 1910:364-70), cosmological (Kant, 1910:370-81), and physico-teleological (Kant, 1910:381-87) arguments—in his *Critique of Pure Reason* opened a new era for a new interpretation of theism.

Kant's argument, in his *Critique of Practical Reason*, that the ideas of God, freedom, and immortality are postulates of practical reason leads to an understanding of confinement of religion within the bounds of reason alone. The assertion that there must be a power (God) who rewards the moral and punishes the wicked after this earthly life connects this confinement to an ethical base. Such a theistic conceptualization of God as a morally necessary being rather than an ontologically supernatural being, within the context of the newly defined connections among ontology, epistemology, and axiology, became the anchor point for the leaning of the rational faith, for the presuppositions of limited theism and for the pragmatic interpretations of religion. Even the image of Christ has been modified under the impact of this reasoning. In *Religion Within the Limits of Reason Alone,* he argues that Christ is not a divine being, but only a symbol of a perfectly moral person who can encourage us to believe that we too can obey the moral law perfectly. His axiological presupposition that nothing can replace our duty to obey the moral law leads him to reject the function of Christ as Savior. Such an image of Christ, which is common among Enlightenment intellectuals, differs from the image in classical Christianity because of its dependency on axiological propositions—the direction of impact has now become epistemology-axiology-ontology. The common element between images of Christ in the medieval era and in the age of Enlightenment, however, is their support for ontological proximity.

Religious trends in the nineteenth century were directly influenced by these inclinations. Barnes' assertion (1965:983) that Kant's influence on Protestantism has probably been exceeded only by that of Martin Luther, is enough to clarify his impact on the religious trends in the nineteenth century. Kant's evaluations in the *Critique of Practical Reason* and the attempts of his chief disciples such as Schleiermacher, Harnack, Constant, Ritschl, McGiffert, and Maurice provided a sophisticated philosophical dignity and moral depth to Protestantism. Ritschl's theological speculations in his masterpiece *The Christian Doctrine of Justification and Reconciliation* might be a typical example for the interconnection and fusion of this impact around pragmatic theistic interpretation for moral betterment, for the understanding of religion as a matter of experience or feeling, and for the practical characteristics of the subjectivist conscientiousness of religion (Barnes, 1965:991).

Being a consequence of a very sophisticated philosophical theism connected to a philosophical system comprehending logic and history, Hegel's definition of religion (1968:327) as the self-consciousness of God—who is no longer a being above and beyond this world, an Unknown, for he has told men what He is (1968:327-8), but an Absolute Idea, a Spirit (1968:348)—was an attempt to provide a philosophical justification for the Christian dogmas[36] of Trinity, Incarnation, Redemption, and Resurrection, which present the Absolute Truth in pictorial form. Hegel, as the founder of a very comprehensive philosophical system, has many-sided influences on the basic trends of philosophy, theology, and science. These many-sided influences of Hegelian thought lead the extremes—and sometimes contradictories—of these trends to approach one another. His system might be accepted as the last attempt at the reconciliation of philosophy and Christian theology. Fraser's (1899:228) conclusion that Hegelian philosophy is Hegelian theology—the two are synonymous—seems fully right when we analyze the place of religion and philosophy in Hegel's system based on the categorization of the Spirit as subjective, objective, and absolute spirits and his evaluation of Christianity within this context (Hegel, 1968:II/328-48).

Hegelian systematization for the reconciliation of his philosophy and Christian theology carries some significant characteristics of ontological proximity, especially in the sense of particularization of divinity, deification of human being, pantheistic tendencies, and imposed logical categories for God, although Hegel also states that there is only one God. Hegel's understanding of God in his *Lectures on the Philosophy of Religion* (1968:III/10) as universal Spirit which particularizes itself and his re-interpretation of Trinity leads to an understanding of the particularization of divinity, while his image of Christ as the God-human assumes an ontological proximity and identification between divine being and humanity.[37] Pantheistic tendencies in Hegelian system have been discussed in detail. Following Collingwood's view, we can say that it "resembles pantheism in that the process of the world is conceived as identical with the process of God's self-creative life; but it differs from pantheism in that God in Himself, as the pure creative concept, is prior to the material world and transcends it as its cause." Using Lauer's (1982:281)

---

[36]For example, he tries to show the divine quality of Christ, arguing that the infinite God becomes God-human in time and space, dies, and rises to show that the finite does not truly exist in independence but is identical with the infinite, a stage in its life.

[37]"Hegel interprets the work of Christ (his life, death and resurrection) from the perspective that he is the God-human. In the life of Christ we see the divine identifying itself with the human to the fullest extent by living a human life. His death shows an identification with humanity to the ultimate degree, for death is the crucial mark of humanity. Christ thus endures death to show the total identification of the divine with the human. Thus the incarnation (the person of Christ) and his life and death (the work of Christ) bring out the full extent of the bond and essential unity of the Infinite and the finite" (Allen, 1985:236-37).

concept, we can say "pan-logism" of Hegel to take the mystery out of God by making God fit into his logical system is an example for the epistemologically defined ontology of Western intellectual tradition within the form of the imposed logical categories for God.

Ontological inclinations in the post-Hegelian period might be summarized in four groups: (i) materialistic atheism parallel to the evolutionary critiques of the new scientific elán in the nineteenth century against supernaturalism, (ii) existentialist response with new philosophical questions and horizons, (iii) the understanding of limited theism based on a new set of epistemologico-axiological presuppositions, and (iv) reformative religious attempts of theologians (especially in Protestantism) in order to adapt to the new intellectual environment by setting up a new functional role for religion. Feuerbach's (1957:270-71) anthropological interpretation of religion leading to the humanization of religion strengthened the epistemologico-axiological grounds of these inclinations through the growing secularization of moral and intellectual life.

Materialism, which was systematized by Hobbes in modern philosophy, reached its zenith in nineteenth century. It was strengthened by the revival of naturalism in science, by the Marxist re-interpretation of Hegelian dialectic, and by the spread of the theory of evolution to all intellectual areas. The scientific tendency against supernaturalism in the nineteenth century was the fundamental component of the hegemony of the nature-centered cosmology and of the peripherality of God and human being in philosophy, even though some of these scientists did not deny that God may possibly exist. Alexander's cosmological view that it is space-time which is the Creator and not God and that God is not creator but a creature, (Collingwood, 1981:164) is a typical conclusion of this response against supernaturalism. In fact, as Pringle-Pattison (1920:219-20) shows from the perspective of pantheism, such an interpretation of God and nature has interesting intellectual and philosophical links with pantheism, and even with polytheism. Alexander's definition of God "as a picture, but a picture eminently worth drawing though nothing actual corresponds to it" (Collingwood, 1981:164) or "as the entire space-time world in nexus toward the next emergent" is philosophically very close to the pantheistic definition of God as "a collective name for a *world of things* which simply exist" (Pringle-Pattison, 1920:253).

Marxist re-interpretation of Hegelian dialectic aims to explain the internal process of becoming in "self-adjusting nature." This positivistic approach to self-adjusting nature aimed to set up a Religion of Humanity based on a complete degradation of God's ontological status formulated by Comte (1858:428): "In a word, Humanity definitely occupies the place of God, but she does not forget the services which the idea of God provisionally rendered."

Existentialism, as a way of doing philosophy rather than a body of doctrines, comprehends a wide range of ontological and theological interpretations constituting a protest against traditional philosophizing. The anchor point of this protest was that "the personal commitment of a thinker be incorporated into his definition of truth" (Roberts, 1960:5). Therefore, there are different approaches within the context of existentialism from the perspective of ontological proximity. The extremes of these approaches are Sartre's atheistic version of existentialism and Catholic existentialism, which has continued to be developed in spite of the fact that existentialism was one of the philosophies singled out for unfavorable mention in the encyclical *Humani Generis* of 1950. Jaspers' existentialist approach developed through interpreting Kant in the light of Hegel, parallel to liberal Protestantism, represents an intermediate position within the limits of these extremes. Although there is a fair distinction between Heidegger and Jaspers (Schrader, 1957:38), Heidegger's conclusion that we can treat even God only as a being—we must objectify and represent him to ourselves—and that we can ask the ontological question about God but there is no hope of an answer might be accepted as a typical existentialist interpretation which is an extension of the Kantian doctrine of the thing-in-itself. Heidegger's (1956:208) presupposition that "Metaphysics thinks about beings as beings" and that "the truth of Being may thus be called the ground in which metaphysics, as the root of the tree of philosophy, is kept and from which it is nourished" especially affected those theologians concerned with demythologizing the New Testament (Macquarrie, 1978:352). Bultmann's *Primitive Christianity in Its Historical Setting* (1956), which aims to picture New Testament religion as having marked affinities to modern existentialism, is a masterpiece for this attempt at synthesis.[38] Heidegger's impact should be evaluated in the light of the fact that "there is much secularized Christianity in Heidegger's thought" or "that "Heidegger's secular thinking does embody elements from Christian thought" (Jonas, 1964:212).

The theoretical links of philosophical and ontological pluralism with polytheistic and pantheistic frameworks provide us very interesting clues for the modification and adaptation of ontological proximity within a modern form of limited theism as the second inclination. As some thinkers (Fries, 1969:136) specify, pluralism is a specific type of contemporary form of polytheism because pluralism assumes that nothing but the plural, the many, the variegated, the manifold is true reality, which is constituted by the association of the many (James, 1909:321). James combines this multicentral understanding of philosophical pluralism with a pluralistic conception of God and universe. His pluralistic conception of God and universe is based on a comprehensive critique of the theistic ontological assumption that God and his creatures are *toto genere* distinct. This theistic interpretation has some collateral consequences for ontology, eschatology, and epistemology. According to James' analysis, the ontological consequence of theism is accepting human being as a mere ontologically outsider subject to God rather than as an intimate partner.

James' alternative pluralistic ontology assumes an alternative conception of God which is a very interesting synthesis of polytheism and pantheism, *Identitätsphilosophie*: "God as intimate soul and reason of the universe has always seemed to some people a more worthy conception than God as external Creator" (James, 1909:28). "We are indeed internal parts of God and external creations, on any possible reading of the panpsychic system. Yet because God is not the absolute, but is himself a part when the system is conceived pluralistically, his function can be taken as not wholly dissimilar to those of the other smaller parts— as similar to our functions consequently" (James, 1909:318). This formulation is, in fact, a very interesting synthesis of polytheism and pantheism which shows transitional links between the idea of mythological "several absolutes" (polytheism), materialistic "no absolute" (because of accepting infinitely many absolutes at the

---

[38]For example, he tries to reinterpret the central Gospel message of salvation, *kerygma*, in the existentialist language of freedom, angst, and authenticity by arguing that authenticity is possible only through the word as revealed in Christ. On the other hand, he argues that "faith involves a new existential understanding of the Self" (1956:102).

same time), and pantheistic "identification with the absolute." James' pluralistic universe appears as a "congregation of psychic macrocosms, in which all human souls merge" (Chuan, 1927:201). This ontological approach leads him to conclude that "because God is limited like other finite beings, therefore his functions are similar to those of men because in other words both God and men are parts of a wider reality, therefore they have the same sort of function to perform" (Chuan, 1927:202).

Reformative religious attempts of theologians for the adaptation to the new intellectual environment aimed to realize two fundamental objects, namely (i) to reconcile Christian theology to the new environment and (ii) to set up a new functional role for religion. The first object, which has epistemological extension, aimed to be reached through the reformulation of the idea of "revelation through nature". The basic presupposition of this reformulation is the argument that "God is the essence of nature". Although it has been argued that such an interpretation is spiritual theism rather than an alliance with pantheism, it carries significant elements of ontological proximity. The analogy that "as our physical organism is moulded and directed by the soul within, so the whole creation is permeated and vitalized by the immanent God and hence the universe is not soulless, but soulfull" (Wood, 1892:37-8) is a syncretic interpretation of the primitive Aryan pantheistic argument that nature was an inspiration, of Platonic World Soul, and of the Christian idea of Incarnation.

The second object, which has axiological extensions, has especially been affected by the interpretations of a new moral base through the idea of the relativity of religion and through the spiritual dimensions of pragmatism. Schleiermacher's advice (1958:94) to the theologians against the attacks of "the despisers of religion" to base the Christian truth not on fact, or critically observable reality, but on subjective experience is the best formulation of the inclination toward the interpretation of religion within a relativistic and subjectivistic framework.

Epistemological particularization of truth: Secularization of knowledge

We have deeply searched the interrelationships among ontological, epistemological, and axiological presuppositions, especially from the perspective of ontological proximity. At this stage, I want to concentrate on a specific characteristic of the Western intellectual tradition which provides the most significant philosophical base for political theories and images, namely the epistemological particularization of knowledge as the origin of the secularization of knowledge.

Bartley (1964:134) specifies that the authoritarian character of the Western philosophical tradition is shown by the fact that the primary philosophical questions have always been: On what grounds do you believe that? How justified is your belief? How do you know that? and so on. All these questions are directly related to the question of the ultimate epistemological source and need authoritarian answers, that is a specification and defense of the authority on which one believes something or claims to know something, whether it is reason, revelation, tradition, experience, etc. The argument that "the history of Western thought is largely a history of attempts to defend the claims of these alternative authorities" and that "rationalism which is the view that only an appeal to an intersubjective authority is allowable, is not a reaction to this authoritarian tradition, as is often supposed, but part of it" (Brümmer, 1981:206) is completely right.

The veiled assumption of these attempts is that these epistemological authorities or sources are alternative to each other, rather than complementary. That assumption is the basis of the particularization of truth in Western intellectual history; while secularization of knowledge is the declaration of the supremacy of reason as the ultimate epistemological source against the others, especially against revelation, within the context of the particularization of truth. The dualistic structure of philosophy and theology in early Christianity was very influential as a pre-Christian legacy in the formation of a specific medieval mind based on a dualistic particularization of epistemology, as well as the formation of medieval educational institutions. The philosophy of the dualistic knowledge and education formulated by Dio Chyrsostom as "there are two kinds of education, the one is divine the other human" (Hatch, 1957:34) has survived in the Christian educational system and has been turned over to modern secular education.The philosophical base of this continuation from the ancient to the modern period via Christianity is epistemological dualism in the essence. This pre-Christian educational understanding created a certain habit of mind because "men who before became Christian had been exposed to the normal educational curriculum of the Graeco-Roman world" (Laistner, 1951:29).[39] The dichotomic character of the corresponding challenge between reason and revelation is a dynamic feature of Western intellectual tradition. It is an adventure from the idea of the absurdity (or irrationality)[40] of revelation to attempts at the rationalization of beliefs or from a vulgar rationalism to a metaphysically justified reason.

This dichotomy has grown out of the imagination of ontological proximity which enables the philosophers to use common criteria or standards of judgement for the outcomes of both reason and revelation. Thus, ontological proximity leads to an equalization of the epistemological spheres, if we do not limit epistemology as the rational reconstruction of knowledge. In fact, such a standardization of judgement is a declaration of the supremacy of reason from the beginning. The failure of the attempts in the history of medieval philosophy to make the revealed truths of Christianity rationally intelligible (Burch, 1962:396-7), should be seen within this context. This failure has been followed by the domain of rational philosophy which has been declared by Martin Luther as following: "What then is contrary to reason is certainly much more contrary to God. For how should not be against divine truth that which is against reason and human truth?" (Beard, 1927:154).

---

[39]The pre-Christian Greek educational system has influenced the Christian educational system not only theoretically but institutionally as well. For example, the designation "professor" originates from the sophists. The use of "chair" to mean a teaching office and "faculty" to denote a branch of knowledge are also of ancient Greek origin. In addition, Greek rhetoric influenced the development of Christian sermons. Justin Martyr indicates the impact of pre-Christian legacy on Christian education when he says, "we teach the same as the Greeks, though we alone are hated for what we teach" (Hatch,1957:126).

[40]Some Christian thinkers (e.g., Tertullian) have glorified in the absurdity of revelation, finding in its very irrationality a sign of the dogma's truth.

Two basic factors might be underlined for this failure: the vagueness of the definition of revelation and the highly complex theology in Christianity as the essence of revelation. Both of these originated from the imagination of ontological proximity and the particularization of divinity. First of all, the question of what revelation is has not been answered homogeneously in Christian theology from the beginning until the modern era. According to Catholics, revelation is given continuously in the living Church under the leadership of saints. According to Protestants, it is given once for all in the inspired scripture.[41] While according to Quakers, God speaks directly to individuals. The challenge of the new scientific elán forced theologians to reinterpret the concept and essence of revelation to overcome the evident contrasts between the judgements of the classical interpretation of revelation and the innovations of reason. Wood's classification of revelation in four groups as (i) revelation through nature, (ii) direct revelation, (iii) biblical revelation, and (iv) revelation through the Son might be noted as an interesting example of these reinterpretations (Wood, 1892:37-116). In particular, the idea of revelation through nature aimed to reconcile with Christian understanding of revelation the assumption of "the self-adjusted mechanism of nature" developed by rationalistic innovations. The argument that "the revelation of God through nature is in full harmony with that which comes through the Son" because "Christ and nature reveal the same Father, but each on a different side" (Wood, 1892:115-6) shows the characteristic of the reasoning for this reconciliation. This interpretation of revelation has strengthened, at the same time, the tendency of the proximation and equalization of the epistemological spheres of God-human being-nature as an extension of ontological proximity.

Catholic interpretation of revelation supported by St. Paul's saying that "we have the minds of Christ" resulted in a highly complex theology of Christian Fathers whose doctrines have been accepted as a part of divine revelation. The formation of such an intermediary source of knowledge between *Deus Revelatus* and human being has transformed Jesus' simple teachings into a contrasting set of dogmas, each of which had been referred to a saint or father who has a special source of knowledge as a part of revelation. This transformation has been analyzed in detail before. Additionally, I want to underline that the absence of a well-defined concept and essence of revelation in Christianity resulted in a dogmatization of the views of the Christian Fathers. This dogmatization has been transformed into a rivalry between reason and revelation, when rationalistic innovations contrasted with these dogmas. Even Luther admits in his *Exposition of the Epistle to Galatians* that "all the articles of our Christian faith which God has revealed to us in His Word, are in presence of reason sheerly impossible, absurd, false" (Beard, 1927:162). The particularization of truth has reached its zenith when this contrast became evident after scholasticism's loss of prestige. The process of the secularization of knowledge has been accelerated step by step parallel to the victory of reason. The question of what the Word of God is emerged as a result of this process. Protestant reinterpretation of revelation mentioned above is a response to the necessity of answering this question in the face of the dilemma that has emerged because of the contrasts between Catholic interpretation of revelation and new rationalistic way of thought.

---

[41]There is a great deal of Islamic influence on the development of this Protestant view of revelation.

The fundamental characteristic of post-Renaissance Western philosophy is the formation of a specific "epistemologically defined ontology" through the centripetal tendencies of "humanized knowledge." So epistemology became the center of philosophy as a determining factor, having the role of the systematization of knowledge. The humanization of epistemology around *cognitio*—whether through empiricism, through materialism, or through logical forms after the reemergence of ancient philosophy—created a relationship of dependency between ontology and epistemology in the Western philosophical tradition. From the perspective of ontological questions, Christianity formed a preparatory stage for this development after the Renaissance. Therefore, in contrast to the common idea, the "epistemologically defined ontology" that emerged after the Renaissance took its sources from Christian theology. As has been shown, the idea of the particularization of divinity was taken from the eclectic belief-structure of the *Pax Romana* and was reformed within a gnostic Christian theology. It included the Incarnation and Fatherhood of God as a legacy from the mystery religions to Christianity, the deification of Jesus within the dogma of Trinity like to the belief of *avatar* in Hinduism, and similar complex ontological problems in Christian theology. This particularization led ultimately to a proximity and identification between the spheres of God and man. Except for some mystical and gnostic fantasies, a systematic idea of *ghayb* (invisibility) as a consequence of a differentiation of epistemological levels between Allâh and man did not emerge in Christian epistemology as it did in Islam. The idea of the deification of man, as in the imperial cult of ancient Rome, or the Incarnation of God as in Docetism—the ancient Graeco-Roman legacy—was based on polytheist and pantheist elements. This was maintained in the Christian ontology within a new form which facilitated the proximity of ontological and epistemological levels by preventing the ideation of an ontological hierarchy as in the Islamic principle of *tanzîh*.

Theological complexities around the particularization of divinity and mysterious aspects of Christian ontology have two significant consequences. One is related to the proximity of ontological and epistemological levels which created an epistemologically defined ontology. The other is related to the popularization process of belief through some agents or autonomous organizations which tended to interpret these theological complexities, namely churches. Catholic interpretation of revelation is very meaningful from this perspective. If we concentrate on the first impact, this proximity of ontological levels produced and accelerated the process of the humanization of epistemology and the secularization of knowledge after the Renaissance and Reformation. From this perspective, there is a continual relationship between ancient philosophy, Christianity, and modern philosophy. Christianity has carried the sources of its antithesis within its theological structure. Therefore a reformation in Christianity was possible developing from a mystery-complex ontology to an epistemologically defined ontology. But this is not the case in Islam. As will be analyzed, all attempts at a reformation in Islam have been easily counteracted by its ontological transparency and by the strong internal consistency between its ontology and its epistemology.

In general, it has been accepted that there are three coordinate sources of ordinary knowledge, namely reason, experience, and revelation. The peripherality of revelation as a source of knowledge resulted in the concentration of epistemology on human sources of knowledge: reason and experience. Francis Bacon's equalization of "Knowledge is power" was the first declaration of the anthropocentric epistemology which became the center of the Western philosophy in modern era. Locke's definition of knowledge as "nothing but the perception of the connection and agreement, or disagreement and repugnancy of any of our ideas" (Gibson, 1931:142) which "are derived from two sources, (a) sensation and (b) perception of the operation of our mind" (Russell, 1962:589) was a new conceptualization of knowledge within the limits of empiricism. Hume's extension of this new epistemological concentration to metaphysical issues was the final blow against revelation as a source of knowledge.

The section "Of Miracles" in Hume's *Concerning Human Understanding* might be accepted as a turning point in Western intellectual tradition. His argument that "our evidence for the truth of the Christian religion is less than the evidence for the truth of our senses; because even in the first authors of our religion, it was no greater; and it is evident it must diminish in passing from them to their disciples; nor can any one rest such confidence in their testimony, as in the immediate object of his senses" (Hume, 1907:II/88) was the ultimate declaration of the centrality and supremacy of anthropocentric epistemology. His suggestion that "a wise man proportions his belief to the evidence" might be accepted as the attempt for a new understanding of revelation. As Polanyi (1983:279) underlines, from Hume until Russell, the belief in the efficacy of doubt as a solvent of error was sustained primarily by skepticism about religious dogma and the dislike of religious bigotry.

The development of nature-centered cosmology as Copernican heliocentrism and anthropocentric epistemology accelerated the process of the formation of a new paradigm through the intrinsic ontological characteristics of Christianity and the impact of the ancient philosophies. Step by step theocentric ontology and revelation as a source of knowledge vacated the stage for the nature-centered and anthropocentric philosophy. Although Kant's anthropocentric approach might be accepted as a response to Copernican heliocentrism, there is a continual link between these philosophies from the perspective of their impact on social and political theories. Copernican heliocentrism, as a new cosmological interpretation, ontologically pushed God and man from the center of philosophy to the periphery. This *imago mundi*, as an incipient form of nature-centered interpretation, opened a new elán not only from the cosmological but also the ontological, epistemological, axiological, and sociological perspectives.

The *principium individuationis* of this elán is an immanent surreptitious will *in* the universe rather than a transcendental will *over* the universe, as in Islamic ontology. From this perspective, this *imago mundi* has some intrinsic pantheist elements. *Cognitio*, autonomous from revelation, has been interpreted as the dominant epistemological tool to interpret the cosmos. The superiority of human knowledge within this *imago mundi* became the core of the anthropocentric epistemology of the Copernican nature-centered ontological approach, which in turn became the origin of the secularization of knowledge. Therefore, Copernican heliocentric cosmology and the emergence of the anthropocentric epistemology are complementary philosophical steps.

This anthropocentric epistemology became the center of modern Western philosophy. Locke's argument that all knowledge comes from our experience, Kant's hypothesis that knowledge is a joint product of mind and external world, Comtean positivism underlying the scientific stage against the theological and metaphysical stages, and James' radical empiricism are several outgrowths of the epistemological foundation afforded by Aristotelian empiricism. Parallel to this anthropocentric epistemology, the proximity of ontological levels growing out of the syncretic atmosphere of *Pax Romana*—which was an intrinsic element within

Christianity—has been philosophically systematized step by step. Hume's interpretation of God as the World Soul, Hobbesian materialism in metaphysics, Mill's theory of "finite or limited Deity," and James' limited theism are interesting phases of the formation of the epistemologically defined ontology of the Western philosophical tradition which rested on a new paradigm.

Thus, particularization of truth led to the process of the secularization of knowledge. A clear-cut mental and institutional segmentation of knowledge has been assumed as the basic feature of the secularization of knowledge. The Christian truths were confined within the boundaries of the churches, while a new definition of epistemology became the basis of the intellectual and axiological secularization of knowledge and life. This new definition assumes the task of epistemology as the rational reconstruction of knowledge. All modern theories of truth—such as the correspondence theory; the coherence theory of the great idealistic system builders such as Spinoza, Hegel, and Bradley and of the logical positivists; the pragmatic theory; and the performative theory—are outcomes of this understanding of epistemology. All of these theories of truth have significant effects on the formation of social imagination and theories in the direction of the secularization of knowledge as an epistemological consequence and secularization of law and life as an axiological phenomenon. Using Ellis' (1979:vi) formulation, we can generalize that all modern epistemologists share "a view of man as a more or less rational agent operating with a priori principles of reasoning upon given data (or in Popper's case upon conjectures and observationally acquired beliefs) to construct the edifice of objective scientific knowledge." As he points out, Popper (1959:31) like the other modern epistemologists, thinks of the body of scientific knowledge as a kind of intellectual superstructure or building erected by us upon more or less firm foundations of items of knowledge or belief acquired directly through sense experience. The fundamental dilemma of this epistemological assumption is that it implies that man, the rational agent, is somehow separate from the physical world which he is trying to understand. That implication is evidently not true, so that the rational agent as a part of the physical world tries to understand the whole, which creates a vicious circle from the perspective of the subject-object relationship in anthropocentric epistemology.

Axiological positivism: Secularization of life and law

Some of the significant interconnections among ontology, epistemology, and axiology have been shown above. Their political implications will be discussed in the following part of this book. At this stage, I want to underline the evolutionary process of axiological positivism as the philosophical base of the secularization of life and law in the Western experience. Two significant sources of this evolutionary stage might be mentioned to frame its historico-cultural continuity.

First, it is a clear fact that any type of secularization necessitates a mental, imaginative, or practical segmentation (or particularization). It has already been shown how a mental particularization of truth results in an epistemological secularization. Axiological secularization of life and law has originated from an ultimate particularization of normative/positive or religious/secular spheres, which is itself a consequence of ontological and epistemological particularization. Second, a purely rationalistic framework of values as an indication of axiological positivism is the essential prerequisite for the secularization of life and law. This prerequisite is theoretically and imaginatively linked directly to the proximation (or equalization) of ontological and epistemological spheres.

The initial forms of the axiological secularization of life and law might be found in Stoicism (especially in the sense of axiological segmentation) and in Epicureanism (especially in the sense of axiological positivism and ethical rationalism). The Stoic assumption that every man is a member of two commonwealths—city and world-city—leads to the Stoic doctrine that for every man there are two laws—the law of his city and the law of the world-city, or in another formulation the law of custom and the law of reason. In particular, Ulbian's ultimate separation of *jus naturale* (the natural law) from *jus gentium* (the law of nations) might be accepted as the cornerstone for the segmentation stage of the process of the secularization of law and life.

The Epicurean contribution to the process of the rationalization of axiology was a substantive one for the seeking of the summum bonum in felicity of life, namely the assumption that happiness consists in nothing but pleasure. This assumption became one of the basic pillars of the process of worldliness of the modern Western value-system because it was the most efficient and sovereign element of the secular segment of the axiology, especially in the form of utility.

Christian ethics was influenced by this Graeco-Roman legacy, both in the sense of segmentation and in the sense of content. There is a clear continuity between the ethics of the pagan philosophers Cicero and Marcus Aurelius and that of St. Ambrose, one of the influential founders of Christian ethics. Marcus Aurelius' formulation "love even those who do wrong" has been Christianized as "love your enemies" (Matthew 5:44). Taylor (1958:77) shows the pagan character of Ambrose's famous work *De Officiis Ministrorum,* underlining its debts to Cicero's *De Officiis.* Hatch (1957:168-170), too, insists that Ambrose's book is less Christian than Stoical. Ambrose's assumption that the ideal of life is happiness, as an extension of Stoic philosophy, might be accepted as the axiological and eschatological basis of secularization resting on Stoic ethics which survived in Christian ethics (Hatch, 1957:170). In particular, Ambrose's argument that there can be no conflict between the *honestum* and the *utile,* since nothing can be *honestum* that is not useful, and vice verse, wherein he follows Cicero, has been extended to the modern utilitarian philosophy as a veiled characteristic of Christian ethics in spite of its contrast with the Augustinian "anti-life" irrationalism.

The interiorization of morality in Christian ethics, together with the effects of the institutionalized exterior Roman law, re-formulated the antagonistic segmentation between ideal and actual, in the philosophical sense, and between Church and Society in practical life. As Taylor (1949:I/370) rightly stresses, whether or not Christ's Gospel set forth any inherent antagonism between the fulness of mortal life and the sure attainment of heaven, its historical interpretations have never effected a complete reconciliation and have always presented some conflict between the finite and the eternal. Fârûqî's (1967:79) assertion that "Jesus' ethic, as a genuine ethic of intent, must abstract or at least de-emphasize, man's community though this may be mankind, and his real relations with that community" might indicate the ethical origin of this antagonism, but it came forth as a sophisticated axiological re-interpretation of Stoic dualism, in the Apostolic Age especially after the formulation of the opposition between the world and the City of

God.[42] Augustine's separation of Church and State in his *City of God* has been the doctrine of the Church ever since. Through the notion of the "two swords,"[43] the dichotomy between Church as the structural institutionalization of the Ideal and Society as the structural institutionalization of the Actual survived as the philosophical and institutional base of the axiological and political particularization of life and law in Western experience. The argument of the traditional theology that the kingdom of God is the Church, not Society, intrinsically carried an assumption of the double-standardization of ethics—one for the members of Church as the kingdom of God and one for the ordinary persons in Society. Repeating Fârûqî's description for St. Augustine, we can say the "anti-life" irrationalism of Christian dogmas strengthened the axiological segmentation throughout the Middle Ages. This "anti-life" irrationalism became a dominant figure especially after St. Augustine's combat against the Pelagians, who argued that man has complete freedom of will and that divine grace merely helps a Christian to accomplish what is already in his power without it. The condemnation of Pelagianism at the Councils of Carthage and the Augustinian interpretation of original sin[44] shaped Christian ethics as an implication of this fundamental principle throughout the Middle Ages. The necessity for a rational axiology in the modern era emerged as a natural antithesis of this "anti-life" irrationalism.

Machiavelli's attempt to emphasize the rational bases of the state as the institutionalization of the Actual and Hobbes' re-systematization of philosophy in three parts (geometry-mechanics, physiology-psychology, and state-society) to find out rationally defined axiological foundations of the segment of the medieval dualistic structure were reactions against this irrationalism, as the members of the other side; namely society. Hobbes' philosophy played the role of cornerstone— with its new setting between physics, axiology and politics—for the development of modern philosophical inclinations.[45] As Strauss (1961:29) shows, Hobbes

---

[42]"Unfortunately, Christian doctrine fell under the dogmatism of Tertullian before, and of Athanasius after, the Council of Nicea. Later on, it was wedded to the 'anti-life' irrationalism of St. Augustine at the Council of Chalcedon. Henceforth the doors were tightly closed. Peccatism, saviourism, millenarianism, and paradox held complete sway. These, not the ethic of Jesus, were the enemies of societism" (Fârûqî, 1967:294).

[43]The emperor, who wields the secular sword, is accepted within the Church, not above it, because he is also a child of the same Universal Spirit of Stoicism and of the Universal Brotherhood of Christianity. From this perspective of the relationship of ethics and politics, Seneca might be accepted as the master of such Christian Fathers as Ambrose and Augustine.

[44]Augustine's understanding of sin in his *Confessions* (1962:27-8) forms a specific philosophy of life: "Who can recall to me the sins I committed as a baby? For in your sight no man is free from sin, not even a child who has lived only one day on earth... if babies are innocent , it is not for lack of will to do harm, but for lack of strength." See Russell's (1962:362) summary of the Augustinian interpretation of original sin.

[45]The place of Hobbesian philosophy in the history of philosophy might be seen in its commentators' interpretation of Hobbes' works as exemplifying almost every inclination and kind of philosophy. In Strauss (1961) there is an intellectual interpretation of Hobbes; in Flew (1964) there is an image of Hobbes as an egoist;

developed a new morality based on "experience" rather than natural science. Hobbes' assumption that human behavior is the result of a reaction toward the attainment of pleasure and the avoidance of pain might be accepted as the most fundamental Hobbesian contribution to the evolutionary process of a new morality and of the secularization of life, because the axiological standards for human behavior began to change in the direction of the independence of morality from religion. His conclusion "that the object of desire is good, of aversion evil" was a revolutionary stimulus for the rationalization of morality and set up morality within the sphere of Actuality and Society instead of within the sphere of the Ideal and the Church.

Hobbes' second assumption—based on the earlier assumption that self-preservation is the supreme good, death the supreme evil, and that to promote the one and prevent the other is the first law of nature—relates directly to his own social experiences. That role of experience for the formation of the axiological set as a mode of morality strengthened the tendency toward realistic interpretation of morality on the one hand and toward understanding the relativity of morality dependent on changes in experience on the other hand. Henceforth, the supremacy of the idealistic and absolute axiology under the governance of Church has been shaken to a great extent.

Thus, axiological conclusions began to originate directly from anthropocentric epistemology rather than from theologically absolute goodness. Especially rationalist and empiricist epistemological schools affected axiological inclinations. For example, Hume mentions reason and sentiment as two fundamental foundations of philosophical inclinations on moral theory in his famous *Enquiry Concerning the Principles of Morals* (1907a:II/170). Using Broad's (1971:108-110) classification, it might be repeated that Hume's relational and psychological theory of ethics is an example of the phenomenalist analysis, rather than causal and a priori concept analysis of the ethical fact. Excluding Spinoza, whose ethical theory is only a part of an elaborate metaphysical theory of the universe (Russell, 1962:620), the ethical theories as the axiological bases of the "new secular life" in modern times generally go along two directions: (i) the empiric-utilitarian approach, systematization of which began with Locke and continued with utilitarian philosophers, and (ii) Kantian causal-a priori systematization.

Locke's fundamental criterion for axiological goodness—that pleasure is the good—was the prevalent view among empiricists throughout the eighteenth and nineteenth centuries. He tries to preserve the link between morality and belief in God in his *Essay Concerning Human Understanding*, but that aims to form a theological justification for his utilitarian approach because Locke admits at the same time that human beings value present pleasure more than future pleasure and pleasure in the near future more than pleasure in the distant future. That view has

---

in Taylor (1965) there is Hobbes the Kantian; in Warrender (1951) and Hood (1964) there is Hobbes the Christian; in Mintz (1969) there is Hobbes the atheist; in Marshall (1983) there is Hobbes the skeptic; in Weinstein (1979) there is Hobbes the Freudian; in Watkins (1965) there is Hobbes the metaphysician. The basic argument of Macpherson's (1962) alternative interpretation of Hobbes is that the central structuring element of Hobbes' political theory is sociological and socio-economic rather than philosophical.

been repeated by the Mill (1951:12) in nineteenth century. Such an admission evidently contradicts the eschatological views of religion.

Adam Smith's consideration of God as a utilitarian in his *The Theory of Moral Sentiments* might be accepted as an extension of this attempt of theological justification for the argument of empiricist utilitarianism. Smith probably views God as a rule-utilitarian, for he argues that "the happiness of mankind, as well as of all other rational creatures, seems to have been the original purpose intended by the Author of Nature. God considers the general consequences of types of conduct and arranges it so that man habitually acts in such a way as to maximize the general happiness. But, of course, God is a utilitarian whose situation is so unlike that of men that it is difficult to compare His utilitarianism with that of man beings. For instance, God does not, presumably, have to choose between His own happiness and that of other beings, and therefore many of the problems of justice versus utility, or private versus public utility, do not arise" (Campbell, 1971:219).

J. S. Mill (1951:26) aims to develop such a theological justification, asserting that "If it be a true belief that God desires, above all things, the happiness of his creatures and that this was his purpose in their creation, utility is not only a godless doctrine, but more profoundly religious than any other." Mill adds that "If it be meant that utilitarianism does not recognise the revealed will of God as the supreme law of morals, ... a utilitarian who believes in the perfect goodness and wisdom of God, necessarily believes that whatever God has thought fit to reveal on the subject of morals, must fulfil the requirements of utility in a supreme degree." These arguments show the mental relationship between the understanding of limited theism and utilitarianism as well as the attempts of utilitarians to obtain a theological justification for the rationalization of axiology.

Bentham, the most sophisticated follower of Locke, substitutes the human lawgiver for God, strengthening the tendency toward secularization of life and law within the context of utilitarianism. Bentham's classification of the sanctions or sources of pleasure and pain in four groups as the physical, the moral, the political, and the religious in *An Introduction to The Principles of Morals and Legislation* might be evaluated as a specific segmentation of axiology as well as the isolation of the religious sanction from the others. His interpretation for the measurement of pleasure and pain was an attempt to objectify his theory within a scientific framework (Bentham, 1965:25,30). This objectification provided a positive base for the absoluteness of the secular axiology and substituted it for the absoluteness of the religious axiology. That is especially meaningful when we accept Berdyaev's (1960:16) definition that "Ethics is axiology, the theory of meaning and values." Thus, the Ideal value-system of Church has been replaced by the Positive-Actual value-system of Society. This is a new process of the dichotomic characteristic of Western experience related to axiology, life, and law.

James' argument (1916:69) that "pragmatism may be a happy harmonizer of the empiricist way of thinking with the more religious demands of human beings" seems to be an attempt at the reconciliation of these dichotomic sides on a new axiological base. Nevertheless, his axiological pragmatism shapes a total system with his ontological pluralism and epistemological radical empiricism. The pragmatic assumption that an idea is true if it possesses some subsequent utility (James, 1916:203-4) shows the assertion of the sovereignty of the Actual value-system, rather than an attempt at reconciliation. He extends this principle even to the imagination of God, arguing that "on pragmatic principles, if the hypothesis of God works satisfactorily in the widest sense of the word, it is true" (James, 1916:299).

From this perspective, he is a follower of the utilitarian approach mentioned above, while methodologically he approaches Kantian moral theology.

On the other hand, the dichotomic characteristic of Western experience is very evident in James' argument (1929:250) that "though the scientist may individually nourish a religion and be a theist in his irresponsible hours, the days are over when it could be said that for Science herself the heavens declare the glory of God and the firmament showeth the handiwork." This argument gives several very significant insights into modern Western mind. First, it offers a mental segmentation within the personality of the scientist. Second, it divides life into responsible and irresponsible hours and sees religious feelings-thoughts as matters to occupy the irresponsible hours. Third, it assumes a full individualization of religious feelings-thoughts. All of these characteristics are fundamental indications for the axiological particularization of mental and social structures of human being under the hegemony of rationalistic axiology based on anthropocentric epistemology. These presuppositions developed necessarily parallel to an ontological proximity in the sense of limited theism.

Kantian synthesism provided very significant elements for the hegemony of the rational axiology and for the re-formulation of the dichotomic structure, though it was theoretically alternative to utilitarianism. Kant's replacement of theological morality with moral theology was a radical attempt both to refute ontological and cosmological arguments for the existence of God and to solve the Euthyphro dilemma—whether what God commands is good because God commands it or is commanded because it is good—in favour of the rational objectification of morality. His argument that the fundamental laws of morality are the same for every rational being—whether man, angel, or God—since the ultimate criterion of rightness is deducible from the concept of a rational being as such, was not only a declaration of the autonomy of morality from religion but also the imposition of a new axiological base for religion within a new epistemological framework.

Kant's division of metaphysics into the metaphysics of nature and the metaphysics of morals in his *Gründlegung der Metaphysik der Sitten* forms the new links between epistemology and axiology.[46] His understanding of the metaphysics of morals, which shook the traditional belief that morality without religion was impossible, is a cornerstone for the rationalization process of axiology. Kant's notion of morality as something categorical and a priori aims to eliminate the alternative interpretations of morality, namely that it is a matter of emotions, that it is a matter of practical consequences, or that it is a matter of obeying God's will. One of the significant corollaries in his *Kritik der Praktischen Vernunft*, that "Pure Reason is practical of itself alone and gives [to man] a universal law which we call the Moral Law" (Kant, 1909b:120), assumes a common rational set of axiological criteria for all rational beings—including Infinite Being (Kant, 1909b:120-21)—which might be accepted as a theoretical justification for the secularization of life and law. He links this justification with a new interpretation of humanism within the context of his fundamental axiom, *summum bonum*. (Kant, 1909b:227-29).

---

[46]"In this way there arises the idea of a twofold metaphysic—a metaphysic of nature and a metaphysic of morals. Physics will thus have an empirical and also a rational part. It is the same with Ethics; but here the empirical part might have the special name of practical anthropology, the name morality being appropriated to the rational part" (Kant, 1909a:2).

Thus, "this moral law is founded on the autonomy of his will, as a free will which by its universal laws must necessarily be able to agree with that to which it is to submit itself" (Kant, 1909b:229).

Kant's reduction of religion to morals gave a new color to the traditional dichotomic mental and institutional particularization through the restoration of the understanding of religion, especially in his *Religion within the Limits of Pure Reason*. This restoration was based on a deistic interpretation of religion (Reese, 1980:121) leading to a definition of religion as the recognition of all our duties (moral obligations) as commandments of God. Such a recognition necessitates a re-interpretation of the separation between natural and revealed religion: "It is revealed religion when through it I must first of all know that something is a commandment of God before I can also know that it is my duty; it is natural religion when I must first of all know that something is a duty before I can know that it is a commandment of God" (Schwegler, 1871:238). Kant's definition of church as an ethical and spiritual community which has for its object the fulfillment and the greatest possible realization of the moral prescripts, assumes intrinsically the dichotomy of Matter-Spirit, Ideal-Actual, and Church-Society and specifies the role of Church within this dichotomic framework *in so far as mere reason permits*.

The new functional role of Church systematized by modern theologians under the impact of the new understanding of morality facilitates both the development of rationalistic axiology and the preservation of the traditional axiological particularization. Schleiermacher's assumption of subjective experience is a good example of this new mentality. Troeltsch's distinction between the religions of law (Islam and Judaism) and the religions of redemption (Christianity and Buddhism) to show the relative superiority of Christianity (1972:107-16), because of the lack of division between the natural and transcendent worlds in the religions of law, is an interesting justification for the withdrawal of Christianity from the sphere of law, which is not a modern artifact but a fundamental feature of Christianity surviving from the Graeco-Roman assumption of two commonwealths. The relationship between Troeltsch's ontological presupposition of redemption through faithful, trusting participation in the person-like character of God and his axiological conclusion as the apathy to law provide meaningful evidence for our argument that there is a mental and imaginative relationship between ontological proximity and axiological particularization.

Thus, the secular element in life and law in Western experience has been re-shaped and the functional spheres of the two commonwealths (which survived as a significant imaginative, mental, and institutional phenomenon in Western tradition from the ancient to the modern periods) has been re-specified. Thus, this secular element is not a new or modern characteristic of Western civilization but a re-formed element which survived throughout the ages within the context of axiological particularization, which has direct links to ontological proximity and epistemological particularization of truth. The surviving elements of these interlinkages among ontology, epistemology, and axiology should be well-analyzed if one is to understand the formation of the Western mind and to follow the internal continuity and consistency of the evolution of Western political images, cultures, theories, and institutions.

CHAPTER 3

ISLAMIC PARADIGM: *TAWHID* AND ONTOLOGICAL DIFFERENTIATION

The ontologically determined epistemology based on a theocentric cosmology provides a specific type of political justification and legitimacy in Islam. It is almost impossible to understand Islamic political culture or Muslim political consciousness without first understanding the Islamic *imago mundi*. The political consequences should be evaluated within this holistic framework of Islam.

The basic principle of Islamic theocentric cosmology is the belief of *tawhîd (Lâ ilâha illa Allâh)* and its conception of Allâh.The principle of *tawhîd*[1] is the main channel from theory to practice, from belief to life, and from ideal to reality in the holistic Islamic *Weltanschauung*. This principle implies that Allâh is one in His essence *(dhât)*, i.e., not composed of parts; one in His attributes *(sifât)*, i.e., not having two powers, two knowledges, etc.; one in His works *(af'âl)*, i.e., not being influenced in any way by anything other than Himself. This principle together with the principle of *tanzîh* (no compromise with the transcendent purity of Allâh) might be accepted as the paradigmatic base of unity among conflicting schools, sects, and traditions in Islamic history.

The principle of *tanzîh,* with the term of *Subhânahu,* which is used to indicate the purity of Allâh from all defects, is the keynote in the discrimination of the "absolute" from the "relative" through the belief in the transcendence and sovereignty of the "Creator absolute" over the "created relatives" *('âlam)*. The negative aspect of the sentence of *tawhîd (Lâ ilâha*—there is no god) is the rejection of the recognition of other sources of transcendence and sovereignty, while the positive aspect *(illa Allâh*—but Allâh) is the obedience of all relative beings to the focus of absoluteness, namely Allâh. This obedience is also the name of the religion, *Islam.*[2]

Zarkashî mentions several arguments on the comparative priorities of the negative *(nafy)* and positive *(ithbât)* aspects of the sentence of *tawhîd* in his epistle *Ma'nâ Lâ ilâha illa Allâh.* The argument that this sentence of *tawhîd* begins with the negative aspect *(Lâ ilâha)* for the cleansing of hearts *(li tathîr al-qulûb)*(Zarkashî, 1986:82) is especially significant in showing the fact that the first stage of the imagination of a real monotheistic framework is the rejection of any type of relationship of ontological proximity and identification between the absolute (Allâh) and the relative (created beings), which is the source of the attribution *(shirk)* of a partner to the absoluteness of Allâh that the Islamic belief system condemns.

---

[1]The root of this word is *wahhada*, which means to declare to be one or, in terminological usage, the action of declaring God to be one.

[2]The root of *Islam* is *salima*, which means to resign, surrender, submit oneself. Hence, the meaning of *Islam* is the act of resigning, submitting oneself. The one who resigns or submits is a Muslim.

Such an attribution may occur in two ways, either through the deification of any part of the relative beings or through the incarnation of the absolute in the form of relative beings. Such a relationship of ontological proximity or identification is the rejection of the negative aspect of the sentence of *tawhīd*, leading to a misimagination and misinterpretation of the relationship between the absolute and the relative. The direct involvement of Elohim—the Absolute—with relative beings in Judaism (e.g., marriage with the daughters of men in Genesis 6:2-4; wrestling with Jacob in Genesis 32:24-30), the Christian doctrines of Incarnation and Trinity, the Hindu principle of *avatar*, and oneness with Tao in Taoism might be evaluated as some types of the relationship of ontological proximity and identification from this perspective of the negative aspect of the sentence of *tawhīd*. Although some sort of relationship between Islam and pre-Islamic monotheistic religions in the Middle East, especially Judaism, has been mentioned (Schimmel, 1976:12) in several studies, the original characteristics of Islamic theology around the principle of *tawhīd* are undeniable. As Hegel (1902:451) specifies, the subjectivist emphasis on the God-man (Jewish community) relationship in Judaism was done away with in Islamic theology because "Allāh has not the affirmative, limited aim of the Judaic God" (Hegel, 1902:452).

Significant consequences for Islamic theoretical tradition and for popular Muslim belief have developed out of this transparently defined concept of Allāh in Islam. First of all, the concept produces an ontological hierarchy between Allāh and man preventing the relationship of identification or proximity between the absolute and relative (created) beings. Together with the cosmological understanding of Islam, this ontological hierarchy might be formulated as "Allāh-man-nature."

It is a common hypothesis that Islamic theology and philosophy owe a significant debt to the Greek legacy. It is impossible to deny that Islamic philosophy especially developed within a cultural-geographical milieu that was influenced by Greek philosophy, but this should not be overestimated. When it appeared, Islam gave a special ontological color to this pre-Islamic legacy. Although there have been several discussions and contradictions among Islamic schools of thought such as *kalām* and *falsafah*, the idea that Islamic philosophy was a simple continuation of neo-Platonic and Aristotelian ways of thinking and that it is therefore impossible to find a common paradigmatic base among these Islamic schools and traditions is an oversimplification. It is based on the misconception that these traditions not only lacked a common base, they also lacked any originality.

In contrast to this superficial view, it can be argued that the accumulated bulk of Islamic theory has a paradigmatic unity with ontologically absolute transcendency. This unity originates from the idea of the unity of divinity, and its consequence is related to Islamic epistemology and axiology. All the Islamic schools of thought tried to show different aspects and proofs of this fundamental ontological argument using different methodologies, techniques, and nomenclatures.[3] Their contradictions are only on a methodological sphere, but they possess this paradigmatic unity.

Although Islamic intellectual tradition used some pre-Islamic sources such as Greek philosophy, it has developed an original *Weltanschauung* around the belief

---

[3]Al-Ash'arī's judgement on his death bed that "I do not call any of this *qiblah* an unbeliever; they point to one God, there is only a difference of terms" (Tritton, 1947:167) shows this fact.

that the ontological transcendence and unity of Allâh are the prime and only cause of all that take place. Almost all analyses by *kalâm* and *falsafah* aim to prove this ontological transcendency and unity.

The belief that the Qur'ân, as *Kalâmullâh* and *Kitâb-i Mubîn* (Clear Book), is also *Furqân* (Discriminator), which specifies and distinguishes between *Haqq* (True) and *Bâṭil* (Untrue), sets up a very strong link between ontology, epistemology, and axiology in the Islamic way of thought. This specifies the impact of ontological antecedents over axiological criteria via epistemological differentiation originating from the belief in ontological transcendence. Now, we can analyze in depth these imaginative and theoretical links among ontology, epistemology, and axiology.

Cosmologico-ontological unity and transcendency

Qur'ânic base

The origin of the ontological color in Islamic history of thought is the original and unique imagination and specification of the relationship between Allâh, man, and nature in the Qur'ân. This imagination depends on a very clear ontological hierarchy based on a cosmologico-ontological unity and transcendency, in contrast to Western ontological proximity[4] based on a cosmologico-ontological particularization and fusion. Allâh's self-definition through His names in the Qur'ân is the first essential source for this understanding of the highly concentrated ontological transcendency and absoluteness. "Allâh," as the center of the semantic system within the Qur'ân, shapes all ontological, epistemological, and axiological links. Therefore it is impossible to understand not only the internal mechanism of Qur'ânic meaning but also the fundamental characteristic of Islamic theoretical accumulation throughout the ages without first understanding the place of the imagination of the belief in Allâh in the process of the formation of Muslim consciousness.[5]

---

[4]This concept of ontological proximity should not be confused with the Islamic ethical concept of *qurbiyyah* which means a moral feeling of nearness to Allâh. Ontological proximity harbors the meaning of the origin of ontological beings, while the other intends to demonstrate a mode of feeling and action in morals to become nearer to the ontologically transcendent being.

[5]Therefore Wensinck's argument (1932:3) that the Qur'ân "does not proclaim a compendium of faith that could serve as a characteristic description of Islam, either in contrast with other religions, or as a means of distinction from the peculiar doctrines of the sects" lacks the essential role of the Qur'ân in the process of mental formation as a specific way of imagination. He generalizes a characteristic of Qur'ânic rhetoric to the essence of the Qur'ânic theocentric system. Qur'ânic rhetoric should not correspond to modern rhetoric. From the perspective of the essence of the Qur'ânic theocentric system, it really gives a very well-defined compendium of faith. The analogy in his following sentence that "in the same way the creeds of the Christian Church could not be directly taken from the New Testament" (1932:3) is an oversimplification because of the essential differences between Christian and Islamic ways of understanding revelation.

Allâh's being the source of all absoluteness is the core of His self-definition, as shown by His names (asmâ' Allâh al-ḥusnâ) in the Qur'ân (7:180; P.). For example, "He is Allâh, than whom there is no other God, the Knower ['Âlim] of the invisible and the visible. He is the Beneficent [Raḥmân], the Merciful [Raḥîm]. He is Allâh than whom there is no other God, the Sovereign Lord [Mâlik], the Holy One [Quddûs], Peace [Salâm], the Keeper of Faith [Mu'min], the Guardian [Muhaimin], the Majestic ['Azîz], the Compeller [Jabbâr], the Superb [Mutakkabbir]. Glorified be Allâh from all that they ascribe as partner [unto him]. He is Allâh, the Creator [Khâliq], the Shaper out of naught [Bâri'], the Fashioner [Muṣawwir]. His are the most beautiful names. All that is in the heavens and the earth glorifies Him, and He is the Mighty, the Wise [Ḥakîm]" (Qur'ân, 59:22-24). Muslim scholars have formulated several classifications of the names of Allâh mentioned in the Qur'ân and hadîths. Although according to some hadîths there are ninety-nine names of Allâh,[6] this does not mean a limitation, as Ghazzâlî (1971:182) and Bayhaqî (Khaṭîb, 1988:16) argue. All of these names of Allâh have been imagined and understood by several Muslim schools and scholars as the ultimate-absolute attributes, which are impenetrable by the limited intellectual capacity of human beings. Several commentaries on these names were written by Muslim scholars to interpret the absoluteness of Allâh within the context of these names.[7]

The name Allâh was used for the high god of pre-Islamic Makkah. That fact is evident in the Qur'ânic verses (e.g., 29:62, 63-5; 31:32) and in pre-Islamic poetry. But the imagination of this high god by Makkan polytheists was completely different from the Qur'ânic description of Allâh. Pre-Islamic Makkan polytheists acknowledged lesser deities together with this high god. This acknowledgement prevented the development of a highly concentrated monotheistic imagination among the Arabs, although the ḥunafâ (pre-Islamic followers of Abraham) did try to maintain the Abrahamic monotheistic tradition. Eliade's conceptualization of the pre-Islamic Arabs' belief in Allâh as deus otiosus because of the fact that "his cult had been reduced to certain offerings of first fruits [grains and animals], which were brought to him conjointly with various local divinities" (1985:III/64) is right from the perspective of the existence of the intermediary deified ontological beings between Allâh (in the Qur'ânic sense) and man. These lesser deities were sometimes regarded as "daughters of Allâh" (banât Allâh) and sometimes as angels who could help (yashfa'unâ ilayhi) worshippers through intercession (shufa'â') and mediation (wasâ'iṭ) with the high god (Ibn al-Kalbî, 1969:13). Thus, such an imagination of divinity carried characteristics of ontological proximity and particularization of divinity similar to those in Western experience.

Islamic ontological color, as the central dynamic of the historical accumulation from the theoretical and practical perspectives, originates from a semantic and

---

[6]For example, Bukhârî (1981:III/185; in Kitâb al-Shurût), and Muslim (1981:III/2063; in Kitâb al-Dhikr) narrate from Abû Hurayrah the number of the names; while Tirmizî (1981:V/530-1; in Kitâb al-Da'wat) adds the list of names in the hadith.

[7]Among many others, Râzî's Lewâmi' al-Bayyinat Sharḥ Asmâ Allâh Ta'âla wa Ṣifât (1984), Ghazzâlî's Al-Maqṣad al-Asnâ fi Sharḥ Ma'ânî Asmâ Allâh al-Ḥusnâ (1971), Qushayrî's Sharḥ Asmâ Allâh al-Ḥusnâ (1986) might be mentioned as examples.

imaginative revolution in the understanding of Allâh realized by the Qur'ânic description. The highly concentrated ontological hierarchy based on the theocentric system of Qur'ân is the basic point of departure between Islam and other religions or philosophies. Thus, Islamic ontological hierarchy and differentiation between the absolute and the relative, or between Allâh and the creature, shapes an original *Weltanschauung* based on a new set of links among Allâh-man-nature completely different from the understanding of ontological proximity. From this perspective, "Islam is the religion of certitude and equilibrium," as Schuon (1963:16) underlines. As Eliade asserts, "from the viewpoint of religious morphology, Muḥammad's message, such as it is formulated in the Qur'ân, represents the purest expression of absolute monotheism" (1985:III/78). This marks the difference between Islam and other religions, especially Western religious traditions, namely Christianity and Judaism.

We can show this fundamental difference through a hermeneutical analysis of Sûrah al-Ikhlâṣ (112, twenty-second *sûrah* in the chronological list): "Say He is Allâh, the One! Allâh, the Eternally Besought of All [*Ṣamad*]! He begets not nor was begotten. And there is none comparable unto Him." As Yildirim (1987:302-3) mentions, there is a continuity between this *sûrah* and Sûrah al-Kâfirûn (109, eighteenth *sûrah* in the chronological list). Al-Kâfirûn ultimately separates the Islamic understanding of divinity from pre-Islamic traditions, while al-Ikhlâṣ challenges all types of ontological proximities through the self-description of Allâh. This is especially significant from two perspectives. First, it shows the original ontological color of Islam as opposing pre-Islamic understandings of divinity. Second, it might be a good example of the semantic revolution that the Qur'ân achieves by setting up new semantic environments around re-defined key-concepts.

The traditions of *asbâb-i nuzûl* (the reasons for the revelation of the verses) related to Sûrah al-Ikhlâṣ show its comprehensive challenge to the pre-Islamic religions. According to the traditions, this *sûrah* was revealed in response to the questions of Arab polytheists[8] and of Jews and Christians (Yazir, 1971:IX/6271-2), who were arguing for some sort of ontological proximity between God and creatures. The relationship of lineage between high god and other deified entities, a significant characteristic of ontological proximity, was a common feature of the pre-Islamic religious traditions in the Near East. Such a relationship was widely accepted in Greek mythology and Syrian-Egyptian religious cults, as has already been shown. Arab polytheists assumed that their lesser deities—such as Lât, Manât, and Uzza—were connected to the high god in such a relation of kinship (e.g., as daughters), while the Jews were asserting that 'Uzayr (Ezra) was God's son, just as the Christians believed that Jesus was the Son of God (Qur'ân, 9:30).

Against this traditional background, Sûrah al-Ikhlâṣ asserted an absolute ontological hierarchy. The inclination toward polytheistic particularism on the sphere of divinity is rejected in the first verse of this *sûrah*—"Say: He is Allâh, the One"—while in the following verses the ontological spheres of the divinity and creatures are completely separated by the description of a highly concentrated

---

[8]The Arab polytheists' question—narrated in a tradition recorded on the authority of Ibn Ka'b (Ibn Kathîr, 1986:565)—on the lineage of the gods parallels the ancient Greek understanding of the lineage of the gods (e.g., in Plato's *Timaeus*), discussed in the previous chapter, and is therefore especially significant for the purpose of showing the Qur'ânic challenge against ontologically proximity.

monotheistic framework opposing any kind of kinship between God and creatures. Therefore this *sûrah* might be accepted as a short summary of the theocentric structure, characteristic of the whole Qur'ânic system, against the ideas of the particularization of divinity and ontological proximity.

From a hermeneutical perspective, the first impact of the Qur'ân was a semantic re-formulation and re-systematization using the same semantic tools (concepts and words) of the same language. This led to a comprehensive imaginative revolution establishing a new set of links between linguistics and mental imagination. The characteristics of the Islamic *Weltanschauung* and its highly flexible and dynamic process of popularization should be examined within this context. The concept of Qur'ânic *i'jâz* (miracle) in its linguistic and semantic capacities is especially meaningful with regard to this re-systematization and re-valuation of words. This re-valuation follows a process in some cases (e.g., the concept of *kufr*),[9] while it occurs with a new use of the word in a single verse in some other cases (e.g., *al-Samad* as a name for Allâh). For example, in Sûrah al-Ikhlâṣ *Allâh* and *Samad* are re-valuated within a new semantic system as the name of the absolute ontological being.

The first verse—"Say: He is Allâh, the One"—rejects the old usage of *Allâh* as the name of the preeminent deity co-existing with other, lesser deities among the pre-Islamic Arabs, arguing that He is not merely the high god but the absolute and only One.[10] This semantic re-valuation of *Allâh* is dominant within the Qur'ânic semantic system as a whole. Therefore, Rubin's assertion that "Muḥammad shared with the pre-Islamic Arabs the same deity" (1984:199) might lead to a misinterpretation if we overlook the fact that the attributes of two understandings of divinity correspond to completely contrasting imaginations.[11] The similarity between Qur'ânic and pre-Islamic conceptualizations of divinity is related to their common base in the Abrahamic tradition, but they differ to a great extent concerning the attributes of the divine being and His ontological position compared with other beings. From this perspective, the theocentric ontological system of the Qur'ân

---

[9]Waldman's article (1968) on the chronological development of the concept of *kufr* is an interesting example for this purpose.

[10]This re-valuation from "high god" to "One God" should be interpreted through an evaluation of the Qur'ânic holistic system. From this perspective, Watt's argument (1979:209-210) that the Qur'ân did not at first deny the existence of the lesser deities because of its emphasis on the powerlessness of the deities rather than on the rejection of their existence and that "therefore the Qur'ân sometimes speaks of the deities as angels" is not correct. In these cases the Qur'ân aims to remind the Makkan people of the true Abrahamic monotheism. On the other hand, the Qur'ânic verses he gives as examples (e.g., 10:18; 30:12-13) deny the existence of divine qualities of these lesser deities arguing their powerlessness which means a total rejection of lesser deities.

[11]His interpretation that "the difference of opinion between Muḥammad and his Arab contemporaries did not relate to the identity of the god who had to be worshipped, but rather to the position of this god among other objects of veneration" (1984:199) lacks the qualitative difference of imagination between ontological particularization of divinity and unity of divinity in the metaphysical sphere. From this point of view, "the identity of the god" could not be separated from "the position of a god among other objects of veneration."

strictly denies intermediary deified beings, such as those in pre-Islamic Arab polytheism, as an ontological category between Creator and creatures.

This semantic re-valuation is valid also for the epithet *Samad*, which occurs only once in the Qur'ân, in the second verse of Sûrah al-Ikhlâṣ. This epithet is an interesting example of the process of this semantic re-valuation from a daily meaning to a metaphysical imagination. Although Ibn Manẓûr (n.d.:IV/2496) gives a long list of meanings for this word in *Lisân al-'Arab*, two of them are especially significant from our perspective. As Râzî (1984:317) summarizes, first, *Samad* is *fa'alun bi ma'nâ maf'ûlun*, from its verb form *ṣamada* (in the meaning of *qaṣada*— to direct, to turn), and in this sense means *al-sayyid al-maṣmûd ilayhi fî al-ḥawâij*— a leader towards whom one turns in cases of emergency and exigency. Second, it means a being to which penetration is impossible (*al-Ṣamad huwa alladhî la jawfa lahu*) or a being to which nothing can penetrate and out of which nothing can come (*wa lâ yadkhluhu shay'un wa lâ yakhruju minhu shay'un*)(Râzî, 1984:318).[12]

After the Qur'ânic re-valuation, this word, as the epithet of Allâh, undergoes a radical change toward a comprehensive metaphysical meaning. That new meaning is far beyond Watt's explanation that "Allâh is thought of as the powerful *sayyid* of a tribe and the lesser deities as other men who are prepared to use their influence with the *sayyid* on behalf of the suppliants of whom they have become the awliyâ' or patrons" (1979:207), when we evaluate it within the context of the places of the epithets of Allâh in the Qur'ânic semantic system. Therefore, Rubin's assertion that Muslim theologians could no longer tolerate the original meaning of *al-Ṣamad*, as the high god toward whom worshippers turn in cases of emergency, carries the same deficiency because of the isolation of a re-valued term from the holistic semantic system of Qur'ân.

The extensive diversification and metaphysical sophistication of the interpretations developed by *mufassirûn* (commentators) on this epithet verify our argument on the re-valuation. Râzî (1984:318) analyzes these comments in two groups as an extension of the literal meaning. The first group contains the meaning of the ultimate absoluteness of Allâh's sovereignty (al-Râzî mentions fourteen different interpretations within this group such as Absolute Knower, Absolute Sovereign, etc.),[13] while the second group is based on the principle of *tanzîh* through the meaning of the rejection of penetration (al-Râzî mentions eighteen different interpretations in this group).[14] This extensive diversification might be seen also in the English translations of the Qur'ân.[15]

---

[12]Rubin (1984: 200-2) gives detailed information on the various pre-Qur'ânic uses of this word.

[13]*Lisân al-'Arab* (n.d.:IV/2596) shows the transformation of meaning from *al-ṣamad al-sayyid alladhi yantahi ilayhi al-su'dad* (the leader in whom the leadership ends) to *Allâh Ta'âla fala nihayah li su'dadihi li anna sudadahu ghayru maḥdûdin* (there is not any limit for the sovereignty of Allâh). Ibn Mas'ûd and al-Ḍaḥḥâk accept this meaning (Râzî, 1984:318).

[14]Significant examples include Sa'îd b. Jâbir's *al-kâmil bidhâtihi*, Hasan Baṣrî's *lam yazal wa lâ yazal*, and al-Muqatil's *al-munazzah 'an kulli 'ayb*.

[15]Pickthall translates it as "Allâh, the eternally Besought of All," Yûsuf 'Ali (1983) as "God, the Eternal, the Absolute," Zayid (1980) as "the Eternal God," and Shâkir (1986) as "Allâh is He on Whom all depend."

The hermeneutical analysis of this short *sûrah*[16] might be extended to the whole Qur'ânic semantic system which shaped (or re-shaped considering the old Abrahamic tradition) a new set of links between linguistic and ontological imagination. The essential characteristics of the Islamic *Weltanschauung* should be understood within the context of the highly concentrated ontological transcendency around the concept of *tawḥîd* which has been clarified by the self-definition of Allâh in the Qur'ân. The relationship between Allâh and man is based on this ontological centrality and supremacy of Allâh.

I want to underline this fundamental characteristic of Islamic ontology when I mention ontological differentiation. Horten's phrase "God's aloofness from the world"[17] does not correspond to this ontological differentiation, because my usage of ontological differentiation implies an ultimate differentiation of ontological spheres rather than an aloofness on the same ontological sphere. Therefore *al-Ṣamad* as an absolute ontological being in Sûrah al-Ikhlâṣ analyzed in the previous lines does not contrast with other Qur'ânic verses in which Allâh says that He breathed into human beings of His Spirit (15:29; 38:73) and that He is "nearer to him [the human being] than his jugular vein" (50:16; cf. 56:85). This subtle distinction might explain the internal dynamic of Islamic thought which compromises the understanding of the highly ontological differentiation between Allâh and man with the imagination of the nearness (*qurbiyyah*) between Allâh and man through a specific type of relationship. It clarifies also the intersecting sphere of imagination and thought among several Islamic schools, while it shows how exoteric and esoteric interpretations of the Qur'ân form a consistent totality of theocentric *Weltanschauung*.

Thus, the relationship between Allâh and man in this *Weltanschauung* is completely different from an ontological proximity which assumes a penetration among ontological spheres. Therefore, the Qur'ânic *Weltanschauung* tends toward ontological supremacy, while Western intellectual history has shifted step by step toward an ontological identification. Izutsu's (n.d., 70-72) analysis of the complex relationship between Allâh and man as two ontological poles in four types and Schuon's definition of Islam[18] in terms of the definitions of God and man are two meaningful interpretations of the novel Islamic ontological relationship between

---

[16]Ringgren's (1962:93-96) linguistic analysis of *ikhlâṣ* verifies this argument of re-valuation.

[17]"The cosmos is an indirect expression of God's concealment. For screens separate from the lower world—'veils of light', light-oceans; these are numbered according to seven motif: 70,700 to 70000. Thus God's aloofness from the world is immeasurably great, and God is 'inaccessible' to men; i.e., 'concealed'. Beneath the light-oceans, the seven planetary tiers, the so-called seven heavens, further isolate God from men" (Horten, 1973:5).

[18]"Islam is the meeting between God as such and man as such. God as such: that is to say God envisaged, not as He manifested Himself in a particular way at a particular time, but independently of history and inasmuch as He is what He is and also as by His Nature He creates and reveals. Man as such: that is to say man envisaged, not as a fallen being needing a miracle to save him, but as man, a theomorphic being endowed with an intelligence capable of conceiving of the Absolute and with a will capable of choosing what leads to the Absolute" (Schuon,1965:13).

Allâh and man. Nieuwenhuijze's (1985) categorization of this relationship as "God-man relationship: revelation as a form; man-God relationship: faith as a lifestyle; and man-man relationship: Islam as a socio-cultural system," is also very interesting because of its socio-cultural implications.

Revelation and socio-cultural system as two specific types of the ontological relationship will be analyzed in the following parts. At this stage we can concentrate on *îmân* (faith) as a positive man-God relationship and *kufr* as a negative man-God relationship. Faith, as a specific type of man-God relationship might be seen as a recognition and consciousness of the ontological supremacy of Allâh. Islam defines two alternative ontological approaches in terms of the dichotomy of *îmân* and *kufr* (and *shirk*). This dichotomy has significant epistemological, axiological, and socio-cultural consequences.

Although it has been argued that *amana,* from which the word *îmân* is derived, originates from Hebrew (Horovitz, 1916:55; Ahrens, 1930:36) or Aramaic (Ahrens, 1930:36), this word, too, has been re-valuated within the semantic system of the Qur'ân. Brawmann's argument that "*amana* was formed in the usual way from *amn* and that it meant 'to seek safety' and 'to be safe' in God for fate and death" (Ringgren, 1951:1) is more trustworthy, although this key-term carries additional meanings. Ringgren's analysis (1951) on the evolution of this Qur'ânic term is especially important from this perspective. Although he differentiates (1951:9) the meanings of amânah as *amn* (security) and as belief (the opposite of *kafara* ["to deny"] or *ajrama* ["to sin"]), the real etymological and imaginative meaning of this word comes out in the interconnected semantic sphere of these two meanings. From this perspective, *al-mu'minûn* (believers) as used in the second meaning—such as in Sûrah al-Baqarah (2:3-5, 283), Sûrah Ali 'Imrân (3:179), Sûrah al-Tawbah (9:71), and elsewhere—are the persons who recognize the ontological security and protection of *al-Mu'min al-Muhaimin* in the sense of the first meaning—the names of Allâh as Faithful, Protector in Sûrah al-Hashr (59:23)—because "Allâh is the Protecting Friend of those who believe, He brings them out of darkness into light. As for those who disbelieve their patrons are false deities [*tâghût*], they bring them out of light into darkness" (2:257, P.).

This interconnected semantic sphere creates a psycho-ontological dimension of meaning in the sense of *itma'anna* in Qur'ân: "Who have believed and whose hearts have rest [*itma'anna*] in the remembrance of Allâh. Verily in the remembrance of Allâh do hearts find rest" (13:28). This psycho-ontological dimension gives a spiritually limitless comprehensive meaning to the word *amânah* beyond Ahrens' interpretation of faith as *Fürwahrhalten* (1930:60). Therefore Baidâwî's declaration that faith is "*Fürwahrhalten* combined with the peace of the heart [*tasdîq ma'a tuma'ninat qalb*]" (Ringgren, 1951:15), which has been accepted by almost all Muslim schools, shows the very strong relationship between ontological consciousness and epistemology in the Islamic imagination of *Weltanschauung.*

This imagination of *Weltanschauung* specifies the basic characteristics of the ontological differentiation of the Islamic man-God relationship through a specific understanding of faith directed by a fulfillment of ontological security. Remembrance of Allâh results in a *qurbiyyah* in the man-God relationship through the resting of hearts, but it does not mean an ontological penetration in this relationship, which would destroy ontological security in the ultimate sense. The ontological status in the Islamic man-God relationship is very definite. Therefore, a person might reject such a relationship and might prefer a negative man-God relationship (*kufr,* in which case he would be a *kâfir*). Nevertheless, it is not only impossible but also inconsistent to impose upon a conscious Muslim who accepts such a relationship between himself and Allâh an epistemologico-axiological framework that denies the spirit of this ontological relationship. As will be shown in the parts on epistemological and axiological consequences, îmân (faith-ontology), 'ilm (knowledge-epistemology) and al-'amal al-ṣâliḥ (good work-ethics) are three interconnected key-concepts in the Qur'ân which set up the relationship of interdependency among ontology, epistemology, and axiology.[19]

Nature is composed of the material environment within which this man-God relationship occurs. Therefore its raison d'etre is directly combined with the purpose of man. Hence, man shares the same ontological sphere with nature because both are creatures, but man ultimately has supremacy over nature because he is the vicegerent of Allâh. Thus, there is an ontological hierarchy of Allâh-man-nature in the intellectual accumulation in the history of Islamic thought around the principle of tawḥîd.

Systematization of the paradigm

This absolute ontological hierarchy and transcendency in the Qur'ânic theocentric system became the essence of the paradigmatic unity among several Muslim schools in the history of Islamic thought. In a very general sense, the members of kalâm, falsafah and taṣawwuf—as fundamental divisions of Islamic thought—aimed to show and systematize several aspects of this fundamental truth using different methodologies and nomenclatures. The detailed discussions on the subject of the attributes of Allâh came out as a result of their attempts to preserve this fundamental characteristic of the Qur'ânic creed during the process of encountering pre-Islamic belief systems after the Islamic expansion to the centers of ancient civilizations. Four are of great importance among the pre-Islamic intellectual centers: the School of Alexandria, the Nestorian School of the East, the School of Harran, and the School of Iranian Jundishapur.[20] Although some scientists argue that the history of

---

[19]This relationship is explained by al-Ghazzâlî in Ayyuha al-Walad (1933:55/58) through the following analogy: "Knowledge ['ilm] is the tree, and working ['amal] is its fruit; and though you studied a hundred years and collected a thousand books, you would not be prepared for the mercy of Allâh the Exalted, except, by working.... O Youth, knowledge without work is insanity and work without knowledge is vanity."

[20]The School of Alexandria, which "was not local, nor even national, but a cosmopolitan" center (O'Leary, 1948:20), was the meeting place of the Hellenic, Jewish, Babylonian, and Egyptian civilizations. The Nestorian School of the East, which emerged after the division of Christianity into Monophysite, Orthodox, and Nestorian churches, was first established in Antioch but later moved to Edessa and then Nisibis. Translating Greek works into Syriac, the members of this school bridged the divide between the Greek, Christian, and Iranian geo-cultural environments. The School of Harran was the center of the Sabaeans, who considered themselves the esoteric followers of the prophet Idris or Hermes, and was significant in the transmission of the Hermetic tradition. The School of Iranian Jundishapur, an institution for medical and philosophical studies established by Khosrau Anosharwan (521-579) and developed with the support of Nestorian

the transmission of ancient Greek classics to Islamic civilization has not yet been adequately documented (Toll, 1976:31), the role of these schools in the transmission process is undeniable.

The history of Islamic intellectual accumulation might be evaluated as the history of challenge that the Qur'ânic ontological, epistemological, and axiological systems posed to these pre-Islamic centers of ancient civilizations around which syncretic geo-cultural atmospheres emerged. Some extremist factions of Khawârij and Shî'a tended toward ontological proximity and identification rather than the Qur'ânic ontological hierarchy and transcendency. These tendencies have been concentrated in two extreme imaginations of the divinity: *tajsîm/tashbîh* (physicalist or anthropomorphist view) and *ta'ṭîl* (negation). Al-Baghdâdî (1935:31-32) analyzes the followers of *mushabbihah* (anthropomorphists) in two categories, one of which likens the essence of the Creator to the essence of other beings and the other of which draws a similarity between His attributes and the attributes of other beings. He gives a long list of the anthropomorphist factions and mentions that the rise of the doctrine of anthropomorphism is linked with several groups among the *ghulât rawâfid*.[21] Al-Baghdâdî argues that all of these groups are excluded from Islam in spite of the fact that they externally claim relationship with it.

Shahrastânî shows the effects of these syncretic geo-cultural atmospheres in his argument that these anthropomorphist factions have been affected by incarnationism (*ḥulûliyyah*) and Christianity.[22] The analogies between 'Ali and Jesus argued by some of the followers of the extremist Shî'a (*ghulât rawâfid*) are especially interesting from this perspective.[23] This argument was transformed into a full

---

Christians (De Boer, 1967:14), played a role in the transfer of cultural elements among the Greek, Christian, Indian, and Zoroastrian traditions.

[21]The list of Al-Baghdâdî might be summarized as following: (i) The Sabbâbiyah who called 'Ali as God and identified him with the essence of god; (ii) the Bayaniyyah, adherents of Bayan Ibn Sam'an who believed that his Worshiped One is a person of light and possesses limbs which have a human form; (iii) the Mughiriyyah, followers of Mughira Ibn Sa'îd al-Ijli who believed that the Object of his Worship possesses limbs and that they are shaped like the letters of the alphabet; (iv) the Khattâbiyyah who profess the divine character of the Imams; (v) the Hululiyyah who believed that God inheres in the person of Imams; (vi) the Mukanna'iyyah Mubayyidah situated in Mawâraunnahr, who assert that al-Mukanna was a god and that he assumes a particular form in every age; (vii) the Azakirah who believe in the divinity of Ibn Abu-1 Azakir who was executed in Baghdad (al-Baghdâdî, 1935:31-32).

[22] For example, the Shî'ite Ghâliyyah liken the Creator to the created. The Mughiriyyah, the Bayaniyyah, the Sabaiyyah and the Hashimiyyah and their followers said that God has a form like the form of men. According to Shahrastânî, (1934:43/103-04), the Ghâliyyah argued that a certain person was God; or that a part of God was incarnate in him, slavishly following the Christians and Incarnationists [ḥulûliyyah] of every community.

[23]"When 'Ali was killed, Ibn Saba held that the slain one was not 'Ali but a devil who appeared to the people in the likeness of 'Ali. 'Ali himself ascended to heaven just as Isa ibn Mariam had ascended there. He said: Just as the Jews and Christians lie in affirming in execution of Isa, so the Nasibs and Khawârij lie in alleging 'Ali's assassination. However, the Jews and Christians saw a crucified

ontological identification of divinity by the members of dhammiyah and 'ulyaniyyah, who believed that 'Ali is God and who reviled Muḥammad by claiming that 'Ali had sent Muḥammad to enlighten the world about himself, but that Muḥammad employed the charge in his own interest (Baghdâdî, 1935:68-9). The belief of the followers of Mufawwiḍah on the divine characters of God, Muḥammad, and 'Ali is a specific formulation of the understanding of the ontological particularization. It carries the mixed characteristics of the Platonic image of God as the Demiurge and Christianized ontological particularization in Western experience.[24]

The second extreme, *ta'ṭîl*, had a potential imagination of God to develop an inactive and limited idea of God in its most ultimate case in the history of Islamic thought. As Shahrastânî (1934:50/123) summarizes, *Ta'ṭîl* can be divorcing (a) the work [of creation] from the Maker, (b) the Maker from the world, (c) the Creator from the eternal attributes which subsists in His essence, (d) the Creator from the attributes and names in eternity, and (e) the plain texts of the Qur'ân and Sunnah from the meanings to which they witness. Such an imagination might lead to an abstract and inactive idea of God as a specific interpretation of soul. Shahrastânî's (1934:51/126) connection of the imagination of Muslim materialists (*dahriyyûn*) to this imagination of *ta'ṭîl* is very interesting to show the links between the idea of an abstract/inactive God and the assumption of self-adjusted nature.[25] Therefore, in a general sense, it might be argued that *tashbîh* and *ḥulûliyyah* corresponded to an ontological proximity within a Christianized form, while *ta'ṭîl* corresponded to the imagination of the ontological proximity of modern philosophy, especially after Newtonian mechanics.

---

person whom they confused with Isa. Similarly those who affirm the killing of 'Ali saw a slain person who resembled him, so that they were of the opinion it was 'Ali. But 'Ali , in truth, ascended to heaven , and he will surely come down to earth and take revenge of his foes" (Baghdâdî,1935:42).

[24]"Concerning the Mufawwiḍah among the Rawâfiḍ: It is made up of a group which maintains that God created Muḥammad, then He committed to him the management of the world and the disposal of its affairs. It is he, and not God, who brought the universe into existence. Then Muḥammad entrusted the rule of the universe to 'Ali ibn Abû Tâlib. He is thus the third ruler. This sect is more ignominious than the Magians, who think that God created Satan and that Satan created all evil things; more shameful indeed than the Christians, who call Isa the second ruler. Whoever reckons the Rafidite Mufawwiḍa among the Islamic sects is on one level with those who count the Magians and Christians as Muslims" (Baghdâdî,1935:68).

[25]"As to (b) the Materialists (*dahriyyah*), who hold that the world pre-existed, say that the pre-existence of the world in eternity implies the divorce of the Maker from His work. This has already been refuted in the discussion of production (*ijad*). Causation is just as impossible as the separation of the Maker from His work. You call your God, cause and principle and necessitator which implies two absurd things: (a) the validity of the relation between cause and effect, and (b) the cause necessitating its perfect per se. The first intention is the existence of the world... through first intention.... The higher does not will a thing for the sake of the lower; therefore causation is refuted" (Shahrastânî,1934:51/126).

The originality of Islamic thought is its specific ontological color which originated from the Qur'ân and was systematized during the process of this challenge. The great founders of several Muslim schools aimed to interpret and preserve Qur'ânic ontological color within a new context of methodology indebted to the pre-Islamic accumulation of these intellectual centers of ancient civilizations. It should be underlined that this theory and imagination of the ontological unity and transcendency has been shared by great Muslim schools and by the overwhelming majority of the Muslim masses throughout the ages, although some synthesis emerged especially in the syncretic geo-cultural atmospheres mentioned above. The fundamental reason for this consistency and continuity might be found in the transparency of the Qur'ân on the definition of Allâh as the source of all absoluteness. Such a transparency is valid also for the definition of Allâh developed by Muslim scholars. For example, Taftazânî's definition of Allâh as the originator of the world,[26] Kindî's definition of Allâh through the method of *via negativa*,[27] Fârâbî's definition of Allâh as *al-Mawjûd al-Awwal*,[28] and Kalabâdhî's definition of Allâh within a Sufi framework[29] show not only this transparency but also the

---

[26]"The Originator of the world is Allâh, the One, the Eternal, the Living, the Powerful, the Knowing, the Hearing, the Seeing, the Desiring, and the Willing. He is not an accident, nor a body, nor an atom; nor is He something formed, nor a thing limited, nor a thing numbered, nor a thing partitioned or divided, nor a thing compounded; nor does He come to an end in Himself. He is not described by quiddity, nor by quality, nor is He placed in place. Time does not affect Him and nothing resembles Him, and nothing is outside of His knowledge and Power" (Taftazânî, 1950:36).

[27]"The True One has neither matter, form, quantity, quality or relation, is not described by any of the remaining intelligible things, and has neither genus, specific difference, individual, property, common accident or movement; and it is not described by any of the things which are denied to be one in truth. It is, accordingly, pure and simple unity, while every other one is multiple" (Kindî, 1974:112).

[28]"Al-Mawjûd al-Awwal huwa al-Sabab al-Awwal li wujûd sair al-mawjûdât kulliha; wa huwa bariyyun min jamî' al-nâqis. Wa kulli ma sivahu fa laysa yakhlû min an yakûna fîhi shay'un min anha al-nâqis,... fa wujûduhu afdal al-wujûd wa aqdam al-wujûd; wa la yumkin an yakûna wujûd afdal wa la aqdam min wujûduhi.... Fa idhan huwa munfarid al-wujûd wahdahu. Fa huwa wahid min hadhihi al-jihât" (Farâbî, 1985:37-40).

[29]"The Sufis are agreed that God is One, Alone, Single, Eternal, Everlasting, Knowing, Powerful, Living, Hearing, Seeing, Strong, Mighty, Majestic, Great, Generous, Clement, Proud, Awful, Enduring, First, God, Lord, Ruler, Master, Merciful, Compassionate, Desirous, Speaking, Creating, Sustaining; that He is qualified with all the attributes wherewith He has qualified Himself, and named with all the Names whereby He has named Himself; that since eternity He has not ceased to continue with His Names and Attributes, without resembling creation in any respect; that His essence does not resemble the essences, nor His attributes the attributes; that not one of the terms applied to created beings, and indicating their creation in time, has currency over Him; that He has not ceased to be Leader, foremost before all things born in time, Existent before everything; that there is no Eternal but He, and no God beside Him; that He is neither body, nor shape, nor

paradigmatic base among Muslim schools of thought around ontological unity and transcendency based on the principles of *tawḥîd* and *tanzîh*.

The systematization of Islamic paradigm on this ontological color occurred during the process of the challenge to the pre-Islamic legacy of ancient civilizations. The formation of '*aqâ' id* and *uṣûl al-dîn* as the codification of Islamic creed and the development of *kalâm* as the systematization of theology are the results of the attempts to re-produce Qur'ânic ontological color within a new holistic consistency as a response to this civilizational challenge. Therefore *'ilm al-kalâm* is not merely "an elaborated polemics of apology without true and primary concern for the rational understanding of the totality of being" or "a kind of sophistry as an art of making contradictions" (Frank, 1968:295) but also and especially a way of explanation of a theological truth. It emerged as a result of the necessity related to philosophical reasoning on the nature and attributes of God and His relation to man and the universe. Therefore, as Frank underlines, "in contrast to a number of writers who have suggested that the earlier *kalâm* is not really a speculative theology, and in contrast to others who have suggested that it is, in the final analysis, unsophisticated, simplistic, and primitive, the language of the *kalâm*, from the earliest time that we can know it in any detail, is extremely precise and its thesis and arguments carefully delimited and refined in their conception and formulation."

So, *kalâm* is not an art of contradiction-making but a way of explaining Qur'ânic ontological color with a specific methodology and rhetoric. In fact, all Islamic sciences have a very interdependent and interconnected structure from this perspective. All of them are like several streets meeting at a junction. This junction is the ontological imagination of Allâh and *'âlam* which is *ism li mâsivâ Allâh Ta'âlâ* (the name of all beings other than Allâh). The semantic link between the etymological origin of *'âlam* "as a mark or sign by which a thing is known" and its meaning of "a class of beings/universe" shows the cosmological imagination of universe as a sign by which Allâh is known. This imaginative link has been underlined by several Muslim scholars in the beginning parts of their books on Muslim theology. For example al-Ṣâbûnî begins his book *al-Bidâyah fî Uṣûl al-Dîn* (1980:19) with the definition of *'âlam* and says *al-'âlam ism li mâsivâ Allâh Ta'âlâ, li annahu 'alamun 'alâ wujûd al-ṣâni'* (the universe is the name of all beings other than Allâh because it is a sign for the existence of the Maker [Allâh]). Therefore, *'ilm uṣûl al-dîn* plays a central role for the formation of the Muslim mind. Hence, Taḥâwî (1987:9) argues that *'ilm uṣûl al-dîn* is *ashraf al-'ulûm* (the most noble science) and that the necessity of this science for human beings is beyond all the necessities because knowing Allâh is possible only through this science. Another name for this science is *'ilm al-tawḥîd*.

Knowing man's ontological relationship with Allâh is the fundamental essence of the Islamic way of belief, thought, and life. Therefore, almost every book in Islamic intellectual history begins with a passage of a specific systematization of the knowledge on Allâh. This characteristic gives us a very interesting clue for the stages of the formation of Muslim consciousness, and it is therefore impossible to isolate any sphere of thought or life from this ontological consciousness, which is

---

form, nor person, nor element, nor accident; that with Him neither junction nor separation, neither movement nor rest;, neither augmentation nor decrease; that He has neither parts nor particles nor members nor limbs nor aspects nor places; that He has not affected by faults" (Kalabâdhî, 1935:14).

the basic obstacle for any type of secular differentiation. The classification of *'ilm al-fiqh* into *fiqh-i i'tiqâdî*,[30] *fiqh-i 'ilmî*,[31] and *fiqh-i wijdânî*[32] (Izmirli, 1981:45) from the time of Abû Hanîfah to the later periods shows these interlinkages among belief, thought, ethics, and law. These three divisions of *fiqh* embrace respectively the sphere of belief, the sphere of law, and the sphere of ethics.

Tawhîd and *tanzîh* are two fundamental principles of this ontological consciousness and of the formation of the Islamic creed. That is the basic characteristic of *'ilm al-'aqâ'id* and *kalâm* beginning with Abû Hanîfah's *al-Fiqh al-Akbar* (1981:58; English trans. Wensinck, 1932:188), the first systematic formulation of Islamic belief. The first passage of this epistle defines the essence of *tawhîd*, while the second passage aims to underline the principle of *tanzîh*—"The heart of the confession of the unity of Allâh (*tawhîd*) and the true foundation of faith consist in this obligatory creed: I believe in Allâh, His angels, His books, His apostles, the resurrection after death, the decree of Allâh the good and the evil thereof, computation of sins, the balance, Paradise and Hell, and that all these are real. Allâh the exalted is one, not in the sense of number, but in the sense that He has no partner. He begetteth not and He is not begotten and there is none like unto Him (112). He resembles none of the created things, nor do any created things resemble Him. He has been from eternity with His names and qualities; those which belong to His essence, as well as those which belong to His action."

These passages affected not only the subsequent members of Abû Hanîfah's school but also the popular belief of the masses throughout the ages. The transparency of these principles closed the gap between systematic theology of the scholars and popular belief of the masses. This is the reason why a church as an institutionalized belief did not emerge in Islamic history and why the socialization process of the belief in Islam—compared with that of other religions—is so speedy. Hegel's interpretation of the relationship of the belief in Allâh, spiritual universality, and human personality in Islam as compared with Judaism's Jehovah is very interesting to show the impact of the transparency on the universalization and socialization process of the belief.[33]

The principles of *tawhîd* and *tanzîh* prevented any type of ontological proximity and strengthened the understanding of ontological differentiation and hierarchy.[34]

---

[30]Other names for this science are *al-fiqh al-akbar*, *'ilm al-tawhîd*, and *'ilm al-kalâm*.

[31]Another name for this science is *fiqh al-sharâi' wa al-ahkam*; this is the most commonly used meaning of *fiqh*.

[32] The other name of this science is *'ilm al-akhlâq wa al-tasawwuf*.

[33]"Jehovah was only the God of that one people—the God of Abraham, of Isaac and Jacob: only with the Jews had this God made a covenant; only to this people had He revealed Himself. That speciality of relation was done away with in Mohamedanism. In this spiritual universality, in this unlimited and indefinite purity and simplicity of conception, human personality has no other aim than the realization of this universality and simplicity. Allâh has not the affirmative , limited aim of the Judaic God. The worship of the One is the only final aim of Mohamedanism" (Hegel, 1902:451-52).

[34]The following sentences from *al-Fiqh al-Akbar* show this highly differentiated ontological hierarchy around the principle of *tanzîh*: "All His qualities are different from those of the creatures. He knoweth, but not in the way of our

This is especially true for the Ahl al-Sunnah, but it is also valid for the members of other sects—except the imaginations of extreme *tashbîh* and *ta'ţîl* mentioned above. In fact, the formation of Islamic *kalâm* is a result of the responses against these deviations from the original Islamic ontological approach in favor of the pre-Islamic geo-cultural syncretic atmospheres.[35] Their discussions concentrate on the subject of finding the most effective way for the preservation of these principles in the process of the challenge to the pre-Islamic legacy. Therefore, an imagination of ontological proximity as a general and common phenomenon like we have examined in the previous chapter related to the Western experience did not emerge in Islamic intellectual history.

The Mu'tazilah, as the first school to have effective contact with Greek philosophy, might be a good example from the perspective of the Islamic ontological approach that transcended its pre-Islamic legacy. The fundamental tenets of this school might be summarized as follows.[36] God's justice necessitates that man should be the author of his own acts. The justice of God also makes it incumbent upon Him not to do anything contrary to justice or equity. God distinguishes good from evil on account of their being good and evil. As God is exempt from place and direction, a vision of Him is possible neither in this world nor in the hereafter. The Qur'ân is a created speech of God. Reason demands that an imam shòuld necessarily be appointed over the *ummah*. Finally, God's pleasure and anger are not attributes but states.

The Mu'tazilah's debt to Greek philosophy is best seen in its assumption of the autonomy of human reason and in metaphysical atomism. Superficially, it might be argued that the assumption of the autonomy of human reason could be transformed to the equalization of the ontological and epistemological levels of Allâh versus that of man. But the members of the Mu'tazilah school who argued in favor of the autonomy of human reason never transformed this idea to an understanding of ultimate conflict between reason and revelation as did the epistemological sources which created the secularization of knowledge in the Western philosophical tradition.[37] In contrast, their interpretation of *tawhîd* led them to a highly

---

knowledge; He is mighty but not in the way of our power; He seeth, but not in the way of our seeing; He speaketh, but not in the way of our speaking; He heareth, but not in the way of our hearing. We speak by means of organs and letters. Letters are created, but the speech of Allâh is uncreated. Allâh is thing, not as other things but in the sense of positive existence, without body, without substance, without accidents. He has no limit, neither has He a counterpart, nor a partner, nor an equal" (1981:59; English trans. Wensinck, 1932:189).

[35]Even after the beginning of the formation of *kalâm*, some tendencies toward ontological proximity survived under the impact of pre-Islamic belief systems (Tritton,1947:137).

[36]I have profited from Valiuddin's article (1963:201-3) on Mu'tazilism for this summary. As he mentions, Ibn Ḥazm adds, in his *al-Milal wa al-Niḥal*, that to be a member of the Mu'tazilah one must regard the perpetrator of a grave sin as an unbeliever.

[37]In fact, the interest of Muslim scholars, and also the members of Mu'tazilah, in the problem of the autonomy of human reason is related to an axiological question, namely whether or not a person who has not been informed by revelation would be responsible to believe in God. This question and its epistemological bases

concentrated ontological transcendence, depending on the belief in Allâh not only as the Creator of the world but also as its constant ground of being. They rejected the separate qualities of God, arguing that such qualities would be separate beings and that such an assumption is against the belief in the unity of God.

Wâṣil b. 'Atâ's argument for eternal oneness on this subject has been systematized by Abû Hudhayl Muḥammad al-'Allâf who taught that "the Qualities were not in His essence, and thus separable from it, thinkable apart from it, but that they were His essence" (MacDonald, 1903:136-7). This was an attempt to avoid the possibility of an approximation to the Christian Trinity as a specific type of particularization of divinity, because according to the Mu'tazilah "the persons of the Trinity have always been personified qualities, and such seems really to have been the view of John of Damascus" (MacDonald, 1903:137). Therefore they called themselves the Ahl al-Tawḥîd wa al-'Adl (people of unity and justice). It is very difficult to support the speculation that a secular way of thinking in Islamic intellectual history would be realized by using Mu'tazilah tradition[38] when we evaluate its epistemological consequences within these ontological premises.

There is widespread variation among the arguments of the Mu'tazilah and it is unnecessary to discuss all of them within such a framework, but it should be underlined that their general theoretical and imaginative attitude concentrated between mu'aṭṭila (followers of ta'ṭîl) and Ahl al-Sunnah from the perspective of ontological unity and transcendency, especially on the subject of divine qualities. The later Mu'tazilah gradually moved toward the ideas of Ahl al-Sunnah. As Tritton (1947:166-7) points out, "the Mu'tazilah had been drawing nearer to the traditional beliefs and al-Ash'arî made the whole turn."

This becomes especially evident in the fifth century of *Hijrah* with the famous leader of the Mu'tazilah, Qâḍî 'Abd al-Jabbâr. For example, as Tritton (1947:193) notes, the argument of his student Muḥammad b. 'Ali al-Baṣrî that the existence of God is His essence—He is different from all else and this difference is due to His essence and is not something added to it—is an approximate repetition of Ash'arite doctrine on this issue. This argument might be accepted at the same time as a sophisticated interpretation of the principle of *tanzîh* without deviating towards the doctrine of ta'ṭîl. Hence, the Mu'tazilah's methodological borrowing from the pre-Islamic legacy did not prevent the development of an understanding of highly concentrated ontological transcendency.

After the reactions of Shâfi'i, Ibn Ḥanbal, al-Muḥâsibî, and Ibn Kullâb against the Mu'tazilah's rejection of divine attributes and their rationalization of Islamic belief, a new rational re-systematization of Islamic belief system as opposed to the extremes of ta'ṭîl and *tashbîh* began to emerge in the beginning of the fourth/tenth century—that is, the formation of the philosophico-theological school of Ahl al-Sunnah.[39] The leading figures of this movement are al-Ash'arî in Mesopotamia,

---

have significant consequences, but these consequences might be interpreted within the mentioned Islamic paradigmatic unity based on ontological justification rather than in epistemological differentiation.

[38]For example, the Mu'tazilah were called *Freidenker im Islam* by Heinrich Steiner, who wrote the first monograph to isolate this school from the other Islamic sects (Goldziher, 1910:100).

[39]There is an approximate consensus among the writers on the classifications of Muslim sects to differentiate Ahl al-Sunnah from the other sects in Islamic history.

al-Mâturîdî in Samarqand, and al-Taḥâwî in Egypt. These three leading scholars aimed to fulfil the need for reconciliation in the theological sphere and resolve the crisis of civilizational challenge by adopting a middle course and a tolerant attitude among different approaches. Their's was a search for a new theoretical and methodological system which aimed to set up a balanced epistemology between reason and revelation. The theological arguments of this school became the most popular both among the masses and scholars.

In his *Tabyîn Kadhib al-Muftarî fi mâ Nusiba ilâ al-Imâm Abû al-Ḥasan al-Ash'arî* (1953:147-8), Ibn 'Asâkir calls this group *muthbitûn* (affirmers) because they "affirmed of God what God affirmed of Himself, and denied of God that which is unworthy of Him". Ibn 'Asâkir argues that their most redoubtable champion among the *muthbitûn* was al-Ash'arî, who avoided the extremes of *ta'ṭîl* and *tashbîh*. The Ahl al-Sunnah's rational re-systematization of the Qur'ânic belief system as *kalâm* differs from the reactions of the Ẓâhirites, the Ḥanbalites, the Muhaddithîn, and others against the Mu'tazilah because of the Ahl al-Sunnah's reliance on the use of reason in defending and explaining religious creeds. Al-Ash'arî strictly rejects in his *Risâlah fi Istiḥsân al-Khawḍ fi 'Ilm al-Kalâm* (A Vindication of the Science of *Kalâm*) the condemnation of these groups that such a rational methodology for the discussions on these issues and *kalâm* as a whole are innovations (*bid'ah*) which did not occur during the period of the Prophet (1953:120-1/Ar.87-8, 1953b:t.94/129).

The fundamental argument of the *muthbitûn* might be summarized as follows. When God describes Himself as being of capable of seeing, hearing, etc., He is using these words in a real sense, because God really sees and hears. But since "nothing is like Him," His attributes, though real, are not like the attributes of human beings or any other created things. This argument strengthened the imagination of ontological differentiation which is immanent in the Qur'ânic ontological color.

The Mu'tazilah aimed at such an ontological differentiation through the idea of "absolute unity," while al-Ash'arî developed the doctrine of *mukhâlafah* or "absolute difference" for a rational systematization of ontological differentiation without denying the divine attributes. This doctrine of *mukhâlafah* means that if any quality, attribute, or term is applied to God, it must be understood in a unique sense and never taken in the sense in which it is normally used when applied to created beings.[40] This doctrine has been expanded to the problem of existence in Ash'arî's formulation, so that the existence of God is not the same as that of the world. This

---

As Seele (1920:I/5) notes, Shahrastânî groups the unorthodox (i.e., other than Ahl al-Sunnah) factions under the four main headings Qadariyyah, Sifâtiyyah, Khawârij, and Shî'ite; Ibn Ḥazm under the headings Mu'tazilah (much the same as Qadariyyah), Murji'ah, Khawârij, and Shî'ite; Baghdâdî under the headings Qadariyyah, Khawârij, Murji'ah, and Shî'ite. There are also several subdivisions of these groups.

[40]There are basically two different interpretations of this difference, as Shehâdî (1964:15) mentions. One interpretation is that God's attributes are different from those of other things, specially man's, in degree only. God's attributes are to some extent like man's, but they are greater and more perfect. The other interpretation is that God's uniqueness is an expression of the utter difference of His nature from all other things.

difference is due to His peculiar essence, not to something added to it.[41] The logical consequence of this doctrine that God's attributes differ from those of the creatures—not in degree but in kind and in their whole nature—specifies the qualitative characteristics of ontological differentiation which strengthens the imagination of ontological transcendency.

Thus, Ash'arite *kalâm* differs from the views of the *mu'aṭṭilah* (negators) because Ash'arî accepts the existence of divine attributes, and it differs from the views of the *mujâssimah* (anthropomorphists) because of Ash'arî's doctrine of *mukhâlafah*. Ash'arî's meticulousness in avoiding these extremes can be seen in the interpretations of *tawḥîd* and *tanzîh* in the beginning chapters of his *Kitâb al-Luma'*.[42] He categorizes divine attributes into (i) *ṣifât-i wujûdiyyah* (existential or positive attributes) and (ii) *ṣifât-i salbiyyah* (negative attributes). The acceptance of *ṣifât-i wujûdiyyah* was a hindrance for the extreme *ta'ṭîl* which might lead to an inactive/abstract God. Additionally, Ash'arî opposes the extreme *ṣifâṭîs* who asserted that even those attributes of God implying His bodily existence are to be taken in their true literal sense in spite of the fact that this view might lead to an imagination of ontological proximity, and he argues that such attributes are to be believed in *bilâ kaifa* (without asking how)[43] and *bilâ tashbîh* (without drawing any comparison). His interpretation of *tawḥîd*, mentioned above, is an attempt to hinder any type of ontological particularization of divinity.

Ash'arite metaphysics is based on a specific interpretation of metaphysical atomism that carries the characteristics of Islamic theocentric ontological color. As Macdonald (1903:203) signifies, the Ash'arites link their theology to their ontology as "thoroughgoing metaphysicians" and as "thoroughgoing theologians." Ash'arite atomism shows at the same time how they differ from the ancient and modern types of atomists because of the effects of the Qur'ânic ontological system. As Hye (1963:240) mentions, the Ash'arite atoms are fundamentally different from those of Democritus and Lucretius because "they are not material; they are not permanent; they have only a momentary existence; they are not eternal but every moment brought into being, and then allowed to go out of existence by the Supreme Being, God, the only cause of everything in the universe." They differ also from Leibniz's system of monadology because "Leibniz had to bring in, in his monadology, a Monad of monads or God, and fall back upon the theory of Pre-Established harmony to bring his monads into harmonious and orderly relations with one another, and this he could do only at the cost of his monadology, and by abandoning his pluralistic and individualistic metaphysic; but the Ash'arites, consistently with their ontology, fall straight back upon God, and found in His will the ground of orderliness and harmony in the universe. They were, thus, more thorough and consistent than Leibniz in their theory of monads."[44] This difference is very interesting to show how a methodological approach and tool in metaphysics

---

[41]One of the later members of Ash'arite school, al-Bâqillânî, rejected this conclusion.

[42]The interpretation of *tawḥîd* is also a response to the eclectic beliefs between Islam and pre-Islamic Iranian dualistic philosophies (Ash'arî, 1953a:t.8/9-10).

[43]He shares this principle with the followers of Ibn Ḥanbal, who believe in the existence of some characteristics of God (e.g., hand)*bilâ kaifa* (Ash'arî, 1980:290).

[44]Maimonides' summary (1928:120) of some of the propositions of the Mutakallim atomists also testifies to their originality.

has been interpreted in two alternative ways of ontological imagination. Ash'arite atomism led to a highly concentrated ontological hierarchy, while a specific ontological proximity survived Leibniz's monadology.

Al-Mâturîdî, the forerunner of the Sunnite *kalâm* in the eastern provinces, systematized Abû Hanîfah's theological views around the basic principle of freedom from *tashbîh* and *tajsîm* without denying divine attributes (*ta'ṭîl*), and his masterpiece *Kitâb al-Tawhîd* might be accepted as a challenge to the extreme eclecticism of some Muslim schools as well as an attempt to build up a rational systematization for the defense of the Qur'ânic ontological color. Al-Mâturîdî shares this feature with al-Ash'arî and Tahâwî, although he also disagrees with al-Ash'arî on certain detailed points. I do not want to repeat some common features among them which shaped the basic principles of Sunnite *kalâm*, but the impact of the ideas al-Mâturîdî both on subsequent scholars and on the masses (especially Hanafiyyah) should not be underestimated.

As a follower of Abû Hanîfah's school, known as *Aṣhâb al-Ra'y wa al-Qiyâs* (the people of reason and opinion) for their legal methodology, Mâturîdî's arguments might be accepted as foundations of the rational systematization of the Islamic creed. His refutation (1981:363-8) of the absolute determinism of the *jabriyyah* (compulsionists) through the argument that the relation between God and man should not be considered the same as that between God and the physical world is a confirmation of the ontological hierarchy of Allâh, man, and nature.

This moderate approach of Sunnite *kalâm* in opposing *mu'aṭṭila* and *mushabbiha* has been strengthen throughout the ages by the followers of these leading figures and has become the dominant way of belief and imagination among the masses. Al-Bâqillânî, Ibn Furâq, al-Isferâinî, and al-Juwainî lead the process of systematization and popularization of the Ash'arite school, while al-Nasafî's epistle *'Aqâid al-Nasafî* became the most essential source of the school of Mâturîdî. The fundamental characteristics of the Sunnite *kalâm* [45] have been shaped during these ages.

---

[45]Al-Baghdâdî provides a long list of the fundamental characteristics of the Sunnite *kalâm* which specifies the common foundation of this school regarding the subjects of knowledge. This list might be summarized as following: (i) the confirmation of the realities and of knowledge, particularly and generally; (ii) the knowledge concerning the creation of the universe including its parts, both accidents and bodies; (iii) the cognizance of the Maker of the universe and His essential attributes; (iv) the knowledge related to His eternal attributes; (v) the knowledge of His names and qualities; (vi) the knowledge of His justice and wisdom; (vii) the knowledge of His messengers and Prophets; (viii) the knowledge of the miracles of the Prophets and the wonders of the Saints; (ix) the knowledge of the bases of Islamic Law on which the community is agreed; (x) the knowledge of the laws of bidding, forbidding and charging; (xi) the knowledge of the inevitable end of every being and his status in the future world; (xii) the knowledge concerning the Caliphate and the Imâmate and the requirements of the leadership. (xiii) the knowledge of the principles of Faith and Islam in general; (xiv) the knowledge of the status of saints and the grades of the pious Imams; (xv) the knowledge of the laws bearing on the enemies among the non-believers and the people of erring fancies. He tries to underline this common foundation through arguing that they agree on their fundamentals but generally differ regarding some of

The second phase of the formation of *kalâm* after al-Ghazzâlî, *kalâm al-muta'akhkhirîn*, will be analyzed in coming pages, but it should be underlined that the members of these two phases share fundamental characteristics with regards to ontological unity and hierarchy. They strongly resisted any type of syncretism of the Islamic God-man-universe relationship with those of pre-Islamic belief systems as leading to ontological proximity and particularization of divinity. Al-Juwainî's criticisms of Judaism and Christianity in his *Shifâ al-Galîl* (1968) and al-Sâbûnî's condemnations (1980:21/65) of the conceptions of God found in Zoroastrianism, Magianism, Christianity, naturalism, and *aflakiyyah* (worship of the spheres as ruling all events) are but two examples of this resistance.

The followers of *falsafah* and *taṣawwuf* also take an intermediate position between the extremes of *ta'ṭîl* (divesting) and *tashbîh* (similitude) around the basic principles of ontological differentiation (*mukhâlafa*) and the unknowability of Allâh's nature. The problems of the philosophers are almost the same of those of the theologians; their differences lie in their methodological approaches and tools. As Arnaldez points out in the *Encyclopedia of Islam* (1965/II: 772), "the first *falsafah* is quite distinct from the *kalâm* which preceded it; although it takes pleasure in the rediscovery of Qur'ânic texts or ideas, it does not make them a starting point, but follows a method of research independent of dogma, without, however, rejecting the dogma or ignoring it in its sources."

It should be added, however, that both the philosophers and the theologians begin and end with the same ontological reality of monism. The fact that their differences are methodological rather than ontological[46] is indicated by Al-Kindî's assertion that revelation and philosophy attain identical truths but in different ways, an assertion that has been repeated by subsequent philosophers as well, in particular by Ibn Rushd in *Faṣl al-Maqâl*. The *falâsifah* are in agreement with the *mutakallimûn* on theological issues, and therefore a complete break between *kalâm* and *falsafah* has never occurred.

We can show this in detail by analyzing the ontological conclusions of the leading philosophers and the relationship of those conclusions to the Qur'ânic antecedents of ontological unity, transcendency, and hierarchy. The parallel definitions of Allâh given by Taftazânî, Kindî, and Fârâbî provide a well-known example. Each of these three aims in his philosophical analysis to prove the ultimate reality of the ontological cause. Hence, like the theologians' definition of *'ilm al-dîn* as *ashraf al-'ulûm*, Kindî's definition of *al-falsafah al-ûlâ* (first philosophy, metaphysics) is *'ilm al-haqq al-awwal alladhî huwa 'illatu kulli haqq* (1950a:98), and he uses the same description—*al-'ilm al-ashraf* (1950a:101)—for this attempt because according to him the final objective of philosophy is the adequate and sure knowledge of God.

Although Kindî is indebted to Aristotelianism and neo-Platonism for some of his methodological and theoretical tools, his metaphysics is very different. For example, though his definition of Allâh in *al-Ṣinâ'at al-'Uẓmâ* benefits from

---

their derived principles to an extent which does not compel mutual accusations of erring and sinning (Baghdâdî, 1935:172).

[46]Craig's (1980:60) summary of the differences between *kalâm* and *falsafah* shows this fact in detail.

Aristotle's discussion of the First Unmoved Mover,[47] his interpretation of creation as *ibdâ'* (ex nihilo)[48] is radically opposed to Aristotle's cosmological evaluations. As Walzer (1957:215) indicates, "al-Kindî the philosopher is in full agreement with the religious view on this issue and differs from all the later Islamic philosophers." Kindî's argument for the unity of Allâh in his treatise *Risâlah fî Waḥdâniyyat Allâh* (1950c:207) is indicative both of his great care to remain on the paradigmatic base of Islam, *tawhîd*, and of the parallels between *kalâm* and *falsafah* on issues related to the supreme being.

Thus, beginning from the first treatises of Islamic philosophy written by Kindî, the members of this school re-valuated pre-Islamic sources—especially Platonic and Aristotelian classics—within a new ontological context. This re-valuation is completely different from their transmitted forms in the medieval and modern intellectual traditions of Western history. Even a terminological transformation of pre-Islamic Greek sources has been realized by Muslim philosophers parallel to this imaginative and theoretical re-valuation.

For example, following the language of the Qur'ân, Kindî identifies "Truth" (*Haqq*) as the ultimate end of philosophy, thereby substituting the Islamic conception of God for Aristotle's Prime Unmoved Mover. Ibn Rushd's transformation of Platonic concepts in his commentary on the *Republic* gives another example, which will be discussed in detail below. Evidence that other Muslim philosophers understood pre-Islamic classics in accordance with Qur'ânic ontological antecedents appears in their commentaries as well. Therefore, it might be argued that there are three different types of Platonic and Aristotelian classics: (i) their original, authentic forms; (ii) their re-valuated Islamic forms that avoid deviating toward ontological proximity; and (iii) their re-invented Western forms within the context of the philosophical continuity between Christianized and modern versions.

The centrality of the ontological consciousness on beings and its relationship to other spheres of thought and life in Islamic philosophy are among its more significant characteristics. Fârâbî is the leading figure of this approach. The internal structures of his famous works are adequate examples of his argument for the dependency of epistemology, axiology, and politics on ontological premises. His two most famous treatises on political philosophy, *Ârâ Ahl al-Madînah al-Fâḍilah* and *Al-Siyâsah al-Madaniyyah*, begin with the analysis of ontological beings within a hierarchical order. The knowledge of *al-Sabab al-Awwal* as the ultimate supreme ontological being within this hierarchical order (*marâtib al-wujûd*) is presented in the first lines (Fârâbî, 1964:31; 1985:37). The epistemological, axiological and political consequences occupy the following parts of these books.

---

[47]"For God, great is His praise, is the reason and agent of this motion, being eternal (*qadîm*), He can not be seen and does not move, but in fact causes motion without moving Himself? This is His description for those who understand Him in plain words: He is simple in that He can not be dissolved into something simpler; and He is indivisible because He is not composed and composition has no hold on Him, but in fact He is separate from the visible bodies, since He... is the reason of the motion of the visible bodies" (Ahwany, 1963:428)

[48]Kindî defines *ibdâ'* in his treatise *Al-Fâ'il al-Haqq al-Awwal* (1950b:183), as *ta'sîs al-aysiyyat min laysa* (to produce real things from nothing).

As Madkour (1963: I/467) mentions, "al-Fârâbî's doctrine is so fully harmonious and consistent that its parts are completely inter-related." His classification of virtue is directly attached to this priority of the analysis on the ontological status of beings in his *Tahsil al-Sa'âdah* (1983:49) because "theoretical virtues consist in the sciences whose ultimate purpose is only to make the beings and what they contain intelligible with certainty" (English trans. from M. Mahdî; 1962:13). Therefore Fârâbî argues in *The Scope of Aristotle in the Book of Metaphysics* that particular sciences restrict themselves to one or several departments of being while metaphysics knows no such restrictions because its field is all reality, namely Being (Hammond, 1947:10).

This supreme being is the absolute One which transcends everything. Hence, Fârâbî's philosophy is entirely theocentric, being based on ontological hierarchy and differentiation. Although he follows Aristotle on many methodological and theoretical issues, he never arrives at an epistemologically defined ontology such as that of the modern Western followers of Aristotle. On the contrary, Fârâbî's statements on the limitation of human intellect in *The Gems of Wisdom* (Hammond, 1947:19) arguing that God is knowable and unknowable, evident and hidden, and the best knowledge of Him is to know that He is something the human mind cannot thoroughly understand, declares the weakness of the human epistemological sources on the ultimate reality of ontology.

On the other hand, as Hammond (1947:21) underlines, "the proof of an immovable mover by Aristotle, which leads to the conclusion that God is a designer and not a Creator, was improved and corrected by al-Fârâbî nearly three hundred years before St. Thomas was born. Starting out from the Aristotelian idea of change, al-Fârâbî was able to arrive at an *Ens Primum* to whom that change is due, while He Himself does not change, because He is pure act." But, his description of *al-Awwal* in *Al-Siyâsah al-Madaniyyah* reaches a highly concentrated ontological unity,[49] differentiation,[50] and hierarchy.[51]

Although Fârâbî has benefited from the neo-Platonic legacy, especially with regards to his emanationist conception of the process of creation (Galston, 1977:17), it should be noted that he does not expand this issue of process to the issue of ontological origin, so that it does not create any type of ontological proximity in his metaphysical system. His argumentation in *The Sources of*

---

[49]"God is only one. For, if there were two gods, they would have to be partly alike and partly different: in which case, however, the simplicity of each would be destroyed.... God is one, because He is free from all quantitative divisions. One means undivided. He who is indivisible in substance is one in essence" (English trans. from Hammond, 1947:26).

[50]"If there was anything equal to God, then he would cease to be the fullness of being, for fullness implies impossibility of finding anything of its kind. For instance, the fullness of power means inability of finding identical power anywhere else; the fullness of beauty means inability of finding identical beauty. Likewise if the first being possesses the fullness of being, this means that it is impossible to find anyone or anything identical with Him. Therefore, there is one Infinite Being, only One God" (English trans. from Hammond, 1947:26).

[51]"Wa amma al-Awwal fa laysa fîhi naqs aslan wa lâ bi wajhin min al-wujûh; wa la yumkin an yakûna wujûd akmal wa afdal min wujûdihi; wa lâ yumkin an yakûna wujûd aqdam minhu" (Fârâbî, 1964:42).

Question against the neo-Platonic dualism of good and evil derived from the dualism of spirit and matter (Hammond, 1947:32), shows his selective approach to pre-Islamic sources in order to preserve the principle of unity. Hence, Hammond (1947:55) is fully right in arguing that "there is a unity of thought throughout the philosophy of Alfarabi, who spared no efforts to make the various parts of his philosophical vision converge towards one living God, on Whom the one and the many, being and becoming, are essentially dependent."

The ontological differentiation in the metaphysical system of Ibn Sînâ has been systematized through the definition of the ontological status of "possible beings" as that of dependence on the "Necessary Being" (1973:48). Ibn Sînâ's Necessary Being is God, the Creator, and the possible beings are other beings of the world. Ultimately, he reaches an idea of an eternal God who is anterior to the universe and transcendent with respect to it. His concentration on the principle that God who is absolutely one and therefore devoid of all multiplicity, together with his idea of transcendency, might be accepted as a re-formulated exegesis of the Qur'ânic teaching. His definition of God in his *al-Risâlat al-'Arshiyyah* verifies this argument (Craig, 1980:97).

Ibn Sînâ's metaphysical conclusion that the Necessary Being is a being whose essence is identical with His necessary existence—unlike contingent beings, in whom essence and existence are distinct—aims to show the ultimate unity of God.[52] Hence, Fazlurrahmân (1963:I/503) argues that Ibn Sînâ's attempt is a rejection of atheistic and pantheistic ways of thought "because unlike atheism, it requires God who should bestow being upon existents; and in order to avoid pantheism, it further requires that the being of God should be radically differentiated from the being of the world." This idea of God has been interpreted within the context of the connection between metaphysics and ontology because, as Nasr (1964a:25) underlines, "everything in the universe, by the very fact that it exists, is plunged in Being; yet, God, or Pure Being, who is the Origin and Creator of all things, is not the first term in a continuous chain and therefore does not have a substantial and horizontal continuity with the beings of the world." The relationship between the transcendency of God and contingency of the universe as a specific type of ontological differentiation affected Ibn Sînâ's cosmology and cosmogony (Nasr,1964a:29).

The essential teachings of eastern Islamic philosophy—that God is *per se* a necessary being, that He has no associates, and that He is the Creator of everything; that everything besides Him comprises the contingent ontological sphere and has emanated from His perfect essence; and that His knowledge of objects is the cause of their coming into being—are also found in western Islamic philosophy in Andalusia, where the leading figures are Ibn Bâjjah, Ibn Tufayl, and Ibn Rushd. By outlining Ibn Rushd's arguments, we can analyze the fundamental characteristics of this tradition on the subject of ontological unity, differentiation, and hierarchy as the paradigmatic base of Islamic intellectual accumulation.

The fundamental characteristics of Ibn Rushd's theoretical approach and conclusions show us his meticulousness in understanding and defending of the Islamic ontological presuppositions mentioned above. First of all, he always avers

---

[52]A detailed discussion of Ibn Sînâ's essence-existence distinction is found in Morewedge, "Philosophical Analysis and Ibn Sînâ's 'Essence- Existence' Distinction" (1972).

the ontological hierarchy based on the absolute sovereignty of Allâh and refrains from any type of ontological proximity. His definition of metaphysics as "the science which studies the relationship of the different existents as regards their hierarchical order of causes up to the Supreme Cause" (Ibn Rushd, 1958:34; English trans. from Sharîf, 1963:I/560) is a reflection of his approach within the context of conceptualization. His classification of beings into three categories in *Fasl* (1973:41) and his answers to Ghazzâlî on the subject of eternity are very interesting to show the common paradigmatic base among these schools around the understanding of ontological hierarchy. In this treatise, he argues that their conflict against the followers of *kalâm* is a problem of denomination (*tasmiyyah*), rather than an essential one.

Ibn Rushd's refraining from any type of ontological proximity or particularization of divinity is especially in his commentaries on Plato and Aristotle. The transformation of some concepts in his commentary on Plato's *Republic* shows not only his personal meticulousness for the basis of the Islamic system of belief but also the ontological color given by Muslim philosophers to the pre-Islamic materials.[53] There are two possible explanations for such a transformation: (i) the changes have been made by translators before these sources reached Ibn Rushd, or (ii) Ibn Rushd has made the changes himself. But neither possibility does away with the argument I am putting forward with regard to the sensibilities of Muslim philosophers on the transmission of the pre-Islamic sources within the framework of the basic Islamic tenets.

Ibn Rushd's sensibility for the purification of Allâh is seen also in his discussion on good and evil. He strictly rejects the Zoroastrian solution that evil is caused not by God but by other persons, a devil, or demons, underlining that such a dualism implies a shortcoming (*taqsîr*) in the Supreme Agent which leads to a specific type of polytheism. When we combine his theoretical explanations for the unicity (*wahdâniyyah*)(al-Ahwany, 1963b:I/549) of Allâh in his famous treatise *al-Kashf* (1964) with this attitude in his commentaries, we can easily say that Ibn Rushd tries to refine pre-Islamic sources based on a new interpretation grounded on the fundamental criterion of the Islamic ontological color. This approach is true, generally, for the members of Islamic philosophy as a whole.

Thus, the paradigmatic base among Islamic schools and sects carries an ontological character, while they differ methodologically and terminologically. An illuminating example is provided by Ibn Rushd's argument in *Fasl* that the existence of three different methodological approaches—rhetorical, dialectical, and demonstrative—in Islamic intellectual history does not prevent the ultimate consensus on three fundamental creeds of Islam, namely belief in the unity of Allâh

---

[53]For example, Plato's "pure spirits" are replaced by "angels" in I/xxviii.5, p.174; Plato's "gods" in 380B and 381B are replaced by "demons" and "angels" in I/xi.4, p.260; "The Delphic Apollo" in 427 B-C is replaced by "what the Most High commanded through prophecy" in I/xxii.10, p.155; and "gods" in 573 C is replaced by "angels" in III/xvii.7, p.240. This transformation may have emerged from the Muslim philosophers' knowledge that pre-Islamic Arabs deified angels, and therefore these philosophers have evaluated Greek "gods" as angels because of this traditional experience in the Near East. But these "gods" might be interpreted in Rome as purely polytheistic elements and passed to the Western theological and philosophical tradition within such a framework.

(ontological principle), belief in prophecy (epistemological principle), and belief in the hereafter (eschatological principle)(1973:40-41). This formulation of the basic creeds of Islam clarifies at the same time the ontological, epistemological, and eschatological dimensions of this paradigm. These dimensions specify also the axiological framework of Islamic social thought.

According to Ibn Rushd, the role of the three methodologies is to define the same ontological reality and to be means of universalization, popularization, and generalization of the same divine truth.[54] His classification of these methodologies lends great weight to my argument that the ultimate contrast among Muslim schools and sects is methodological rather than ontological or essential. Ibn Rushd's understanding of prophecy within this context is that prophecy embraces all of these methodologies in order to deliver the Holy Message to the whole of humanity regardless of race, capacity, age, etc.[55]

The metaphysical and mystical parallelism between *falsafah* and *taṣawwuf* lies in the dialectic of ontological differentiation and mystical nearness between Allâh and man (as a contingent being). Ibn Bâjjah, like the followers of *taṣawwuf*, advises three things to achieve nearness to God: "(i) charge our tongues to remember God and glorify Him, (ii) charge our organs to act in accordance with the insight of the heart, and (iii) avoid what makes us indifferent to the remembrance of God or turns our hearts away from Him" (al-Ma'ṣumî, 1963:522).

Qushairî indicates this psychological and imaginative balance between ontological differentiation and mystical nearness in his discussion, in his very famous classical work *al-Risâlat al-Qushairiyyah*, of the Ṣûfî's relation to God. First and foremost, one's belief in God should contain no element of doubt.

---

[54]"For every Muslim the Law has provided a way to truth suitable to his nature, through demonstrative, dialectical and rhetorical methods. Since all this is established, and since we, the Muslim community, hold that this division of ours is true, and that it is this religion which incites and summons us to the happiness that consists in the knowledge of God, Mighty and Majestic, and of His creation, that [end] is appointed for every Muslim by the method of assent which his temperament and nature require. For the natures of men are on different levels with respect to [their paths to] assent. One of them comes to assent through demonstration; another comes to assent through dialectical arguments, just as firmly as the demonstrative man through demonstration, since his nature does not contain any greater capacity; while another comes to assent through rhetorical arguments, again just as firmly as the demonstrative man through demonstrative arguments" (Ibn Rushd, 1973:34; English trans. from Hourani, 1976:49).

[55]"Thus since this divine religion of ours has summoned people by these three methods, assent to it has extended to everyone, except him who stubbornly denies it with his tongue or him for whom no method of summons to God the Exalted has been appointed in religion owing to his own neglect of such matters. It was for this purpose that the Prophet, peace upon him, was sent with a special mission to 'the white man and the black man alike'; I mean because his religion embraces all the methods of summons to God the Exalted." (Ibn Rushd, 1973:35; English trans. from Hourani, 1973:49). He refers to the following Qur'anic verse to support his arguments: "Call unto the way of thy Lord by wisdom [hikmah], by good exhortation [al-mawizah al-hasanah], and by debate [al-jadal] with them in the most effective manner" (Qur'ân, 16:125).

Second, a person's relation to God should be so thorough, comprehensive, and intimate that it would lead him to feel as if he lives and does everything not because he is doing it all, but because God is doing it all. The Ṣûfî's relation to God is a pure relation in the sense that it is a relation just between him and his God without any material link. This relation rids man of all occupation with affairs worldly and mundane. Finally, the Ṣûfî must regard himself as having been created for no one and nothing but God (Ḥamîduddîn, 1963:317).

The meticulousness related to ontological differentiation is a common characteristic beginning from the time of al-Muḥâsibî, a significant forerunner of taṣawwuf. His tri-level cosmology in Kitâb al-'Ilm (1983:141) of this world (hadhihi al-dâr), the hereafter (dâr al-baqâ') and Allâh is a good example. According to Kalabâdhî's report in his masterpiece Kitâb al-Ta'arruf li-Madhab Ahl al-Taṣawwuf on the fundamental doctrines of the followers of taṣawwuf in his time, their doctrine of the attributes of God was very similar to the centralist doctrine of kalâm based on the principle of mukhâlafah.[56] Hence, in taṣawwuf "the relation between the 'Creator' and the 'Created' is not one of 'Identity', but is definitely that of 'Otherness'" (Valiuddîn, 1974:13).[57] Therefore, it is very difficult to analyze Ash'arite transcendency and Sufi immanence in the relationship between God and man within a categorical differentiation because of the fact that Sufis strictly believe in the absolute transcendence of God. In both views God is the only absolute reality whereas universe and soul are dependent and subordinate realities.

Jâmî expresses this point in his Lawâ'iḥ (1914:21), a later treatise on Sufism, thus: "When one says that the 'Truth' most glorious comprehends all beings, the meaning is that He comprehends them as a cause comprehends its consequences, not that He is a whole containing them as His parts." As Naṣr (1972:146) mentions, "the doctrine of unity, or tawḥîd forms the axis of all Sufi metaphysics, and it is in fact the misunderstanding of this cardinal doctrine that has caused so many orientalists to accuse Sufism of pantheism.... Sufi doctrine does not assert that God is the world but that the world to the degree that it is real can not be completely other than God; were it to be so it would become a totally independent reality, a deity of its own, and would destroy the absoluteness and the Oneness that belong to God alone." Thus, Sufism differs completely from pantheism, within which the ontological relationship is based on a relationship of identity, and such an

---

[56]"They are agreed that God has real qualities, and that He is qualified by them, these being: knowledge, strength, power, might, mercy, wisdom, majesty, omnipotence, eternity, life, desire, will, and speech. These are neither bodies nor accidents nor elements, even as His essence is neither body nor accident nor element. They also agree that He has hearing, sight, face, and hand, and reality, unlike hearing, sight, and faces."(Kalabâdhî, 1935:16) Kalabâdhî's argument that the attributes of God, are neither He nor other than He; and that the assertion of their being does not imply that He is in need of them, or that He does things with them, is a repitition of the central position of Kalam.

[57]Valiuddin expresses this "otherness" as the relationship of the One and the many, Khâliq (Creator) and makhlûq (created beings), Rabb (Lord) and marbûb (slaves), Ilâh (the Worshipped) and ma'lûh (worshipper), Mâlik (the Master) and mamlûk (servants). As he argues, Islamic mysticism solves the problem of the One and the many with the assumption that in existence there is unity but in essences there is multiplicity.

interpretation of *tawḥîd* strengthens the imaginative feeling of ontological transcendency and absoluteness because its doctrine claims that there is only one ontological source and that the universe has no existence of its own apart from the reality of God.

Al-Ghazzâlî is the person who set up a new balance among *kalâm*, *falsafah*, and *taṣawwuf*. His works affected the directions and tendencies within these fundamental Islamic schools to a great extent. The process of the systematization of the paradigm in the sense of the intellectual movement toward the central gravity on the basis of ontological transcendency has almost been completed after him. His criticisms of the philosophers in his famous *Tahâfut al-Falâsifah* (1927) has strengthened the feeling of deliberateness in relation to pre-Islamic philosophical background even within this school. From this point of view, Ibn Rushd is nearer to the center than Ibn Sînâ. The new tendency in *kalâm* after Ghazzâlî, *muta'akhkhirîn*, became much nearer to *falsafah*, especially in benefiting from its terminological and methodological tools to express theological realities compared with pre-Ghazzâlian *kalâm*, *mutaqaddimîn*. His works on *taṣawwuf* had two significant effects on this school: first to specify the supremacy of Sharî'ah over mystical experience by setting the limits of mystical contemplation and second to accelerate the popularization of *taṣawwuf* among the masses.

These interconnected effects are the fundamental origins for the surnames given to Ghazzâlî in Islamic intellectual history, such as Ḥujjat al-Islam (Proof of Islam), Zayn al-Dîn (Ornament of Religion), and Mujaddid (Renewer of Religion). Sharîf's (1963) title for the chapters on Ghazzâlî as "The Middle-Roaders" and Obermann's (1921:197) description of Ghazzâlî's works as "eine Regeneration des Religiösen Gedankens" are fully correct when we think on his critical place in the re-systematization of the Islamic paradigm. Borrowing Eaton's (1927:vii) description of Descartes' place in Western thought, we can say that Ghazzâlî stands where the streams of Islamic thought meet.[58]

After Ghazzâlî's re-systematization, the central characteristics of the Islamic paradigm based on ultimate ontological unity, differentiation, and hierarchy have been strengthened as the factors of gravity of mental, ideological, and imaginative formation which has social, economic, and political reflections. As Shehâdî (1964:20-1) clarifies, the classical doctrine of *mukhâlafah* (uniqueness, utter difference) of God has been interpreted by Ghazzâlî in four senses: God is (i) absolutely the only One, (ii) necessarily unique, (iii) absolutely unlike all others, and (iv) unique in total nature. This interpretation depends on the assumption that "God belongs to a unique category of Being" (Ghazzâlî, 1986b:123). His differentiation of the strata of reality as *al-wujûd al-ḥaqîqî*, *al-wujûd al-'ilmi*, and

---

[58]Ghazzâlî's criticisms of various schools of thought in *Tahâfut al-Falâsifah*, in *Kitâb Faḍâil al-Baṭiniyyah wa Faḍâil al-Mustaẓhiriyyah*, in *Fayṣal al-Tafriqa bayn al-Islam wa al-Zandaqa*, and in *al-Munqidh min al-Ḍalâl* might be accepted as a challenge to the intellectual environment. He tries to show his own system especially in *Al-Iqtiṣad fi al-I'tiqâd* and *Iḥya al-'Ulûm al-Dîn*. *Mi'yâr al-'Ilm* and *Al-Qisṭâs al-Mustaqîm* show his methodological reasoning on theoretical issues. *Mishkât al-Anwâr* and *Kimyâ al-Sa'âdah* might be mentioned as two significant books on *taṣawwuf*.

al-wujûd al-lisânî is attached to this assumption.[59] That means an ultimate and total rejection of any type of ontological proximity.

Using Watt's analogy it might be said that "in passing from al-Ghazzâlî to the immediately following period there is a sense of passing from bright sunshine to murky obscurity" (1972:125) because of the lack of detailed works on the theological and philosophical leanings and their forerunners apart from Ibn Taymiyyah and Ibn Khaldûn. That is perhaps a natural result of the fixed idea that Islamic intellectual history has a significance only as a transmitter of ancient classical sources to the modern era. Nevertheless, three significant characteristics might be mentioned for the post-Ghazzâlî period.

First, as I have mentioned earlier, there is a tendency toward synthesis of *kalâm, falsafah,* and *tasawwuf.* Râzî's synthesis of *kalâm* and *falsafah* and Ibn al-'Arabî's great synthesis of *falsafah* and *tasawwuf* are two significant attempts within this framework. Ibn Taymiyyah's vitalization of *salafiyyah* was a reaction against these attempts at synthesis. His criticisms of *muta'akhkhirîn* (e.g., 1988:169-79) are based on a methodological ground because he argues that it is impossible to attain the knowledge of God by rational methods, whether those of philosophy or of philosophical theology. His argument that God should be characterized as He characterizes Himself and as His Prophet characterized Him without similitude, figurization or divesting (*bilâ tashbîh bilâ tamthîl wa bilâ ta'tîl*)[60] is a repetition of the centralist approach opposing the followers of the various extreme positions regarding the attributes of Allâh. I do not want to go into detail related to these discussion, but it should be underlined that these discussions did not prevent the process of strengthening and stabilization of the paradigm around the basic principle of the ontological unity, differentiation, and hierarchy. On the contrary, they accelerated this process by moving towards the center and avoiding any type of ontological proximity in the sense of *ta'tîl* (divesting), *tashbîh* (similitude), or *tamthîl* (figurization).

Thus, the second characteristic is the stabilization of the paradigm on the basis of the Qur'ânic ontological color around the fundamental principles of the ontological unity, absoluteness, and hierarchy of Allâh. This stabilization created the third characteristic of this period, the concentration of the chief effort of theologians on commentaries, super-commentaries, and glosses on earlier books and treatises.[61] The fundamental thinkers from this period to the modern era aimed to preserve this stabilization. Among them, al-'Îjî,[62] al-Taftazânî,[63] al-Talamsânî,[64]

---

[59]Gatje gives a brief summary in his article (1974:161-6) on Ghazzâlî's differentiation of reality (*Seinschicten*) into what he calls "*die reale , gnoseologische und sprachliche Wirklichkeiten..*"

[60]A brief summary of Ibn Taymiyyah's arguments on the unity and perfection of Allâh (1983:21,40ff) together with his criticisms of the followers of ta'tîl (1983:19) can be found in his *Al-Risâlah al-Akmaliyyah.*

[61]For example, Brockelmann lists about a dozen commentaries, about thirty glosses, and about twenty super-glosses on *'Aqâid al-Nasafî* (Watt,1972:149).

[62]Al-'Îjî's famous works are *Al-'Aqâid al-'Adudiyyah,* in which he summarizes the Islamic creed, and *Mawâqif,* in which he deals with several philosophical questions.

[63]Taftazânî's commentary on *'Aqâid al-Nasafî* has been used as the basic textbook in madrasas.

al-Dawwânî,[65] Muḥammad Birgivî,[66] Ḥasan al-Bosnawî,[67] al-Laqqânî,[68] al-Fadalî,[69] and al-Gümüshânawî[70] might be mentioned as some of the characteristic personalities. Ibn Khaldûn, too, as the most sophisticated and productive scholar of the post-Ghazzâlî period, preserved this stability of the systematization of the paradigm rather than discuss it. Hence, M. Fakhrî's (1983:325) argument that Ibn Khaldûn followed al-Ghazzâlî rather than Ibn Rushd on theoretical ground is completely correct.

The ontological relationship between God, man, and nature based on the principle of *tawḥîd* is the central issue also for the Muslim scholars and intellectuals of this age, who faced the second challenge of Western civilization. Beginning with al-Afghânî's *Answer to Renan* and *Refutation of Materialists*, all counteractions against this challenge carry the characteristics of a clash between two alternative *Weltanschauungs* rather than of a pure political competition. As Mahdî (1972:106) mentions, Afghânî's basic propositions in these attempts are: "(i) Religion is that which constitutes a nation, a culture, or a civilisation, forms its basis and foundation, and provides the most secure bond that holds it together; (ii) The conflict and tension between science or philosophy and religion is embedded in human nature." These propositions are defended by Afghânî in an age of the absolute sovereignty of rationalism over religion. It should not be forgotten that Afghânî has Islam in his mind when he speaks of religion.

The famous modernist of Egypt, 'Abduh, also tried to counteract this challenge through rationalization in the methodological sphere without deviating from the principle of *tawḥîd*. His *Risâlat al-Tawḥîd* carries the basic characteristics of the

---

[64]Talamsânî's most famous work, the short treatise *al-'Aqâid al-Sughrâ*, is a good example of the blending of *falsafah* and *kalâm* as philosophical theology. Since Talamsânî asserts that every believer must know twenty attributes necessary in respect of God and twenty attributes impossible for Him, he expects even the average believer to have some philosophical sophistication (Watt, 1972:155).

[65]Dawwânî wrote philosophical, theological, and mystical works, as well as commentaries on al-'Îjî's and al-Jurjânî's books.

[66]Muḥammad Birgivî, who was very influential in the socio-political life of his time, is best known for *al-Ṭarîqat al-Muḥammadiyyah*.

[67]Ḥasan al-Bosnawî wrote a commentary on *'Aqâid al-Taḥâwî*.

[68]Laqânî's famous work *Jawhar al-Tawḥîd* has many of the same characteristics as the previously-cited works.

[69]Fadalî's medium-length exposition of the Islamic faith has been translated into English by D. B. Macdonald (1903:325-351). He gives fifty articles in this work related to belief in God and prophecy. Twenty of them are necessary in God, twenty are impossible in Him, and one is possible. Four qualities are necessary, four impossible, and one possible in the case of the apostles. It is one of the most sophisticated works in later period, showing the continuity from the time of al-Ghazzâlî to the modern era.

[70]Gümüshânawî's *Jâmi' al-Mutûn* is especially significant for seeing how the paradigmatic characteristics of the Islamic creed have been interpreted by a Ṣûfî leader of Naqshibandiyyah. It also shows the convergence between *kalâm* and *taṣawwuf* throughout the ages.

traditional paradigm mentioned above. His definitions of theology[71] and unity[72] might be mentioned for the verification of this judgment. These definitions are reflections of his assertion that "Qur'ân describes the attributes of God, by and large, with a far surer accent of transcendence than the earlier religions" (1966:31). However, it should be underlined that the methodological rationalization of modernists is time-dependent, reflecting the characteristics of their periods.

Iqbâl's *The Reconstruction of Religious Thought in Islam* is a sophisticated response to the civilizational challenge based on an alternative *Weltanschauung*. Its originality arises from his theocentric interpretation of absolute unity in the sense of combination of ontological differentiation, transcendency, and nearness (*qurbiyyah*). From this perspective, it is a modern version of attempts to compromise the understanding of highly concentrated ontological transcendency and nearness mentioned before. Hence, although Hegelian impact on Iqbâl has been mentioned frequently (Raschid, 1981:8), it should not be forgotten that such an approach might be found also in the history of Islamic thought, especially related to the synthesis of the theological and mystical imaginations. Iqbâl's criticisms of the cosmological, teleological, and ontological arguments (1934:28-29) of scholastic philosophy together with his original interpretations of the spirit of Muslim culture as an analysis of tradition, are attempts to open the way for the reconstruction of religious thought in Islam. Therefore, the intellectual and imaginative link between belief, thought, and life has been set up by a dynamic interpretation of *tawhîd*: "The new culture finds the foundation of world-unity in the principle of *tawhîd*. Islam, as a polity, is only a practical means of making this principle a living factor in the intellectual and emotional life of mankind. It demands loyalty to God, not to thrones. And since God is the ultimate spiritual basis of all life, loyalty to God virtually amounts to his own ideal nature" (1934:140).

The other Muslim scholars and activists of this age, such as Sa'îd Nursî, Sayyid Quṭb, and Mawdûdî, also try to set up a direct link between ontological and social imaginations by preserving the traditional paradigm around the belief of *tawhîd*. Nursî's basic assumption that the fundamental problem of Muslims in this age is the the issue of belief, Quṭb's identification of *kalimah al-tawhîd* with the Islamic way of life in his famous *Milestones* (1978:97), and Mawdûdî's description of the names of Allâh to underline the link between *tawhîd* and life in his works—especially in *Four Terms According to the* Qur'ân (1979)—are but a few examples for the continuation of the paradigmatic base around the belief of *tawhîd* in our age.

Thus, the conflict and irreconcilability between Islamic and Western civilizations originates from the reality of being based on alternative

---

[71]'Abduh defines theology as "the science that studies the being and attributes of God, the essential and possible affirmations about Him, as well as the negations that are necessary to make relating to Him" (1966:29).

[72]'Abduh's definition of unity is parallel to the understanding of transcendence: "The Necessary Being is One, in His essence, His attributes, His existence and His acts. His essential Unity we have established in the foregoing denial of composition in Him, whether in reality or conceptually. That He is unique in His attributes means that no existent is equal to Him therein.... Neither do they equal him in the attributes which belong with existence. By His Unity of existence and action we mean His uniqueness in necessity of being and in His consequent giving of being to contingents" (1966:51).

Weltanschauungs. In fact, socio-political resistance among Muslim masses and elites against Western ways of life and political structures is a social reflection of this clash. Islamic theoretical and imaginative tradition based on Qur'ânic ontological color which has been systematized throughout the ages as a very consistent paradigm provides both an internal consistency among methodologically competing Muslim schools and an effective potentiality for the reproduction of social and political imaginations and theories as reflections of this consistent *Weltanschauung* within any new framework of natural and social environment.

Epistemological unity of truth: Harmonization of knowledge

Three most significant characteristics should be mentioned related to Islamic epistemology: (i) the relationship of dependency between ontology and epistemology which creates an "ontologically determined epistemology," (ii) differentiation of epistemological levels, and (iii) harmonization of epistemological sources to attain the unity of truth. In fact, all of these characteristics have theoretical and imaginative interconnections which form a totalist web of *Weltanschauung.*

The origin of the "ontologically determined epistemology" in Islam should be sought in the Qur'ânic system of semantics. Even the number of occurrences of the most frequently used terms in the Qur'ân provides us significant indications for this specific link between ontological and epistemological imaginations. The six terms occurring most often—in all their derivations—in the Qur'ân are *Allâh* (2800 times), *qwl* (to say, 1700 times) *kwn* (to be, 1300 times), *Rabb* (950 times), *amn* (888 times), and *'ilm* (to know, 750 times). Following these, with approximately 450-550 occurrences each, are the four terms *aty* (to come), *kfr* (to deny, to conceal, to cover [the truth]), *rsl* (to send a messenger) and *'ard* (earth).[73] These terms form a web of meaning which specifies the ontological differentiation between Allâh and other beings in the sense of *kawn* as well as the origins and types of relationship between Allâh and human beings as a specific communication of *qwl-rsl-'ilm* [Allâh-man]/*amn-kfr* [man-Allâh]. The etymological kinship among *'ilm* (knowledge), *'alam* (sign, mark), and *'âlam* (world) is another interesting clue for this dependency between ontological and epistemological imaginations.[74] Al-Baghdâdî's (1981:34) definition of *'âlam* as "as everything that has knowledge and sense perception" and al-Zamakhsharî's definition of *'âlam* as "the totality of bodies [substances] and accidents of which the Creator has knowledge" are examples of the kinship between *'ilm* and *'âlam*, while al-Juwaynî sets up a semantic link between *'alam* and *'âlam* by defining *'âlam* as "an indication set up to indicate the existence of the owner of the *'âlam*" who is Allâh (F. Rosenthal, 1970:19). It should not be forgotten that one of the beautiful names of Allâh is *'Âlim* (e.g., Qur'ân, 6:59, 34:26). Thus, within the framework of this semantic system, it is impossible to separate the context of knowledge from the context of

---

[73] I have taken the numbers from F.Rosenthal (1970:19-20), except *amn* which I have counted from Abdulbâqiy (1984:81-93).

[74] See Isfahani's *Müfradât* (1921: 344-345) for this etymological kinship.

being. Therefore, the definition, origin, and categorization of knowledge in Islamic intellectual history has directly been attached to the ontological antecedents.

The highly differentiated ontological hierarchy mentioned above necessitates a differentiation on epistemological levels, so that the *al-'ilm min Allâh* (the knowledge from Allâh) can not be interpreted on the same epistemological level as the knowledge of man. Such a differentiation of epistemological levels forms a strong internal consistency with the principles of *tawḥîd* and *tanzîh* as the bases of *'aqâid* because Allâh as *'Âlim* (the Absolute Knower) is the origin of knowledge. This differentiation of epistemological levels has been supported by a doctrine of *ghayb* (invisible, unseen) in the Qur'ânic system, because it has been revealed that "with Him are the keys of the invisible and none but He knows them" (6:59). Therefore, a relationship of co-penetration among these levels is impossible. The application of different sets of criteria for each epistemological level prevents the development of common criteria which could be applied for both levels so that a secular base for anthropocentric epistemology could emerge. Al-Muḥâsibî's correlation between ontological and epistemological levels to systematize the categorization of knowledge is a very indicative example for the relationship of the dependency between ontological and epistemological differentiation.[75] In his system, each kind of knowledge is oriented to one of the three levels of reality in his tri-level cosmology. Al-Baghdâdî's categorization of knowledge as divine and animal knowledge within a hierarchical framework might be mentioned as another example of the systematization of this principle of epistemological differentiation on behalf of theologians (Wensinck, 1932:253).

Ibn Rushd's interpretation of the interconnection of ontological and epistemological differentiation is clear enough to exemplify our argument of "the ontologically determined epistemology" in Islam. His argument that human knowledge must not be confused with divine knowledge because of their essential differences and that "true knowledge is the knowledge of God" (Ibn Rushd, 1973:49) shows the epistemological differentiation and hierarchy as a result of strict ontological hierarchy in Islamic thought. This understanding prevents the formation of common criterion for both human and divine knowledge, which might be the first stage for the secularization of knowledge. Islamic thought depends on this specific link between ontology and epistemology through the understanding of prophecy (*nubuwwah*): "What the religious laws in our time think of this matter is what God wills. The only way to know what it is that God wills in respect of them is [through] prophecy"(Ibn Rushd,1966:185). He underlines in the same paragraph that this knowledge is divided into two parts; namely abstract knowledge such as religious laws regarding the perception of God and practical knowledge, such as the ethical virtues it enjoins. This understanding of *nubuwwah* is his one of the

---

[75]Muḥâsibî "relates three kinds of knowledge to a tri-level cosmology: *hadhihi al-dâr* or this world [*dunyâ*; *dâr al-baqâ'* or the hereafter [*al-âkhirah*]; and Allâh or God Himself.... The first knowledge is external in nature, appropriate to this world, and related to the law and its application. On this basis the first kind of knowledge is external. The second kind is an inner knowledge which results in *al-'ibâdah al-qulûb* or *al-'ibâdah al-bâṭiniyyah*.... The third knowledge, relative to God Himself, is *al-'ilm bi-Allâh wa aḥkâmihi* (or *tadbîrihi*) *fî khalqihi fî al-dârayn*. This final kind of knowledge is scarcely mentioned since it is ultimately impenetrable" (1983:132, Librande's intr.).

characteristic differences from Plato in his commentary on the *Republic*.
E. Rosenthal's evaluation that "the difference in religious thought between a
Muslim and a Greek is the difference between Revelation and Myth" (1951:274) is
an exact conclusion from this perspective. Ibn Rushd's criticism of Plato as being
confused by mythological tales and his exclusion of some parts of the *Republic*
from his commentary (Ibn Rushd, 1966:251) are evidence of this contrast between
Islamic revelation and Greek myth.

The principal difference between *nass* (incontrovertible proof) and *ijtihâd*
(intense exertion to arrive at a rule of law) in the axiological sphere can only be
understood from the perspective of the differentiation of the epistemological levels
in the Islamic prescriptivist methodology of *fiqh*. Attempts at reforming Islam by
transforming the rules of Islamic jurisprudence cannot be successful in the long run
since the internal consistency of Islam, which is based on this differentiation of
ontological and epistemological levels, could very easily eliminate those instances
of *ijtihâd* that conflict with *nass* as the ultimate source of *fiqh*. The strong resistance
of Muslims to pyramidal and superstructural reformation attempts should be
evaluated within the context of the ontologico-epistemological dimension of Islam.

This internal consistency between Islamic ontology and epistemology has been
brought to completion with the ideas of the revelation and mission of prophecy. The
classifications of the causes of knowledge in Islamic theology assume the absolute
priority of *wahy* (revelation) which is the narrative of the Messenger aided by an
evident miracle, and brings about deductive knowledge, and the knowledge
established by it resembles the knowledge established by necessity in certainty and
in fixity (Taftazânî, 1950:15). The collections of the true knowledges of this
specific cause are the books of Allâh [*kutub*] which He has sent down by His
prophets, and in them He has shown His positive commands and His prohibitions,
His promise [*wa'd*], and His threat [*wa'iyd*] (Taftazânî, 1950:135). The Qur'ân, as
the last and most complete source of revelation originated from the divine
knowledge of the Absolute Knower, constitutes the top of the epistemological
hierarchy.

As Nieuwenhuijze (1985:41) mentions, in Islam revelation is an ongoing, in the
sense of repetitive, proposition. It accompanies mankind throughout its existence,
from Adam to Muhammad (peace be to him). Thus, the prophets form a spiritual
brotherhood, and in many traditions Muhammad (peace be to him) talks about other
prophets as his brothers. The Qur'ân insists on the continuity and consistency of
revelation, arguing that "every scriptural revelation in its pristine purity was in
essence Islam" (3:66, 78-9; 4:64; 27:25-9; 42:13) and "we make no distinction
between any of them" (2:136, 285; 3:33, 83). The victory of the supporters of the
argument that the Qur'ân is the *Kalâmullâh* (Word of Allâh) against the Mu'tazilah,
who argued that the Qur'ân is a creation of Allâh, strengthened the link between
ontology and epistemology in preserving this epistemological differentiation.

The conception of the Prophet as a messenger—not as a hero, a semi-divine
being, an *avatar*, or Son of God—together with this interpretation of the Qur'ân as
Kalâmullah has strengthened the tendency toward a differentiation of ontological
and epistemological levels. In comparisons between Islam and Christianity, it
should not be forgotten that in Islam *Kalâmullâh* is scriptural revelation in the form
of Qur'ân, while in Christianity Jesus himself is the revelation. This fundamental
difference effected both ontological and epistemological consequences in these
religious traditions. The place of the Prophet in the channel of communication
through revelation has been specified very clearly by Qur'ân: "Say: The knowledge

is with Allâh only, and I am but a plain warner" (67:26). This Qur'ânic specification has been repeated by the followers of *kalâm* as "in sending of messengers there is a wisdom, and Allâh has sent Messengers of mankind to mankind announcing good tidings, and warning, and explaining to people what they need [to know] of the matters of this world and of the judgement" (Taftazânî, 1950:127).

Another significant assumption related to this issue is the rejection of ultimate conflict between these epistemological levels. All Muslim scholars and philosophers try to show and keep the balance between revelation as the source of absolute truth and the reason as the means of interpreting revelation. From this perspective, scriptural revelation delineates the scope, function, and limitations, of different sources of knowledge. As a natural result of this fundamental principle of the harmonization of knowledge, it has been accepted that "false consciousness and unfair rationalisations are not the product of pure reason and pseudo-religions alone" (Husaini, 1980:7). As an extension of ontological unity, the possibility of an ultimate contradiction between revelation and pure reason has been denied by almost all Muslim schools by assuming that the unity of truth originates from the absolute unity of divinity. They have insisted strongly on a complementary, rather than competitive, relationship between revelation and pure reason. Kindî, as the founder of *falsafah*, is the champion of this understanding of the harmonization of the sources of knowledge, arguing that "knowledge produced by the true prophet is identical with that produced by the competent philosopher" (Hitti, 1968:192). Ibn Tufayl's masterpiece *Hayy ibn Yaqzân* (1905) is one of the best examples of an attempt to show the complementarity of revelation and reason.[76] Ibn Tufayl concludes this treatise by asking God "that He would please give us the true and certain knowledge of Himself, for he is gracious and liberal of His favors" (1905:69). Such a conclusion implicitly assumes the epistemological hierarchy which presupposes the supremacy of divine knowledge like the classification of Baghdâdî as the leading figure of *kalâm*.

On the other hand, Ibn Hazm's argument in his *Al-Milal wa al-Nihal* that "that the Qur'ân is true is known from true premises founded on reason and sensation, the only true bases of knowledge. When God gives a revelation, He creates in the recipient knowledge of its truth" (Tritton, 1965:620) shows the place of reason as a means to prove the truth of revelation as well as the harmonization of these sources. Al-Ash'arî's following judgement (1953b:95t., 131) tries to guarantee the preservation of this fundamental principle of the harmonization of the epistemological sources in the cases of the difficulty on the intellectual harmonization of the epistemological sources: "When new and specific questions pertaining to the basic dogmas arise, every Muslim ought to refer judgement on them to the sum of principles accepted on the ground of reason, sense experience, intuition, etc., not confounding the rational with the traditional [revealed], or the traditional [revealed] with the rational."

---

[76]"And when he understood the condition of mankind, and that the greatest part of them were like brute beasts, he knew that all wisdom, direction and good success, consisted in what the messengers of God had spoken, and the Law delivered; and that there was no other way besides this, and there could be nothing added to it" (Ibn Tufayl, 1905:68).

Thus, epistemology has been limited and determined by ontological antecedents in the Islamic way of thought. Such a relationship between ontological and epistemological presuppositions necessitates an understanding of the unity of truth via harmonization of the sources of knowledge. This theocentric ontology and this epistemology are the bases of the paradigmatic unity in the accumulated bulk on Islamic theory. Even conflicting theological and philosophical schools agree on this principle of ontological transcendency and on the evaluation of Islamic epistemology based on this fundamental principle. The specification of the places of reason and sensation together with revelation in Islamic intellectual history to attain the ultimate truth prevented the segmentation of epistemological sources based on the assumption of the ultimate contrast, such as occurred in the Western epistemological tradition.

Axiological normativeness: Unity of life and law

The genuine core of the comprehensive totalist system of Islam is the interconnection of ontological, epistemological, and axiological imaginations. The Islamic value system is directly attached to the ontological and epistemological premises mentioned above. Therefore, the fundamental key-concept of the Qur'ânic value system, al-'amal al-ṣâliḥ (good work-ethics) constitutes an indivisible unity with the other key-concepts of îmân (faith-ontology) and 'ilm (knowledge-epistemology).

The fundamental characteristic of Islamic axiological normativeness is its interpretation of man's responsibility on earth which forms the imagination of the unity of life and law by preventing any type of compartmentalization of the different sections of life. Islamic morality has been directly attached to the ontological antecedents via specification of man's place in the universe as the basic element for the divine responsibility. Man, who has not been created except to serve Allâh (Qur'ân, 51:56), has a specific responsibility (amânah) on earth. "Lo, we offered the trust unto the heaven and the earth and the hills, but they shrunk from bearing and were afraid of it. And man assumed it" (Qur'ân, 33:72). Born with innocence, the human being is capable of fulfilling this responsibility because "Allâh does not charge a person with more than he can bear" (Qur'ân, 2:286). As von Grünebaum (1970:11) clarifies in comparison with Christianity, "Obedience to the Lord, fulfillment of His order justified the individual existence, the more so that no inner rent called for atonement and redemption—the Muslim was a man without original sin, in need of guidance, but not of reparation."

Hence, Islamic understanding of man's moral responsibility has been connected directly to his ontological place in the universe. Therefore, for example Fakhraddîn al-Râzî begins Kitâb al-Nafs wa al-Rûḥ, his treatise on moral philosophy, with clarification of man's degree (martabah) in the hierarchy of beings (marâtib al-mawjûdât), which he divides into four groups according to their possessions and tendencies. Man is distinguished from angels, animals, and plants by his possession of *'aql* (reason) and *ḥikmah* (wisdom) and the tendencies of *ṭabī'ah* (nature, disposition) and *shahwah* (desire), so that he has moral responsibility.[77] This understanding of divinely based moral responsibility results in an ultimate unity of life. This indivisibility of life has been supported by a vision of eschatology which assumes a relationship of continuity between this world and the next. Ghazzâlî's (1910:43-4) analogy makes this point evident: "this world is a stage or market-place passed by pilgrims on their own way to the next.... While man is in this world, two things are necessary for him: first, the protection and nurturing of his soul; secondly, the care and nurturing of his body. The proper nourishment of the soul is the knowledge and love of God, and to be absorbed in the love of anything but God is the ruin of the soul. The body, so to speak, is simply the riding-animal of the soul, and perishes while the soul endures." This approach is fully consistent with Qur'ânic eschatology, which assumes this world as a place for preparation to the hereafter: "Whoso desires the life of this world and its pomp, we shall repay them their deeds herein, and therein they will not be wronged. Those are they for whom is naught in the hereafter save the Fire. All that they contrive here is vain and [all] that they are wont to do is fruitless" (11:15-16). Such an imagination of the unity of life together with such an eschatological perspective is absolutely different from the imaginative bases of secularization of life and law.

This imagination of the unity of life, as opposed to the secular divisibility of the sectors of life, and this divinely based moral responsibility provide theoretical and imaginative bases for the highly concentrated axiological normativeness in Islamic intellectual and social history. Political and economic mechanisms, applications, and institutions could be justified only through their role in the process of the realization of this axiological normativeness. Therefore, they have never been imagined as independent sectors of life existing on their own. That fundamental difference, compared with the secularization of life in Western experience, will be held in the following chapters, but it should be underlined at this stage that axiological normativeness in Islam plays the role of channel between ontologico-epistemological antecedents and socio-political and economic mechanisms. The superiority of the Islamic all-embracing jurisprudence (*fiqh*) cannot be understood if one omits the role this imaginative channel. Hence, prescriptivism has been supported by a very consistent normativism, and this is the characteristic that provides strong resistance among Muslim elites and masses against the process of Westernization based on a counter-prescriptivism of Western ways of life that emerged from an understanding of the divisibility of the sectors of life.

The interpretations on the aim of life developed by Muslim jurists, philosophers, and theologians intersect on this fundamental issue. The Qur'ânic norm-centered structure is the prerequisite of the prescriptivist parts of the supreme law. Law is directly attached to this value system, while social mechanisms and institutions are expected to be determined by the interconnected sphere of this axiological normativeness and prescriptivism. The aim of life is the realization of these values in whole parts of life. Law itself and institutional mechanisms as the

---

[77]Râzî (1978:178) divides beings into four groups: (i) those possessing *'aql* and *ḥikmah* but not *ṭabī'ah* and *shahwah* (i.e., angels), (ii) those possessing *ṭabī'ah* and *shahwah* but not *'aql* and *ḥikmah* (i.e., animals), (iii) those possessing none of these (i.e., plants), and (iv) those possessing all of them (i.e., human beings).

social consequences of the application of this law are only the means for the realization of the sovereignty of this value system.

Even very detailed mechanisms have been attached to this value system and its ontological antecedents. Al-Khâzinî's *Kitâb Mizân al-Ḥikmah* (Book of the Balance of Wisdom) is an excellent example of these imaginative and theoretical channels. The essential aim of this book is to explain how the mechanism of the water-balance works, but it begins with a very sophisticated part on the philosophy of justice and its relationship to the cosmic balance under the control of the absolute sovereignty of Allâh together with its ontological and epistemological reflections: "Justice is the stay of all virtues, and the support of all excellencies. For perfect virtue, which is wisdom in its two parts, knowledge and action, and in its two aspects, religion and the course of the world, consists of perfect knowledge and assured action; and justice brings the two [requisites] together. It is the confluence of the two perfections of that virtue, the means of reaching the limits of all greatness and the cause of securing the prize in all excellence. In order to place justice on the pinnacle of perfection, the Supreme Creator made Himself known to the Choicest of His servants under the name of the Just; and it was by the light of justice that the world became complete and perfected, and was brought to perfect order—to which there is allusion in the words of the Blessed: "by justice were the heavens and the earth established" (Khâzinî, 1860:3-4). His connection of this understanding of justice to the power of "self-government" as an ethical quality[78] and to the Holy Book as a supreme canon[79] shows the intersection of ontological, epistemological, and axiological premises and how a specific *Weltanschauung* leads to a totalistic unity of life and law via a specific prescriptivism directed by normativism. The veiled assumption of such an approach is that all mechanisms might be controlled only by a very well defined morality based on an axiological normativism. Thus, the value of a norm cannot be determined by the mechanism itself; on the contrary the mechanism might be controlled only by a supreme normativism based on a specific ontologico-epistemological source. Al-Khâzinî's work is only a typical example of this approach on a comparatively detailed issue. It might be extended to the whole Islamic intellectual tradition. As will be discussed in following chapters, this characteristic has significant reflections on socio-political imagination, theory, and culture.

Qur'ânic ethical structure, based on opposed categories as the classes of positive and negative moral properties (Izutsu, 1966:105) and their connections to the basic dichotomy of believer and unbeliever, forms an imagination of human life

---

[78]"Justice in action is two-fold: (1) self-government, which is the harmonizing of the natural endowments, the maintenance of equilibrium between the powers of the soul, and the bringing of them under beautiful control—agreeably to the saying: "the most just of men is he who lets his reason arbitrate for his desire" and it is a part of the perfection of such a man that he dispenses justice among those inferior to himself, and wards off from others any injury which he has experienced, so that men are secure as to his doing evil; (2) control over others" (Khâzinî, 1860:5).

[79] "The Glorious Book of God, which, from the beginning to end, is without any admixture of error, is the supreme canon, to which both legal rules and doctrinal principles refer back, the arbiter between the Supereminent and the subject creature, to which the tradition of the Blessed Prophet is the sequel" (Khâzinî, 1860:6).

as a dynamic circle between being of the best stature (*ahsani taqwîm*) and the lowest of the low (*asfala sâfilîn*)(95:4-5). Thus, the Qur'ân offers an ethical set of norms for the perfection of the human being, who was created by Allâh as of the best stature. The attainment of happiness in Islamic ethics constitutes a consistent totality with Islamic law from this perspective. The perfection of human being might be attained through the attainment of *sa'âdah*[80] which is directly dependent on the realization of Qur'ânic positive moral properties under the protection of a comprehensive law.

Thus, the Islamic divine law has unique characteristics compared with other systems of law as legal codifications. It is a theoretical and imaginative consequence of the specific ontological, epistemological, and axiological framework. The Hanafî definition of *fiqh* as "the knowledge of the rights and duties whereby man is enabled to observe right conduct in this life, and to prepare himself for the world to come" connotes the dependency of law to the unity of life within this consistency. Hence. its legal codes are only meaningful within this framework and a total particularization of this structure such as in the case of the process of the secularization of law in Western experience is impossible. As Santillana (1965:288) mentions, "submission to this law is at the same time a social duty and a precept of faith; whosoever violates it, not only infringes the legal order, but commits a sin, because there is no right in which God has not share. Judicial order and religion, law and morals, are the two aspects of that same will, from which the Muslim community derives its existence and its direction; every legal question is in itself a case of conscience, and jurisprudence points to theology as its ultimate base." The prescriptivist dimensions and sources of Islamic law have been determined by Muslim jurists according to this fundamental characteristic.[81]

Interpretations of the objectives of Sharî'ah reflect this comprehensive axiomatic base of Islamic law. In Ibn Rushd's explanation, which is a typical example, the objective of Sharî'ah has been defined as attaining true knowledge and true practice (*al-'ilm al-haqq wa al-'amal al-haqq*)(1973:49). As al-Ahwany (1963:I/545) mentions, this judgement "reminds us of the definition of philosophy given by al-Kindî, which remained current all through Islamic philosophy." This definition embraces the theoretical and imaginative channels between ontology, epistemology, and axiology. *Al-'ilm al-haqq* directed by *nubuwwah* as the fundamental epistemological source specifies *al-'amal al-haqq* guaranteed by Sharî'ah through a specific axiological normativeness.

The contrast between Islamic Sharî'ah and Platonic *nomos* in Ibn Rushd's commentary on the *Republic* is especially meaningful within this context. Sharî'ah, as the expression of the will of God, shows the highest good of man and his end as rational being because God alone knows the obstacles that prevent man from attaining happiness. The supremacy and perfection of Sharî'ah over man-made laws consists in its epistemologically divine character, according to Ibn Rushd. This is another dimension of Islamic paradigm accepted by several Muslim sects and schools. As Rosenthal (1953:261) mentions, "Ibn Rushd should give the same definition of prophecy and prophets and make the same assertion about the Sharî'ah

---

[80]As I have clarified in chapter 1, I intend its widest sense in the Islamic philosophico-theological tradition when I use *sa'âdah* rather than happiness only.

[81]See Shâfi'î's *al-Risâlah* (1961) for this systematization.

in an admittedly philosophical treatise, written in defence of the *falâsifah* against al-Ghazzâlî's attack upon them" (cf. Ibn Rushd, 1978:316).

Ibn Rushd's presupposition that the philosopher aims at knowledge identical with that which God demands in the Sharî'ah shows a "parting of the ways" between Islamic *hikmah* and Greek philosophy. But this parting on ontological ground does not prevent the attempts of the followers of Islamic *hikmah* from finding methodological, terminological, and axiological reconciliation without distorting this ontological color. Rosenthal's argument (1953:261) that the aim of the Sharî'ah is identical with that of political science as defined by Aristotle in the *Nicomachean Ethics* and repeated by al-Fârâbî in his *Kitâb Tahsil al-Sa'âdah* and by Ibn Rushd in his commentary on Plato's *Republic* should be evaluated within this context. The essence of happiness as the purpose of Sharî'ah and philosophy should not be confused with the technique applied for the analysis of this aim. As Leaman (1980:170) concludes, "Ibn Rushd used the same technique which Aristotle employed to combine social with intellectual virtues in his account of happiness, but in the case of the Islamic philosopher, happiness was discussed in relation to religious and intellectual virtues."

The contrast between the elitist interpretation of happiness formulated by the philosophers and the general validity of Sharî'ah has been eliminated by Ibn Rushd through popularization of happiness based on his thesis that the Sharî'ah is required of everyone, but philosophy is not.[82] He defines happiness as an action belonging to the rational soul performed with virtue (Ibn Rushd, 1966:188; cf. 275, Rosenthal's note). His classification of the perfections (Ibn Rushd,1966:189) aims to show that the human perfections are more than one.

Thus, the holistic structure of Islamic law around the basic principle of the unity of life and its general validity originates from a highly sophisticated axiological normativeness supported by ontological and epistemological antecedents as a comprehensive *Weltanschauung* based on the belief of *tawhîd*. Axiological normativeness constitutes the third fundamental dimension of the Islamic paradigm, along with ontological unity and epistemological harmonization, shared by almost all Muslim schools and sects.

---

[82]"Ibn Rushd's discussion of the relationship between happiness and philosophy solved a problem in Islamic social philosophy which bedevilled the *falâsifah*... The problem originates with Plato and his assertion that theoretical reason (*sophia*), is the highest activity of man, and man's happiness lies in the exercise of reason.... This Platonic doctrine created the problem with which Ibn Rushd was confronted, which is that it seems at the very least arguable that one has to be a philosopher to know how to do good, or to achieve happiness. This difficulty in Plato's ethics struck the *falâsifah* particularly clearly, since they held that the Qur'ân contains the whole of the knowledge of the content of morality" (Leaman,1980:167).

PART II

POLITICAL CONSEQUENCES

JUSTIFICATION OF THE SOCIO-POLITICAL SYSTEM: COSMOLOGICO-ONTOLOGICAL FOUNDATIONS

Political ideas and theories, like all other ideals, can be justified only through appealing to some sort of norm as a comprehensive set of intrinsic values—a part of a complete way of thought, a *Weltanschauung* comprising cosmological, ontological, epistemological, and eschatological presuppositions. Attempts to justify the state as a socio-political institution in contrasting Islamic and Western political theories give us significant clues for our argument.

We can analyze and compare attempted justifications in two groups, (i) those based on arguments from the origin of the state as a socio-political system and (ii) those based on arguments from the aims of the state as a socio-political institution. The interesting link between ontology, axiology, and politics is clearly related to the problem of justification. From this perspective, God-centered Islamic political justification and nature-centered Western political justification are two alternative ways of justification, depending on different theoretical and philosophical backgrounds.

Western way of justification

Two ancient bases of Western attempts at the justification of the state as a socio-political system are the Aristotelian methodology and the Stoic ethics. Aristotle, as the founder of the "realistic justification" depending on empiricism, might be accepted as the forerunner of the modern "state of nature" and "social contract" theories for the justification of the state through speculations on its origin. Aristotle's political philosophy has been directly related to his epistemological approach, which is parallel to his cosmological-ontological arguments. In the epistemological sense, his empiric methodology was aimed at understanding the mechanism of the actuality of the cosmological teleology rather than at developing speculations on the ontological origins of potentialities. Therefore he conceptualizes the First Unmoved Mover as a part of cosmological actualities rather than as a transcendental creator of all cosmological substances. This central position of empiric epistemology became one of the fundamental characteristics of all types of justifications throughout the ages, not only political justification. The modern version of such a historical legacy is the central idea of modern empiricism that "if there is to be such a thing as justification at all, empirical knowledge must be see as resting on experiential foundations" (Williams, 1980:243).

Aristotle's empiricism in political theory might be accepted as a continuation of this epistemological attitude toward ontology. His affinity to the actualities of the cosmos on an ontological level and to the political actualities on a social level have the same epistemological tool, namely empiricism. This empiric epistemology is a delicate channel from an ontological to a political sphere. He ascends to the First Unmoved Mover by observing moved and perishable substances and depended on motion as a fundamental cosmological reality. Using the same methodology in his political analysis, he reaches an understanding of the "best practicable state" by observing several political structures and constitutions based on political actualities. Therefore we can say that these two reflections on the ontological and political spheres both using the same epistemological and methodological tools.

Origin of the socio-political system

Bluntschli (1901:283-302) classifies the speculative theories on the origin of the state into five categories: (i) the state of nature, (ii) the state as a divine institution, (iii) the theory of force, (iv) the theory of contract, and (v) the natural sociability and political consciousness of man. These speculative approaches are, at the same time, the foundations for the justification of the socio-political system from the perspective of its origin. Theories on the state of nature and on the social contract are the most significant modern versions of the justification because the others might be reduced to these interpretations. However, as will be shown, the justification of the state through arguments that it is a divine institution should not be confused with the Islamic paradigm of the unity between ontological and political spheres due to the fact that Western divine justification presupposes the categoric differentiation of the authority into state and church. Contrary to the Islamic case, in which ontological and religious imaginations are strictly unified, Western justifications of the state as a divine institution have been developed and used by secular authorities to attain their independence from the supreme authority of the Church. This process will be analyzed in chapter 7, to show its impact on the formation of the nation-state system as radically opposed to the Islamic notion of *ummah*.

The theories on the state of nature to justify the existence of the state as a socio-political system are very indicative of the political consequences of the Western paradigm analyzed in chapter 2. As Bluntschli (1901:283) summarizes, this philosophical speculation is fond of imagining a primitive condition in which men lived without government and then asking how from that condition mankind has arrived at the state. This state of nature has been imagined by some of the philosophers as a state of war while by others as a golden age.

The leading figure of the former view is Hobbes, whose *nouva scienza* of man and state is "the first peculiarly modern attempt to give a coherent and exhaustive answer to the question of man's right life, which is at the same time the question of the right order of society" (Strauss, 1961:1). In his *Leviathan* (n.d.:64), Hobbes reaches the conclusion of the state of war through his analysis "that in the nature of man, we find three principal causes of quarrel. First, Competition; Secondly, Diffidence; thirdly, Glory. The first, maketh men invade for Gain; the second, for Safety; and third for Reputation. The first use Violence, to make themselves Masters of other men's persons, wives, children, and cattle; the second, to defend them; the third, for trifles, as a word, a smile, a different opinion, and any other signe of undervalue, either direct in their Persons, or by reflexion in their Kindred, their Friends, their Nation, their Profession, or their Name. Hereby it is manifest, that during the time men live without a common Power to keep them all in awe, they are in that condition which is called Warre; and such a warre as is of every man, against every man."[1]

Hobbes' mechanistic psychological interpretation of the state of nature carries indications of the new method by which Galileo's understanding of the supremacy of physics in the hierarchy of sciences and the emergence of the modern naturalistic cosmology became possible, as well as of ancient and Christian ways of thoughts. A sophisticated analysis on the material sources of Hobbesian political philosophy might provide us significant clues for the survival of the basic theoretical and imaginative elements to verify our argument of the continuity, rather than the revolutionary progression, of the Western paradigm throughout the ages as the basic parameter of Western civilization. Bluntschli's simile between the state of war and Christian idea of fallen humanity,[2] Dilthey's assertion of Stoic impact on Hobbes' political philosophy, and Strauss' emphasis on the indebtedness of the Hobbesian analysis to the new method[3] are explanations of the several faces of the same reality. Therefore, there is no contradiction between the facts that "nearly half of the Leviathan is devoted to an exposition of the theological and ecclesiastical principles that supplement its moral and political theory" (Dunning, 1916:297) and that almost all modern secular ideologies can be philosophically reduced to Hobbes' political philosophy.

Nevertheless, the impact of the re-formed Western paradigm on the Hobbesian understanding of the state of nature is very evident. The re-emergence of the epistemologically defined ontology together with the new resolutive-compositive method provided the epistemological and methodological tools for Hobbes' *nouva scienza*. His new morality reflects the process of the centralization of epistemology because it absolutely depends on his own experience as the basic epistemological source. His analysis on human nature and on state of nature is a consequence of his empiricism in an age of civil war: "Whatsoever therefore is consequent to a time of Warre, where every man is Enemy to every man; the same is consequent to the time, wherein men live without other security, than what their own strength, and their own intention shall furnish them withall." Although he argues that the only

---

[1]Hobbes' reasoning from the state of nature to the emergence of the natural state with its moral basis upon "natural appetite" and "natural reason" may be represented by the following steps: from (i) naturalistic reasoning to (ii) self-preservation to (iii) avoidance of death to (iv) agreement with companions against enemies to (v) dominion of the master (the victor who has safeguarded his honor) over servants to (vi) the natural state.

[2]"This philosophical idea [i.e., the state of nature as a state of war] found a welcome confirmation in the theological speculation which regarded the State not as the organization of Paradise, but of fallen humanity" (Bluntschli, 1901:284).

[3]"It would thus seem that the characteristic contents of Hobbes' political philosophy—the absolute priority of the individual to the State, the conceptions of the individual as asocial, of the relation between the state of nature and the State as an absolute antithesis, and finally of the State itself as Leviathan—is determined by and, as it were, implied in the method. As this method, however, was applied only subsequently, only in imitation of Galileo's founding of the new physics, Hobbes' achievements, from this point of view, however great it may be, is nevertheless of the second order—secondary in comparison with the founding of modern science by Galileo and Descartes" (Strauss, 1961:2).

example for his state of nature is the conditions of life among the American Indians (n.d., 65), his own life gives clear witness of the impact of the anarchic conditions of English civil war, when the hypothetical model of *homo homini lupus* was a fact. Macpherson's interpretation of Hobbes to show the congruency between his environmental conditions and his theory of the state of nature might be more meaningful within the framework of this epistemologico-methodological transformation of the re-formed paradigm.

Spinoza, too, agree on this hypothetical model of the state of war. But, he imagines a more ethical case of the state of war in his *Tractatus Theologico-Politicus* and *Tractatus Politicus*. The fundamental differences between Hobbes and Spinoza on this issue are their views on the existence of sin and liberty in the state of nature. Unlike Hobbes, who argues that nothing can be unjust in the state of nature, Spinoza insists that men cannot break the laws of nature, for these laws are inviolable.[4] This difference is a natural consequence of Spinoza's metaphysical pantheism formulated as *Deus siva Natura,* because in his argumentation men can not sin against God, for God is not a king who lays down laws that men can break, which means that natural laws have been identified with the divine teleology. This characteristic is a very significant indication of the critical position of Spinoza in the history of Western philosophy where theology and natural cosmology intersect as well as an indication of the effects of ontologico-cosmological presuppositions on socio-political imaginations and theories.

Thus, Spinoza (1965a:125,127) opens the ways from divine teleology to natural teleology and from divine laws/rights to natural laws/natural rights by identifying the divine with nature, *Deus siva Natura.* "For there is no doubt that nature in the absolute sense has a perfect right to do everything in its power, i.e., that the right of nature extends as far as its power; the power of nature being nothing but the power of God, who has perfect right to do everything". This identification is consistent with his definition of the right and law of nature as the rules of each individual thing's nature, the rules whereby we conceive it as naturally determined to exist and act in a definite way. Such an identification of the divinity with nature implies the ontological insignificance of man as a "tiny part of the eternal order of the whole nature" because nature is not bounded by the laws of human reason. It also assumes the epistemological incapacity of man because he knows things only in part, being almost entirely ignorant of how they are linked together in the universal system of nature.

Spinoza argues that the state of nature is prior to religion both in nature and in time. So, the state of nature should not be confused with a condition where religion and law exist, but must be conceived as without religion or law (Spinoza, 1965a:143). It is impossible to imagine such a state of nature within an Islamic

---

[4]"There is no sin in the state of nature; or rather, that if anyone sins, it is against himself, and not against others. For the law of nature obliges nobody to do the will of another unless he so desires; it obliges nobody to count anything good or bad save what he himself decides to be such in accordance with his own nature and judgement; and it forbids absolutely nothing that is within human power."(Spinoza, 1965b:279) As a natural consequence of this understanding of the law of nature, he reaches to the conclusion that sin, justice and injustice are inconceivable except in a state, where what is good and bad is determined by civil laws which are common to all.(Spinoza, 1965b:283)

framework because it absolutely contradicts the Islamic concept of *dîn* based on the absolute sovereignty of Allâh, but it is a counterpart of the naturalistic interpretation of cosmology and forms a consistent integrity with the secularization of epistemology and of socio-political life.

The followers of the second version of the state of nature "dreamed of a golden age of Paradise, in which there were as yet no evils and no injustice, while all enjoyed themselves in the unlimited freedom and happiness of their peaceful existence. In this primeval condition there was supposed to be no property, since the superabundance of nature gave to every one in sufficiency all that his unsophisticated and uncorrupted tastes could require. As yet there was no difference of ranks, nor even of callings. Every one was like another. Then too there was neither ruler nor subject, nor magistrate, nor judge, nor army, nor taxes" (Bluntschli, 1901:283). The leading figures of this hypothetical model are Locke, Rousseau, and Marx.

Locke's *Two Treatises of Government* reflects this way of justification not only through its content but also through its structure. Locke (1965:319-21) assimilates the understanding of political power and natural law to each other after a description of this hypothetical model: "To understand Political Power right, and derive it from its Original, we must consider what State all Men are naturally in, and that is, a State of Perfect Freedom to order their actions, and dispose of their Possessions, and Persons as they think fit, within the bounds of the Law of Nature, without asking leave, or depending upon the Will of any other Man. A State also of Equality, wherein all the power and Jurisdiction is reciprocal, no one having more than another"(1965:319). The state of nature as a state of peace, good will, mutual assistance and preservation, and the state of war as a state of enmity, malice, violence, and mutual destruction are two categorically differentiated social prototypes in his hypothetical model. The state of nature is composed of men living together according to reason, without a common superior on earth, with authority to judge between them, whereas force or a declared design of force upon the person of another is the foundation of the state of war, where there is no common superior on earth to appeal to for relief.

Thus, as Dunning (1916:345) points out, the state of nature as conceived by Locke is a pre-political rather than pre-social condition because, rejecting the incisive distinction made by Hobbes between the law of nature and real law, Locke follows the Grotian doctrine and declares the law of nature to be a determining body of rules for the conduct of men in their natural condition. Locke's interpretation of the state of law based on the assumption of natural law and reason might be accepted as very indicative of the continuity in the Western paradigm, as well as of the impact of the new epistemological tendencies around the transformed cosmologico-ontological framework, during the process of the justification of the state.

The idea of natural law as a way of justification is one of the basic indications of the continual imagination of Western mind from the ancient to the medieval and modern periods, related to the impact of ontological and epistemological presuppositions on socio-political philosophy and culture. Stoic postulation of human reason as the revealer of the laws of nature and as thus the judge of right conduct, the Thomistic argument that "every law framed by man bears the character of a law exactly to that extent to which it is derived from the law of nature" so that "if on any point it is in conflict with the law of nature, it at once ceases to be a law [and] is a mere perversion of law" (Tawney, 1950:41), and Locke's following statements differentiating the state of liberty from the state of licence, might be accepted as several reflections of the same imagination: "But though this be a State of Liberty, yet it is not a State of Licence, though Man in that state have an uncontrolable Liberty, to dispose of His Person or Possessions, yet he has not Liberty to destroy himself, or so much as any Creature in his Possession.... The State of Nature has a Law of Nature to govern it, which obliges every one: And Reason, which is that Law, teaches all Mankind, who will but consult it, that being an equal and independent, no one ought to harm another in his Life, Health, Liberty or Possessions" (1965:309-11). Therefore, Russell's argument that Locke's political theory was not original, might seem true. But it should be added that, with the increasing tendency of ontological proximity within the framework of naturalistic cosmology and the strengthening of the centralistic position of epistemology just before Locke, the stress of the *Weltanschauung* shifted towards nature and reason.

This idea of natural law is the basis of the assumption of natural right which led to the second way of justification for the existence of the state, namely social contract theories.[5] As Locke formulates, the basic assumption of social contract theories is that no one can be put out of the estate, and subjected to the political power of another, without his own *Consent* because men are all free, equal and independent by nature: "The only way whereby any one divests himself of his Natural Liberty, and puts on the bonds of Civil Society is by agreeing with other Men to join and unite into a Community, for their comfortable, safe, and peaceable living one amongst another, in a secure Enjoyment of their Properties, and a greater Security against any that are not of it.... When any number of Men have so consented to make one Community or Government, they are thereby presently incorporated, and make one *Body Politick,* wherein the *Majority* have a right to act and conclude the rest" (Locke, 1965:375). As Jones argues, such a justification of the state through the idea of the natural right is purely utilitarian: the state is justified because it is to men's advantage that it should exist. Thus, it embraces the justification of state through the specification of its aims, f.i. to guarantee a comfortable, safe, and peaceable life.

Rousseau agrees with Locke's imagination of a pre-political state of nature but insists that its base is emotion rather than reason because reason is itself the outgrowth of the artificial life of men in organized society. As Gettell (1959:254) indicates, Rousseau's justification of state through the idea of social contract carries the marks of the influence of Hobbes and Locke, "the method of Hobbes and the conclusions of Locke being curiously combined." For Rousseau, the state is a necessary evil emerging from the rise of inequalities among men. Therefore, he aims to explain how such a mechanism came about. The justification of state through a social contract seems to him a solution for this purpose: "To find a form of association which may defend and protect with the whole force of the community the person and property of every associate, and by means of which each, coalescing with all, may nevertheless obey only himself, and remain as free as before. Such is the fundamental problem of which the social contract furnishes the solution. In short, each giving himself to all, gives himself to nobody; and as there is not one associate over whom we do not acquire the same rights which we concede to him

---

[5]These too provided the axiological/juristic dimensions of the legitimacy of an existing state, which will be examined in the following chapter.

ourselves, we gain the equivalent of all that we lose, and more power to preserve what we have" (Gettell, 1959:254).

In short, all of these attempts at justification through setting up a speculative theory on the origin of the state reflect the transformation of the Western paradigm within a new formulation of ontological proximity. A *natural current situation* rather than a *transcendental ontological will* is the center of this "realistic justification" which depends on the empiricist epistemology. This led Western political philosophers to *understand* the natural mechanism of the current situation rather then to *direct* it for the fulfillment of some politically substantive ideals. Hypothetical models related to the state of nature for the justification of state and socio-political systems are the applications of this nature-centered justification through empiricist epistemology. This way of justification intrinsically assumes a natural teleology which is a consequence of the cosmological-ontological interpretation examined in chapter 2.

This understanding of natural teleology without being directed by ontological transcendency, as in Diderot's assumption of self-adjusting nature in place of God, could not coexist with the idea of a transcendental sovereign God as in Islam. The understanding of God as an abstract idea—not as the Living Being (*Ḥayy* in Qur'ânic terminology)—of Descartes, Hume, and Kant, has the same consequences as the atheism of Holbach, from the perspective of a self-adjusting natural teleology due to the common sense that our world is a closed material system with a specific causality independent of the impact of the will of a transcendental sovereign God. We find that polytheism, pantheism, and atheism meet in this understanding of a self-adjusting teleology. Contrary to this Western philosophical experience, Islamic understanding of teleology is always directly linked to the belief of Allâh via the key-terms *'âdatullâh* and *sunnatullâh* to show the ontological origin of causality.

This assumption of a self-adjusting natural teleology together with the Aristotelian empiricist epistemology for the understanding of the "real world" became two significant bases for the justification of the state and the socio-political system. The Hobbesian interpretation of the state of nature depending on a psychological analysis of human nature is a very typical example of this type of justification. Because of this accommodation to the common philosophical base of Western tradition for the problem of justification, Hobbes became the theoretical origin for several, even conflicting, political theories and ideologies in Western political history such as individualism and totalitarianism.

Adam Smith's "invisible hand" theory for the justification of liberalism, with its self-adjusting market mechanism, is based on the same nature-centered paradigmatic assumption. Western humanism should be evaluated within this assumption of nature. The humanization of epistemology and the secularization of knowledge developed parallel to the "naturalization" of cosmology and ontology. In fact, each of the processes strengthened the other. The humanization of epistemology could only be meaningful through the assumption of an intrinsic will for the teleology in nature (pantheist element). Otherwise using human epistemological sources to understand the "real world" could not be justified. Western humanism developed through the dialectic between man and nature based on the ideal of "understanding" and "inventing" the realities of nature to be sovereign over nature. This ideal could not coexist within a centripetal theoretical framework which has an idea of transcendental God at the center. The justification of the state and the socio-political system in Western political thought was based on this paradigmatic assumption related to its origin.

Aim of the socio-political system

The justification of the state through the arguments related to its aims originated mainly from Stoic, neo-Epicurean, and Christian ethics. The Stoic influence should be emphasized for this type of justification. The axiological continuity leading to a secular justification could be followed within the continuity from the Roman legacy, influenced by Greek philosophy, to Christianity and through to the modern period.

The influence of the Greek legacy on Roman religion through Stoicism and Epicureanism was fundamentally practical rather than theoretical. An original ethics emerged in Rome through the effects of Stoicism, while Epicureanism dealt directly with the problem of happiness rather than cosmological speculations. Greek Stoicism under the leadership of Zeno had been manipulated in the Roman understanding of life to comprise ancient polytheism and a particularization of divinity. Therefore Roman Stoics argued that gods could be worshipped as the manifestation of Divine Reason, which was the source of peace and wisdom. These ideals led to a humanizing process of life and law beyond their deep theoretical and intellectual consequences.

Seneca and Emperor Marcus Aurelius hold the key positions in this marriage of Greek philosophies with Roman polytheism and paganism. The Stoic Emperor Marcus Aurelius (n.d.:IX/23), who tried to use Stoicism for the reformation of Roman polytheism through a cooperation based on a specific ethics, argued that since the Intelligence of the universe (God) is social, human society functions as a phase of cosmic coordination. This is interesting especially as an example of cosmologico-ontological justification of the socio-political system.

Stoic concentration on the theoretical foundation of the achievement of virtue as the aim of life, and the idea of living in conformity with nature by dealing with ontological and theological problems to answer the question of man's place in the universe, extended also to Christian ethics and theology as its basic principles. Its cosmopolitan character opened the way for the triumph of Christianity in the Roman Empire with a new syncretic form.

The Stoic doctrine that every man is a member of two commonwealths—the civil state of which he is a subject and the greater state composed of all rational beings—because of his human character was systematized by Seneca, whose fundamental assumption on this subject was that the greater commonwealth is a society, rather than a state, and its bases are moral and religious rather than legal and political. This philosophico-political pluralism (dualism) became the *principium individuationis* of the justification process of the city and the law of the world-city. The law of custom and the law of reason of the Middle Ages were based on this Stoic transformation of Christianity which formed the superstructure of feudalism as well as a socio-political and socio-economic system.

The secular interpretation of individual happiness in the modern era to justify actual political systems has its origin in the amalgam of a neo-Epicurean understanding of life and a Stoical-Christian ethics. Ambrose's assumption that the ideal of life is happiness as an extension of Stoic philosophy might be accepted as the axiological and eschatological bases of the secularization resting on Stoic ethics which survived in the form of Christian ethics. A process of materialization has been experienced in the modern era related to this concept of happiness. It should be underlined as a fundamental difference that such a process of materialization did not emerge in Islamic imagination and thought, whether at its first stage when these ancient concept were internalized by Muslim philosophers or at its extension to other spheres as the general Islamic concept of *sa'âdah*. The very strong eschatological dimension of Islamic *Weltanschauung* and its understanding of *ghayb* might be mentioned as two basic hindrances to such a process of materialization.

The philosophical speculations on natural law as the theoretical and imaginative origin of the idea of natural right provided a new framework for the Western process of the materialization of happiness. The details of this framework will be discussed in the following chapter on the process of political legitimacy. Nevertheless, I want to underline its vital role in the specification of the end of the state as a way of justification of the socio-political system. This relationship is obvious in the American Declaration of Independence, which states "We hold these truths to be self-evident, that all man are created equal, that they are endowed by their Creator with certain inalienable Rights, that among these are Life, Liberty, and the Pursuit of Happiness, that to secure these rights, Governments are instituted, deriving their just powers from the consent of the governed" (ADI, 1776). It also appears in French Declaration of the Rights of Man, which maintains that "Men are born and continue equal in respect of their rights. The end of political society is the preservation of the natural and imprescriptible rights of man. These rights are liberty, property, security, and resistance to oppression" (DRM, 1791).

Secular systematization of these continuing elements as an amalgam has been clarified by Hobbesian materialist methodology and Kantian disengagement of morality from theology. This-worldly happiness of the individual alone—as the basic criterion of the secularization of life—became one of the significant bases of justification of the socio-political system by assigning a mission to the state for the fulfillment of this aim. Modern individualism, liberalism, utilitarianism, and pragmatism are several attempts of this type of justification. This amalgam could be traced back to Grotius' liberalism based on the idea of natural rights, to Hobbes' individualism motivated by the psychological stimulus of self-preservation, to Bentham's utilitarian psychological assumption that men actually seek pleasure and happiness in life, to Mill's understanding of morality grounded on happiness, and to James' pragmatism assuming that an idea is true if it possesses some subsequent utility. This assumption of this-worldly individual happiness implies a specific ontological approach leading to indifference toward eschatological problems. The segmentation of life in the Western philosophical tradition, as against the Islamic understanding of unity of life, should be evaluated within these ontological-eschatological considerations, which lead to an alternative type of justification of state and socio-political systems.

Islamic way of justification

In contrast to the case in Western philosophical-political justification, the process of justification in Islamic political theories is a reflection of the basic paradigm analyzed before, namely theocentric ontological transcendency. This is true for almost all sects and schools in Islamic history. It is almost impossible to find a political justification without reference to the absolute sovereignty of Allâh.

The ontological hierarchy as "Allâh-human being-nature" implies a socio-political hierarchy as "Allâh-human being-political system" in the Islamic way of political thinking. Therefore the justification of the political system is directly referred to the understanding of the trusteeship of man given to him by Allâh—as the origin of axiology and absolute normativeness. The fundamental tools for the justification of the state as a socio-political institution are the meta-historical covenant for its origin and the fulfillment of the mentioned divine responsibility on earth for the aim of the state.

Origin of the socio-political system

The justification of state as a socio-political institution through interpretations of the origin of the socio-political system in Islamic political imagination and theorization is directly attached to the Qur'ânic terms of *'ahd*, *'aqd*, and *mîthâq*.[6] A social contract to establish a socio-political system has been, and could only be, justified through the meta-historical covenant between Allâh and man. This meta-historical covenant was a declaration of obedience by man to Allâh. The establishment of political authority on earth, and obedience to it, has been accepted as an extension of this meta-historical covenant for the realization of the set of axiological presuppositions revealed by Allâh through the mission of prophecy.

The usage of the concept of *khalîfah* both for man as vicegerent of Allâh and as a political authority on earth is an interesting indication of this holistic link between the ontological and political spheres. The belief in absolute truth, originating from the divine being through one chain of prophecy, implies a certain divinely-responsible man who had not been created in vain, but with a serious end (Qur'ân, 44:38) determined by the meta-historical covenant. As the vicegerent of Allâh on earth, the human being has taken a divine responsibility of trusteeship (*amânah*) on earth that must be fulfilled (Qur'ân, 33:72).

Thus, *'ahd*, *'aqd*, *mîthâq*, *amânah*, *wilâyah*, *ummah*, *khalîfah*, and *walî al-amr* constitute a semantic, imaginative, and theoretical set for the linkage of the ontological and political spheres to justify a necessary socio-political organization. As Ahmed (1971:84) summarizes, "interpreted in terms of social contract theory, a covenant between a prophet and his followers created a *millah*, and a covenant between God and His devotees laid the foundation-stone of a moral order (*dîn*) among human beings, but a social contract among different religious communities gave birth to the *ummah*." Although Ahmed's systematization might be disputed, it is right that the concepts of *millah*, *dîn*, and *ummah* in the Qur'ân are fundamentally based on the idea of covenant. State as an organization of man-man relationship in the form of covenant is a reflection of the man-Allâh relationship in the form of primordial meta-historical covenant. The basic principle in the cosmologico-ontological sphere, that all authority in the universe lies with Allâh because He alone created it, results in a socio-political consequence that only Allâh is to be obeyed. Thus, the primordial covenant between Allâh and man should be extended to social life as a covenant between man and man. The corollary of this conclusion

---

[6]There are several verses in the Qur'ân (e.g., 5:1) underlining the importance of fulfilling these undertakings.

is that a social contract between man and man should be consistent with the primordial contract between Allâh and man.

The term *khalîfah* plays a very significant role both for the justification of socio-political system and for the imaginative links between ontological and political spheres. Margoliouth (1922:322) mentions the pre-Islamic forms of this word in the Assyrian, Hebrew, Aethiopic, and Greek languages, but the word gains a new semantic field together with other political key-terms in the Qur'ân. It continues to have the meanings it has in pre-Islamic Arabic sources, but within a new context. It occurs in the Qur'ân twice in its singular form *khalîfah* (2:30; 38:27) and seven times in the plural form—four of them in the form *khalâ'if* (6:166; 10:15, 74; 35:39) and three in the form *khulafâ'* (7:69, 74; 27:62).

There is a wide diversity of commentaries on the philological and political meanings of this term. As Watt (1968:32) argues, the difficulty experienced by the commentators arises from the fact that the root of *khalîfah* has had a rich and varied semantic development in Arabic. Al-Qâdî (1988:398-402) sums up its meanings in five main groups: (i) to succeed, to follow, to come after another; (ii) to replace, to substitute, to take the place of another; (iii) to substitute, to replace, to take the place of another, but normally after this other is gone (destroyed, dead, etc.); (iv) to inhabit, to cultivate (*sakana, 'amara*); and (v) to govern, to rule, to be king. The commentators tend to interpret this key-term as a title for the whole of humanity, rather than only for Adam, to clarify humanity's comprehensive mission on earth. Ibn Kathîr's (1986:I/60-71) quotations from earlier commentators, especially from Ibn Jarîr, give important indications of this common theoretical and imaginative base for the understanding of this term. Modern commentators such as Rashîd Ridâ (1954:I/257-9), Yazir (1971:I/299-300;3/2116), and Qutb (n.d:I/14-5) follow this view, while M. Vehbî assigns this mission especially to the prophets in the personality of Adam (1966:I/90-1) and to the *ummah* of Muhammad after the *ummahs* of previous prophets (1967:IV/1574).

There is much discussion on the origin of *khalîfah* as a political title, beginning with the election of Abû Bakr, who is generally held to have taken the title of *khalîfah rasûl Allâh* (the caliph of the messenger of Allâh). It is very difficult either to prove or disprove that Abû Bakr's political title came from the ordinary secular use of the word rather than from its Qur'ânic usages, but it is impossible to deny that these Qur'ânic usages affected the process of the transformation of the political imagination and culture in the direction of the development of the political justification of socio-political system through an ontological relationship between Allâh and man.

The first usage of this word in the Qur'ân, related to Adam's creation, specifies the ontological status of man on earth. The second usage, related to Dâwûd, connects this concept to a socio-political responsibility; namely judging (*fa'hkum*) justly between people. This second usage clearly connotes a socio-political status for being *khalîfah* in the personality of Dâwûd. Suddî interprets this verse "we have made you a *khalîfah*" as "He made him king (*mallakahu*) on earth" (Al-Qâdî, 1988:404) is related to this imagination.

The fact that "the early exegetes in the Umayyad period did not equate the Qur'ânic *khalîfah* with the head of the Islamic state" (Al-Qâdî, 1988:409) does not mean the rejection of such an imagination of political authority within the context of ontological antecedents. It might be related to the meticulousness of the 'ulamâ' in avoiding the use of the title of *khalîfah Allâh* (caliph of God) for the Umayyads, who tried to exploit such an imagination to legitimate their political authority.[7] As Bartold (1963:124) underlines, such a title is completely foreign to early Islam. This avoidance begins from the time of Abû Bakr, who used the title *khalîfah rasûl Allâh*, and especially from the time of 'Umar, who strictly rejected such a title and preferred to use *amîr al-mu'minîn* (prince of the believers), as Badî' al-Zamân Hamadhânî mentions in his *Rasâ'il*.[8]

On the other hand, Qur'ânic use of the plural forms of *khalîfah* strengthens this imagination of setting up a very strong relationship between divine responsibility of man grounded on his ontological status as vicegerent of Allâh on earth and socio-political responsibility to form a just socio-political community, because almost all instances of the plural are related to the succession by new nations of those nations (of 'Ad, of Noah, etc.) who have been destroyed for not fulfilling their divine responsibility.

The verse "He it is who has placed you as viceroys of the earth and has exalted some of you in rank above others, that He may try to you by [the test of] that which has been given you" (Qur'ân, 6:166) hints at a hierarchy between man and man within the imaginative framework constituted by being viceroy of the earth and fulfilling divine responsibility. This term has been understood within such a framework especially in later works on political theory: "This clarifies what the caliphate means. Natural political [royal] authority means inducing the entire people [to the actions] required by purpose and desire. Political authority means [aims] to induce the entire people [to the actions] required by rational insight to obtain worldly welfare and to avoid any harm in that respect. The caliphate means to induce the entire people [to actions] required by religious insight for their well-being in the other world as well as in this world. [Worldly affairs] have bearing upon [the affairs in the other world], since according to Lawgiver [Muḥammad] all worldly situations are to be considered with regard to their value for the other world. So, the caliphate, in reality, is a successor of Lawgiver [Muḥammad] to

---

[7]Mawârdî quotes in his *Kitâb Adab al-Dunyâ wa al-Dîn* a poem from the Umayyad poet Farazdaq in which the title caliph of God has been used for Caliph Sulaymân (715-17). The title caliph of God appears on coins as early as the second half of the seventh century (Walker, 1956:30). "In 'Abd al-Mâlik's currency reform, only quotations of a religious nature were put on the gold and silver coins, and no attempt was made to put the name of the Caliph next to the names of Allâh and Muḥammad. This clearly shows that the rulers had still not decided to transfer the concept 'Caliph of God' from the sphere of court flattery and rhetorical salutation into the sphere of law" (Bartold,1963:125).

[8]"When the Apostolate came to an end, and the Sovereignty (Imamate) came in, the honor fell to the latter. Abû Bakr was addressed: Caliph of the Apostle of God. God made the Caliphate the badge of Abû Quhâfah's family, and no one except the representative of that family received the title; then Abû Bakr appointed as his Caliph (successor) 'Umar. A man addressed him as Caliph of God. He said: God confound you! That is God's prophet David. The man then addressed him as Caliph of the Apostle of God. 'Umar said: That is your departed master (Abû Bakr). Then the man addressed him as Caliph of the Caliph of the Apostle of God. 'Umar said: That is my right title, only this is too long. 'Umar proceeded to style himself Prince of the Believers" (Margoliouth, 1922:323-24).

protect the religion and to exercise leadership of the world" (Ibn Khaldûn, n.d:191).

Thus, the Qur'ânic conceptual structure forms an ontologico-political semantic field constituted by such concepts as *khalîfah, mîthâq, 'ahd, 'aqd, wilâyah, amânah,* and their derivatives. All of these concepts have been used both for the Allâh-man relationship as the determinant of the ontological position of man and for the man-man relationship as the determinant of the socio-political position of man. There is the concept of *khalîfah* at the center of this semantic field. This ontologico-political semantic field of the Qur'ân created the strongest imaginative link in human history between ontological and social beings and their positions to each other.

The secret of the extraordinary development of Islamic civilization within a very short period of time after the seventh century—both in the sense of theoretical richness and in the sense of political expansion parallel to a highly complex institutionalization—should be sought in this unique characteristic of it in human history. This strong imaginative link between ontological and political spheres has affected all dimensions of the theoretical and practical dimensions of Islamic civilization. This characteristic accelerates the process of reproduction of political theory and culture even after the periods of crisis. This reproduction of political culture provides both a feeling of resistance to foreign elements and a dynamic element for attempts to achieve the crisis through the re-adjustments of the institutions for the realization the value system based on ontologico-epistemological characteristics mentioned above.

Thus, this ontologico-political semantic field and its imaginative consequences provide the basic elements for the justification of the existence of a socio-political system. This way of justification of political system is very evident also in the writings of Muslim scholars on political theory. The ways of justification of the socio-political system from the perspective of its origin in these political writings might be summarized into three groups: (i) the meta-historical arguments, in which the origins of socio-political system have been attached to the meta-historical covenant between Allâh and man; (ii) the logical arguments, in which the origins of socio-political system have been explained in this argument through syllogistical analysis on teleological structure of the macrocosm, microcosm, and socio-political system; and (iii) the historical argument, in which the origins of socio-political system have been explained as depending on the characteristics of human nature, especially on man's natural disposition to be in need of others. We explained the first way within the framework of the Qur'ânic ontologico-political conceptual structure. Now, we can give examples of the second and third ways of justification in the political writings of the fundamental Muslim schools.

The political theory of the *falâsifah* assumes a clear-cut differentiation between the ideal state and others. The justification of the ideal state in this tradition is directly attached to ontological antecedents, especially through a channel of teleological arguments. Fârâbî's masterpiece *Al-Madînah al-Fâḍilah* contains the clearest examples of the second and third ways of justification. Its structure is itself the best indication of the second way of justification through syllogistic analysis of the teleological structure.

Fârâbî develops an analogy between cosmic teleology, the human body, and the ideal state. He specifies (1985:37), at the very beginning of his treatise, the origin of the teleology in the cosmic system, namely *al-Sabab al-Awwal,* and explains the cooperation of the elements of cosmos according to the direction of this First Cause. Then he applies the same method to the teleology in the human body

(1985:78-100) and shows that "heart" has the same function for the cooperation of the elements of the human body. His logical conclusions on the teleological structure of the universe as macrocosm and human body as microcosm become the basis for his theorization of the structure of the ideal state. Although, as Walzer asserts (1962:246), the Platonic legacy might have some effect on the development of this theorization, it should not be forgotten that Islamic *falsafah* emerged within an intersected intellectual sphere where the accumulation of pre-Islamic legacy reconciled with the basic Islamic system of creed. Hence, this theorization shows the veiled assumption of the process of internalization of pre-Islamic sources during the formation of the Muslim schools.

Fârâbî differentiates the origin of the ideal state from the causes of the formation of ignorant and imperfect states. He mentions realistic causes—such as force, patriarchy, and material relations—for the formation of states other than the ideal state, which is thought of as an ideal form of the extension of the absolute teleology of macrocosm and microcosm.

The analogy between macrocosm and political structures might be found also in the political writings of other representatives of *falsafah*. For example, Ibn Rushd applies his presuppositions on ontological beings to political beings. His specification on the permanence of the ideal state is a typical example for this type of application (Ibn Rushd, 1966:219). The impact of teleological argument led Muslim scholars (f.i., Baghdâdî, 1935:213) to argue that the Imamate can rightly belong to only one person throughout the entire land of Islam, unless a barrier lies between the provinces, such as an ocean, or an enemy that cannot be coped with, when the people of the two districts are not able to lend each other aid .

The third way of justification has been applied to the explanation of both the origin and the aim of the state. The necessity of political association as the origin of the socio-political system can be found in all political writings of the *falâsifah*, of the *fuqahâ'*, of the *mutakallimûn*, and of the writers of *siyasatname*. Fârâbî underlines man's need for mutual help and cooperation in the part of *al-Qawl fî Iḥtiyâj al-Insân ilâ al-Ijtimâ' wa at-Ta'âwun* (1985:117) of his masterpiece, before analyzing the ideal state, and argues that they organize different societies by uniting their individual efforts for different objects. The same point has been explained in *Taḥṣîl al-Sa'âdah* (1983:61-62; English trans. from Mahdî, 1969:23): "It is the innate disposition of every man to join another human being or other men in the labor he ought to perform: This is the condition of every single man. Therefore, to achieve what he can of that perfection, every man needs to stay in the neighborhood of others and associate with them. It is also the innate nature of this animal to seek shelter and to dwell in the neighborhood of those who belong to the same species, which is why he is called the social and political animal." Nâṣir al-Dîn Ṭûsî (1964:190) uses almost the same reasoning for the necessity of civilized life: "Now, since it is impossible to conceive the species to exist without cooperation, while cooperation without combination is an absurdity, therefore the human species is naturally in need of combination." According to Ṭûsî, this type of combination, is called 'civilized life' which is what the philosophers mean when they say that man is naturally a city dweller, i.e., he is naturally in need of the combination called 'civilized life' [*tamaddun*].

The necessity of human cooperation has been explained by Muslim thinkers on the basis of the virtue of love rather than the natural feeling of competition as the basic psychological stimulus, such as found in Machiavellian or Hobbesian theory.

Tûsî's (1964:198) attachment of justice to love marks this intrinsic characteristic: "Again, since Man has been created with a natural direction towards perfection, he has a natural yearning for the synthesis in question. This yearning for the synthesis is called Love. We have already alluded to the preference to Love above Justice. The reason for this idea is that Justice requires artificial union; at the same time, the artificial in relation to the natural is like an outer skin, the artificial imitating the natural." His differentiation between love and friendship and his argument that the reason for the friendship between young men is the quest for pleasure while the reason for the friendship of the old men and persons of like nature is the quest for profit mark one of the essential differences of such a political culture from utilitarian philosophy.

Due to the fact that at the top of the hierarchy of love is the divine love, the explanation also embraces a teleological element based on the core of love: "In man, however, there is to be found a simple, divine substance having no affinity with other natures, and he can enjoy thereby a class of pleasure having no similarity to other pleasures. The love producing this pleasure is excessive in the extreme, being like to distraction, and it is known as Utter Passion and Divine Love. Certain of those who assimilate themselves to God lay claim to this love.... Thus, where the love to God is concerned, to associate any other therewith is sheer polytheism" (Tûsî, 1964:198, 205).

This love-centered social imagination has affected Ottoman political thought and culture to a great extent. A detailed comparison between Kinalizâde's *Akhlâq-i 'Alâ'î* and Machiavelli's *Prince* or Hobbes' *Leviathan* might provide significant clues for the impact of alternative *Weltanschauungs* on political theories and cultures. Kinalizâde represents the stability of the classical Ottoman political culture and therefore aims to preserve the social balance of the system around the principles of love and justice, whereas Machiavelli aims to provoke the dynamic element of the political culture of his society in order to radically change the existent status. Kinalizâde attaches his political philosophy to a very well-defined understanding of love and strengthens the dependency of politics to ethics in the sense of an ultimate degree by defining the basis of the socio-political system as love. In absolute opposition to this, Machiavelli, who lived at almost the same time, concentrates his energy on the ultimate separation of politics from ethics.

The *mutakallimûn* and *fuqahâ'* use both religious and rational arguments for the justification of a socio-political system under the authority of an *imâm*. As Taftazânî (1950:145) concludes, the position of agreement is that it is necessary to appoint an *imâm*. The difference of opinion is on the question whether the appointment must be by Allâh or by His creatures, and whether the basis for the appointment is authority or reason. The common position is that the creatures must appoint a *khalîfah* on the basis of authority because of the statement of the Prophet, "whoever dies not having known the Imâm of his time, dies the death of the days of Ignorance [*al-Jâhiliyyah*]."[9]

---

[9] Several versions of this *hadîth* have been used for the justification of the necessary existence of the socio-political authority; cf., e.g., Ibn Hanbal's *Musnâd* (1982:IV/96) and *Sahîh al-Muslim* (1981:II/1475-1480).

Shahrastânî (1934:151) and Ibn Khaldûn (n.d.:192) report that, with the exception of the Mu'tazilah, Abû Bakr al-Aṣamm, and certain Khawârij,[10] all Muslim schools agree on the necessity of a political authority. The argument of these schools that the imâmate is a command (*farḍ*) from God is a juristic reflection of the ontologico-political imagination mentioned before. The Sunnîs extended this judgement that "it [imâmate] was a duty [*farḍ*] which all Muslims must carry out" (Shahrastânî, 1934:151). It has also been discussed whether the imâmate is one of the principles of the faith. Ibn Khaldûn's conclusion on this subject aims to support Sunnî argument that the election of the political leader is a subject of free choice of Muslims, rather than being divinely ordained (the Shî'ite position): "Some wrongly claim that the Imamate is one of the principles of the faith. It is one of the public affairs which should be performed by the people. If it were one of the principles of the faith, it would be something like prayer, and Muḥammad would have appoint a representative, exactly as he appointed Abû Bakr to represent him at prayer" (n.d.:212-13).

Ibn Khaldûn (n.d.:191-92)) prefers the religious justification of the socio-political system together with a historical proof taken from *Asr al-Sa'âdah*: "At the death of the Prophet, his companions proceeded to render the oath of allegiance to Abû Bakr and to entrust him with the supervision of their affairs. It was same at all subsequent periods. In no period were the people left in a state of anarchy. This was so by general consensus, which proves that the appointment of *imâm* is an imperative.... The appointment of an *imâm* is required by the religious law, that is, by the consensus." The same way of justification of the socio-political system and hierarchy was used by Shahrastânî before Ibn Khaldûn via the following statement: "The institution of the Imamate is attested by catholic consent from the first generation to our day in the words: 'The earth can never be without an *imâm* wielding authority.'... Such a consensus of opinion is decisive proof of the necessity of the office....When Muḥammad died none contested Abû Bakr's statement that a successor must be appointed, and all know the story of 'Umar's homage to Abû Bakr. When the latter died it never occurred to any one that an *imâm* was not indispensable. 'Uthmân and 'Ali were next chosen. All this goes to prove that the first generation unanimously agreed that there must be an *imâm* . The office has gone on from then until now either by general consent of the people, or by agreement and testament, or by both. Such a consensus of opinion is decisive proof of the necessity of the office" (1934:151-52).

Thus, there is an idea of an ideal state at the basis of justification in several Islamic political theories, in contrast to the hypothetical models of the state of nature developed through empirical and actual facts of the Western philosophical tradition.

---

[10]The logical reasoning of these groups also reflects the dependency of politics to religious antecedents from the perspective of the ontological position in spite of its contradistinction to the consensus of other sects. The Najdite section of the Khawârij, and the Qadarites like Abu Bakr al-Aṣamm, and Hishâm al-Futawî hold that the Imamate is not obligatory in law so that sin is incurred if it is not established. On the contrary it rests on the conventions of society. They argued that if men behaved justly and did their duty, there would be no necessity for an *imâm*. because one man is as good as another in religion, in Islam, in knowledge, and in private judgement [*ijtihâd*]; they are like the teeth in a comb. Therefore there is no necessity to obey a man like oneself, according to them.

Even the historical way of justification developed by Shahrastânî and Ibn Khaldûn has been directly attached to the existence of the socio-political system and hierarchy as a historical realization in an ideal period (*'aṣr al-sa'âdah*). The logical and rational justifications of theologians and jurists are linked to ontological interpretations. This reality created a contrast between the idea of a secular state justified through historical facts in Western political theories and the idea of a substantive state justified through ontological antecedents based on a meta-historical covenant between Allâh and man in Islamic theories.

Aim of the socio-political system

The justification of the socio-political system via the explanation on its aim is directly related to the ontological, epistemological, and axiological framework analyzed in the third chapter. The aim of the socio-political system is directly attached to the aim of human life. The belief that man is chosen by Allâh as the vicegerent on earth (Qur'ân, 6:166) with a special mission implies the principle of the unity or indivisibility of human life. The mono-centric conception of man in the Qur'ân and the centripetal tendencies of Islamic theological structure lead to a comprehensive style of life rejecting separation of the "sacred" from the "profane," the "religious" from the "secular," or the "temporal" from the "moral" branches of human life. There is no clear-cut distinction between spiritual and material lives in Islam.

Thus, there are two aspects of the unity of the responsibility of man on earth. The first is related to the quality of this responsibility of man which is unique, having both spiritual and material parts, while the other is related to the fact that every man is charged with the fulfillment of this responsibility. These two aspects of the unity and objectivity of the responsibility of man are the bases of the two distinctive characteristics of Islamic political understanding.

The first aspect is the Islamic view of the "unity of life," which rejects the separation of spiritual and material parts. The rhythm of the Islamic life is specified directly by religious responsibilities which unify the quantitative parts of life in the sense of time (day, month, year, etc.) to remind man of his qualitative mission in life, as opposed to such a qualitative compartmentalization of spiritual and material parts in the secular sense. "The rhythm of the daily round is determined by the five prayers which the Muslim is enjoined to perform at set hours in a set fashion and preferably with his fellows behind a prayer-leader in a mosque. The rhythm of the year is determined by Ramaḍân, the month of fasting, with the reduced living of its strained and edgy days, and the religious exercises of the nights. And the rhythm of the believer's life is determined by the pilgrimage to Makkah which, circumstances permitting, he is to undertake at least once" (Von Grünebaum, 1962a:52). This rhythm of life provides a psychological re-production of the feeling the self-consciousness and of the meaning of life as a unity together with its eschatological dimension.

The second is the essence of the socio-political community in Islam which is formed by human beings who accept this responsibility without any discrimination among themselves and who reject special responsibilities related to one group of scholars (theocracy), or to one class (capitalism and socialism), or to nation (nationalism). The understanding of the unity of life is a logical consequence of the ontological belief in the unity of Allâh and the epistemological assumption of the unity of truth.

Islamic theocentric humanism—as opposed to nature-centered Western humanism—could be evaluated within this way of justification, grounded on the responsibility of man which at the same time assumes a relative free will and sovereignty on earth. This has been limited only by the absolute will and sovereignty of Allâh, as the Living Being (al-Hayy), in contrast to the abstract and inactive image of God in the Western philosophical tradition developed by Descartes, Hume, and Kant. Islamic humanism has been supported by an understanding of liberty. As De Santillana (1965:292) argues and Von Grünebaum repeats, "'in Islam, the original state of man is liberty and it is the exigencies of social life that compel the abridgment of this liberty:' "Allâh wishes to make it easy for you, and does not wish to make it difficult for you" (Qur'ân, 2:181). The Prophet's common sense discouraged exaggeration of any kind. Law is intended as the complement of faith regulating man's actions even as faith regulates his beliefs. Happiness and its transcendental counterpart, salvation, reward the believer" (Von Grünebaum, 1946:144).

Political structure is a consequence of the use of this combination of relative will and liberty. Thus, sovereignty based on a given right and responsibility originating from the covenant between Allâh and man create a political covenant between man and man for the fulfillment of the divine responsibility. In other words, a political covenant has been justified by an ontological covenant. Therefore, it should have a substantive character. This substantive character is the basis of the justification of the socio-political system through the evaluations on its aim. At this point an imagination of life intersects with a specific understanding of law and politics. The parallels between the Hanafî definition of fiqh as "the science of law is the knowledge of the rights and duties whereby man is enabled to observe right conduct in this life, and to prepare himself for the world to come" and Ghazzâlî's definition of politics in his Maqâsid al-Falâsifah as aiming at "man's welfare in this world and bliss in the next, only attainable if government is rooted in the legal ['ulûm shar'iyyah] and completed by the political sciences ['ulûm siyâsiyyah]"[11] shows the impact of the imagination of life on law and politics. This is also a very clear indication of the dependency of politics on axiology, which is always accepted as a determinant of ontological consciousness, and of its epistemological consequences in the process of justification.

This intersected imaginative and theoretical relationships is valid also for the falâsifah. For example, Ibn Rushd connects justification of the state directly to the ontological antecedents and their axiological consequences. His following analysis (1966:183-4) is a typical example of this trend in Islamic political thought: "since man is one of the natural existing things, he must needs have a purpose for the sake of which he is existing. For every natural existing thing has a purpose in accordance with the explanation in Physics; all the more so man, who is the most distinguished of them. Since man can only exist in the State, he can attain this his end only in so far as he is a part of the State". The most critical question at this stage is what the human end is. After evaluating several opinions on the human end mentioned by Plato in Republic, Ibn Rushd concludes (1966:185) that what the

---

[11]The English translations of these definitions have been borrowed from E. Rosenthal (1973:1-2).

religious laws of this matter is what God wills. His assumption that even the philosopher can attain highest perfection and ultimate happiness as the purpose of the human being only within society is another way for the justification of the state as a socio-political entity, from the perspective of its aim which necessitates a consistent linkage between ontological and axiological frameworks.

'Adâlah (justice), as a key-term, clearly symbolizes this substantive mission of the Islamic state. Justice has a very deep imagination in the formation of Muslim mind beyond its importance as an ethical virtue. Al-Khâzinî (1860:6) extends its importance to all branches of life because "justice is the support of both religion and the course of the world, and the stay of future as well as present felicity; so that whoever takes hold of it, or one of its branches, takes hold of a strong handle to which there is no breaking." He connects this idea of justice to the mercy of Allâh (Al-Khâzinî, 1860:6-7). The critical position of this idea of justice at the intersection of ontological, epistemological, and axiological imaginations is signified by his classification of sources answering to the several divisions of justice as (i) the Glorious Book of Allâh, (ii) the guided leaders and established doctors, and (iii) the balance.

This way of justification makes justice a channel between axiological presuppositions justified by ontological antecedents and the prescriptivist character of Islamic political theories, cultures, and structures. In this way, the interconnects between law and politics are meaningful through this fulfillment of substantive mission. Thus, Islamic ontologically justified political power creates a political culture suitable for the justification of the transcendental substantive state.

The aim of the state is the fulfillment of justice on behalf of Allâh on earth. For some Muslim scholars, justice is a more significant characteristic of a state than that the state be composed of Muslims. Ibn Taymiyyah argues that Allâh will help a just state even though it may be composed of non-Muslims, while He might not help a tyrannical state that happens to be composed entirely of Muslims. This is a clear example of the central character of this mission for the justification of political authority. This is also true for Ibn Abi al-Rabî', Mawârdî, Fârâbî, Ibn Bâjjah, Ghazzâlî, Ibn Rushd, Kinalizâde as the members of several Islamic schools.

Mawârdî, the writer of one of the significant documents of Islamic political thought, specifies that the real motive of the state is the rule of justice and truth; while Nizâm al-Mulk, as a scholar and active politician, argues that Allâh the Almighty is pleased with a governor only when he treats his people with justice and kindness. Ghazzâlî underlines justice and law as two bases for the legitimacy of a political authority; while the mission of justice imposes a system of rights in Ibn Abû al-Rabî's political theory dependent upon three fundamental rights, namely (i) rights due to Allâh, (ii) rights due to the living, and (iii) rights due to the dead.

This idea of the ideal state with an ontologically defined substantive mission is another paradigmatic assumption in the history of Islamic political theory. The perfection of the individual is connected to the fulfillment of this mission by an ideal state in the writings of several Muslim scholars. Their fundamental assumption is the necessity of a political community as an extension of theocentric teleology on earth. From Ghazzâlî to Ibn Rushd almost all Muslim scholars agree on this assumption. Fârâbî, Ghazzâlî, Ibn Bâjjah, and Ibn Rushd strictly rejected the possibility of the isolation of the individual from the community due to the assumption that there is an interaction between man's perfection and that of the state.

Fârâbî and Ghazzâlî, although members of different Islamic schools, argued in a completely parallel manner that the individual needs the assistance of other men within a political community. As Afnan (1958:178) mentions, Ibn Sînâ sets up a direct link between the human being's need for a socio-political structure to attain perfection and the divine law with an ultimate end to realize justice as a substantive mission. The theoretical link between *tadbîr al-mutawaḥḥid* and *al-madînah al-fâḍilah* in Ibn Bâjjah's political philosophy is meaningful in showing this interconnected relationship between the perfection of the individual as Allâh's vicegerent and the socio-political life. This is at the same time a way of justifying the political system. Ibn Rushd extends this relationship to a specific understanding of citizenship by arguing that man is a part of the state and therefore cannot live without it and must contribute his share to its maintenance and functioning.

Intellectual and social virtue have been combined in Ibn Rushd's approach to an ideal socio-political system. This leads him to a material and spiritual identification of man and state. His assertion (1966:163) that the man endowed with the nature of this ideal State will be of utmost virtue, just as this State is of the utmost virtue, illuminates not only this spiritual identification of man and state but also one of the characteristics of the way of justification of Muslim philosophers for the socio-political system within the context of the aim of the state.

Like Plato, Ibn Rushd uses these axiological conclusions on virtue as evidence for the oneness of the ideal state. The correspondence of the axiological and political categorization is another significant feature of the Islamic socio-political thought. "Virtue is thus a kind of health and beauty, and vice is a kind of sickness. Just as health is one, so is virtue one. Therefore the ideal state is one. The vices, however, are many and varied, just as diseases are many and varied. The ignorant States are also many and varied; but they can be summarized in four classes" (Ibn Rushd, 1966:164). The same correspondence might be seen also in Abû al-Najîb Suhrawardî's *Nahj al-Sulûk fî Siyâsat al-Mulûk* (1974).

In some other treatises the justification of setting up a political authority has been connected to the specification of the functions of this authority. Taftazânî's explanation might be quoted as an example: "The Muslims must have an Imâm, who will carry out the administration of their decisions, the maintaining of their restrictive ordinances, the guarding of their frontiers, the equipping of their armies, the receiving of their alms, the subjugation of those who get the upper hand and robbers and highwaymen, the performance of worship on Fridays and Festivals, the settlement of disputes which take place among creatures, the receiving of evidence based on legal rights, the giving in marriage of the young men and maidens who have no guardians, and the division of the booty" (1950:145). The same issue has been underlined by Baghdâdî in *al-Farq bayn al-Firaq*,[12] by Shahrastânî in *Nihayah al-Iqdam*,[13] and by Abû al-Mu'în al-Nasafî in *Baḥr al-Kalâm*.[14]

---

[12]"The Imamate is a duty incumbent on the community, because the appointment of an Imam establishes judges and executives. He guards their frontiers, leads their armies in raids, apportions the booty among them, and vindicates the one wronged against the wrong-doer" (Baghdâdî, 1935:210).

[13]According to Shahrastânî, (1934:151) the fundamental functions of the political leader are as following: (i) to administer the laws; (ii) to protect the country; (iii) to command the army; (iv) to divide their spoil and alms; (v) to arbitrate in

disputes; (vi) to punish wrong-doers; (vii) to appoint officials; (viii) to warn sinners and bring them back to the right path; (ix) to take steps to cleanse the land of error with the sword .

[14]"Another indication is the fact that when the Prophet died, the Companions assembled in the portico of the Banû Sa'îd and said: whosoever dies seeing not an *imâm* [ruling] over him, is dying the death of the times of Ignorance,... the reason why this is so [i.e., why they are in unbelief] is because there are some among the regulations [laid upon all believers] whose being put into operation is bound up with *imâm*, e.g., the Friday service, the two feasts, and the marriage of orphans" (Nasafî, 1962:441).

CHAPTER 5

LEGITIMATION OF POLITICAL AUTHORITY: EPISTEMOLOGICO-AXIOLOGICAL FOUNDATIONS

The principal difference in the development of legitimacy between Islamic and Western political theories might be analyzed from three perspectives: (i) epistemologico-axiological, (ii) prescriptivist, and (iii) institutional differences. The basis of all these differences is an epistemologico-axiological dimension which is bound directly to the ontologico-cosmological evaluations mentioned previously.

The most effective and permanent dimension of the legitimacy of an established political authority is the fitting of the basic norms of persons in the political mechanism to those of the people. Since every norm originates from a specific approach to the epistemological sources, the basic issue in the process of legitimation is this epistemologico-axiological dimension. A prescriptivist or procedural means of legitimacy may be valid and has a real value if it fits this dimension. Voluntary obedience to a socio-political system in the sense of legitimacy might occur only through appropriate prescriptivist and procedural means to this basic parameter and origin of the legitimacy. A prescriptivist or procedural means for political legitimacy cannot survive in the long term unless it originates from such an origin, while an epistemologico-axiological legitimacy can overcome all institutionally supported ways of legitimacy.

The ultimate epistemological authority for the legitimacy of political authority is the principal question related to political legitimacy. The source and essence of political legitimacy can not be understood without appealing to the ultimate epistemological authority. That is the main conflict between the principle of *shûrâ* in Islam and the mission of parliament in Western political tradition, as the basic procedural means for the legitimation of political authority. The functional similarity of these two means of political legitimacy is very deceptive and superficial if we omit the philosophical and epistemological dimensions of the problem. The principle of *shûrâ* has been interpreted in Islamic political theories as appealing to the cosmological and ontological integrity and its epistemological consequences, in contrast to the ontological apathy of the Western trend related to this issue. This is the main reason for the inadaptability of the Western democratic philosophy to Muslim societies, in spite of the structural similarity. Muslims do not resist democracy—if we limit democracy to a political structure that aims to create political participation—but resist the ontological apathy of Western democratic philosophy.

The source of the ultimate epistemological authority and its relationship with the axiologico-political framework is the anchor topic of these conflicting issues. The origin of this conflict is, in fact, the disagreement between the meaning of truth in Western epistemology based on compartmentalization of truth creating secularization of knowledge and the unity of truth in Islamic epistemology, together with its sources appealing to Haqq and 'Alim as names of Allâh in the Qur'ân.

Western way of legitimation

Epistemologico-axiological dimension

Talcott Parsons (1958:204) defines legitimation as "the appraisal of action in terms of shared or common values in the context of the involvement of the action in the social system" (D'entreves, 1963:688). Such a definition seems adequate to underline the place of common value in the legitimation process, but the question of the legitimacy is correlated to the essence and the origin of this common value. Therefore, this definition necessitates the clarification of this key-concept. The basic question is: Which characteristics of a value make it common? I think that a sophisticated deliberation on this question leads us to discuss the validity of some traditionalist assumptions that the question of legitimacy is a question of fitting of an action to the sovereign law, and therefore the approval of this law by the majority of a society makes it common as the basic standard of value. The delicate difference between legitimacy and legality should not be forgotten as we seek the real basis of legitimacy. Rather, I insist that the real base of legitimacy is the fitting of a value to the epistemologico-axiological imagination of a society and that the legitimation process is that of harmonization between them. Therefore, the Western paradigm described in chapter 2 might provide a theoretical framework for the question of legitimacy.

The modern identification of legitimacy and legality assumes the norms of the current law as the basic criteria of legitimacy. This does not explain how the current law gained such a superior position. In fact, this identification carries the indications of the re-formed epistemologico-axiological paradigm of Western civilization, and therefore we must inevitably distinguish between legitimacy and legality if we are to compare Western and non-Western phenomena.

Weber's specification that legality is the prevailing type of legitimacy in modern society underlines this phenomenon. But if we accept this as the anchor point for our analysis of political legitimacy in non-Western societies, we may fall into two significant misconceptions. First, we might conclude that political authorities in non-Western societies have no legitimate base. Second, we might conclude that there is no legal framework as the prescriptivist base for legitimacy in non-Western societies. But historical experiences, at least in Islamic history, show that these conclusions are not true. Hence, the real anchor point for such a comparative analysis of Islamic and Western experiences of legitimacy should be their epistemologico-axiological bases.

Such misconceptions might occur when we assume the Weberian classification of legitimacy as presenting inevitable stages of a historical process. But as Mardin (1983:19) rightly clarifies, all Weberian categories on legitimacy might be found in every society at any stage. They only aim to underline the dominant way of legitimation. Therefore, these categories should be held merely as ideal types rather than inevitable stages of a natural historical process. There is no need to discuss this issue in detail because we aim to explain the place of the Weberian categories in the Western way of political legitimation, rather than to discuss their validity as a sociological methodology. It is enough to stress that this methodology might mislead researchers if it is improperly applied.

In fact, the priority of legal forms in the legitimation process indicates an imaginative transformation in Western epistemologico-axiological presuppositions around the basic paradigm. Weber's classification of legitimacy as charismatic, traditional, and rational implicitly marks such a transformation. His identification of rational legitimacy with legality answers two critical questions related to the problem of legitimacy: What is the ultimate epistemological source? and What is the critical role of axiological norms between this epistemological source and the institutional mechanism?

The answers to these questions show the common base of the rationalistic and deterministic ways of political theorization which have been accepted by Friederich (1941:593, 167) as alternate approaches to political theory (Rogowski, 1974:27). Rationalism specified the ultimate epistemological source within the context of the humanization and secularization of epistemology. Meanwhile, the deterministic metaphysics of the new political science assigned a new role to this ultimate epistemological source, especially under the impact of the corpuscular perspective of science in the Newtonian and post-Newtonian period (to use Kuhnian terms [1962:24]) to understand the natural mechanism of social life, which is independent of any supreme will of God or of human beings. The scientism of the political theory might be accepted as an intellectual consequence of this new role together with the empiric methodology (Denisoff, 1972:7). Thus, the ways of the empiricists and the theorists of order during the early modern period intersected in our age.

This new role is the answer to the second question. Thus, a political action is legitimate only if it originates from rational reasoning or a rational choice consistent with the natural mechanism of social life.There is no place within this framework for any eternal value originating from a super-human epistemological source. The mechanism-based legitimation in Western experience originates from such an epistemologico-axiological base, as a veiled imagination. Legality means, within this context, having a legal corollary consistent with the natural mechanism of socio-political life. Thus, identification of legitimacy with legality, as the prevailing type of legalism, is a counterpart of the supremacy of mechanism-based legal forms over the value-system which becomes a dependent variable in the legitimation process. Post-Kantian theological inclinations towards subjectivization and individualization, based on the idea of the subjectivist conscientiousness of religion after the replacement of theological morality with moral theology, might be accepted as the declaration of this axiological secularization by the theologians.

Rogowski's (1974:27) assertion that Weber is the leading figure—in the 1950s and 1960s—of the new political science, the metaphysics of which is deterministic, and Beetham's (1974:55) denomination of Weber as protagonist of bourgeois values are meaningful from the perspective of mechanism-based legitimacy. In fact, Weber is not a vulgar protagonist of any system of values. Rather, such an attitude is a counterpart of the assumption of the internal dynamics of abstract self-adjusting mechanisms to produce their value-systems.

Such a mechanism-based legitimacy is a modern artifact; but its origins might be traced back to the Aristotelian methodology underlining the central position of epistemology and to the particularization of truth as an ancient and medieval phenomenon. The epistemological secularization of knowledge as well as the axiological secularization of life and law are the basic prerequisites of this modern way of legitimation.

Before searching for the ancient and medieval sources of the Western political legitimation process, we must repeat our earlier statement that any type of secularization necessitates a mental, imaginative, or practical segmentation (or particularization). It has been already shown how a mental particularization of truth results in an epistemological secularization. Axiological secularization of life and law originates from an ultimate particularization of normative/positive or religious/secular spheres, which is a consequence of ontological and epistemological particularization. In addition, we must also repeat that a pure rationalistic ethical framework, as an indication of axiological positivism, is the essential prerequisite for the secularization of life and law. This prerequisite is theoretically and imaginatively linked directly to the proximation (or equalization) of ontological and epistemological spheres.

The origins of epistemologico-axiological legitimacy in Western political philosophies can be found in the Aristotelian legacy. The relativity of ontology through empiric-realistic epistemology in Aristotle's philosophy resulted in an axiological classification of potentialities and actualities which might be accepted as a primary form of the categorization of the "normative-positive" or "ideal-real." These categorizations could be regarded as the axiological ground of secular differentiation of intellectual levels. The Aristotelian process for legitimation of a political system through the assumption of the "best practicable state" based on empiric epistemology, leading to observation of existing states around the axiom of "political actuality," is a good example of epistemologico-axiological legitimacy. This ontologically impenetrable way of legitimation became the fundamental type of legitimacy via historical relativism and evolutionism in modern political philosophy after the modern interpretation of the Aristotelian legacy.

The Christian way of legitimation contributed to this legacy an institutional dimension, supported by a specific bicompartmentalization of life into the spiritual and the material. Thus, the legitimation process has been determined through institutional relationships between the state and church, or (in Augustinian terminology) between an earthly city on the one hand and a celestial one on the other. Celestial authority as the perfect image of the divine ideal has the right to legitimate the imperfect earthly city created by sinful man or to refrain from doing so. This dualistic structure, formulated as the doctrine of the "two swords", has philosophical origins in Stoicism, as we have already pointed out.

There are several philosophical leanings in the origins of this dualistic structure. Stoic duality of matter/spirit and body/soul was extended to Roman eclectic geo-cultural atmosphere by Posidonius of Syria and Cicero. Together with the effect of neo-Pythagoreanism under the impact of Nigidus Figilus, which merged with oriental ideas, ethical dualism became the essential feature of the pre-Christian period. On the other hand, this dualistic process has been strengthened by neo-Platonism, which was the last ancient attempt to explain the dualism of appearance and reality. Thus, the influence of Greek philosophy through neo-Epicureanism, neo-Pythagoreanism, neo-Platonism, and Stoicism; of oriental mystery cults, especially through those of the Iranian Mythra and the Egyptian Isis; and polytheistic Roman paganism shaped an eclectic theoretical base around dualism and multi-central cosmologism before the spread of the institutionalization.

This dualistic philosophy was translated into medieval political understanding through the Augustinian system. Thus, the state was accepted as a natural and legitimate institution, and therefore every subject owed obedience and loyalty to the earthly state which began to be responsible to the leaders of the greater society, namely the Church. This legitimation process of current political structure led to an ethical base for the legitimation also of feudalism, because of the aristocratic elements within the Church. This bicompartmentalization of life opened the way for the secularization of life. The lack of a comprehensive law in Christianity forced the leaders of the Church to leave the sphere of the earthly life to that of secular authority, step by step. With Martin Luther's argument that the rule of the secular authorities can never be legitimately resisted came the declaration of the legitimacy of the final step of this divorce. The belief that final authority belongs to the Church became a symbolic slogan in the course of time because kings, as the representatives of the secular authority, began to declare not only their absolute sovereignty but also their divine quality. James I stated that the monarchy was supreme on earth—that not only were kings God's lieutenants upon earth sitting upon His throne, but that they were called gods even by God Himself.

Dynastic legitimacy was overturned by a re-formed epistemologico-axiological legitimacy around "reason." Re-endorsement theories, especially relativism and evolutionism, set up a bridge between actual political structures and this new epistemology, assuming the centrality of rational knowledge in the whole of life. A new axiology and ethics emerged depending on this epistemology or the process of political legitimation. The age of the supremacy of human reason isolated religion within the Church and transformed the idea of the divisibility of life into a new form, cutting up the links between ontological transcendency and socio-political life in the legitimation process. Hobbes' assumption of "self-preservation," Locke's axiom of the "natural rights of the individual," Kant's rational morality, Mill's and Bentham's utilitarianism, and James' pragmatism—all of which have the same epistemological anchor point—became the axiological bases of political legitimacy.

A re-definition of the terms knowledge and truth around the Enlightenment principles of reason, experience, and nature within the framework of relativism and evolutionism divorced the legitimation process from the divinely normative axiology by denying the idea of eternal norms. The institutional procedures for political legitimacy in Western political systems as political participation, the mission of parliament, and constitutionalism should be evaluated within this political-philosophical framework based on the humanization of ultimate epistemologico-axiological sources. This epistemologico-axiological re-formulation of the Western paradigm together with the mechanistic cosmology opened ways for a new imagination of socio-political legitimacy as a synthesis of rationalism, empiricism, and determinism. The priority of legality as a prescriptivist dimension and its mechanism-based origins during the legitimation process are natural consequences of such an imaginative and theoretical background.

In short, Weber's classification of legitimacy and his assertion that legality is the prevailing type of legitimacy in modern society is absolutely correct from the perspective of the internal consistency and historical continuity of Western civilization. But if we try to apply the same tools to the Islamic legacy, we are facing a very essential problem because the problem of legality is a sub-subject of the legitimation process which assumes direct control of the epistemologico-axiological dimension over prescriptivist/legal and mechanistic/institutional dimensions in Islamic tradition.

Prescriptivist dimension

The prescriptivist dimension of Western political legitimacy might be attached directly to the essential characteristic of the Western paradigm, namely secularization of knowledge, of life, and of law as a result of particularization in the epistemological and axiological spheres. The axiological categorization of normative/positive or ideal/positive and its epistemological sources are the theoretical and imaginative bases of the practical prescriptivist legitimacy which might be understood as legality in a narrower sense. Hobbes' statement that "law created morality, not morality created law" is a reflection of the axiological secularization in the sense of the formation of the positive law. Sidgwick's (1929:200, 208) following explanation underlines this categoric differentiation, as well as its role as a factor in prescriptivist legitimation: "I incidentally noticed the distinction between Ideal Morality or the true moral code—by many conceived and spoken of as the "Law of God"—and positive Morality, or the rules of duty supported by the sanctions of public opinion in any given age and country.... The moral opinions and sentiments prevalent in any community form so important a consideration in practically determining how its government ought to act, that it is desirable to survey the general relations of Positive Morality to Positive Law in a modern State.... I, following Bentham and Austin, regarded as 'legal' those rules of which the violation is repressed, directly or indirectly, by the action of Government or its subordinates; whereas the violation of a rule of positive morality is only punished by general disapprobation and its social consequences.... Positive morality, in a well-ordered State, does not only support the action of Government: it has, of course, the further important function of regulating conduct in matters beyond the range of governmental coercion." Such a categorization of ideal and positive morality, and its extensions in the legal structure as a code of law, marks one of the basic differences between this tradition and Islamic tradition, which assumes an identification of ideal and positive axiological sets. Therefore, it is almost impossible to develop a prescriptivist legitimacy based on absolute imagination of a secular axiological set independent from the divinely revealed ideal morality within an Islamic framework which did not have such a categoric differentiation in its historico-cultural legacy.

Thus, such a secularization of law, as a basis for political legitimacy, emerged from the medieval categorization of law into *jus divinum* (divine law), *jus naturale* (natural law), *jus gentium* (law of nations), and *jus civile* (civil law). St. Isidore's categorization of law as human and divine, based on the assumption that divine law is established by nature and human law by custom (*mores*), became the legal foundation of the doctrine of "two swords" throughout the Middle Ages. Gratian's subsequent twofold division "of divine or natural law on the one side and human law, which is founded on custom, on the other" (Carlyle, 1950:II/98) is a very significant identification of divine and natural laws within this framework of categorization. The modern version of ontological proximity—the extreme formulation of which was Spinoza's *Deus siva Natura*—provided the imaginative base for political legitimacy through the idea of natural law as the ultimate criterion for the formation of human law, which became the legal code to specify legitimate and illegitimate political actions.

The modern version of the prescriptivist dimension based on the idea of the positive law came out in the process of the re-emergence of the natural law within this framework. One of the first formulations of the basic principle of this modern version was developed by Hobbes, although its philosophically most consistent interpretation was achieved by Spinoza. The following basic principles of Hobbes' laws of nature can be extracted from *Leviathan* (n.d.:67-81): (i) that all human beings ought to seek peace; (ii) that all human beings are to defend themselves by whatever means available, (iii) that all human beings ought to perform their covenants; (iv) that one ought to avoid giving harm to those who show one good will; (v) that one ought to strive to accommodate oneself to others; (vi) that one ought to pardon past offences of the repentant, on expectation of similar treatment for oneself in the future; (vii) that, in punishing, one ought to look not at the greatness of past evil to be revenged but at the greatness of future good to be achieved; (viii) that all human beings ought to avoid any declaration of hatred or contempt for one another; (ix) that all human beings ought to acknowledge their natural equality; (x) that, at the entrance into conditions of peace, one ought to expect for oneself only such rights as one is willing to see granted to others; (xi) that one ought to deal equally between the parties involved in matters in which one has been entrusted with rendering judgement; (xii) that indivisible goods ought to be perpetually enjoyed in common, if possible, or else proportionate to the number of those that have a right to it; and (xiii) that diplomats must be allowed safe conduct.

Hobbes accepts these "Lawes of Nature" which are "Immutable and Eternall," as the basic criteria for the formation of any legal code, "For Injustice, Ingratitude, Arrogance, Pride, Iniquity, Acception of persons, and the rest can never be made lawfull," and "it can never be that Warre shall preserve life, and Peace destroy it" (n.d.:82). Thus, prescriptivist regulations in the form of a legal code should be consistent with these natural laws.

Spinoza's ontological statement, *Deus siva Natura*, as the ultimate case of ontological proximity provided a consistent theory for the philosophico-theological base of the secularization of the idea of natural law as the set of criteria of prescriptivist political legitimacy. Spinoza's presupposition that God is not a legislator or king who lays down laws for men,[1] led him to the very important conclusion that the laws of God or nature are scientific laws (1965b:267), not commands or prescriptions. They operate whether men apprehend them or not, and they are inviolable. Thus, laws of nature are ultimate truths beyond all religious laws: "No doubt when we disregard the unknown ways in which things are connected in the system of nature, and, confining our attention to the dictates of reason which concern religion, regard them as revealed to us by the voice of God in our own hearts, or, indeed, as revealed to the prophets in the form of laws; then, speaking in the manner of men, we say that a man obeys God when he loves him with a sound mind, and sins when he is led by blind desire. But we must always remember that we are in the power of God like clay in the power of the potter, who

---

[1]Spinoza concludes that the description of God as a legislator, king, just and merciful is the result of the stupidity of the masses because God acts and directs everything by the necessity of his own nature and perfection alone which logically necessitates that his decrees and volitions are eternal truths, and always involve necessity (Spinoza, 1965a:83).

from the same lump make some vessels for honorable, and others for dishonorable use; and hence that, although a man can *transgress* the decrees of God which have written as laws upon *our* minds or the minds of the Prophets, he *can* in no wise transgress the eternal decree of God which is written upon universal nature, and which has regard to the system of nature as a whole" (1965b:281-83). Thus, no obligation can stand against a law of nature.

In Spinoza's system, rejection of the absolute authority of the religious law is followed by a synthesis of natural and human law as an evident verification of the secularization of law. "Although I fully admit that all things are determined to exist and act in a fixed and definite way by universal laws of nature, I still say the laws of the second type depend on the will of men, and for two reasons. I. Since man is part of nature, he forms part of nature's power. Everything, therefore, which follows from the necessity of human nature, i.e., from nature itself conceived in the determinate from of human nature, follows, albeit necessarily, from human power. Hence the institution of these laws may well be said to depend on the will of men, because they largely depend on the power of the human mind, yet, unlike necessary laws as I have just defined it, need not be contained in an adequate conception of the human mind as perceiving things under the form of truth and falsity. II. My second reason for asserting that these laws depend on the will of men is that we ought to define and explain things through their proximate causes, since general considerations about necessity and causal connection can give us very little help in forming and arranging our ideas about particular things" (1965a:67).

These sentences aim to harmonize two rising tendencies of that critical period: anthropocentric epistemology and mechanistic/deterministic interpretation of ontological proximity. The human base of the natural law is very apparent in Hobbes and Locke as well. Hobbes (n.d.:66) stress that a law of nature "is a precept or general Rule found out by Reason," while Locke (1963:253) identifies the law of nature with the law of reason. This synthesis might be traced back to the Thomistic understanding of natural law as a mediaeval legacy (Regan, 1986:24).

Locke deviates from tradition by denying that the natural law is inscribed in the minds of men and that it can be known from men's natural inclination or from the universal consent of men, to say nothing of tradition. The only way of knowing the natural law is by ascending from the sensibly perceived things to God's power and wisdom as to what God wills man to do (Strauss, 1959:198). Locke's emphasis on empiric epistemology to find out the laws of nature as the natural constitution of man, in his *Essay on the Law of Nature*, is a very significant contribution to these attempts at synthesis. Empiric epistemology and naturalistic determinism intersected in this synthesis and co-effected the prescriptivist dimension of political legitimacy through the formation of positive law based on the necessity of the actual social mechanism.

One of the most fundamental consequence of this idea of natural law is the set of precepts of natural rights, which form the theoretical and juristic core for the prescriptivist dimension of political legitimacy up to the present. Locke's assumption that natural law constitutes the natural constitution of man shows the direct link between the presuppositions of natural law/natural right and the prescriptivist dimension of political legitimacy.

Many of these precepts of the natural law are similar to those of the ethical prerequisites of political legitimacy in Islamic political theories written many centuries before Hobbes. But the fundamental difference among them is the direct impact of the alternative *Weltanschauungs*. The axiological foundations of Islamic political legitimacy are eternal values given by a supreme divine being which is sovereign over the human being and nature. Thus, the set of these axiological norms is an object itself, rather than being a subject or dependent variable of a specific imagination of nature. On the contrary, the set of precepts of the natural law became the subject of changes in the imagination of nature throughout the ages. Thus, they have been transformed according to the transformation of the world views related to the natural and social mechanisms.

For example, although Hobbes denominates his set of natural law precepts as eternal and immutable, it has been re-formulated by Locke and subsequent philosophers according to their own imaginations of nature, which directly correlated with their ideas on social and political mechanisms. Spinoza's ideal form, which resulted in the identification of the laws of science with the laws of nature, proved the relativity of these laws as a dependent variable of the scientific achievements. Thus, prescriptivist dimension began to be directed by the necessities of the new socio-political and socio-economic mechanisms and environments, especially after the extension of the idea of natural mechanism to the socio-economic and socio-political sphere parallel to the fundamental assumption that social life has an independent internal mechanism beyond a supreme will over it by God or by man. I think the basic factor for such a transformation is the essential characteristic of Western tradition, namely ontological proximity, which creates an imagination of identification between God and nature. The eternity of Hobbesian natural laws originated from their divine nature, but changes in the imagination of nature parallel to the new re-formulated central position of epistemology not only transformed the precepts of the natural law, but also the imagination of God.

Institutional dimension

The institutional dimension of political legitimacy might be examined under two sub-headings: (i) religious ceremonies as symbolic declarations of the acceptance of political authority and (ii) secular procedural means, such as bilateral acts in feudalism or selection in the sense of political participation in the modern democratic tradition, to show the consent of the governed people for the distribution of political authority.

The first of these was one of the basic means for legitimation of political authority in the Middle Ages, as well as during the formation of absolutist monarchies after the Reformation. It was a part of the medieval particularization of the divine and earthly authorities. As Tellenbach mentions, the general conviction prevailed that kings were essentially different from all other laymen until the time of the Investiture Controversy because it has been assumed that they had a special mission from God and in them God's ruling will was peculiarly active, ennobling their persons. He refers to the ancient conceptions of divine kingship, to Germanic religious sentiment and to the biblical stories and commands as the origins of this veneration of the sovereign prince. So, these formative sources of the european mediaeval mind shaped the belief that the king's rule is holy and that his person is sacred because he is set up and put down by God: "In pictures of mediaeval rulers God's hand is sometimes seen over the king's head as a symbol of his religious eminence. The Church took account of this in ceremony of royal consecration, which was reckoned among the sacraments in the early Middle Ages, and so drew kingship into its spiritual territory. In the ceremony of consecration, it was held

God gave the king something of His power through His servants the bishops, and as a result the king became 'a new man'.... Royal theocracy was only possible if the king was given a place in the hierarchy above the bishops. In Carolingian times the king was commonly regarded as the equal of the pope, sometimes even as his superior. If, in early medieval royal portraits, bishops also appear, they are always smaller than the king; they show a respectful mien and a humble bearing, and the very arrangement of the figures indicates their lower rank. In the later Middle Ages this is entirely changed; from this period we possess paintings of archbishops of Mainz at imperial coronations, and the prelates are larger than the kings who stand beside them, whereas in earlier painting the only figures which overshadow the king are those of Christ and the saints. On ceremonial occasions the king took the first place, unless the pope himself was present. The glorification of the king reaches its highest point when, like Christ, he is depicted seated in a mandorla, the symbol of the incarnation, or when the dogmatically impossible assertion is made that the bishop is merely the representative of Christ, the king the vicar of God the Father himself" (Tellenbach, 1970:57-60). Ritual coronations by the pope—such as that of Charlemagne by Pope Leo III—had such a role for procedural legitimacy.

The forerunners of dynastic legitimacy during the period of absolutism used the same ceremonial means provided by religion to legitimize their political authority in the eyes of laymen. The process of the nationalization of the churches after the experiences of the royal councils was an attempt to benefit from religion in the process of institutional legitimacy. It might be said that the Protestant Reformation was provoked by monarchs to use religious symbols and institutional means for the legitimation of their political authority.

The origins of this type of institutional legitimacy as a specific relationship between religion and politics to develop a legitimate base for the supremacy of monarches as the centers of secular power can be found in the reconquest of the Roman political legacy. In particular, the Augustinian revival in Rome provided a historical experience to transform the base of legitimacy through the use of religious reformism. There was a close relationship between religious and political images, especially in the late Roman imperial period, when the imperial cult was the essential characteristic of religious life. Religion in Rome was used as a mechanism for the process of internalization and popularization of the socio-political system. Thus, it was used as a sub-system providing a base of legitimacy to the super-system of socio-political institutionalization. Therefore, almost all movements to reform and re-strengthen the state aimed first to revive religious consciousness in the direction of this attempt. The fundamental characteristic of Roman religion was its direct correlation with the pragmatic aims of the socio-political system rather than with the sophisticated cosmological and ontological question.

The Augustinian revival of ancient Roman religion was really more a political than a religious attempt at re-establishment of ancient Roman virtues through the recreation of the state cult. Through these reforms, the emperor Augustus tried to prevent the expansion of oriental mysterious religions in Rome. He took the religious title of *pontifex maximus*, which became the sign of the headship of the state religion after him, both for his pagan and Christian successors. Many temples and a new college (*Augustales*) of priests were built for his cult after the proclamation of his divinity by the Senate. His successors from Tiberius to Diocletian continued to use the imperial cult for the same pragmatic political aim: to test loyalty to Roman political authority. The main reason for the persecution of Christians in Rome was their refusal on the basis of their religious beliefs to take part in emperor worship, which was interpreted as treasonous by the Roman political authorities.

Roman religion remained a matter of formal state ritual rather than of cosmological and ontological faith because of the practical and unimaginative character of Roman culture. Priests were officers of the state. Roman religion was also characteristically a class religion due to its socio-political function, and the conflict between patricians and plebeians originated from both religious and political sources. Plebeians were largely excluded from public ceremonies as a natural result of Roman polytheism, which assumed a differentiation of gods according to the social status of men. The fact that in our own time there continue in some places to be separate Christian churches for blacks and whites might be interpreted as a continuation of the kind of religious-social stratification found in ancient Rome.

This idea that the Roman emperors possessed divine qualities gained strength from an infusion of Mithraic elements after Roman expansion into Asia. "We have record of Roman generals in Asia who were honored with sacred rites and these were merely the forerunners of the long list of deified emperors of Rome" (Laing, 1963:147). Thus, the idea of "sacred majesty" and "divine rights of the kings" as a specific way of political legitimation used for the absolute monarchy of Europe originated from the Roman and Mithraic legacy.

The subtle but essential differences between the Roman legacy, which is the origin of the secularization of legitimacy in Western Europe, and Islamic religious-political unity should not be overlooked merely because of their superficial institutional similarities. Although both assume a complete unification of political and religious authority, the manner in which their socio-political systems are justified and their provisions for political legitimacy are radically opposed to one another.

First of all, Roman centralization of religious and political authority did not presuppose a very well-defined value base for the epistemologico-axiological legitimacy of the socio-political system. Rather, it assumed a pragmatic function for religion in the socio-political legitimation process. Therefore, the institutional unification of religious and political authority did not create real and objective images in the political culture in the sense of the identification of religious and political values in an autonomous set. Hence, it was very difficult to re-produce this political culture around the same images, if political actualities necessitated another epistemologico-axiological framework for legitimacy, because the political leaders or posts were looked upon as having divine qualities rather than the value-system of the political culture.

The Islamic case is absolutely different. The Islamic value-system has absolute priority over political institutionalization because its epistemologico-axiological dimension is divine in quality rather than the corresponding leaders or posts in this dimension. This characteristic provides an internal dynamism for Muslim masses to reproduce their value-based political culture even when they are in opposition.

Second, Roman religious-political centralism assumed that religion was in the service of politics, while Islamic political imagination insists on an absolute identification of these spheres as an extension of its ontological-cosmological justification of the political system around the belief in *tawḥīd*. Hence, the modern revival of the Roman legacy of politico-religious centralism was used against papal authority to secularize of the legitimation of political authority in Europe, whereas Muslim masses managed to reproduce the basic parameters of Islamic political culture against the secular political culture imposed by Westernized elites in the process of modernization.

Moving now to the second aspect of the institutional dimension of political legitimacy, procedural means to show the consent of the governed to the distribution of political authority, we might attach these directly to the idea of the social contract. Secular procedural legitimation is intended to moralize and legitimatize the act of obedience to the political authority and to law, in that by giving his consent to the law-making authority, an individual gives himself a moral reason to obey the law freely. Thus, obedience to law becomes, by virtue of consent, an act which an individual voluntarily ought to perform if he is to act morally (Richards, 1971:198).

This consent carried traditional elements in the medieval experience of the bilateral act as the basis of the contractual understanding to specify rights and obligations in the feudal structure because the Teutonic tribes had no sense of the state as a distant, impersonal continuing source of law (Gettell, 1959:104). Although, it is an evident historical fact that the mission of parliament is indebted to a great extent to this medieval experience, the procedural dimension of political legitimacy gained its real importance after the emergence of the transformed epistemologico-axiological dimension and its prescriptivist extensions in the sense of natural law and natural right.

Political participation as a mechanism of this dimension became a central phenomenon as a counterpart to rising democratic feeling, and its basic assumption is the axiom that "every man is the best judge of his own interest, and therefore best knows what sort of government and what laws will promote that interest and that those laws and that government will presumably be the best for a community as a whole which are desired by the largest number of its members" (Bryce, 1921:44). Thus, consent as the mark of political legitimacy is manifested in the liberal-democratic electoral process: "The democratic method is that institutional arrangement for arriving at political decisions which realizes the common good by making the people itself decide issues through the election of individuals who are to assemble in order to carry out its will" (Schumpeter, 1962:250).

The development of such a procedural legitimacy evolved parallel to the rising of two mechanisms, one political and the other economic. The political mechanism is the formation of a new base of sovereignty: national or popular sovereignty. The rising importance of this mechanism led to a shift in political theory toward finding the best way to fulfill this aspect of procedural legitimacy. Liberal democratic tradition and socialist/popularist democracies began to defend the supremacy of their systems due to their appropriateness for political participation rather than due to their attachment to a value-system. Thus, political participation as a means of political legitimation became a value by itself and began to reproduce the norms of political life. The idea of positive morality together with the axiomatic moral neutrality of the new political science provided an imaginative base for the supremacy of the procedural type as a mechanism-based form of political legitimation.

The economic mechanism which accelerated this process is that of the market. Therefore, democratic political participation is the counterpart of capitalistic evolution based on market mechanisms. First of all, such procedural legitimation necessitates two significant axiomatic prerequisites: equality and freedom. Positivistic/materialistic interpretations of these prerequisites emerged as a natural consequence of the market mechanism because it assumes an equalization of human beings in the sense of labor as a factor of production, while freedom has been accepted as fundamental for the most productive economy to attain material happiness. The justification of democracy by utility is a theoretical reflection of this phenomenon.

The socialistic solution tried to manage the highest degree of political participation in order to show that it is the most perfect type of procedural legitimation by setting up a new morality and a new bureaucratic structure to control the evils of capitalistic tendencies on behalf of the rationalistic prerequisites. But this bureaucratic mechanism has taken over the role of the market mechanism in the sense of the production of its own norms and reproduction of them within a consistent and independent mechanistic structure.

Such human necessities as freedom and equality were discussed in the pre-capitalist period within a metaphysical rather than a positivistic/materialistic framework. Thus, such a bicompartmental division of human happiness is a natural result of the dualistic structure of the Western paradigm. The fundamental contrast between Islamic and Western ways of legitimation and the basic reason why the transfer of Western institutional ways of legitimation to Muslim societies did not gain a real base for political legitimacy might be understood on this point: Western political culture and theories moved toward a mechanism-based legitimacy consistent with the Western historico-cultural legacy, while Islamic societies continued to be attached to a political imagination and culture that are highly value-dependent and reject any type of compartmentalization related to their epistemologico-axiological foundations.

Islamic way of legitimation

In contrast to Western experience related to political legitimacy, the epistemologico-axiological basis of political legitimacy in Islam has been directly attached to ontological antecedents. Belief in the unity of human responsibility and the unity of life originates directly from the belief in the transcendental unity of Allâh. These are the two basic grounds upon which all processes of socio-economic and socio-political legitimation in Islam are based.

Epistemologico-axiological dimension

The most distinctive characteristic of the Islamic way of legitimation is its normative character. The highly concentrated ontological and epistemological differentiation in Islam create a very persistent set of eternal values that has been firmed throughout Muslim historical experience. The fundamental problem of the Islamic way of legitimation is whether or not institutionalization of political authority fits these values, while the basic dynamism of Islamic socio-political history is the realization of these eternal values via the best institutional mechanism. Therefore, the anchor point of Islamic legitimacy is this set of eternal values, while the efficiency or rationality of the political mechanism is a secondary and dependent variable to it.

This characteristic is especially important in the periods of civilizational challenge. The basic Islamic epistemological sources, the Qur'ân and Sunnah, do not offer any definite and tight type of socio-political mechanism. Therefore,

Muslims do not hesitate in benefitting from the institutional experiences of other civilizations. This is a natural result of the Qur'ân's fundamental concern with broad normative issues of right and wrong or good and evil rather than with narrow questions of detail. Muslims have always tried to adapt borrowed institutions and mechanisms to the above-mentioned epistemologico-axiological dimension. Such a civilizational challenge resulted in a reproduction of a socio-political culture, so long as it preserves these eternal values within this process of institutional transformation. The rich diversity of socio-cultural mechanisms in Islamic civilizations from Andalusia to India is in many ways unique in the history of civilization.

The following statements from Ibn Khaldûn show how a Muslim scholar sees the relationship between this epistemologico-axiological dimension and the process of institutionalization. "The religious law does not censure political [royal] authority [mulk] as such and does not forbid its existence. It merely censures the evils deriving from it, such as tyranny, injustice, and pleasure-seeking. No doubt, these evils which are the concomitants of political [royal] authority have been forbidden. The religious law praises justice, fairness, the fulfillment of religious duties, and the defence of religion which will of necessity find their reward. All these things are concomitants of political [royal] authority, too. Censure attaches to political [royal] authority only because of some of its qualities and conditions, and not others. [The religious law] does not censure political [royal] authority as such, nor does it seek its abandonment completely. Likewise, it also censures concupiscence and indignation in responsible persons, but it does not aim to abandon these qualities altogether, because their existence is naturally necessary. Its purpose is the proper use of them in accordance with the truth. Dawud and Sulaiman who were prophets and belonged, in the view of Allâh, among the most distinguished human beings that ever existed, possessed royal authority such as no one else ever possessed." (Ibn Khaldûn, n.d.:192).

But this receptiveness to borrowed institutions does not mean that Islamic political structures are mere imitations of pre-Islamic ones. On the contrary, it stress the priority of the epistemologico-axiological dimension and the dependency of the institutionalization process on this dimension. The originality of Islamic institutionalization is based on this characteristic.

For example, the caliphate as the ultimate religious-political institution is a purely original Islamic socio-political structure. Arnold's (1965:11) correct comparison between the Holy Roman Empire and the caliphate underlines this fact: "The Holy Roman Empire was consciously and deliberately a revival of a pre-existing political institution that had been in existence before the birth of Christianity and was now revived under a specifically Christian character. Charlemagne assumed a title which had been held by heathen emperors before him.... Unlike the Holy Roman Empire, the Caliphate was no deliberate imitation of a pre-existent form of civilization or political organization. It was the outgrowth of conditions that were entirely unfamiliar to the Arabs, and took upon itself a character that was exactly moulded by these conditions. The Caliphate as a political institution was the child of its age, and did not look upon itself as the revival of any political institution of an earlier date." Thus, Islamic expansion towards the geo-cultural and socio-political axis from the Nile to the Oxus[2] created an original institutionalization based on a specific epistemologico-axiological dimension.

This approach based on the centrality of the epistemologico-axiological dimension during the process of institutionalization might be applied for the institutional transformation in the modern era, but the fundamental problem of Muslim societies, especially the Western-oriented elites of these societies, during the modern challenge of Western civilization is the fact that modern Western socio-political and socio-economic mechanisms produce their own values. This means that it is impossible to accept any eternal value within such a social organization composed of self-valuing mechanisms, so Muslim societies face the dilemma of either denying their eternal values or resisting imposed foreign institutions.

The first period of this civilizational challenge seemed to be a victory for the Western-oriented elites, but in the long run, the secret power of the eternal values re-emerged as the origin of resistance by the traditional socio-political culture. The dimension of this mechanism/value imbalance related to the social change will be discussed in the following chapter, but at this stage I want to underline that the basic dichotomy of the socio-political structure of Muslim societies today is the impossibility of the legitimacy of the institutional political structure via eternal values. There is not a relationship of correspondence between value base and institutional structure which is the essential condition for a stable legitimation process.

Throughout history, Muslim scholars have tried to check political mechanism via a very stable and resistant value structure and to re-establish them. Now, Muslim scholars and masses face a new phenomenon: the ultimate dependency of value structure on the mechanisms. This new phenomenon prevents both checking the institutional mechanisms through the direction of the eternal values and preserving a stable value structure. This creates an obscurity related to the process of legitimating socio-political authority and socio-economic mechanisms.

The idea of the responsibility of man is *principium individuationis* of Muslim society (*ummah*) as a socio-political unity. This is an open society for any human being, regardless of his origin, race, or color, who accepts this responsibility which is the basis of the identification and political socialization process of a Muslim in an Islamic socio-political environment. This political identification and integration process in an Islamic society is the main difference in comparison with the state tradition in Western civilization—as nationalist, communist, or liberal-democratic—where the basis of political identification and integration occurs through a national or class consciousness. The achievement of legitimacy in such a socio-political unity is, therefore, directly related to the question of whether the political authority in the society provides the requirements for the fulfillment of this responsibility. From this perspective, "ideal/real" and "positive/normative" socio-political images and structures should intersect due to a given axiological base through a divine epistemology originating from God's will.

---

[2]See Hodgson (1974:I/103-146) for the pre-Islamic characteristics of this axis.

Prescriptivist dimension

The epistemologico-axiological base of political legitimacy in Islam imposes a comprehensive legal order revealed by Allâh to be applied within the framework of the unity of life. This is another distinctive characteristic of Islamic legitimacy. The doctrine that is most universally accepted by Muslim schools and sects is the rejection of the compartmentalization of life and law. This is another paradigmatic unity among Islamic political theories originating from their ontological evaluations.[3] This paradigmatic unity has been strengthened by a very strong eschatological dimension.

Ibn Khaldûn's following interpretation (n.d.:190-91) gives a clear indication of the holistic consistency between eternal norms, eschatology, law, and politics. "It is imperative to have reference to established political norms [qawânîn siyâsiyyah], which are consented by the entire people and to whose laws it submits.... If these norms are established by the intelligent and leading elite of the state [dawlah] having insight, it will be a politics based on rationality [siyâsah aqliyyah]. If they are established by Allah through a lawgiver who regulates them as religious laws, it will be a politics based on religion [siyâsah diniyyah], which is useful for life in both this and the other world because the purpose of human beings [creation] is not only their worldly well-being. No doubt, this entire world is trivial and futile ending in death and annihilation.... The purpose of human beings is their religion, which leads them to happiness in the other world... Religious laws have been revealed to induce them for this purpose in all their affairs with regard to the worship [to Allah] and to the conducts [with their fellow men]. This [principle] also applies to political authority [mulk], which is natural in human social organization. These [religious laws] guide it along the method of religion, so that [all affairs] will be conducted from the perspective of the religious law. Any conduct [of the political authority] pursuant to force, superiority, or the derelication of the power of ʿaṣabiyyah, is tyranny and injustice and considered blameworthy by [the religious law], as it is also blameworthy by the essentialities of the political wisdom [al-ḥikmah as-siyâsiyyah]. Any conduct [of political authority] pursuant to the political considerations and rules without guidance of the religious law, is also blameworthy, because it is ignoring the divine light.... All political and other actions will come back to the relevant human beings at the Resurrection. Political laws consider only worldly interests, while the intention the Lawgiver is their well-being in the other world, too. Therefore, it is imperative [of the religious law] to induce the entire people to act in accordance with the religious laws in all their affairs related to this world and the other world. The authority to do so was

---

[3]Some orientalists have tried to show that there were two contrasting laws, *shar'* and *'urfî*, in Muslim states, especially in the Ottoman socio-political system, and to make this an anchor point for their speculations on the secularization of law in Muslim societies. But because that *'urf* is considered one of the sources of Sharîʿah (e.g., by Abû Ḥanîfah) so long as it does not contradict the more fundamental sources (the Qurʾân and Sunnah), a regulation based on *'urf* is part of the juridic scheme, *fiqh*. Therefore, such speculations could not have any meaning without referring them to the methodology of Islamic law.

possessed by the experts of the religious law, the prophets and by those who took their place, the caliphs."

Islamic comprehensive law based on eternal norms consists of a prescriptivist dimension of political legitimacy. The legitimacy of a political authority can be checked through its attitude related to the application of this law, such as Ibn Khaldûn insists. Mawârdî argues that the real motive of the political leadership (*imâmah*) is the following of the "straight path," while Ghazzâlî underlines two conditions for the legitimacy of a political authority: justice and law.

These eternal norms, as the fundamental axiological framework, have an epistemological basis for their justification in the process of becoming a conviction. The superiority of divine law as the prescriptivist formulation of these norms depends on this extraordinary origin of knowledge, namely *nubuwwah* (prophecy). This is basically assumed by *falâsifah*, as well as by *fuqahâ'*. For example, Ibn Sînâ attaches his systematic binding between man's happiness/perfection, justice as the basic norm and divine law, to the belief in Allâh and *nubuwwah*.[4] Likewise, Ibn Rushd connects his political theory with the idea of the superiority of Sharî'ah which is the law of the Muslim state and aims at the happiness of all its citizens, the philosophers as well as the masses. His argument that the perfection and superiority of Sharî'ah over man-made laws consists in its divine character shows the ontologically-defined epistemological dimension of his conception of political legitimacy. Parallel to these scholars, Ibn Taymiyyah, redefining the key-term *wilâyah*, specifies that the object of *wilâyah* is to order what is permissible and to prohibit what is not, aiming at the rule of justice and the well-being of the people.

Obedience to a legitimate authority in matters of right and justice and within the legal limitations is, according to the Qur'ân (4:58) a continuation of the obedience to Allâh. So, the legitimacy of a political authority is related to its obedience to the legal order of Allâh. But no one has the right to command obedience in the service of sin.

This is the axiological basis for a legitimate opposition in Islamic political theories. Abû Hanîfah's creed in this matter was (i) that the caliphate of an unjust incumbent was basically wrong and insupportable and deserved to be overthrown; (ii) that people not only had the right but the duty to rise in rebellion against it; and (iii) that such a rebellion was not only allowed but obligatory, provided that it had a realistic chance to succeed in replacing the tyrant with a just, virtuous ruler and not merely fizzle out in lose of lives and power (Mawdûdî, 1963:688).

---

[4]"Man lives in society, Avicenna argues; no one is happy entirely alone. And in a human society men are bound to have constant association with one another. These relations must be governed and directed so that justice may prevail. To dispense justice there must needs be law and to lay down laws there must be a lawgiver. To be a lawgiver, a man must rise to become the leader of men, and devote his life and efforts to the problems of society. And to be chosen for that mission he must possess merits that others either do not have at all or have to a lesser extent than he. By these merits he must win the submission and support of his fellow men. Having gained these, he can attend to their needs and apply the 'order of the Good' provided for them by God. Obviously this leader could not be a human being like all the rest; except that he is chosen, authorized and inspired by God who makes his holy spirit descend upon him" (Afnan, 1958:178-79).

For some scholars, this common judgement has been extended to the personal affairs of the political leader. For example, according to Shâfi'î, the imâm—like any judge or commander—may be removed on the grounds not only of tyranny but also of personal wrong-doing (Taftazânî, 1950:150). This right of the community to depose of an unjust caliph from leadership is verified in the words of Abû Bakr at his election to the caliphate: "You have put me in power, though I am not the best among you. If I do well, help me, and if I do wrong, then set me right."

Rashîd Riḍâ connects this idea of legitimate opposition to the power of community and to consultation (shûrâ) as a procedural means. He (1988:22-3) uses the arguments of the classical scholars to bolster his view: "[It has been mentioned] in the text of the Mawâqif of 'Aḍud that the Community may depose its leader in case of necessity. Yet, the lesser of two evils should be preferred if that will lead to a civil strife [fitnah]. Its commentator As-Sayyid Al-Jurjânî mentions the disorder in the conditions of the Muslims and the relapse of the matters of religion to describe the reasons.... The argument of al-Râzî [on this subject] is that the supreme authority belongs to the ummah, which may depose the Imâm [the caliph] if it sees the necessity for such an action. Al-Sa'd says, he intends by ummah those with power to loose and bind, that is, those who represent the ummah by possession of leadership and authority which extends to the other individuals in the ummah . Al-Râzî makes it clear in his commentary on the verse 'Obey God, His Messenger, and those in authority among you' (4:58) that those in authority means those who may loose and bind and represent the power of the ummah .... It is necessarily known that 'those in authority' at the Prophet's time who were consulted in the public affairs; were not [merely] from 'Ulamâ' of the Law, from commanders, or from judges, but from men of counsel among the leading Muslims".

The prerequisites for being imâm or caliph and his duties after the election show the epistemologico-axiological base of the legitimacy of a political authority in Islam very clearly. Ibn Khaldûn (n.d.:193-94) formulates the prerequisites governing the institution of the imâmate as (i) knowledge, (ii) probity, (iii) competence, and (iv) freedom of the senses and limbs from any defect that might affect judgement or action. His interpretations of these qualifications prove the importance of the epistemologico-axiological dimension as a premise of political legitimacy.

The systematization of falâsifah on the necessary qualifications of the political leader has twofold importance: from the perspective of the dependency on the epistemologico-axiological foundation of its prescriptivist reflections related to the question the legitimacy and from the perspective of how they internalize pre-Islamic sources in the process of the imagination of the political leadership and its legitimacy. Ibn Rushd enumerates the following qualifications which the ruler of the ideal state should possess by nature, in his commentary on Plato's Republic : (i) he should be disposed by nature for the study of the theoretical sciences to recognize in his nature what a thing is in its essence and to distinguish it from that which is by accident; (ii) he should preserve things in his mind and should not forget them; (iii) he should love study, choose it, and desire to inquire into all parts of science; (iv) he should love truth [sidq] and hate falsehood because he who loves the knowledge of reality as such loves truth and hates falsehood; (v) he should loathe the sensual desires; (vi) he should not love money because money is a desire and desires are not proper for the political leaders; (vii) he should be high-minded to desire knowledge of everything and of all existing things; (viii) he should be courageous; (ix) he should be so disposed that he moves of his own accord towards everything which he considers good and beautiful, like justice and other such virtues; (x) that he should be a good orator to express whatever is in his mind; (xi) he should have proper physical conditions in the sense of strong physique and fitness. (Ibn Rushd, 1966:178-179).

These are almost the same qualifications mentioned by Plato in *Republic*. Ibn Rushd formulates these qualifications within a new context in the third treatise to bring them into line with Islamic premises through insisting that five basic conditions of an absolute ruler and of a true government are wisdom, perfect intelligence, good persuasion, good imagination, capacity for waging *jihâd* and no physical impediment to the performance of actions in connection with *jihâd*. (Ibn Rushd, 1966:207-08)

This classification is a repetition of Fârâbî's argument in *Fuṣûl al-Madanî*. "He is the first chief and it is he in whom are combined six conditions: (a) wisdom; (b) perfect practical wisdom; (c) excellence of persuasion; (iv) excellence in producing an imaginative impression; (e) power to fight the holy war [*jihâd*] in person; (f) that there should be nothing in his body to prevent him attending to the matters which belong to the holy war. He in whom all these are united is the model, the one to be imitated in all his ways and actions, and the one whose words and councils are to be accepted" (Fârâbî, 1961:50). A similar classification might be found in his *Kitâb Ârâ Ahl al-Madînah al-Fâḍilah* (1985:127-28). The epistemological dimension is very evident where Fârâbî argues (1961:51) that the ideal ruler "should possess knowledge of the ancient laws and traditions which the first generations of Imâms acknowledged and by which they ruled the city."

Borrowing from Fârâbî, Ibn Rushd (1966:283) insists on the expression "king of the laws" because he gives a vital place to the art of jurisprudence in his political philosophy. He even provides for division of authority if one person does not possess both of the qualifications because it may not happen that both these qualifications are found in one man, the one capable of *jihâd* [*mujâhid*] being another than the legal expert, *faqîh*. Ibn Rushd suggests in such a situation that they should share in the rule and he underlines that this is the case with many of the Muslim states. (Ibn Rushd, 1966:208-9).

Institutional dimension

The Imâmiyyah and Ismâ'iliyyah, as the fundamental Shî'a sects, argue that the appointment of a socio-political authority is of Allâh via a *naṣṣ* (indication), while Ahl al-Sunnah say that the method of conferring the Imâmate on the Imâm is selection by the Muslims, by seeking the most qualified person among themselves (Baghdâdî, 1935:210).

The historical experiences of selecting the first four caliphs provide several options for the establishment of a legitimate authority in the political theory of Ahl al-Sunnah. The election of Abû Bakr was accepted as a model for the participation of the whole community. In this election three competing political groups were formed: the Ansar in support of Sa'd ibn 'Ubâdah, the Muhâjirîn in support of Abû Bakr, and Banû Hâshim in support of 'Ali. After discussion on their respective candidates, 'Umar proposed Abû Bakr and all agreed. The procedural base of the legitimacy of this election has been approved through a *bay'ah 'âmma* (public confirmation). This application of general consensus has been supported by the idea of *ijma'* and became the first model for the procedural base of the legitimacy of establishing a socio-political authority. This procedural model has been generally accepted by classical and modern political theorists as the best way of establishing a political authority. This historical experience as a way of legitimate election has been used as the basic argumentation especially for the modern theorists whose basic problem of legitimacy is the expansion of political participation. J. Iqbâl's description (1986:42) of the election of Abû Bakr as "a conference which sought to maintain a dialogue for political consensus, realized through mutual consultation" is a well-defined example for these attempts.

The election of the second caliph was a model for the popular approval of a nomination. Prior to his own death, Abû Bakr suggested 'Umar for the political leadership, and this suggestion was approved by the public. This way has been used to legitimate the dynastic nominations during the Umayyad and Abbasid periods, but such an analogy has also been criticized by some Muslim scholars on the ground that Abû Bakr's nomination was merely a suggestion, while dynastic nomination was a consequence of political power. 'Abdul Rahmân b. Abû Bakr's remark to Marwân, governor of Madînah, that the decision of Mu'âwiyah to nominate his son Yazîd to the caliphate was more like the practices of Khusrau and Caesar than those of Abû Bakr or 'Umar is an example of this criticism (J. Iqbâl, 1986:44). Thus, dynastic nomination was not accepted as an ideal form of the procedural means for political legitimation; rather it has been interpreted as an existent political reality.

Therefore, the attempts of scholars to regulate dynastic nomination might be seen as efforts to restrict such political action through the limitations of the juristic scheme. The anxiety to prevent the abuse of political power is very evident in the political works of such scholars as Mawârdî and Ibn Taymiyyah. They aimed to limit political reality within the framework of the prescriptivist legitimacy under the patronage of law, rather than diverting law to provide a procedural base for the legitimation of an existing political authority. For example, Ibn Taymiyyah (1988:14-6) strictly rejects the nomination of a close relative to even an ordinary position, arguing that such a nomination—because of the possibility of a psychological infirmity—is a breach of trust which is strictly condemned by the Qur'ân (8:27). This example shows the importance of the epistemologico-axiological base for the legitimation process beyond its procedural and institutional bases.

The election of the third caliph, 'Uthmân, through an electoral college of the probable candidates provided another means of establishing a legitimate political authority. It might be said that the theory of *ahl al-hal wa al-'aqd* is inspired from this historical experience. It seems the most viable option from the perspective of the jurists because the required qualifications to be caliph were similar to those for an elector. For example, Mawârdî (1973:6) and Abû Ya'lâ b. al-Farrâ' (1983:19) mention almost the same conditions for being elector, namely justice and knowledge on the requirements of being caliph and on the qualifications for an effective public policy.

The election of the fourth caliph contributed a significant principle to the legitimation process: the openness of *bay'ah* (allegiance) as the procedural means. 'Ali refused the private *bay'ah* of 'Abbâs, his uncle, and argued that if Muslims wanted to take an oath of allegiance to him as the caliph, it should be openly performed in the Prophet's mosque.

Now, we can analyze the principal institutional prerequisites and key-concepts for legitimacy in Islam mentioned above: *bay'ah 'âmma* (confirmation of the authority of the ruler by the public), *ijma'* (consensus of the community), and *shûrâ* (the mechanism of consultation between ruler and ruled).

Bay'ah 'âmma is a bilateral act through which a political ruler promises to fulfill his duties, determined by law based on the "straight path" of justice, and through which the people promise to obey that which is right and just. Without such a bilateral act of *bay'ah*, the political authority and hierarchy could not be legally installed. This prerequisite for political legitimacy has its origins in historical experience of Muslims beginning from the time of the Prophet.

The first and second pledges of al-Aqabah (Hamîdullah, 1987:46-51) might be accepted as a socio-political and religious contract before the establishment of the state in Madînah, between the Prophet and his followers from Madînah. Some women participated in this bilateral act, and the Qur'ân commanded the acceptance of the pledge of allegiance from women as well as men. This application of *bay'ah* was repeated in *Bay'ah al-Riḍwân* at Hudaybiyah in the year of 6 AH and after the conquest of Makkah in the year of 8 AH. Thus, it became a *sunnah* as a bilateral act. But, it should be noted that these *bay'ahs* between the Prophet and his companions were not merely political contracts, due to the ultra-political role of the Prophet. This application became a procedural means for the legitimate establishment of a political authority, especially during the elections of the first four caliphs after the death of the Prophet.

Ibn Khaldûn (n.d.:209) describes this act thus: "It should be known that the *bay'ah* is a contract to render obedience [through which] the person who renders the oath of allegiance with his *amîr*, surrenders supervision of his own affairs and those of the Muslims to him and [promises] that he will not contest his authority and that he will obey him by [fulfilling] all the duties with which he might be charged, whether agreeable or disagreeable. When people render the oath of allegiance to the *amîr* and make the contract, they put their hands into his hand to confirm the commitment. This [procedure] is similar to the action of buyer and seller. Therefore, the oath of allegiance was called *bay'ah*, the infinitive of *bâ'a* [to sell/buy]. The *bay'ah* was a handshake. Such is its meaning in customary linguistic terminology and the accepted usage of the religious law which is the purpose in the hadith on the *bay'ah* of the prophet during the night of 'aqabah and near the tree..."

Although the etymological and traditional origin of this bilateral act might be sought in pre-Islamic background, especially in south-Semitic development (Brawmann, 1972:213-220), it should be added that such an act has been re-valuated within a semantic and imaginative framework of the ontologico-political semantic field of Qur'ân mentioned before. The verses in the Qur'ân related to this key-concept reflect the color of this semantic field, which set up a direct relationship of meaning between ontological and political spheres. This ontologico-political semantic link is very clear (48:10; 9:111; 60:12). Hence, it is very difficult to find a in Western medieval experience thorough correspondent to its re-valuated meaning within this semantic field.[5]

The Islamic version of this act carries additional characteristics originating from the epistemologico-axiological base of legitimacy mentioned above, and it is therefore beyond a reciprocal relationship such as in its pre-Islamic usage or in the corresponding medieval European ceremonies. Moreover, pre-Islamic *bay'ah* was life-long and impossible to dissolve from the side of the subject, while Islamic

---

[5]Brawmann's argument (1972:216) is to be criticized on exactly this basis.

bay'ah presupposes the supremacy and objectivity of law which gives the right to dissolve this act in any case against the epistemologico-axiological and prescriptivist base of political legitimacy.

In fact, in the Islamic version of *bay'ah*, both parties of agreement are attached to each other for the formation of an ideal substantive state, within which citizens could perform their responsibilities assigned by Allâh. Combining the idea of the unity of life with Islamic eschatological presuppositions, we have to underline the condition that rulers in an Islamic political society are not responsible only for the people's worldly happiness, but also their otherworldly happiness in so far as they are to provide a socio-political atmosphere for the fulfillment of *amânah*. This is very different from the medieval Western reciprocal relationships between feudal elements and modern utilitarian/individualistic philosophy due to their eschatological dimension and political consequences, especially related to this issue of legitimacy.

The other two essential prerequisites and key-concepts of Islamic political legitimacy, *shûrâ* and *ijma'*, have a common imaginative and theoretical base due to the fact that the latter, as an informal activity, owes its origin to the former as prescribed by the Qur'ân.[6] Although there was a similar institution of consultation in pre-Islamic Arab tradition, *dâr al-nadwa* , the origin of this principle as a way of legitimacy is the Qur'ânic command and its application during the period of 'Asr al-Sa'âdah. Therefore, contrary to the origin of the tradition of Western parliament, its theoretical origin is not historical experience itself; but historical experience has been legitimated through the Qur'ânic command. As A. Hassan mentions, the term *shûrâ* is the antithesis of *fawdâ'* (chaos, anarchy). Hence, it is "a collective endeavor for seeking an objective truth" (1984:26).

The principle of *shûrâ* is not only accepted as a guarantee for the political participation of the people but is also interpreted as a mechanism to prevent tyranny in socio-political life, because it has been assumed that this principle can be realized only via freedom of thought and expression.[7] The existence of several different opinions has been supported due to the prophetic tradition that "the difference of opinion in my *ummah* is the blessing of Allâh." As Hassan (1984:27) reports, it is a historical fact, especially in the period of the first four caliphs, that the *shûrâ* council functioned as a legislative body representing the community, though not through formal elections.[8]

Modern scholars, such as Rashîd Ridâ (1988:21), insist on this prerequisite to stress the importance of the collectivity in political life through referring to Qur'ânic

---

[6]There are five Qur'ânic verses including the key-concept *shûrâ* and its derivatives. Two of them (3:159; 42:38) are direct commands for the realization of this principle.

[7]Abû Yûsuf narrates in his *Kitâb al-Kharaj* (1973) that Caliph 'Umar once addressed a meeting of his *shûrâ* council thus: "I have called you for nothing but this, that you may share with me the burden of the trust that has been reposed in me of managing your affairs. I am but one of you, and today you are the people that bear witness to truth. Whoever of you wishes to differ with me is free to do so, and whoever wishes to agree is free to do that. I will not compel you to follow my desires" (English trans. from Sharîf, 1965:16).

[8]See Dacca's article (1955) for a summary of the application of *shûrâ* in pre-Islamic and Islamic history.

verse on mutual consultation as the basic principle of the social interaction: "And who answer the call of their Lord and establish worship and whose affairs are by mutual consultation..."(42:38). He underlines that the Qur'ân prescribes law for the collectivity of Believers [jamâ'ah], on the matters of the common interest and that it orders obedience to those in authority representing them.

The principle of *ijma'*, as the third legal source, provides an impressive inspiration to modern Muslim thinkers to form a new socio-political mechanism leading to a more comprehensive political participation as an effective way of political legitimacy. Iqbâl's (1934:164) following statements are one of the first attempts for this purpose: "The third source of Mohammedan Law is Ijma which is, in my opinion, perhaps the most important legal notion in Islam. It is, however, strange that this important notion, while invoking great academic discussions in early Islam, remained practically a mere idea, and rarely assumed the form of a permanent institution in any Mohammedan country. Possibly its transformation into a legislative institution was contrary to the political interests of the kind of absolute monarchy that grew up immediately after the fourth Caliph. It was, I think, favorable to the interest of the Omayyad and Abbaside Caliphs to leave the power of Ijtihad to individual Mujtahids rather than encourage the formation of a permanent assembly which might become too powerful for them. It is, however, extremely satisfactory to note that the pressure of new world forces and the political experience of European nations are impressing on the mind of modern Islam the value and possibilities of the idea of Ijma. The growth of republican spirit, and the gradual formation of legislative assemblies which, in view of the growth of opposing sects, is the only possible form Ijma can take in modern times, will secure contributions to legal discussion from laymen who happen to possess a keen insight into affairs. In this way alone we can stir into activity the dormant spirit of life in our legal system, and give it an evolutionary outlook."

For some of the modern scholars who try to reconcile this Islamic way of political thought with modern political mechanisms, these procedural means for legitimacy are adequate to close the institutional gap between Islamic and Western ways of political understanding that emerged during the phase of civilizational challenge. But it should be underlined that these procedural conditions, too, have epistemologico-axiological bases directly attached to ontological transcendency and therefore philosophically and methodologically are different from similar procedures in Western political institutions. Their legislative function and power are only meaningful within the context of the epistemologico-axiological legitimacy mentioned before.

The fundamental essence of the issue of political legitimacy is whether or not these epistemologico-axiological presuppositions have been realized. The elitist approach of *falâsifah* in the process of the establishment of political authority and the relatively more democratic approach of the jurists through these procedural means intersect on this basic characteristic. Thus, the historical experiences during the election of the first caliphs and their applications provide several alternatives for the richness of the procedural legitimation of a political authority, but the essential core continued to be on the epistemologico-axiological base, and these procedures have had their true meanings as long as they reflect this fundamental base. On the other hand, the prescriptivist dimension of political legitimacy has been used especially by the scholars as a direct and indirect means to check constituted political authority from the perspective of this epistemologico-axiological base.

The contrast between Western institutions imposed by Western-oriented political elites in Muslim societies and the political images of Muslim masses not only cannot be eliminated but also cannot be understood without an appreciation of the significance of the epistemologico-axiological bases of these political images that emerged because of being referred to ontological transcendency.

CHAPTER 6

POWER THEORIES AND PLURALISM

One of the fundamental questions related to structural modernization in Muslim societies is whether or not a socio-economic functional pluralism might be internalized by these societies. This is not only a subject of institutionalization but also of political culture. It is almost impossible to internalize institutions within a society, in the long run, unless those institutions are supported by a socio-political culture.

From this perspective, the subject of power theories and pluralism is an interesting issue to operationalize our theoretical inquiries related to Islamic and Western paradigmatic unities. The contrast between Islamic religious-cultural pluralism, based on ontologically justified political power, and Western socio-economic functional pluralism, based on an ontologically impenetrable justification of political power, can give us significant clues not only to the influences of imposed institutional functionalization within Muslim societies after the application of pyramidal modernization strategies, but also to the interpretation of historical practices such as the "millet system" in Muslim socio-political structures which could not be set up within a comparative framework of Western experiences. These contrasting interpretations of political power should be compared by relating them to their philosophical and ontologico-axiological antecedents to clarify their ultimate effects on political images, cultures, theories, and institutions.

Ontologically impenetrable justification of political power and Western socio-economic pluralism

Ontologically impenetrable political power

The theoretical background of pluralism, as a special interpretation of the notion of power, is as long as the history of political thought. Therefore the core of pluralist thought is related to the understanding of the notion of power. As Dahl (1957:201-02), one of the leading figures of the pluralist approach, specifies very clearly, the concept of power and its equivalences in several languages such as *Macht, pouivior, pussance, Gewalt, Herrschaft, imperium, potestas, auctoritas, potentia,* etc., are as ancient and ubiquitous as that which any social theory can boast. The awkward word power, which has no verb form in English, derives from Latin and French words meaning "to be able," while the German word *Macht* derives from *mögen* and has almost the same meaning (see Dahl, 1957:79-80; Wagner, 1969:3). Due to the fact that the essential issue of a semantic analysis of a key-concept is its process of gaining a conceptual meaning, we have to concentrate both on the historico-theoretical and on the semantic basis of the concept of power.

The notion of power in ancient Greece, "that every man has power who does that which he wishes at the time when he wishes" (Krieger, 1969:3), is a reflection of the idea that power exists only in the realization of the good because it is "a good of the possessor," as has been defined in Plato's *Gorgias* (1937:I/524-7). Plato's fundamental assumptions on the idea of power might be summarized as the inseparable union of power and the moral purpose of power. His principal conclusion that power is a good was predicated on the assumption that the primary ingredient in power is knowledge.

Aristotle's contribution to the notion of power has theoretical and methodological dimensions. His theoretical contribution, depending on the ethical necessity concerning power in terms of an ideal end, strengthened the substantive and moral idea of power through generalizing the teleological dimension of power. His definition of power "as a source of movement or change, which is another thing than the thing moved or in the same thing qua other" in *Metaphysics* (esp. 1941:764-6, 820-5), shows his analysis related to the potentiality of power. But, his most effective contribution to the interpretation of power, which has been extended to the modern era, is related to the methodological dimension in analyzing the actuality of power which implies a neutrality during the process of analysis in the actual dispersion of power.

When we compare the concepts of power in ancient Greek and Roman political thought, we can say that the Greeks accepted the generic notion of power while the Romans evaluated it as a purely political notion. The Greeks had no authentic notion of political power.[1] The Romans accepted a distinctive conception of political power by emphasizing its neutrality to the ethical and teleological type of power. This created an ontologically impenetrable understanding of power.

The origins of this understanding should be sought in the structure of the Roman law, which strictly separated public from private life. An autonomous sector of the public sphere where power, *potestas*, became an accepted legal category referring to rights and duties, emerged through this separation of public from private life. Power began to be used as an autonomous political concept after this legal usage transformed the Greek idea of ethical power into the Roman idea of political power.

The modern idea of political power may be accepted as a detailed re-emergence of the Roman understanding of political power after a break in the Middle Ages, when the understanding of political power came nearer to the Greek concept than the Roman because of the acceptance of and ethical usage of the notion of power, although the medieval theorists took both the Roman notion of political power as defined by its sources, and the Greek notion of power as defined by its end.The theoretical history of the Middle Ages related to the notion of political power was a transformative process in three stages: (i) the unbalanced emphasis on a legitimate, Christianized power; (ii) the synthesis of legitimate political power with teleological/ethical power; and (iii) the unbalanced emphasis upon Christianized ethical power. That is a process from St. Paul's doctrine that "there is no power but of God and the powers that be ordained of God," to Augustine's understanding of "God as the Creator of all powers," and finally to the synthesis of Thomas Aquinas who interpreted the dignity of the teleological and ethical notion of power within a context of the political sphere (Krieger, 1969:20-2).

---

[1]Arendt (1958:84-97) explains this lack of the authentic notion of political power in ancient Greek by arguing that the egalitarian *polis* left the Greeks with no idea of political authority, which is essential to the notion of political power, because it forced them to borrow surrogates from the non-political authority of fathers over families, reason over experiences, soul over body.

The transformation of the Christian interpretation of in the Middle Ages provided justification for the power structure that existed in the feudal ages. The coexistence of the doctrines both of papal sovereignty and theocratic kingship asserted the plenitude of powers based on the idea of divine appointment, which was used by these centers of power for the justification of their own political purposes (Ullman, 1961:34, 130; Krieger, 1969:22). This plenitude of power in the Middle Ages has been accepted as a special type of legal pluralism by some political scientists (Chuan, 1927:260), although in the epoch of feudalism the political unit was no longer the clan or the people but the district under the control of a seigneur or lord, who was the final wielder of legal power (Jenks, 1898:22).

The idea of divine appointment justified this power structure of legal pluralism originating from socio-economic and socio-political differentiation of feudalism, despite the superficial characterization that power was monopolized theoretically in God's sovereignty. This doctrine of the segmentation of power is also relevant to the content of the power in the hands of the monarch. First it had a theocratic power that, it was claimed, originated from the grace of God. Second, it had a feudal power that was claimed by virtue of contract. In contrast to the Islamic understanding of power, the Christian theory of power aimed to support the coexistence of this plenitude of powers both in an institutional and in a theoretical sense by balancing them rather than reorganizing them in a hierarchical order through an ontological justification. Therefore the Roman understanding of ontologically impenetrable political power could implicitly exist and be effective in the Christian theological interpretation. It easily appeared as a fundamental characteristic of Western political theories when real socio-economic and socio-political forces began to shake papal sovereignty as a symbol of the power structure of the Middle Ages.

The attempts of John of Paris, Philip the Fair, Marsiglio of Padua, and William of Ockham to strengthen royal authority against papal authority might be seen as the first indications of this process. This conflict between papal and royal authorities seeking to be the source of power demolished the medieval synthesis of the notion of by denying the assumptions that the power of the Church was also political and the political power of the state was divinely instituted. This in fact put an end to the impact of teleological assumptions on the notion of political power, and may be accepted as a rediscovery of the Roman ontologically impenetrable and morally neutral definition of power.

The top figure in this rediscovery was Machiavelli, who assumed the notion of political power as an autonomous process categorically divorced from any non-political justification or legitimacy but related to its origin and purpose. This approach resulted in a completed differentiation of ontological, axiological, and political spheres during the process of the interpretation of political power. This Machiavellian trend became the dominant trend in the modern era in the notion of political power and also became the basis of both monist and pluralist interpretations of the secular state, although some others attempted to combine ethics and power. Among these, Spinoza and Rousseau attached an ethical connotation to the very meaning of political power.

This Machiavellian trend to interpret political power based on the differentiation of these spheres became a common methodological ground for both monist and pluralist approaches in modern political theories. For example, Hobbes' monist argument depending on the interpretation of power as a possession enabling its owner to secure some apparent future good has the same methodological background as Benthamite utilitarian pluralism, which opposes Hobbes' notion of power by arguing that the possession of it might become a "national or constitutional evil" due to the reality of the greater quantity of power possessed. In fact, these two conflicting interpretations of power might be accepted as the foundations for the justification and theoretical reasoning of monist and pluralist types of socio-political structures and states, but they conflict with each other in the institutional sphere rather than in philosophical and methodological spheres. These conflicting views in the institutional sphere are two different aspects of the same philosophical-methodological tradition that emerged after the rediscovery of Aristotelian methodology and Roman understanding of ontologically impenetrable political power. Aristotelian methodology led modern power theories to concentrate on the analysis of power, rather than speculating on its essence and mission. This methodology has been supported by the theoretical consequence of the divorce of politics from ontology and axiology.

The evaluation of political power developed by Hobbes was another significant attempt to separate the sphere of politics from ethics. Hobbes defined power in *Leviathan* (n.d.:43) as a possession enabling its owner to secure some apparent future good, while Locke accepted it as a right rather than a possession and bound it with public good rather than the possessor's good. According to him, political power is a right of making laws with penalties of death and consequently all less penalties, for the regulating and preserving of property, and of employing the force of the community, in the execution of such laws and in the defence of the commonwealth from foreign injury. He insists in the same definition that this right should be used only for the public good. (1965:308).

Bentham, whose philosophy of utilitarianism became one of the significant bases of pluralist political thought, opposed Hobbes' notion of power by arguing that the possession of it might become a "national or constitutional evil" in his *Leading Principles of a Constitutional Code* (1843:II/269-72): "The national or constitutional evil is that which has place in so far as the subject matter of the distribution is power. It has placed in this way : the greater the quantity of power possessed, the greater the facility and the incitement to the abuse of it. In a direct way this position applies only to power. But, between power and wealth such is the connection, that each is an instrument for the acquisition of the other, in this way therefore, the position applies to the wealth likewise." In fact, the conflicting interpretations of power might be accepted as the foundations of justification and theoretical reasoning of monist and pluralist type of political structure and state.

These methodological and theoretical characteristics have been systematized since the modern scientific approach in politics through a methodist point of view. Weber's relational interpretation of power (1948:78) is the fundamental contribution of this new approach to the theory of political power. His formulation that "power [*Macht*] is the probability that one actor within a social relationship will be in a position to carry out his own will despite the resistance of the others" (Weber, 1947:152) is a sophisticated formulation of the analytical methodist way of understanding the existing relational power structure through ethical neutrality. This approach differs methodologically from Hobbes' traditional possessive interpretation, but it shares the common theoretical background related to the autonomous character of political power from ontological and ethical antecedents. Tawney (1931:229) enlarged this definition arguing that "power may be defined as the capacity of an individual or a group of individuals to modify the conduct of other individuals or group in the manner which he desires and to prevent his own conduct being modified in the manner in which he does not."

Mills' and Dahl's definitions of power follow the trend set by Weber's relational notion of power, although they are members of opposite approaches from the perspectives of elitist and pluralist political interpretations. The conflicts between this relational interpretation of power and the possessive interpretation, which has been extended from Hobbes to the present by Lasswell and Kaplan, could not eliminate the paradigmatic unity of the theoretical sphere assuming ontologically impenetrable political power, or the methodological sphere assuming an empiric-positivist analytical framework. They have institutional and sociological dimensions rather than philosophical.

There is no essential contradiction between Mills' (1959:9) argument in *Power Elite* that the powerful are "those who are able to realize their will, even if others resist it" and Dahl's (1957:201) intuitive idea of power that "A has power over B to the extent that he can get B to do something that B would not otherwise do." Their conflict is related to the characteristics of the existing power structure rather than to the origins and essence of it. This methodist approach leads to technical evaluations to solve the problem of measurement rather than deep theoretical and philosophical interpretations. As Polsby (1971:11) underlines very clearly, power is conceived by sociologists as one dimension of social life along which people may be stratified, while political scientists have traditionally concerned themselves with power and with the institutional order specialized to the exercise of political power in social life, the state.[2]

In spite of the existence of different interpretations of political power, there is a very significant common base among them. All of modern interpretations might be accepted as reflections of the dominant philosophico-theological inclinations and of the imaginations created by them. Three stages in the post-Machiavellian modern era can be underlined related to the evolution of theories on the political power.

The first stage is the theorization of the ontologically impenetrable power which emerged as a counterpart of the divorce of politics from ontological and ethical antecedents. This stage began with the Machiavellian attempt to set up an autonomous politics under the impact of the rediscovery of the Roman understanding of realistic political power. Hobbes' *nouva scienza* has strengthened the theoretical foundation of this stage, while Locke's interpretation of political power contributed to it a legislative/juristic element. The fundamental characteristic of this period is its rationalistic element, although the impact of Locke's empiric epistemology on his interpretation of political power is also quite evident. As I have shown related to the issue of political legitimacy, a synthesis of empiric and rationalistic elements in the Western paradigm related to its epistemological dimension opened the ways for the second stage.

Second stage can be summarized under the title "relational/observational interpretation of political power." The implicit assumption of this approach is that there is an autonomous social mechanism and that political power is an element of

---

[2]Polsby presents K. Mayer's *Class and Society* (1955), M. Gordon's *Social Class in American Sociology* (1958), and H. Pfantz's "The Current Literature of Social Stratification" (*American Journal of Sociology*, 1953) as examples of the sociologist's approach and Easton's work as an example of the political scientist's approach.

this mechanism. The fundamental problem of this approach is to find the best methodological tool for analyzing the dimension of political power of this mechanism, rather than to check it within the framework of a set of value. Such an approach is very consistent with the dominant philosophical tradition of its background, namely mechanistic world view. Horovitz's following specification is very interesting from this perspective: "Both the empiricists and the theorists viewed the power with awe, as some sort of divine lever by means of which the social system becomes self-regulating. The laissez-faire economic world of Adam Smith became transformed into laissez-faire vision of society as a whole" (Mills, 1974:9-10) Polsby's definition of power as "a subsidiary aspect of the community's social structure" in his *Community Power and Political Theory* (1971:7) might also be taken as an interesting expression of this phenomenon.

The argument that power is never the property of an individual but rather belongs to a group and remains in existence only so long as the group stays together is also a natural consequence of this mechanistic view. Arendt's assertion that power needs no justification, being inherent in the very existence of political communities, but does need legitimacy connects this approach to the Athenian and Roman understandings of power. T. Parsons (1969:252), the leading figure of structural functionalism, defines power within the context of legitimation and obligation by arguing that "power then is generalized capacity to secure the performance of binding obligations by units in a system of collective organization when the obligations are legitimated with the reference to their bearing on collective goals and where in case of recalcitrance there is a presumption of enforcement by negative sanctions—whatever the actual agency of that enforcement." As Horovitz specifies very interestingly "the dominant wings of American sociology during the period between 1940-1960 tended to translate all claims of conflicting power into a delicately system of pattern-maintenance and tension-management" (Mills, 1974:9).

Beside this relational interpretation of power, the possessive interpretation of Hobbes has been extended by some other thinkers. Russell's definition of power as "production of intended effects" (1938:35) and the definition of Lasswell and Kaplan as "simple property... which can belong to a person or group considered in itself" (1950:75) might be mentioned among these.

Bachrach and Baratz (1974:19) criticize this approach on three fronts: (i) this argument fails to distinguish between power over people and power over matter, (ii) one cannot have power in a vacuum but only in relation to someone else, and (iii) the common conception of phenomena mistakenly implies that possession of the instruments of power is tantamount to possession of power itself. But beside this generalization, Lasswell and Mills might be seen as members of another of trend accepting power as a zero-sum phenomenon "which is to say that there is a fixed quantity of power in any relational system and hence any gain of power on the part of A must by definition occur by diminishing the power at the disposal of other units, B, C, D" (1969:252). This interpretation carries the characteristics of the third stage. In spite of these attempts to objectify and to standardize the notion of political power as a reflection of the mechanistic world view and empiric-rationalistic scientism, it never reached a fully illuminating theorization.[3]

---

[3]Because, as Karl Loewenstein (1965) says, "we know what power does but we are unable to define its substance and essence," William Riker (1964) argues that we ought to banish the notion of power rather than redefine it. But, following

The third stage is an extreme extension of this approach: namely, the attempts to prove the measurability of political power, systematized especially by the behavioralists. This stage is a reflection of the movement of scientism in the social sciences. Some of the definitions are very technical, contrary to the theoretical interpretations. The fundamental aim of these technical interpretations is solving the problem of measurement. The definition of the mathematician Shapley and the economist Shubik (1954:787-92) relates only to the power resulting from the right to vote in a system in which voting, and only voting, determines the outcomes. March (1957::222-26), as a political scientist, tries to define the concept of power by measuring comparative amounts of influence, while Cartwright (1959:183-220), as a social psychologist, defines and measures power as an ability to force others to do one's binding, which is very close to the definition of Dahl given above. Karlsson's (1964:341-49) definition of power in terms of utilities depends on the ability to decrease alters utility reversely to the idea of Shapley and Shubik whose definition of power rests on the ability to increase ego's utility.

Social change/dynamism and the imagination of unilinear progress: Institutionalization of power

One of the most significant imaginative elements of modern Western culture is its implicit assertion of the unilinear progress of human beings throughout history, which makes social change an inescapable necessity. Thus, a natural dynamism has been assumed in time and space. If justice and movement are the two essential concepts of ancient philosophy, it might be said that the human imagination has generally shifted toward the side of movement, which assumes a dynamic process of change, as opposed to justice as cosmologico-ontological and social-political harmony and stability.

Two basic origins of this characteristic of modern imagination are the theory of motion during the Renaissance, especially after the rediscovery of the ancient idea of movement, and the Newtonian mechanistic cosmological imagination with its new set of necessities. With the ascendancy of the theory of motion and its Newtonian transformation into an inescapable natural phenomenon, the necessity of movement became the center of both cosmological and social imagination. The idea of the unilinear progress reached the status of dogma in the Enlightenment, and the grand theories of the nineteenth century on the history of mankind, such as those of Hegel and Marx, were based on this fundamental assumption.

A belief in unilinear progress involves the assumption that a pattern of change exists in the history of mankind, that this pattern is known, that it consists of irreversible changes in one general direction only, and that this direction is towards improvement from a less to a more desirable state of affairs (Van Doren, 1967:4-6; Pollard, 1971:9). Such a presupposition of unilinear progress and irreversible change within a mechanistic flow of history led to an idea of the institutionalization of power specified by the dynamic elements of this flow. This in turn meant the justification as necessary phenomena of the existing power structures. The imagination of determinative links changed parallel to this phenomenon, and

---

Mills' claim, we have to say that power as the realization of human will remains the critical axis about which the social commonwealth spins.

economics began to be accepted as the greatest determining factor in social change because of its reflection of the existing power structure related to the material environment. The rise of scientism in economics during this period is not a coincidence. The relativity of moral values as a reflection of the secularization of axiology and the idea of limited theism as the counterpart of the liberal theories of those, such as J. S.Mill, who assigned a determinative role to economics are philosophico-theological reflections of this phenomenon.

As will be shown in the following lines, the most characteristic contrast between Islamic and Western civilizations rest upon this fact of the links of determination from the most determinative factor to the least one. Islamic civilization strictly assumes a determinative link from ontology to epistemology, from epistemology to axiology, from axiology to politics, and from politics to economics. In the modern West, this scheme is just the opposite.

The consequences of this Western phenomenon related to the institutionalization of power might be summarized thus: (i) the assumption of unilinear progress; (ii) dynamic pluralistic adventure of social change; (iii) the determinative supremacy of economics over politics; (iv) socio-economic pluralism, in the sense of economic stratification, as the basic parameter of socio-political differentiation; and (v) institutionalization of power as a reflection of socio-political autonomous institutional pluralism based on the socio-economic dispersion of material power, namely the formation of interest groups.

Phenomenological background of pluralism

Beginning with the Greek and Roman period, it should be underlined that these societies carried some basic origins of philosophical and socio-political pluralism, although these origins might be traced back to the Indo-European culture in the from of polytheism and pantheism as the philosophico-theological base for the evolution of the philosophical pluralism that will be analyzed in the following lines. Greek political culture was an example of monism, in the institutional sense of state organization, because of the absence of rival groups and organizations as a natural consequence of being a city-state in which life and politics were simple, although the pluralistic elements, both in the sense of socio-economic stratification and in the sense of philosophical pluralism (cosmologico-ontological particularization of divinity), were implicitly contained. The Stoic ideal of a universal system under one government carried this institutional monist structure of Greek city-state politics into the Roman imperial state structure, but philosophical pluralism continued to be strengthened as an indication of socio-cultural continuity.

The Middle Ages was the period at the end of this institutional monism, when Western societies disintegrated into a thoroughly pluralistic order, especially in the legal structure, because of the effect of diverse private laws which created a three-fold division of law into civil, religious, and commercial. The civil law also disintegrated because of territorial decentralization. The feudal structure of the political system with its vast hierarchy of quasi-autonomous kings and lords, the establishment of the Christian Church as a new ethical socio-cultural and socio-political organization, and the nucleus of the emerging socio-economic class perceiving the need of organization after the gradual development of craft industry and sea commerce created a segmentation of political, economic, and religious spheres, each with its own independent system of law and government and internally autonomous organization.

Beside these nuclei of institutional pluralism, philosophical and ontological bases of political pluralism began to be theorized in the form of the theory of "two swords." This legitimated and justified the current pluralistic structure on a reformed philosophical and ethical ground after the transformation of early rebellious Christianity into an institutionalized Church as a new factor in political life. St. Paul's view that "there is no power but of God" and "the powers that be are ordained of God" and St. Augustine's understanding that "God is the Creator of all powers" were interpreted as an ontological justification of the existing power structure rather than as an ontological-political unity as in Islam. Therefore the arguments of such leading figures as Marsiglio of Padua and Philip the Fair on the absolute authority of secular organizations were fundamentally religious and translegal. The justification of the power structure, changed after social and economic developments, rested on the same philosophical-ethical base as in the Middle Ages.

In this way, the pluralistic entity of the medieval period continued to strengthen its position within Western social life until the industrial era, although the absolutist sovereign states which began to be formed in the fourteenth century set up a superficial monist structure upon a pluralist philosophical justification and upon a weak, but living, socio-economic pluralism. For example, for Hobbes, the prince of the monistic thinkers, there is a clear demarcation between the sphere of religion and politics—the political state should be absolute in its own sphere. In fact, this is a continuation of the ontological-political pluralism of Western political thought, while according to Islamic political understanding almost all social and political issues should be interpreted on the basis of ontological-political unity.

The institutional particularization of the political structure in its own sphere occurred parallel to the rise of a new economic class in Western Europe which created a transformation from the medieval guild system to modern labor-industrial organizations. Thus, pluralism began to be effective as a natural result of the increase in economic associations and organizations, as new structural factors in social life began to be accepted as the central mechanism in favor of freedom, against despotism or misuse of power. Political pluralism, in the sense of division of power, began to be accepted as the first condition of liberty. Lamennais's saying "who says liberty, says association" together with Proudhon's formulation of "multiply association and be free" (Nisbet, 1962:268) are indications of political pluralism's resting on the increase of association-type economic organizations. The institutional particularization within the state was theorized by Montesquieu as an extension of the argument that "the only safeguard against power is the rival power." Lord Acton combined political pluralism with liberty saying that "liberty depends upon the division of power" (Nisbet, 1962: 270).[4]

---

[4]This associational and institutional particularization of the socio-political system has been explained by Tannenbaum very clearly: "In the balance of institutional power lie the possibilities for a harmonization of personal freedom and associative authority. The road to social peace is the balance of social institutions and a wise statesmen would strengthen those institutions that seemed to be losing ground, for the only way to peace in this world of fallible human nature is to keep

This associational and institutional particularization of the political system in Western societies was directly connected to the dispersion of socio-economic power in the hands of some functional interest groups and classes after industrial societies, as compared to pre-industrial societies, led to a concept of a pluralistic society made up of various institutionally isolated sectors which emerged with the dispersion of socio-economic wealth as a realization of material power. The social roles and identities of individuals began to be defined by these functional groups and classes.

Socio-economic pluralism: Basic parameter of socio-political differentiation

Although the pluralist approach might be divided into several schools of thought, the systematization of modern political pluralism has been realized primarily by two groups, namely European and American political pluralism.

European political pluralism. The main representatives of European political pluralism are legal historians, such as F. W. Maitland in England, Otto von Gierke in Germany, and L. Duguit in France; the English economist G. D. H. Cole; the English political scientist H. Laski; the English clergyman J. N. Figgis; a professor H. Krabbe; and French statesman J. P. Boncour. These persons rejected "both the Hegelian notion that the modern state as a virtual monopoly on legitimate authority and the 19th century liberal belief that the individual exists in a social vacuum" (Kelso, 1978:11). Pluralist theorists such as Maitland, Cole, and von Gierke drew their arguments and illustrations from the example of the Middle Ages, a time characterized by the inability of the predecessor of the modern state to extend its control over such autonomous entities as the Church, the universities, the guilds, and the free cities (Merkl, 1972:69-70). Von Gierke and Maitland tried to transform the idea of the independence of associational structure into a consistent theory of political system and state by assuming associations as real personalities having a collective consciousness and a will independent of the minds and wills of its several members. According to these two, such associations, as originating agencies in the development of law, may function as organs through which common beliefs of a legal character find their way into rules of law (Burns, 1960:112). These ideas have two significant consequences: (i) there are other units beside individuals, like associations and organizations, of which society is composed, and (ii) the state does not have all-inclusive sovereignty over the interconnections between these units.

Figgis (1914:58), speaking on behalf of the Christian Church as an autonomous group, tried to interpret these associational views within a theoretical and religious context and was interested in the independence of the Church, although he also insisted upon the independence of other social groups, such as trade unions, colleges, and families. Assuming that the best social structure is that which gives the individual the best opportunity for self-development, he argues that the real personality of groups must be realized in order not to prevent the self-realization of the individuals. Associational freedom is much more significant than individual

---

all human institutions strong, but none too strong, relatively weak, but not as weak as to despair of their survival" (Nisbet, 1962:270).

freedom in Figgis' theory because of the assumption that self-realization may be achieved in groups.

Boncour gives great significance to occupational and professional associations because they have arisen spontaneously in all countries and have developed rapidly to a stage in which they impose rules upon their own members and dictate conditions to the rest of the society. He claims that the existence of several sovereign professional associations can prevent the exploitation of majorities in a democratic system because of the lack of ability of the majority to perceive the interest of the whole population.

In the theory of the British pluralist Laski, these arguments all rest on a different base, namely individualism, and Laski's theory might therefore be called individualistic pluralism. Laski's pluralism assumes a different idea of human society. Contrary to Cole and Figgis, who claim that man develops his personality in various associations and the functional organizations of society, Laski argues that man is morally autonomous: "he can determine in what his self-realization consists, that is, each man can choose his own way and ends. The condition that the society has to put up with is one in which different men pursue different ends differently" (Laski, 1931:47).

Cole, who argues that pluralism should be established in order to safeguard freedom and to ensure justice, was the leading figure of Guild Socialism. Again his notion of pluralism has been systematized around a key concept of human personality which depends in Cole's theory on the assumption that "man in society is a complex being, complex essentially in the interests and the groups with which he associates" (1966:31). Arguing that a democratic society should satisfy men's wants in an orderly system and at the same time save their freedom, he gives a special significance to the functions of associations as "any group of persons pursuing a common purpose of aggregation of purposes by a course of cooperative action extending beyond a single act and for this purpose laying down in however a rudimentary form" (Cole, 1920:37) shows their key position as intermediary mechanisms between individual and society, which according to him is made up of a multiplicity of associations of various kinds. Due to the fact that these associations are formed by a common interest, these ideas reflect the organizational structure of socio-economic pluralism. Although he criticized the understanding of state as sovereign body, he contrarily suggests a Democratic Supreme Court of Functional Equity (Cole, 1920:135) which will be a joint body to coordinate all the main function of society.

Another group of pluralists in Europe were interested chiefly in the juristic consequences and characteristics of the theory in the beginning of the century. The leading figures of this group were Leon Duguit and Hugo Krabbe. Duguit's pluralistic views rest on a specific notion of law which has no necessary relation with state. He strictly opposes the idea that the state has a law-making function, arguing that the state itself is composed merely of a group of governors who are themselves limited by law. His rejection of the assumption of a naturalistic law as a higher law of nature inherent in the order of the universe and embodying the indefeasible rights of the individual led him to refuse the sovereignty of bodies with sacred rights together with the rejection of the special mission of the state. Contrary to Laski, Duguit's pluralism is collectivist rather than individualistic. Law, with the function of providing social solidarity, is not only superior to the state but also to the individual in Duguit's interpretation of pluralism.

American political pluralism. Although the pluralist school of philosophers reached the height of its popularity in the first quarter of this century in Europe, the past three decades have seen American political scientists grow more deeply interested in pluralist theory and interest-group theory. The internal consistency and theoretical framework of American pluralism after World War II was much stronger than that of the early pluralist movement in Europe, which had significant differences and contradicting ideas among the members. The main representatives of this pluralistic intellectual trend in the United States are R. Dahl, D. Riesman, V. Key, D. Truman, W. Sayre, H. Kaufman, E. Banfield, C. Lindblom, W. Kornhauser, A. Downs, D. Braybrook, and J. Coleman. This group of American pluralists has been especially affected by the legacy of Tocqueville, Madison, and Arthur Bentley.

David Riesman's *The Lonely Crowd* (1953) and C. Wright Mills' *Power Elite* (1955) are the typical examples of the two dominant rival tendencies in American political thought, the pluralist and elitist interpretations of American political system. Mills argues that there is a tendency toward increasing concentration of power in the hands of a unified power elite composed of men whose positions enable them to transcend the environment of ordinary men and women and that this power elite determines all major policies. He interprets the pluralistic way of thinking thus: "There are of course other interpretations of the American system of power. The most usual is that it is a moving balance of many competing interests. The image of balance, at least in America, is derived from the idea of the economic market: in the 19th century the balance was thought to occur between a great scatter of individuals and enterprises in the 20th century it is thought to occur between great interest blocks" (Mills, 1974:30).

Riesman, on the other hand, claims that the tendency is toward increased dispersion of power in American politics. Rejecting the existence of a power elite, he argues that "there has been in the last fifty years a change in the configuration of power in America in which a single hierarchy with a ruling class at its head has been replaced by a number of veto groups among which power is dispersed" (Riesman, 1953:239). This tendency toward dispersion of power creates a diversified and balanced plurality and monopolist competition among organized interest groups. Riesman's view is diametrically opposed to Mills' ideas on the coincidence of interests among major institutions of economic, political, and military order.

As Richards (1972:35) specifies, American pluralism originates from the assumption that a modern industrial society is differentiated into a wide range of sub-groups, the members of which share certain interests in common and provide the potential for coordinated action. According to Dahl (1967:24): "The fundamental axiom in the theory and practice of American pluralism is, I believe this, instead of single center and sovereign power there must be multitude centers of power, none of which is or can be wholly sovereign. Although the only legitimate sovereign is the people, in the perspective of American pluralism even the people ought never to be an absolute sovereign, consequently no part of the people such as a majority ought to be absolutely sovereign.... [This dispersion of power] can settle conflicts peacefully: because one center of power is set against another, power itself will be tamed civilized, controlled and limited to decent human purposes; because even minorities are provided with opportunities to veto solutions; because constant negotiations among different centers of power are necessary to make decisions... not merely to the benefit of one partisan to all the parties to a conflict."

So conflict is a very significant key-concept in pluralist theory to show the dynamic element of the understanding of social change led by socio-economic groups as the centers of the institutionalization of power. Socio-economic pluralism as the basic parameter of socio-political differentiation in Western society has been justified through this argument based on the implicit assumption of the inevitability of social change. The concept of conflict is the common element of pluralist and monist interpretations of state.

It is very interesting that the concept of conflict in pluralist theory, especially in Dahl's interpretation, has been affected by the Hobbesian understanding of human nature. Following Hobbes, who was the pivotal figure in stratification and sovereignty theories, Dahl argues that conflict seems to be an inescapable aspect of community life and hence of human being because men have diverse interests. This idea of diversification of abilities and interests originated with James Madison, the leading pluralist figure during the establishment of the American constitutional system.

According to pluralistic theory, man, whose existence as a social being is conditioned by a set of contradictory tendencies that make him a member of some political system, is unable to live with others without conflict, and therefore communities search for ways of adjusting conflicts so that community life will be possible and tolerable. The assumption that conflict is a natural and inescapable fact of human life leads to a following assumption that factions, parties, and groups are natural facts of social life. When someone says he opposes every faction and party, what he usually means is that he opposes every fraction, every party, every interest except his own. This assumption of the naturality of plurality in socio-economic life might be accepted as an intrinsic extension of the philosophical assumption of pluralist universe.

The pluralist theory draws its inspiration from the group-interaction approach to politics, and it maintains that policy is the product of group interactions and conflicts in which a stable, generally salutary balance among group interests is approximated. This argument implies a fairly open, competitive bargaining process. As Kelso (1978:13) specifies very well, the representatives of political pluralism, like their laissez-faire counterparts in economics, view the political arena as a competitive market place in which any entrepreneur can gain entry to merchandise his views. They see political life as a multiplicity of functionally specialized centers of influence competing for and appealing to several publics and their elected officials. In the theoretical framework of political pluralism, the leaders of these private and public organizations and groups do not constitute a power elite because they lack the means for communicating among themselves or for coordinating policy outcomes.

Lindblom (1977:258), one of the representatives of political pluralism, claims that these functionally specialized centers of influence and groups are bound together by Durkheim's organic solidarity, by differences that make them dependent one another. Likewise, Dahl tries to point out in his book *Who Governs* (1961) that there is a considerable functional specialization by issue areas like education, highways, etc., although small numbers of people still do most of the governing. The competitive situation forces the participating groups to be dependent upon legitimate public officials, who have a balancing relationship in his theory. Thus resolution of major conflicts is referred to and frequently guided by men elected in accordance with them, while these men, in turn, must be sensitive not only to the balance of active group interests, but also to the less articulated interests that can manifest themselves in many responses and election-day consequences.

This group structure creates a self-regulating and self-correcting political system, similar in the theory to Adam Smith's invisible hand, so that if particular groups do start to accumulate excessive amounts of power, countervailing forces are likely to become active to prevent the abuse of power by checking and limiting their actions. Truman (1951:114) considers this phenomena of "potential groups and coalitions" as the main obstacle against the monopolization of power. This coalition between interest groups should be time bounded to prevent the establishment of a group of elite. Sayre and Kaufman (1970:710) argue that the self-regulating nature of the political system drives from the existence of multiple decision-making points.

This theoretical explanation of political pluralism rests on a specific interpretation of power, as analyzed above. There are two essential presuppositions of the pluralist approach related to the interpretation of power. The first basic presupposition is that nothing categorical can be assumed about power in any community, rejecting the stratification thesis that some group necessarily dominates a community. The second presupposition runs counter to stratification theory's assumption that power distribution is a more or less permanent aspect of social structure. Pluralists believe that power may be tied only to issues and that issues can be fleeting or persistent, provoking coalitions among interest groups and citizens ranging in their duration from momentary to semi-permanent (1971:115).

So, the fundamental cornerstones and properties of the current pluralist theory resting upon the philosophical background discussed before, might be summarized as (i) group interaction approach to politics, (ii) the differences of the pattern of influences and interactions due to issue and scope, (iii) the rejection of the categorical assumptions about power, (iv) different and competing structures of interests, (v) accepting the political life as a multiplicity of functionally specialized centers, (vi) the lack of the means for communicating among the leaders of groups, (vii) the absence of unified, coordinated, mobilized organizational activity, (viii) the semi-permanent characteristics of power distribution, (ix) the human behavior as a result of inertia, (x) time-bounded characteristics of the coalitions, and (xi) the diversification of the leadership roles.

Depending these philosophical background and assumptions the pluralist theory, as being the defender of the pluralist democracy in United States, provides a rejoinder to the theory of the ruling elites and to those who see the capitalist system "as corrupt and exploitative."

Philosophical background of pluralism

According to Spinoza, the order of ideas is the same as the order of things (*ordo idearum est ac ordo rerum*). The philosophical background of pluralism, as a special interpretation of the notion of power (dispersion of power), is as long as the history of political thought, even though many scholars argue that modern pluralism flourished only in the first quarter of the twentieth century, in the sense that "regarding the state as only one of a number of sovereign agencies to which the members of a modern community render allegiance, went back to the theories of Otto von Gierke and Maitland in the late 19th century" (Burns, 1963:112).

According to the traditional view, the highly segmented and differentiated social structure of industrial society, as compared to pre-industrial societies, led to a concept of "pluralistic society standing for the notion that industrial society is made up of various institutionally isolated sectors which require from the modern individual the ability to play disparate roles, thus imprinting on him disparate identities" (Zijdervald, 1972:127). The current discussion occurs around these sociological and technical interpretations and lacks the philosophical background and origin of the pluralistic approach. But neither this assumption that pluralism is an artifact of industrial society nor the classical approach that political pluralism is a response or critique to the idea of sovereign state based on abstract monism can explain the inherent cultural philosophical continuity of Western political thought and pluralism within its context. We can explain the philosophical background of the political pluralism referring to our analysis on the Western paradigm in chapter 2.

Although the historical accounts of pluralism trace its source in various fields back to W. James (philosophy), to the Middle Ages and Otto von Gierke's studies on this theme (law), to the encyclical of Pope Leo XXIII, to various church movements in the nineteenth century and to syndicalism (politics), if we accept the key assumption of pluralist thought as "multiple center of powers" or a "dispersion of power" the philosophical background of pluralism related to the justification of political power should be searched for a complete analysis of the methodological an theoretical paradigmatic unity of Western philosophical-political tradition.

From the cosmological and ontological perspective, philosophical pluralism has some significant relationships with polytheistic and pantheistic *Weltanschauungs*. Pluralism has been accepted as a specific type of contemporary form of polytheism by many thinkers due to the pluralistic assumption that "nothing but the plural, the many, the variegated, is true reality" (Fries, 1969:139). James combines this multi-central understanding of philosophical pluralism with a pluralistic conception of God and the universe based on a comprehensive critique of a theistic cosmological and ontological understanding that God and his creatures are *toto genere* distinct. According to James' analysis, the ontological consequence of theism is accepting man as a mere ontological outsider to God rather than as an intimate partner. His alternative pluralistic cosmology, ontology, and epistemology, grounded in an alternative conception of God, is an interesting synthesis of polytheism and pantheism as an *Identitätsphilosophie*: "God as intimate soul and reason of the universe has always seemed to some people a more worthy conception than God as external creator" (James, 1909:28). "We are indeed internal parts of God and external creations, on any possible reading of the pan-psychic system. Yet because God is not absolute, but is himself a part when the system is conceived pluralistically, his functions can be taken as not wholly dissimilar to those of the other smaller parts—as similar to our functions consequently" (James, 1909:318).

The synthesis originated from ancient times and is a transition from the idea of several absolutes (polytheism), or no absolute (because of acceptance of several absolutes at the same time), to the idea of the identification with the Absolute (pantheism). The contradiction of James' philosophical pluralism is that he tries to reject certain qualities which traditionally pertain to an absolute. For example, he images an absolute which is not all-inclusive, but he does not explain clearly how a being will be absolute without being all-inclusive, because the lack of all-inclusiveness means, logically, relativeness at the same time. James' pluralistic universe appears as "a congregation of psychic macrocosms, in which all human souls merge" (Chuan, 1927: 201).

There is an evident relationship between this pantheistic conception of God and anti-teleological interpretation of philosophical pluralism: "There is no really inherent order, but it is we who project order into the world by selecting objects and tracing relations so as to gratify our intellectual interests" (James, 1909:10). The axiological and methodological extensions of this ontological pluralism are pragmatism and radical empiricism.

Radical empiricism is the epistemological dimension of philosophical pluralism. James argues that empiricism means the habit of explaining the wholes by parts and that rationalism means the habit of explaining parts by wholes. Rationalism thus preserves affinities with monism, since wholeness goes with union, while empiricism inclines to pluralistic views: "since we actually find many discontinuities in our experience, the hypothesis of a block universe that is integrated through and through into one single system is totally untenable" (James, 1909:217-22). Contrary to this view, the members of the opposite side argue that pluralism disrupts the connections and relations which constrain it and brings "the many and manifold into a reciprocally hostile position" (Stahlin, 1961:146). These conflicting ideas are extensions of the conflict each-form of pluralism and all-form of monism. James concludes (1909:324) that in the each form, a thing may be connected by intermediary things with a thing with which it has no immediate or essential connection while the all-form allows of no taking up and dropping of connections, for in the all, the parts are essentially and eternally co-implicated.

Pragmatism, assuming that an idea is true if it possesses some subsequent utility, is influential over the representatives of political pluralism, while empiricism becomes a methodological tool to discover and justify the existent power structure of "the real world." His pragmatism was, in fact a response to the traditional monistic way of thought in the form of Hegelian and neo-Hegelian idealism (Hsiao, 1927:177). There is a very close theoretical and imaginative connection between pragmatism and utilitarianism which can be "traced back in modern form at least into seventeenth century and one can include within it on the one hand conservative thinkers such as Paley and on the other hand virtual anarchists such as Goodwin" (Bramsted & Melhuish, 1978:13), although it has been systematized by Bentham whose basic psychological assumption was that what men actually seek in life is pleasure and happiness. Bentham's essential value-judgement was that pleasure is the only thing which can be reached in itself. The indebtedness of James as pragmatist to J. S. Mill shows the preparatory process for the idea of pragmatism as the axiological base of the modern political pluralism.

All of these basic ontological, epistemological, axiological, and methodological characteristics of philosophical-political pluralism, such as philosophical pluralism, pragmatism and radical empiricism, might be accepted as modern extensions of ancient polytheism, Epicureanism, and Aristotelian empiricism within the continuity of the Western tradition.

In short, we can say that the philosophical background of modern political pluralism should be analyzed within the context of ontological polytheism and pantheism, axiological pragmatism and utilitarianism, and methodological radical empiricism. The absence of any idea of ontological transcendency as an absolute and living being in polytheistic and pantheistic ontology leads to an interpretation of the powers of God(s) and the power of the other beings as existing on the same ontological sphere. The resemblances between ancient Greek myths which showed a relationship between the gods and the aristocratic way of life have direct theoretical and imaginative links with this *Weltanschauung* based on cosmologico-ontological particularization and proximity. This approach forms a way of justification of the existent power structure without appealing to an ontological transcendent within a hierarchical framework creating an ontologically impenetrable justification of political power. The particularization of divinity as a result of polytheistic and pluralistic ontology in a philosophical sphere results in the justification of the pluralistic power on a social sphere through a process of *Weltanschauung*, while the image of an intimate God as a final assumption of pantheism becomes a basis of justification of existing power structures through the understanding of a natural teleology directed by the "invisible hand". The understanding of the ontologically impenetrable power of Western socio-economic pluralism implicitly cuts down the link between ontology and politics, together with these implicit pantheistic and polytheistic elements, and systematizes it through a methodology of radical empiricism.

Ontologically justified political power and Islamic religious-cultural pluralism

Ontologically justified political power

In contrast to Western experience, the Islamic tradition has a complete theocentric interpretation and justification of political power, which becomes the theoretical background of religious-cultural pluralism and institutional monism in Islamic history. The ontological transcendency around the concept of Allâh as a living presence implies an ontologically justified political power in Islamic political culture and images which assumes a very strong and direct link between ontological transcendency and political power. The ontological antecedent that the totality of power and authority belongs only to Allâh causes a political consequence that political power could be justified only through an ontological interpretation of power. This understanding of power forms a holistic framework from a philosophical-political way of thought together with the idea of the human responsibility and the unity of life.

The strong and direct link between ontological transcendency and political power has its origin in the Qur'ân and the *hadîths* as the sources of '*aqâ'id* and *fiqh* as comprehensive theoretical and juridic schemes. The Qur'ânic call (4:59) for Muslims to obey God, the Prophet, and "those of you who are in authority [*ulul amr min kum*]" became the basis not only of the link between ontology and politics but also of the ontological justification of the political power in the writings of all Muslim political theorists. This Qur'ânic calling has been supported by several *hadîths*: "He who obeys me, obeys Allâh and he who obeys the Imâm obeys me, and he who rebels against me rebels against Allâh, and he who rebels against the Imâm rebels against me," and "Fear Allâh and obey Him, and if a flat-nosed, shrunken-headed Abyssinian slave is invested with power over you, hearken to him and obey him," (Abû Yûsuf, 1977:10) are two significant samples of the *hadîths* providing this theoretical link.

There is almost no attempt in the Islamic political accumulation to justify political power without appealing to its ontological dimension. The parallelism between ontological and political approaches in Islam on the issue of political power is the basic differentiating characteristic compared to the Western philosophical-political tradition. It implies not only a specific political identity given to individuals, but also the mission of the state as the institutionalization of political power and its limitations. The principle specified by the *hadîth* that even an Arab noble on occasion should obey a flat-nosed, shrunken-headed Abyssinian slave should be accepted as revolutionary when compared to age of feudalism in Western Europe, where socio-political identifications and orientations were determined only through caste-like socio-economic differentiation. This fact could be interpreted only through the dependency of socio-political identification on the ontological identification in confrontation with ontological transcendency. The distinctive character of Islamic socio-political and socio-economic equalitarianism is an axiological result of its ontological dimension that every human being is on the same ontological sphere as every other and therefore does not have any privilege except the fulfillment of his divine responsibility (*taqwa*).

The idea that the totality of power and authority belongs to Allâh implies at the same time the temporality and relativity of the power in the forms of economic materials or political status on this earth. Therefore the exercise of power could appear only after the justification of it via appealing to the absolute power of Allâh. The concept of *wilâyah* used by Ibn Taymiyyah is a typical key-term to show this approach to political power. His argument that all exercises of authority (*wilâyah*) as a realization of power are actions of piety by which man, as the vicegerent of Allâh, approaches Allâh and by which those who are invested with authority are the representatives of Allâh is a good formulation of the parallelism between ontological and political hierarchies. This term is not used merely for the authority of the caliph as the person at the top of the political hierarchy but also for general public authority, including all levels of government. According to Ibn Taymiyyah (1988:18), this chain of ethico-political responsibility is based on the *hadîth* that "all of you are shepherds, every shepherd is responsible [*mas'ûl*] for his flock" (Bukhârî, Ahkâm, 1; Muslim, Imâra, 20). Such an interpretation means enlargement of ethico-political responsibility and socio-political authority throughout the whole society, since each man becomes master and servant at the same time, as Fârâbî argues.

The understanding of ontologically justified political power has two significant consequences, one related to the origin of power and the other to the exercise of power. The question of the origin of power is an issue of *'aqâ'id*, while the question of the exercise of power is an issue of *fiqh* and the institutionalization of political power. The interconnected relationship of *'aqâ'id* and *fiqh* within the holistic framework makes ontologically justified political power the anchor point of the Islamic political theories and cultures. The antecedents related to the origin of power appealing to the sovereignty of Allâh specify the mission of the state as the ultimate institutionalization of political authority. Therefore we can say, using the "ideal types" of modern state theories, that the Islamic state as the locus of the political authority is ontologically instrumental and institutionally transcendental. It is ontologically instrumental because it is a governmental instrument to form a socio-political atmosphere within which the ontological relationship could be set up best between Allâh as the absolute sovereign and His creatures. Therefore, in contrast to some types of state-centered Western totalitarianism, the state in Islamic political theories does not have a meaning as an abstract institution, but its existence can be justified only through its instrumentality for the realization of the ontological relationship.

Social balance/stability and imagination of circular evolution: Institutionalization of power

This theoretical instrumentality created transcendental institutionalization in Islamic political history due to the exercise of ontologically justified political power for the fulfillment of the substantive mission formulated by Ibn Taymiyyah as upholding the authority of Allâh to provide the conditions to enlist man in His true service. Institutional transcendentalism as a result of the concentration of political power to fulfill this substantive mission has been theoretically justified by setting up a correlative relationship between cosmological teleology and political order. Fakhraddîn al-Râzî, Fârâbî, and Ghazzâlî provide typical examples of this relationship in their organismic interpretations of the political order through biological similes, arguing that the whole governmental structure is akin to the human body.

They used this organismic argument to support their arguments for the qualifications of the imâm. Fârâbî's (1968) *al-raîs al-awwal* and Râzî's *al-sâyis al-mutlaq* should be as perfect as humanly possible due to the reality that the qualifications of the political leader became the central question of such concentrated power structure. Al-Jâhiz (1969) argued that ideally the imâm should possess outstanding intellectual and moral qualities, while Fârâbî (1964) likened his supreme head to God because he put everyone and everything in the most suitable place. Fârâbî's argument is an interesting adaptation of cosmological teleology to political order.

This meticulousness in creating a socio-political order as an extension of cosmological teleology has four significant results in the theory and practice of Islamic political history: (i) subordination of economics to politics; (ii) understanding of the circular evaluation of social stability and order as being centered in justice, compared to the dynamic pluralistic adventure of social change; (iii) equalitarian-solidarist views of social structure (*ta'âwun*), compared to socio-economic stratification which emerges from the abuse of wealth in the hands of some socio-economic groups; and (iv) concentration of power through institutional centralization of the governmental organs to maintain political order, compared to a socio-political autonomous institutional pluralism based on the socio-economic dispersion of material power.

The first and second consequences are important in understanding Muslim political consciousness, which accepts political activity as a special mission in establishing justice over the whole world. In the political writings of Islamic history, there is a common approach in favor of the subordination of economics to politics. In fact, politics has always been linked directly to axiological presuppositions through a specific understanding of ethics. The direction of the theoretical and imaginative impact might be formulated as from ontology to epistemology, from epistemology to axiology (ethics), from axiology to politics, and from politics to economics (material world).

This Islamic subordination of economics to politics has some parallels in Platonic political analysis. Ibn Rushd's conclusions in his commentary on the *Republic* are very significant indicators of the Islamic mentality, its relationship to the organismic interpretation of society,[5] and its opposition to the socio-economic pluralism in Western civilization: "The bad states are in reality many states, even though their area may be in one locality, because in them the political administration is only for the sake of the economy, and not economics for the sake of the politics. So if a state is called one, it is by accident. For the Ideal State with its parts is like the body as a whole; before speaking of the whole body, the hand or the foot, for example, exists only for the sake of the limbs which are parts of it. But with those States the situation is exactly opposite; for their political community exists in general only by a sort of compulsion in order to preserve the economy." (Ibn Rushd, 1966:151). He argues that this is self-evident for anyone who is even a little versed in this science.

His argument, parallel to Plato, that justice consists in every one of its citizens doing only that for which he is destined individually, (Ibn Rushd, 1966:160) strengthens the assertion of the subordination of economics to politics for the stability of the social structure and for the permanency of the ideal state.[6] The hierarchical categorization of arts is another clear evidence for the subordination of economics to politics in Ibn Rushd's political philosophy which based on the assumptions that the art of politics as the art of governing states is absolute master over all the other arts, and that there exists a master intellectual faculty which is the faculty through which the actions of this art come into being in material things. (Ibn Rushd, 1966:194). The other practical arts, which are parts of economic life, are subordinated to the master art, namely politics.

The idea of unilinear development through the enlargement of material power in Western political consciousness, which developed especially in the Age of Enlightenment, does not have any place in the axiological base of this mentality. The circular interpretation of social stability focused on justice formulated by Fakhraddîn al-Râzî, Ibn Khaldûn, and Tursun Beg demonstrates this fundamental difference.

Fakhraddîn al-Râzî understands social stability in the following way. "The world," he says, "is a garden, whose waterer [abar] is the dynasty [dawlah], the dynasty is an authority [sultân], whose guardian [hâjib] is the Sharî'ah, the

---

[5] His arguments that there is nothing which brings more evil and confusion to the State than when its citizens say of something 'this is mine' and 'this is not mine' and that the whole body feels pain when one finger is in pain, so that through this pain the condition of the whole body is determined are two illuminating examples from the many passages in which Ibn Rushd presents his organismic interpretation. (Ibn Rushd, 1966:171).

[6]"This is civic justice; just as wrongdoing in States, which is the cause of injustice, is simply that every one of its citizens grows up with more than one occupation, and transfers from one thing to another, from one occupation to another and from one grade to another." He concludes that the harm of this transfer of occupation is clearly visible when the classes transfer from one to another, as when one who is parsimonious and wealthy is moved, thanks to his parsimony, so as to enter the order of the warrior class, or even more that of the ruling class -Plato's guardian class- (Ibn Rushd,1966:160-1). His analysis might illuminate the process of the deterioration of the seyfiyye (especially yeni-cheris) of the Ottoman state due to the historical fact that it was a very dynamic military force until an occupational transfer has been established between this warrior class and economic groups.

Sharî'ah is a policy [siyaset] which preserves the kingdom [mulk], the kingdom is a city which the army brings into existence, the army is guaranteed by wealth [lasker-ra mal kafalat kunad] wealth is acquired from the subjects, the subjects are made servants [banda] by justice as the axis of the well-being of the world." This is very similar to Ibn Khaldûn's formulation, "the world is a garden the fence of which is the dynasty [al-dawlah], the dynasty is an authority [sultân] through which life is given to proper behavior [al-sunnah]. Proper behavior is a policy [siyaset] directed by the ruler [al-mâlik]. The ruler is an institution [nizâm] supported by the soldiers [al-jund]. The soldiers are helpers [a'wân] who are maintained by money [al-mâl]. Money is sustenance [rizq] brought together by the subjects [al-ra'iyyah]. The subjects are servants ['abîd] who are protected by justice. Justice is something familiar [ma'lûf] and through it, the world [al-'âlam] persists. The world is a garden [bustân]" (Lambton, 1985:137). Tursun Beg, Ottoman statesman and historian of the late fifteenth century, extended this circular understanding of social stability as being dependent upon justice to the Ottoman political philosophy, setting up a circular relationship beginning and ending with justice: power for justice, soldiers for power, money for soldiers, well-being for money, and justice for well-being (Inalcik, 1964:43).

A threat to justice as the basic value of the political teleology through the destruction of socio-political stability and order could not be justified within such a framework, even if such an action could provide huge material benefits. Such an understanding of the circular evolution of social stability has been supported by an equalitarian and solidarist social philosophy (ta'âwun) binding all Muslims together by in brotherhood throughout history until the final judgement as specified in the Qur'ân. This solidarist view emerged from the idea of ontological-metaphysical solidarity transformed which was the reality of socio-economic and socio-political solidarity through moral solidarity, determined by a holistic Weltanschauung and an all-inclusive law which, for example, imposed zakât as a right of poor Muslims over rich Muslims. The function of hisbah as the conscience of the community, fard kifâyah for the individual Muslims, and fard 'ayn for muhtasib is the socio-psychological dimension of this teleological stability around the unity and equality of society composed of equal beings in the same ontological sphere. Therefore the abuse of power and wealth in certain hands as a result of the socio-economic stratification of class formation, such as the emergence of the bourgeoisie in Western societies, and tyrannical attitudes have been highly criticized in Islamic political theories and culture by arguments that the pharaoh, as a symbol of the abuse of political power, and Qârûn, as a symbol of the abuse of economic power, have been condemned in the Qur'ân.

The need to concentrate power through an institutional centralization of governmental organizations in order to fulfill the substantive mission of the state and the necessity at the same time of setting up of a political system that prevents the abuse of power is the fundamental dilemma of Islamic political culture and history. Muslim statesmen and political theorists tried to accompany these contradicting aims with a strong ethical base and with protection for the supremacy of the law and the autonomy of judicial authorities.

Ibn Taymiyyah argues that wilâyah connotes power, so that everyone must respect the law aimed at preventing the abuse of power, while al-Jâhiz's maintains that the duty of obedience lapses when the sovereign, who is an ordinary human being and may be guilty of some error and sin, is neglecting his duties and abusing his power. These ideas, along with Ghazzâlî's ethical prerequisites for political order, might be accepted as the formation of a theoretical base for a legitimate opposition to tyranny. Although Ghazzâlî and Ibn Jamâ'ah accepted the theory that the caliphate includes coercive power, according to them such an exercise of power should be legitimated by the juristic scheme. Almost all Muslim scholars argued in favor of the autonomy of judicial authority to prevent the abuse of political power, maintaining that after the appointment of a judge he should be seen as the deputy of the *ummah* rather than of the imâm and that hence the imâm may not dismiss him without some valid reason, because even the imâm does not have immunity from the judicial judgment and process.

Religious-cultural pluralism and institutional monism developed side by side in Islamic socio-political history. These superficially contrasting characteristics can be brought together only in reference to the antecedents of this *Weltanschauung*. Historical factors or material infrastructure can not explain it thoroughly, since these characteristics did not appear in other societies with the same infrastructure. The historical reality that several different cultural and religious communities could survive and coexist with their authentic cultures throughout the centuries under the patronage of Muslim states, whereas the tolerant society in Western political history is a modern artifact, shows us that the relationship between these two alternative political structures is not a relationship of different stages, but a relationship originating from different political cultures and images as extensions of alternative *Weltanschauungs*.

The substantively missionary character of the state in Islam together with the responsibility to establish an equalitarian philosophy created a socio-political duality of *askerî* and *ra'iyyah* (governors and governed people) in Islamic political history. The group of *askerî*, *wujûh al-nâs* (with Ibn Jamâ'ah's term consisting of *umarâ*, *'ulamâ'*, and *ruasâ*), had the responsibility to direct and control the fulfillment of the substantive missionary state. Due to the necessity of a huge political and military power for the establishment of justice all over the world, the concentration of power in the hands of this group as the political center could be logically justified. The duality of the society from the administrative perspective might be seen as a sociological reflection of the ontological hierarchy. The "intra-elite" character of the duality of socio-political life creating intra-elite political power distribution and power conflict could be directly linked to the concentration of power.

Related to the institutional-political monism in Muslim societies through the concentration of political power it should be underlined that Islamic institutional-political monism is philosophically and methodologically very different from Western political monism which is an alternative to pluralism only within the Western philosophical-political tradition mentioned above. Therefore Islamic institutional-political monism in history opposes both the approach of the Western tradition and the pluralist approach. Hobbesian monism in the Western tradition is an institutional monism originating from the craving for order and unity to avoid disorder and anarchy. This is a pragmatically justified monism through an inductive interpretation and carries a strong secular character. The fundamental differential characteristic of Islamic institutional-political monism is the existence of a strong theoretical link between cosmological-ontological monism in the form of the belief of *tawḥîd* and political monism. Western monist and pluralist thoughts have been shaped from the same philosophical paradigm, and Western monism is therefore a "secular monism" systematized by the synthesis of the epistemological segmentation of truth via the secularization of knowledge and institutional integration. The conflicts between the epistemological segmentation of truth and institutional monism have been eliminated through an ontologically impenetrable justification of political power based on ontological particularization and proximity of divinity. This is in absolute opposition to the concentration of power in Muslim states.

Islamic institutional transcendentalism depends on fundamental meticulousness to preserve the axiological base of communal life rather than to control private and communal life to strengthen the power of state as an abstract institution. Therefore *maḥabbat* (love) has been mentioned as the basic parameter for social coherence and stability. This model of social order suggests a trilateral social interaction: (i) the love of a ruler for a subject should be a paternal love; (ii) the love of the subject for the ruler should be filial; (iii) the love of subjects for each other should be fraternal. Ṭûsî describes this trilateral social interaction and its behavioral model as follows: "the ruler, in dealing with the subject, should model himself on the sympathetic father in respect of sympathy and compassion, solicitude and graciousness, nurture and indulgence, and in his quest for best interests, his warding off of unpleasantness, his attraction of good and his prohibition of evil; that the the subject, on the other hand, should follow the example of an intelligent son in giving the father obedience and good counsel, esteem and veneration; and, finally that [the subjects] in their generosity and kindness to each other should behave like brothers in agreement" (Ṭûsî, 1964:203). The imagination of *Devlet baba* in Turkish political culture has such a deep ethico-political source as a historical factor.

This characteristic is the area of intersection of theoretical instrumentalism, substantive transcendentalism, and religious-cultural pluralism of Islamic polity. Therefore, when Goitein (1970:102-3) states that "The Muslim state, in its classical period, conformed to Wilhelm von Humboldt's definition of ideal libertarian state, one which is least felt and restricts itself to one task only: protection, protection against attack from outside and oppression from within", he is not contradicting our analysis of social order. On the contrary, his statement indicates the impossibility of the definition of Islamic state tradition within a pure Western conceptual framework due to its unique characteristics. From the perspective of some of the characteristics of the Islamic state tradition this similitude might be criticized, but from the perspective of some others it reflects the historical realities: "In short, the Muslim government felt itself obliged mainly to perform one duty: to protect its people. For this purpose, it concerned itself with three objects: the army, the judiciary (including police and market supervision), and above all—and this is a point often misunderstood by modern historians—the court itself, for the power and splendor of the ruler was a safeguard against enemy attack from outside and a guaranty for the upkeep of authority and peace within the state" (Goitein, 1970:103). This description underlines the same crucial contrast mentioned above: the axiologically framed institutional transcendentalism of Islamic tradition which does not prevent religious-cultural pluralism and theoretical instrumentalism, as opposed to secular monism through identification of the socio-political system on behalf of a party of the socio-economic pluralism. Using Roszak's description (1971) it might be said that technocracy as a hegemony over the private life of human being is the institutional continuation of the absolutist transcendental monism of abstract idea of state in the sense of Hobbesian theory. The substantive mission of the state and its transcendental consequences in Islamic history completely differ from such a hegemonic monism. From the perspective of the restrictions of the state—especially related to communal and private life—within an axiological framework, of which state is also a subject like the individuals and autonomous communities, Goitein's statement is completely correct. At this intersection, we see the contrast between mechanism-dependent and value-dependent socio-political cultures. The Roszakian critique of technocracy is a response to the modern artifact that the personal fortunes and wills of the individual citizen are affected, determined, and checked by a socio-economic mechanism day in day out. "State" as an abstract entity such as in the Hobbesian or Hegelian sense is a supreme socio-political reflection of the supremacy of mechanisms. Today, both welfare states and totalitarian states restrict human will by a set of mechanisms. Western institutional transcendentalism—totalitarianism in its extreme form—in socio-political life depends on such mechanistic imagination, whereas institutional transcendentalism in Islamic political thought is attached directly to the substantive mission of *ummah* as the socio-political unity within a framework of axiological set. Such socio-economic mechanisms as *ḥisbah* have only the function of checking social life from the perspective of the realization of these values.

Religious-cultural pluralism: Basic parameter of socio-political differentiation

Thus, throughout Islamic history concentration of political power at the center did not form a socio-cultural monism. The multiplicity of socio-cultural groups within the territories of Muslim states is in fact a counterpart of the ontologically-defined political power structure which assumes a horizontal segmentation of governed people according to their ontological approaches. An Islamic state, from this perspective, is a confederation of several socio-cultural groups (millets) under the patronage of the political center where power is concentrated. The political center gives a socio-political identity to every religious-cultural group according to its ontological approach which is bound to the system with a specific act of citizenship (dhimmiship).

The privilege of becoming a protected minority via an act of dhimmiship was only given to the followers of a prophet to whom a sacred book had been revealed. Therefore, these communities have been called *ahl al-kitâb*. This denomination and the rights of these communities have been specified by the Qur'ân. At the beginning, Jews and Christians were accepted as *ahl al-kitâb*. After the Islamic expansion, members of several other religions such as Zoroastrians, Hindus, Buddhists, the gnostics of Harran, and pagan berbers of North Africa were also accepted as protected minorities.[7]

Even some Qur'ânic justifications were found for a comprehensive interpretation of the concept of monotheistic religion. For example, in the verses

---

[7]Al-Baladhurî reports in his *Futûḥ al-Buldân* that when a group of Brahmans approached Muḥammad b. al-Qâsim for the protection of their lives and temples after the conquest of Sind, he granted them the status of the *dhimmis* by declaring: "The Hindu temples are just like the Christian churches, Jewish synagogues, and the Zoroastrian fire-temples" ('Ali, 1982:108). Abû Yûsuf (1973:210-14) gives some information on the status of Zoroastrians and Sabians in his time, arguing on the basis of several hadiths that they might be accepted as a protected minority in return for poll-tax but that it is forbidden to marry with them because of their tradition of consanguineous marriage.

"By the fig and the olive, by Mount Sinai, and by this land made safe" (45:1-3), the olive is taken to refer to Jesus, Mount Sinai refers to Moses, and this land made safe is a reference to Makkah and thus to Muḥammad. The mention of the fig has therefore been accepted by some as an indication of the prophecy of Buddha.[8]

This comprehensive extension of the concept of *ahl al-kitâb* is the basis of such multi-national and multi-cultural Muslim states as those of the Umayyads, Andalusia, the Abbasids, and Muslim India. The Ottoman millet system is the last and most developed version of this religious-cultural pluralism. As Watt mentions (1968:51), "the problem of minorities in the contemporary Middle East is a legacy from the millet system and an indication of the failure so far to find any adequate replacement for it." It should be added to this judgement that it is not a bare problem of institutional replacement but rather a natural result of the challenge of two alternative political cultures. Beginning from the constitution of Madînah as the first agreement with another religious group, the Jews of Madînah, Muslims managed to develop and to re-produce a political culture which is suitable for a real co-existence of several cultural groups, until the victory and expansion of Western socio-economic pluralism together with a highly provoked national consciousness as the base of the unity of the nation-state.

The origin of the application of millet system goes back to this constitution of Madînah, the first written constitution in human history (Hamîdullah, 1981:21). This constitution, the text of which has come down to us complete, specifies very clearly that everyone was to be not only free in respect of the dogma and practice of religion but also free to comply with the laws of the community to which he belonged: Jews were to be judged by Jewish law, Christians by Christian law, and so on. "25. The Jews of Banû ʿAwf are a community along with the believers. To the Jews their religion and to the Muslims their religion. [This applies] both to their clients and to themselves, with the exception of any one who has done wrong or acted treacherously; he brings evil only on himself and on his household. 26. For the Jews of Banû al-Najjâr the like of what is for the Jews of Banû ʿAwf, etc." (Hamîdullah, 1987:59-64; English trans. Watt 1968:130-4). On the other hand, by the agreement with the Christians of Najrân during the period of the Prophet, Christians were permitted to practice the rules of their religion and run their own affairs, on condition that they paid a fixed tax, gave hospitality to the Prophet's representatives, provided support in the form of supplies to the Muslims in cases of war, and refrained from usury (Hamîdullah, 1987:176).

The respect for this act of citizenship is a part of the divine responsibility of the substantive missionary state and depends on several verses of the Qur'ân and *hadîths*. The famous Qur'ânic command "there is no compulsion in religion" (2:256) has been clarified by several *hadîths* such as "God forbids you to enter into the home of the people of the Book without [their] permission; to beat them; to take away their crops when they have fulfilled their obligations" and "Behold, he who oppresses a *dhimmi* [a covenantor, a non-Muslim citizen, or an ally], cheats him, or imposes upon him [a duty] which is above his capacity, or usurps his possessions, I shall be his tormentor in the Day of Judgement" (Abû Dâwud, 1981:3/437; Abû Yûsuf, 1977:145-7)

Abû Yûsuf specifies the following rules related to the relationship with the non-Muslim subjects: "(i) whatever agreement is made with them has to be faithfully

---

[8]See Hamîdullah (1972:459) for this line of argumentation.

observed; (ii) the responsibility for the defence of the State does not lie on them, but
on the Muslims alone; (iii) they should not be burdened with excessive poll-tax and
land revenue; (iv) the poor, the blind, the old, the recluse, workers at the houses of
worship, women, and children are exempt from poll tax; (v) there is no *zakât*
[prescribed charity] chargeable on the wealth and cattle of the non-Muslims; (vi) no
one is allowed to resort to beating or inflicting other physical tortures on them for
exacting the capitation, as the maximum punishment for its non-payment is only
imprisonment; (vii) to realize more than the fixed amount from them is unlawful;
(viii) the poor and the cripple among them are to be supported from the State
exchequer" (Abû Yûsuf, 1977:129-37, 150-61; English summary from Mawdûdî,
1963:700).

Although some commentators, such as Zamakhsharî, interpret the payment of
jizya as a sign of Muslim sovereignty and of the belittlement of non-Muslim
subjects (Lewis, 1984:14), the poll-tax has been accepted by most jurists as a
special payment in return for the responsibility of protection fulfilled by Muslims.
For example, Abû Yûsuf mentions (1973:224-5) as proof of this that Abû
'Ubaydah returned poll-taxes to the non-Muslim subjects in Hims when he found
himself unable to ensure their protection in the face of an enormous army raised by
the Roman emperor Heraclius.[9] Abû 'Ubayd (770-830), the author of *Kitâb
al-Amwâl*, a significant classical treatise on taxation, emphasizes that the *dhimmi*s
must not be burdened beyond their capacity, nor must they be caused to suffer
(Lewis, 1984:15). Shaybânî insists that, "as to the blind, the crippled, the
chronically ill, and the insane, the *jizya* is not to be levied on them, even if they are
rich" (1966:276) and that "if one of them dies and part of his *jizya* has not been
paid, it should not be deducted from his estate nor should it be collected from his
heirs, because the *jizya* is not considered a debt" (1966:275).[10] The argument of
Ibn Taymiyyah (1966:219) in his letter to Moghul invaders of that Muslim state
shows the most serious obligation (*a'zam al-wâjibât*) of releasing Jewish and
Christian prisoners from the hand of the enemy[11] is another interesting example of

---

[9]Abû Yûsuf (1977:150) narrates Abû 'Ubaydah's letter to the leaders of the
non-Muslim subjects in this situation: "We are returning you poll-taxes which you
have paid to us, because we have been informed that the Byzantians prepare a
powerful army for war. We were taking poll-tax from you in return for the
protection of your life, country, and property. However, we are not powerful
enough to fulfill this responsibility and therefore we are returning them to you. If
Allâh will help us and we will be victorious in this war, we will be devoted to our
previous agreement with you."

[10]"If a portion of the *jizya* is deferred, the balance should be collected in the
following year.... If anyone becomes blind or poor and is no longer able to pay the
remainder of his *jizya*, it is waived and he is no longer obliged to pay it.... *Dhimmi*
women and children do not have to pay the *jizya*, nor do those of them who are
blind, crippled, helplessly insane, chronically ill, too old to war, or who are too
poor to be able to pay. Priests, monks, and abbots are to pay if they own property.
But *dhimmi* slaves, *mudabbar*s, and *mukatab*s do not have to pay the *jizya*"
(Shaybânî, 1966:275-76).

[11]"All Christians know well how I have asked the Tatar to liberate our
prisoners. The Tatar, nevertheless, liberated the Muslim prisoners only. Ghazan
and Qutlusha will accept; I have informed my prince of it. The Tatar, however, will

the protective obligations of the Muslim state to the religious-cultural groups within its territory. The respect to the non-Muslim subjects has also been emphasized by modern Muslim scholars as one of the characteristics of socio-political life in Islamic history.[12]

Mez mentions in his famous work on the tenth century of Islamic history, *Die Renaissance des Islams* that "relying upon agreements and rights resulting therefrom, churches and synagogues always remained as something foreign to the state and never could form part of it" (Mez, 1922:29/eng.32; cf. 1922:40 on legal autonomy). On the other hand, there was a free exchange of thoughts among the leaders of these religious-cultural groups. Ṭabarī quotes in *Kitâb al-Iḥtijâj* that Bishr b.Ghayyat al-Mârisî (218/813) took part in disputations in the presence of Ma'mûn and that at one of these debates were present "the catholicus, the followers of Zoroaster, the chief herbad, the head of the dispersion, the leaders of the Sabians, Anastasius the Greek, the theologians and 'Ali Riḍâ" (Tritton, 1947:73).

Hence, repeating Goitein's conclusion as a consequence of his studies on the inner organization of Jewish community in Egypt during the tenth through the twelfth centuries, it might be argued that the Christians and Jews living under Islam formed a state not only within the state, but beyond the state, inasmuch as they owed loyalty to the heads and the central bodies of their respective denominations (1970:109). He goes further and argues that the Christian and Jewish communities were even stronger than the shapeless, amorphous masses of Muslims because they carried over from Hellenistic and Roman times civic forms of communal organization, which gave the individual member opportunity to be active in public life. His inferences from the historical sources of Jewish community related to their application of minority self-rule provides us significant details on the characteristics of this religious-cultural pluralism together with its dimension of the legal autonomy and of the survival of the authentic lifestyle throughout ages: "The concerns of the community were manifold. The upkeep of the houses of worship and the seats of religious learning, as well as the appointment and payment of the various community officials required much attention and effort. Secondly, law in those

---

deliver only the Muslims, and say 'we have only Christians whom we captured in Jerusalem; we refuse to release them.' I have replied, 'all Jews and Christians who are in your hands are our subjects. We must release them. We shall not wait, therefore; nor shall we leave in your hands even one prisoner, be he a Muslim or *dhimmi.*' We are determined to succeed in liberating a considerable number of Christians. That is our manner of conduct, and such is our generosity. God gives the recompense" (English trans. from Makari, 1976:213).

[12]"When non-Muslim powers conquered a kingdom they used to follow the army of conquest with an army of preachers of their faith, who took up quarters in the houses and occupied their councils, in order to impose the conqueror's religion. Their argument was force and their evidence conquest. It was not so with Muslim victors: such things were quite unknown in all their history. There were no preachers with the official and special duty to undertake propaganda and give their whole energies to urging their creed on non-Muslims. Instead the Muslims contented themselves with mixing among other peoples and treating them kindly. The entire world witnessed that Islam counted the proper treatment of conquered peoples a meritorious and virtuous thing, whereas Europeans regard such behavior as weak and despicable" ('Abduh, 1966:144).

days was personal rather than territorial; an individual was judged according to the law of the denomination to which he belonged. Almost the entire field of family law, and also cases of inheritance and commercial transactions were handled by the courts of the various religious communities. It is natural that individual Christians and Jews often applied to the qâḍî, especially when Muslim law was favorable to their case, as happened especially in litigations over inheritances. In order to forestall such occurrences, the denominational courts would adopt their legal practice to that of the government courts, and a most interesting interplay of law ensued."(1970:111)`

Goitein also describes the mechanism of self-administration under Islamic political order which had unique characteristics different from both localized mediaeval/feudal European experience and drastic central control of the territorial modern nation-states. The appointment of the leaders of the community occurred through the full participation of the laity, especially in the eleventh and twelfth century, which has in its hands not only the collection of the fund but also their administration and distribution under the supervision of the communal courts that formed the highest authority. The local officials were chosen by, or under vivid participation of, the laity, a system which was acknowledged by the religious communities. He provides examples of the acknowledgements by the highest Jewish councils in Jerusalem and Baghdad. As he underlines, a community had plenty of means to get rid of a leader who proved to be unacceptable for one reason or another (1970:112). In theory and practice, Muslim government did not interfere in the internal affairs of the community and "acted only, and then very reluctantly when approached by one of the rivalling parties within a non-Muslim community" (1970:109). Therefore, Goitein denominates this religious-cultural pluralistic system as a "medieval religious democracy" interpreting it as a successful application of the liberal-instrumentalist type of state theorized by Wilhelm von Humboldt in the nineteenth century. It is very interesting to note that when some Muslim governors (Ma'mûn) aimed to extend these democratic principles of minority self-rule to all religious groups composed of at least ten persons, the other great Christian communities did not accept it and tried to prevent the granting of the certificate of installation of new self-ruling minority groups (Mez, 1922:38).

Contrary to the universalization and monopolization of life style, even dressing of these protected minorities has been preserved as a mark of cultural identity. It is very difficult to accept Cohen's assertion that "the very fact both Christians and Jews in various ways maintained their separate religious identity implies, by definition, a certain degree of estrangement from the society as a whole" (1982:10) because, as he argues in the same article, "Christians engaged in trade on all levels and of different kinds" and "among Jews we find high officials and physicians, blacksmiths, silversmiths and goldsmiths, butchers and meatsellers, millers and tailors, bankers and moneysellers" during the sixteenth century in the Ottoman state (1982:11). This diversification of protected minorities in socio-economic activities necessitates a comprehensive involvement in the sense of social relationships within the society as a whole. If we compare this socio-economic situation with the relationship among the intra-religious sects in Europe in the same period, it marks a highly extended socialization process among the communities without destroying the cultural identity because it is impossible to manage these socio-economic activities within the limitations of only one community. Therefore, the psychological stimulus for the survival of the millet system should be sought beyond the purposive actions of the political center to estrange the protected minorities from the society as a whole. Rather, it is a natural result of a specific administrative spirit and mechanism to guarantee social balance by keeping alive religious-cultural pluralism as the basic parameter of socio-political differentiation in this socio-political life and institutionalization.

We should not interpret this historical fact within the framework of modern parameters of socio-economic pluralism. The secret forces of this religious-cultural pluralism might be understood within its own mechanism which depends on a specific political culture. Platonic interpretation of justice as "giving to every man his due/preserving every man in his place" and Islamic adaptation of cosmological teleology to the social life might provide us significant indications for the development of such a socio-political imagination and culture which facilitates a suitable atmosphere for the administrative institutionalization of religious-cultural pluralism. The act of dhimmiship as a practice of Islamic history beginning from the time of the Prophet provided both a prescriptivist legitimacy and of a historical accumulation of experience to form such a comprehensive institutionalization of millet system applicable within a huge territory in the Ottoman state.

This pluralistic character also applied to a great extent to various Muslim sects. Though there had been some disputes among the members of competing Muslim sects, it should be underlined that these disputes never erupted into open warfare, as happened in Europe. Additionally, the mere fact that the governor of a state belonged to a specific Muslim sect did not necessarily mean that the overwhelming majority of the population of that country belonged to the same sect. Von Grünebaum's statement that Iranian or Moroccan Islam is not an organic unit but merely a stenographic expression to denote the type or types of beliefs and practices that are prevailing within the territories of somewhat accidental boundaries, is correct due to the fact that "not only do the frontiers of those political entities fail to coincide with the boundaries of one or the other specific modifications of the Muslim faith but within the independent Muslim states, [in some cases] different ethnic or social strata will adhere to different versions of the Prophets message" (1962:42). For instance, Imâmî Twelver Shî'ism, the official religion of Iran, reaches into Iraq, and Sunni Muslims are strongly represented on Iranian soil.

CHAPTER 7

THE POLITICAL UNIT AND
THE UNIVERSAL POLITICAL SYSTEM

The idea of the political unit and its relationship to the universal political system is another significant aspect of the political extension of philosophical-doctrinal differences between Islamic and Western traditions. The comparison of the continual philosophical bases of the evolution from the incipient national states, *res publica*, to the formation of the modern nation-state as the universal political unit, on the one hand, with the doctrinal bases of the bicompartmentalization of the universal political system into *Dâr al-Islam* and *Dâr al-Ḥarb* in Islamic political theories, on the other, can provide us with significant insights into the Islamic historical-cultural response to the universalization of Western political ideals.

Western multicompartmentalization: Nation-states

Such a comparison first of all presents us with a conceptual and etymological problem. Because "nation-state" is a purely Western artifact, there was a problem of finding corresponding terms in non-Western languages during the challenge and impact of Western institutions over other communities. The problem is especially apparent related to Muslim languages. Similarly, it is very difficult to find an adequate corresponding term in Western languages for the term *ummah* as a socio-political unity because of its uniqueness in Islamic political history and culture.

Etymology of nation-state

An etymological analysis of the concept of "nation-state" leads us to the semantic fields of the concepts of "nation" and "state." While "people" is a wider term for any aggregation of individuals, "nation" used in English has two senses, giving special substance to this aggregation of individuals. The first usage of the concept of nation is for a conscious aggregation of individuals to compose a socio-political community united under one government, while the other is for a community which has some common characteristics like race, religion, language, and tradition. The former usage shows the socio-political orientation and identification of a group of individuals. In that sense, it has been used in the intersection of the semantic field of the concept of "state." The latter sense, which is not used within this semantic field of the concept of "state," is used for any aggregation of individuals united because of some other characteristics. We will use the concept of "nation" in the sense of the former usage.

The concepts of *Nation* or *Volk* in German and *nation* in French have almost the same meaning as in English. However, there have been some semantic changes in the usage of *Nation* and *Volk* in German. *Nation* was formerly used in German in the cultural rather than in the political sense of the word, but *Volk* began to be used for this purpose in the 1930s. *Volk* extends the notion of the family to a wider plane. It is mainly an ethnocentric term denoting a body of men who are physically, and thereof spiritually, of common descent and historical consciousness. In the semantic system of the German language, there is a close relationship between *Volk* as "an organic being" and *Staat* as "a form of organization." The same clear distinction between socio-politically and socio-culturally oriented conceptions of nation can be seen in German as *Kulturnation* indicating culture and language and *Staatsnation* indicating socio-political identification.

In French, the terms *nation, etat,* and *peuple* form a similar semantic relationship. *Nation* signifies a community of men linked by the tie of a will to live together in a *patrie* which is the territory inhabited by the nation. The link between the *state* and *nazione* is almost indissoluble in Italian. This was especially so during the period of Mazzini. According to the Encyclopedia Italiana, although a *nazione* either is or tends to become a state, the state tends to create the *nazione* as well as is created by it.

The etymological analysis of the concept of "state" leads us to the expressions of *status* in Latin which has been used in Emperor Justinian's text as *"statum reipublicae sustentamus "*, and *stato, etat, stat* in Teutonic languages. With Pufendorf, and his translator Baybeyrac, the concept of state (*status, etat*) definitely becomes a part of the theory although it has been used before to correspond to several expressions in ancient time as *polis, civitas, regnum* by Plato, Aristotle, Cicero, and St. Augustine. The Greeks signified city and state by the same word *polis* which shows that the conception of state in the Greek language was based and limited by the city within a moral context. So, in the Greek language, *"polis* has the meaning of state and church together" (Bluntschli, 1892:23). The Roman view of the universal state that was dependent on a legal element was very different from the Greek city-state. St. Augustine used three terms to differentiate the types of state, especially in Italy, while *regnum* was used by him to describe the territorial monarchies. *Res Publica* was reserved in most cases for describing a wider community: i.e., *Res Publica Christiana* united all believers in one sheepfold. (D'entreves, 1967:3). This key-concept was first used in its modern sense by Machiavelli. His definition of state as the proper object of politics as a collective unit, although its shape and form of government may vary, might be accepted as the first formulation of the modern sense of this concept.

When we combine these two concepts, nation-state is a special type of the government of a community or people whose members are bound together by a sense of solidarity through a common culture and national consciousness as a socio-political identification. It presupposes "the existence of a centralized form of government over a large and distinct territory" (Kohn, 1969:4). Therefore the legitimacy of the nation-state as a political unity and the consciousness of nationalism is purely a modern artifact although it has its nuclei and philosophical origins from ancient times in the sense of being a reflection of a specific *Weltanschauung* and socio-political imagination.

Historical legacy of the idea of state

The idea of state in ancient Greece was depending on the mentality of city-state which was a moral and political order in which human nature fulfills its end. The idea of state in ancient Greece may be accepted as the first formulation of the organic theory of state. This organic theory of state led to an imagination of state as a human being. That might be traced back to Platonic doctrine that the best state is that which approaches most nearly to the conditions of the individual. Thus, if a part of the body suffers, the whole body feels the hurt and sympathizes all together with the part affected. In the Platonic idea the state is highest revelation of human virtue. Assuming that man is by nature a political animal, Aristotle defined the state as the association of clans and village-communities in a complete and self-sufficing life.

Because of the acceptance of the state as embodying highest virtue, the idea of state in ancient Greece depended on a pyramidal-hierarchical relationship between state and subjects (citizens). The citizen was nothing except a member of a city-state. There was not any moral or legal limit to state power. Hence, it was almost impossible to develop a national understanding upon which the legitimacy of the state could be grounded.

The universal empire of Alexander the Great became a marriage of Greek city-state mentality and Eastern divine kingdom. This created a highly mobile cultural and institutional transaction between east and west, which would be taken over and developed by the Roman Empire for the same idea of universal empire in contradistinction to the limited mentality of city-state.

The Roman idea of state, best expressed by Cicero, resembles the Greek idea of city-state in assuming an organic theory of state and in believing that the city-state is the highest product of human virtue. But there were also some significant differences between these two ideas of state which may be accepted as the first indication of the modern national idea of state. First of all, legal organizations became the focus of the idea of state as a natural result of the distinguishing of law from morality. Secondly, the strict hierarchical order and identification between citizen and city-state in ancient Greece had been changed in the Roman idea of state. Individual rights, such as private property, were better protected in Roman idea of state against the arbitrary exercises of public authority through the supremacy of law and legal organizations. Individual and family life became more free, although the welfare of the state continued to be accepted as the highest law (*salus populi supreme lex*). The Roman idea of state contributed much to the modern national idea of state, declaring that the will of the people should be the source of all law depending on the assumption that state is nothing but people organized. The Roman state was not a commune contradictory to the city-state, but an incipient national state (*res publica*) aiming at *Pax Romana*. So, with this aim the national *jus civile* had been supplemented by *jus gentium*.

The characteristics of the early medieval idea of state were shaped by two significant new elements, the rise of the papacy with the spread of Christianity throughout the Roman Empire as the dynamic spiritual vitality and the Teutonic-barbarian attacks as the temporal force. These were the leading elements to force the super-structure of state in the age of feudalism as a new socio-economic system. The rise of the papacy in Rome after the weakening and destruction of the Western Roman Empire was in fact a reemergence in spiritual form of the Roman idea of universal *dominium*. This idea of state found a new religious ground after the dominance of the papacy. As Bluntschli clarifies very well, with these events "the Roman Empire was renewed in medieval form, but represented in superior form by the Roman Church, and in an inferior by the Holy Roman Empire of the German people under the governance of Teutonic princes" (1901:42). By the end of the sixth century, the Christianization of Europe by the papacy and the segmentation of the old Roman Empire by Teutonic influences had been completed. This completion was in fact a beginning of formation of Europe as nucleus.

The idea of the state was weak in that time because the Teutonic tribes had no sense of the state as distant, impersonal continuing source of law. Then had no sense of loyalty to large and general institutions although they had strong loyalty to persons, kings, and chiefs as a natural result of nomadic tradition. This tradition was the basis of contractual understanding to specify rights and obligations in the feudal structure. The segmentation and particularism in Europe had been increased with Teutonic effects after the destruction of Roman Empire. This particularism prevented the emergence of the idea of nation-state because of the conflicting claims of territories, estates, and dynasties.

The Christianization and particularization of Europe in the Middle Ages created a problem of ultimate sovereignty among the ecclesiastical and clerical hierarchy (*sacerdotum*) and temporal kings (*regnum*). This struggle was fundamental in the formation process of the nation-state. In the early Middle Ages the supremacy of *sacerdotum* could not be discussed. This can be seen in the letter of Pope Gelasius I written to Byzantine Emperor Anastasius very openly: "There are two powers, August Emperor, by which this world is chiefly ruled, namely the sacred, authority of the priests [*auctoritas*] and temporal power [*potestas*]. Of these, that of the priests is the more weighty, since they have to render an account for even the kings of men in the divine judgement.... [therefore] you should be subordinate rather than superior to the religious order, and... in these matters you depend on their judgement rather than wish to force them to follow your will" (Viorst, 1965:20).

This idea of two swords was strengthened after Pope Leo III's crowning of Charlemagne, who defined his task as "to defend by armed strength the Holy Church of Christ everywhere from the external onslaught of the pagans and the ravages of the infidels and to strengthen within it the knowledge of the Catholic Church." This ritual of crowning by the pope continued during the time of Otto I presenting the permanent association of the Christian Roman Empire with Teutonic kingdoms.

So up to the early eleventh century, the idea of state depended on the doctrine of the two swords, which was the main obstacle to the formation of the nation-state. But some socio-political, socio-cultural, and socio-economic changes emerged in eleventh century that began to destroy this traditional structure in favor of temporal authority which would be the forerunner of the nation-state.

Formation of the European nation-state system as the basis of political unity and the universal political system

The nation as an ethnic entity and national feeling can be traced back to very early in human history. The feeling of ethnic discrimination in ancient Aryan culture[1] which was institutionalized as the caste system in the socio-political sphere and the idea of

---

[1]This ancient legacy has survived throughout the ages. For example, *barbara* which means non-Aryan in Sanskrit has been extended to Greek political thought and culture as *barbaros* meaning strange or foreign. The usage of this term to distinguish groups that do not take part in the same national feeling continued to be used in Western political culture and thought throughout the ages.

the missionary supremacy of Jewish community as an ethno-religious entity[2] are two significant examples of this. Nevertheless, the system of nation-state, the political legitimacy of national sovereignty, and the political theory of nationalism developed after the destruction of the traditional feudal order of the Middle Ages. The first stirrings of the development of the nation-state system as an international universal system began to occur in the eleventh century, while the definite entry of the nation-state into the system of Europe was completed in the mid-seventeenth century after the Treaty of Westphalia in 1648.

The political systems before this period, such the *polis* in ancient Greece or the king-state combination in Babylonia, fell short of a nation. The political systems of the Alexandrian and the Roman empires were the representatives of the multinational and universal political mentality combining the political legitimacy of the deification of the emperors. The Roman state was not a community but an incipient national state (*res publica*) aiming at *Pax Romana*. The political mentality in the Middle Ages was shaped by Christianity around the idea of the Christian commonwealth. Christianity, having consecrated the structure of Roman Empire, developed the idea of two swords as divine political legitimacy under the rule of pope and holy Roman emperor as the representatives of the dual political structure. The imaginative link of continuity between this medieval legacy and modern nation-state system is very clear because such a compartmentalization opened the way for the concentration of political power in secular and religious centers. The formation of the nation-state system is a natural consequence of this compartmentalization on behalf of the secular forces. Such a transformation of political power became possible and legitimate because of the theoretical and imaginative continuity in the sense of ontological-epistemologico-axiological foundation.

During the Middle Ages the concept of *natio villa* was used for a group of kinsmen. The first time it was used was by the Baron of Oxford who used the phrase *natio regli Anglia* for the kingdom of England in 1258. Germany began something of an independent state under the Saxon dynasty in 919, whereas the Capetian monarchy started on its long career in France in 987, and William I began to form a new England after 1066 (Barker, 1927:120).

The period of the institutionalization of the nation-states from the tenth to the fifteenth centuries was a complementary fact in the process of a socio-political transition from towns to national units. After the incipient and transitional period, the traditional order was destroyed and a new socio-cultural, socio-economic and socio-political system appeared in Europe. The ethical-religious base of this new system was Protestantism; the intellectual-scientific base was Galileo's theory of motion; the socio-political base was national royal absolutism within a specified territory; the socio-economic base was mercantilism. The nation-state system was a complementary artifact of this new order of Western civilization with the same philosophical background, and it carries the fundamental characteristic of the Western paradigm examined in chapter 2. The internal structure of the nation-state, from a theoretical and institutional perspective, has been systematized by Machiavelli, Bodin, and Hobbes, while the principle of the international system in

---

[2]Kohn's statement (1969:120) that "the purely vegetative group feeling developed for the first time into a national consciousness which received its inspiration from the ancient classics and Old Testament" is absolutely correct from this perspective.

which nation-states became political units was set up by Grotius who used and acknowledged Braun, Vasques, Suarez, and Gentilis.

The development of the nation-state as the basic political unit and the multi-compartmentalization of the universal system has the same characteristics as the Western philosophico-political tradition mentioned above. The autonomy of political culture and structure which lacked a direct link with the ontological approach, the socio-political identification through real factors without appealing to an axiological holistic framework, the ultimate authority of humanistic epistemology in the form of national will, all are several aspects of the specific relationship between the philosophical-political tradition as a paradigmatic unity and the system of nation-state as its institutional counterpart.

The internal impact of the nation-state is mainly related to the concept of citizenship according to certain criteria, while the external impact is the necessity for an institutional system consisting of several nation-states. The divorce of politics and ontological antecedents is a *sine quo non* for the establishment of such a system which could be easily manipulated according to the existent power structure.

Now, we can analyze briefly the periods of the formation of nation-state system in Europe to show the continuity of the philosophical and imaginative features.

Inception. The cultural, economic, and social changes that occurred in eleventh and twelfth centuries were the first stirrings of the modern phase of Western civilization. From this point of view, this period was the first renaissance in Western history. First of all, great changes in socio-economic life began to shake the old contractual feudal structure. The new agricultural techniques improved the methods of food cultivation which led to a huge increase in food production, never seen before this period. The population began to increase parallel to this increase in food production which encouraged the process of urbanization and commerce. The development of towns through this process of urbanization affected the socio-cultural and socio-political life of Western societies to a great extent. The new monetary connections between lords and peasants necessitated a new type of socio-economic system which would shape mercantilism in further ages.

The socio-political structure of feudalism as small and limited units began to be shaken because of the growing necessity in the direction of centralization and coordination. The new socio-political elements began to emerge in towns which would force the governing elites to set up national units in further steps. But it should be underlined that the philosophical and imaginative backgrounds of these units has been sprang from the same origin of the ancient and feudal accumulation, i.e., they did not originate from a revolutionary attempt. In other words, the previous philosophico-theological system provided a continual theoretical and imaginative base for the process of the legitimation of the new socio-economic and socio-political units.

Parallel to these socio-economic changes, Europe had been brought into existence as political divisions. After the second barbarian waves in the tenth century, the nuclei of modern European states began to be shaped in the eleventh century. The Kingdom of France was in being, adjoining Germany in the Holy Roman Empire. The kingdoms of England, Scotland, Denmark, Norway, and Sweden had also taken form. The small Christian kingdoms in northern Spain and Italy had been formed as independent political units. In East Europe, the kingdoms of Bohemia, Poland, and Hungary came into existence through the process of crowning rituals by the pope. Meanwhile, Slavic, Russian, and Bulgarian kingdoms became independent members of the Eastern Orthodox Christian commonwealth.

The rivalry among the sacred and temporal authorities to lead these socio-economic and political changes accelerated the conflict of sovereignty between church and state. The monarchial structure of the Church was also strengthened in these socio-economic processes because of its being the greatest landowner in Europe . Therefore the popes at that time tried to strengthen their supremacy. These attempts of ecclesiastical authority were documented by Gregory VII's *Dictatus Papae* in 1075 against German monarchs. The most significant articles of this *Dictatus Papae* might be quoted as follows: "(1) The Roman Church was founded by God alone.... (8) The Pope alone may use the imperial insignia. (9) The Pope is the only person whose feet are kissed by all princes.... (12) He has the power to depose emperors..... (16) No general synod may be called without his consent. (17) No action of a synod and no book may be considered canonical without his authority..... (19) He can be judged by no man..... (27) The Pope has the power to absolve the subjects of unjust rulers from their oath of fidelity" (Viorst, 1965:20).

Henry IV's reply in 1076 to this *Dictate* created an irreparable conflict between papacy and monarchies. In this struggle Gregory VII forced Henry IV into submission to the papacy through the declaration of excommunication. That was the failure of the first national attack against papal supremacy. The leading figures of papal supremacy in this period were Agobard, Bishop of Lyons; Hincmar, Archbishop of Rheims; Pope Nicholas I; Pope Gregory VII; Manegold of Lutterbach; St. Bernard; John of Salisbury; St. Thomas Aquinas; and Pope Innocent III.

The temporal rulers opposed these attempts at ecclesiastical supremacy on two grounds: divine and legal. First of all, they argued that political society was of divine origin and that kings, as agents of the divine purpose, were responsible to God alone. Second, with the revival of Roman law and corporate organic theory of state, they insisted on the supremacy of monarchs because the Roman law taught that the emperor governed the whole civilized world.

Although Henry IV's attempt at German nationalism was defeated by Gregory VII, the Charter of Lorris in 1155 might be accepted as a triumph of French nationalism to set up centralized nation-state within a specified territory, Ile de France, the chief city of which was Paris. Interurban trade was encouraged, property rights were preserved, taxation was legalized and, a bill of rights was declared with this charter (Viorst,1965:69).

Transition. The transitional period in the formation process of the nation-state system occurred from the twelfth century to the time of Machiavelli in the late fifteenth century. The Charter of Lorris was the first indication of this transition. In this period, monarchs dealt with the inner organization of their kingdoms through the formation judicial, monetary, military and political institutions.

The kings instituted royal courts to attain judicial autonomy. This assertion of legal jurisdiction and military force became the main pillar of secular/royal power. To obtain money necessary for governmental machinery, a system of taxation began to be applied. The taxation was purely a result of the revival of Roman law because it was quite unknown to the Teutonic peoples and feudal tradition.

Royal councils of the feudal period gradually transformed into parliaments and spread all over the Europe by the thirteenth century. The new assemblies were called *cortes* in Spain, *diets* in Germany, *estates general* or provinced estates in France, and parliaments in the British isles (Palmer & Colton, 1978:30). The kings called these assemblies as means of strengthening royal rule. Parallel to urbanization, a burgher class was added to the lords and bishops in parliament. But parliament as the basic legal/procedural means for the legitimation of political authority in the nation-state system gained its importance after the epistemological transformation in Western civilization toward epistemologically-defined ontology under the patronage of the centrality of epistemology.

The balance between church and monarches under the theoretical systematization of the compartmentalist idea of two swords began to change in favor of monarches in this period. The leading figures against papal supremacy in this period were Frederick II of Germany and Philip IV of France. Frederick II claimed superiority for the empire not only over other kings but even over the pope, aiming to make himself supreme in spiritual as well as temporal affairs.

As Kohn underlines, ancient Rome served as a source of inspiration to Frederick II second only to the Bible. He coined money like Augustus to show financial independence. The rediscovery of Roman law by the jurists of the University of Bologna resulted in the growing of the idea that the king, as the supreme head of mankind, could not be called to justice except by God. Soon after the revival of Roman law, the jurist Martinus ascribed to the emperor a true ownership of all things and therefore a free power of disposal over the rights of private persons (Gierke, 1958:79).

These ideas in favor of the centralization of political power and their corresponding political theories were the similitudes of the Islamic theories which assumed the concentration of political power in the hands of the caliph as the religio-political leader. This similarity marks a very indicative impact of Islamic political thought and institutionalization on Europe at that time, after the experiences of the secular royal authorities during the Crusades.

Kohn (1969:89-90) argues that Frederick II was influenced by Islamic civilization at that period, which he loved and admired for the breadth of its views and greater freedom of its intellectual atmosphere. Furthermore, he signed a treaty on just and equal terms with the sultan of Egypt and this treaty was called as an unpardonable crime by the Church. Even Dante, who was in favor of Frederick's actions for the supremacy of royal power, placed him among the faithless in the *Inferno*.

However, these attempts at the centralization of power in the hands of monarches did not create a religio-political unity such as that in Islamic experience because of the paradigmatic differences of the two different *Weltanschauungs*. Rather, they led to the supremacy of the secularization of political power because the Catholic Church did not leave religious authority to any other institution in spite of the theories on the divine rights of the kings and councils. Even the leading figures of the independence of the monarchy, as opposed to papacy, insisted on the preservation of the balance of two swords. For example, Ockham insisted that the spheres of spiritual and temporal jurisdiction must be kept sharply from each other.[3] Thus, the beginning of the shift of political power toward the temporal authorities occurred within the categorization of the two swords, which is a natural result of the ontologico-epistemologico-axiological imagination and continuity of Western civilization analyzed in the first part of this book.

---

[3]See McGrade (1974).

The conflict between Pope Boniface and Philip IV the Fair of France accelerated the growing spirit of national unity and the establishment of centralized nation-states. The dispute began when Philip IV tried to apply taxation to the French Church in order to finance the war against England. Pope Boniface threatened Philip IV with the sentence of excommunication in the bull *Clerics Laicos* (Viorst, 1965:70), like Gregory VII had earlier done against Henry IV of Germany. But this time, the pope could not be successful because of the growing national feeling: this dispute ended with the supremacy of the monarches. Thus, the supporters of the secular authority, for centuries on the defense, began to show growing self-confidence: Philip IV applied this taxation and even decided to depose Pope Boniface.

The main supporters of secular supremacy and the establishment of nation-states were Marsiglio of Padua, William of Ockham, Pierre Duboes, Dante Alighieri, John Wyclif, John Huss, and John Gerson. Many of these thinkers were directly influenced by Ibn Sînâ and Ibn Rushd. Lerner identifies Dante and Marsiglio in particular as Averroists.

Marsiglio of Padua, who became rector of the University of Paris in 1313, was willing to push the theocratic influence out of politics to attain good government. Marsiglio, in his *Defensor Pacis* (1963), suggested that people with different languages should form separate states and that wars among states were a wise provision of nature. Being a practical thinker, he desired internal peace. These ideas opened the way for the nation-state system. His ideas had also some democratic elements, which would be developed in further ages. For example, he made a clear distinction between ultimate sovereignty in the state, which he located in the people, and the form of government chosen to execute the laws. Therefore he suggested an elected monarchy.

Wicksteed mentions (intr. part of Dante, 1963:419) that the alleged Averroism of Dante's *On Monarchy*[4] is founded in part on his use of the doctrine of the possible intellect in chapter three of Book I (Dante, 1963:422). But it should be added that his departure from the teaching of Aristotle by advocating the establishment of a monarchy or world government as a means of eliminating strife among cities and nations carries the characteristics of Ibn Rushd's conciliation of Greek political thought with the Islamic institution of the caliphate.

Dante defined temporal monarchy as a unique princedom extending over all persons in his time and stressed that "it is necessary for the best disposition of the human race that there should be a monarch in the world and consequently for the well-being of the world that there should be a monarchy" (1963:435). According to him the role of monarchy is to keep peace. As God is the monarch of all creation, so the emperor is the monarch of temporal kings. Gierke (1958:30) underlines that there was a consensus among philosophers at that time on this basic argument. Ockham argued that the emperor is bound to conform to the laws common to all

---

[4]Dante deals with three significant questions in this treatise as the key issues of the supremacy of royal power. "And now it seems to me that I have sufficiently attained the goal that I set for myself. For I have searched out the truth concerning the three questions that were raised: whether the office of monarch is necessary for the well-being of the world, whether the Roman people rightfully claimed the Empire for itself, and finally whether the authority of the monarch derives immediately from God or from someone else" (Dante, 1963:437).

nations. With this argument he became the forerunner of international law within a system of national states.

John Wyclif in England and John Huss in Bohemia, affected by the arguments of Marsiglio of Padua and William of Ockham, were the other representatives of the national, anti-papal, and democratic movements in this process of transition to the nation-state system. Wyclif argued that both state and church were directly authorized by God and that the pope and clergy had no right to exercise political power. The theory of Wyclif proposed a national state with a national church subordinate to it. That idea became the basis of the establishment of the Church of England by Henry VIII. As Gettle emphasizes, Wyclif's theory foreshadowed in its exaltation of the state the doctrines of Bodin and Hobbes. Together with Huss, Wyclif was one of the significant forerunners of the Reformation (Skinner, 1978:II/34-42).

Through the efforts of these thinkers, the new elements in Western social, economic, and political life that emerged in the eleventh and twelfth centuries were legitimated. With these developments the basis of legitimacy began to change through the destruction of feudal structures and the establishment of new socio-economic and socio-political structures. The socio-economic structure might be called pre-industrial mercantilism, while the socio-political structure might be called centralization of monarchies around the nation-states with increasing supremacy of temporal forces over papal authority.

Maturation. The early fifteenth century is sometimes called the conciliar period in reference to the various councils that became instrumental in the maturation of the nation-state system. The councils of Pisa in 1409, Constance in 1415, Pavia in 1423, Basel in 1431, and Bourges in 1438 had three significant results in Western political history. First of all, after these councils the Church began to be accepted as a human society rather than an extra-ordinarily organized divine being. For example, John Gerson favored a system of limited monarchy in church organization while Cardinal Nicholas of Cues argued that a representative council should be set up as the central organ in both church and state (Gettell, 1959:140). Thus, the organizational structure of the Church began to be discussed and criticized. Second, the idea of national church began to develop as a very significant complementary factor in the formation of nation-states. Third, the development of national churches in the period of the Reformation resulted in the absolute supremacy of temporal power over papal authority.

The Council of Constance in 1414 asserted its supremacy over the pope, while the Pragmatic Sanction of Bourges in 1438 denied papal claims of superiority. The most significant articles of this sanction might be summarized as follows: (i) The authority of the general council is superior to that of the pope in all that pertains to the faith and the reform of the church in both head and members. (ii) Election is reestablished for ecclesiastical office but the king or the princess of his kingdom, may take recommendations when elections are to occur. (iii) The popes shall not have the right to reserve the collation of benefices. (iv) Those who shall have received benefices shall be punished by the secular power (Viorst,1965:78).

The independence and sovereignty of secular-national monarchies had been declared by several bilateral agreements in the fifteenth and sixteenth centuries. The Concordat of 1418 between the reunited papacy under Martin V and *nations* present at the Council of Constance, the Concordat of Vienna in 1448 between Frederick II of Austria and Pope Nicholas V, and the Concordat of Bologna in 1516 between Francis I of France and Pope Leo X were "negotiations between equal sovereign powers rather than arrangements between the head of the church and spiritual sons" (Morrall, 1958:133).

The writers of conciliar period, such as John Gerson, Nicholas of Cues, and Aenean Sylvius, were the bridges from the transitional period to the emergence of nation-states. Although they contributed much to this emergence, especially the concepts of the state of nature, natural rights, social contract, and representative government, the real forerunner of the national state theories was Machiavelli.

Machiavelli's most significant contribution to Western intellectual history and the emergence of the national state was his clear-cut definition of the state as an artifact created by human beings. That idea became the intellectual base of secularism and absolute supremacy of the national state over ecclesiastical authority because Machiavelli made safety and success of the state the paramount issues of political life. From this perspective he was a pragmatic philosopher, thinking on the theory of the preservation the state rather than on the theory of the state itself. Therefore the philosophical qualities of his theory may be discussed, but it can not be denied that he was the founder of the realistic approach in the history of political theory. His masterpiece, *The Prince* , became the cornerstone of the process of the nation-state theory dealing with the mechanics of government in absolute national states.

In fact, the time of Machiavelli, and the Renaissance in general, was the period during which "the purely vegetative group feeling developed for the first time into a national consciousness" (Kohn, 1969:120). From this point of view, the period of the Renaissance and the Reformation swept away the obstacles of the traditional feudal structure to set up the system of nation-states. But the completion of this new political order occurred in the early seventeenth century.

The fifteenth century was a century of civil wars. The Hundred Years War, the Hussite Wars, and the English Wars of the Roses created an atmosphere of political chaos in this century. These wars led monarches to strengthen their royal powers. At the beginning of the sixteenth century the nation-states in Europe had not been completely formed. Government in England, France, Germany, and Spain was partially local and decentralized. But three issues developed in the fifteenth century which would be effective in the formation of nation-states in the seventeenth century. These were the foundation of the taxation system, bureaucracy, and capital cities as very significant organs of centralized nation-states.

Royal monarches developed taxation systems to finance their wars. A new type of public servants, secretaries and ambassadors, appeared as the first indication of modern bureaucracy. Parallel to these developments the most significant indication of the trend toward the formation of nation-states was the emergence of recognizable capital cities. Paris, London, Lisbon, and other such cities became the seats of governments and the centers of economic, cultural, social, and political life.

These enormous changes in the idea of state continued and accelerated in the sixteenth century. The intellectual transformation of the Renaissance toward a reason-centered mentality, the economic transformation of mercantilism around cities toward a nationwide commercial capitalism, and religious transformation of the Reformation toward nationalization of churches depending on a clear-cut sphere of religion as an individual matter were the main dynamics of the sixteenth century for the formation of new socio-political and international structures depending on the nation-state system in the early seventeenth century.

The Renaissance questioned the traditional assumptions of the feudal system and increased the idea of worldliness. The invention and spread of the printing press accelerated the development of national languages and cultures. In particular, Francis I created a French cultural nationalism as a base of the nation-state in France. Some French authors even went so far in praise of the monarch as to declare that the name *langue françoise* was derived from the royal name Françoise (Kohn, 1969:130). After the period of Renaissance the center of intellectual life became reason rather than divinity. This transformation created a philosophical ground for the formation of the nation-state system.

The main contribution of the Reformation to the nation-state system was the destruction of the traditional idea of unity in church and empire. This event resulted in the reorganization of Europe territorially into distinct national states. Thus, the center of the idea of state shifted from world empire to territorial state and from ecclesiastical to civil predominance. The main leaders of the Reformation were Martin Luther, Melancthon, Zwingli, and Calvin. The main contributions of Luther to formation of the nation-state were "the clear distinction he made between political and spiritual authority, the emphasis he laid upon the secular as against the ecclesiastical power and the importance he placed upon passive obedience to the established order in state and society" (Gettell, 1959:156).

The nationalization of churches as one of the main complementary facts of the maturation of the nation-state system in Europe was successfully completed after the Reformation. The cornerstones of the process of nationalization of churches were England's Act of Supremacy (1534) and continental Europe's Peace of Augsburg (1555). The conflict between Henry VIII and Pope Clement VII over the former's desire to divorce his older brother's widow whom he had married resulted in the breaking of ties between Canterbury and Rome. Henry VIII established the Anglican Church with the king as its head through a series of parliamentary statutes in 1534. England's Act of Supremacy was a very significant step toward nationalization of the church and establishment of a completely independent nation-state: "Albeit the king's majesty justly and rightfully is and ought to be the supreme head of the Church of England, and so is recognized by the clergy of this realm in their convocations, yet nevertheless for corroboration and confirmation thereof... by the authority of this present parliament that the king, our sovereign lord, his heirs and successors, king's of the realm shall be taken, accepted, and reputed the only supreme head in earth of the Church of England, called *Anglicane Ecclesia*" (Viorst, 1965:117).

Meanwhile, the Peace of Augsburg signed after the religious wars between Catholic and Protestant countries empowered the idea of national church in continental Europe through declaring that each prince had the right to determine the religion of his subjects. Lutheranism had been legalized as the only permissible form of Protestantism in Germany after this agreement which also confirmed all seizures of Catholic property by Protestant churches prior to 1552.

The document of James I's claim of divine right in 1609 may be accepted as the ultimate end of ecclesiastical supremacy in favor of the absolutism of royal powers: "The State of Monarchy is the supremest thing upon earth, for kings are not only God's lieutenants upon the earth, and sit upon God's throne, but even by God himself they are called gods... Kings are also compared with the fathers of families, for a king is truly *parens patrie* , the politic father of his people."

Completion. The ultimate transformation from locally organized feudalism to the nation-state system was completed in the late sixteenth century and especially in the first half of the seventeenth century. France was the first consolidated nation-state, and the French philosopher Jean Bodin was the forerunner of modern idea of national sovereignty. In his masterpiece on political theory, *De Republica Libri Sex* (1576), he specified nine true marks of sovereignty—the power to legislate, to make war and peace, appoint higher magistrates, hear final appeals, receive homage, coin money, regulate weights and measures, and imposed taxes. He concluded that the concept of sovereignty must be taken to denote just a high and absolute power over the citizens. He formulated the power of government as so strong that it transcends the particular interests both of provincial autonomy, that perennial obstacle to the policies of the French crown, and even of religious belief. According to him, the existence of such a type of sovereignty is what distinguishes the state from any other kind of human association. Bodin's great work embraces a clear definition of sovereignty through the definition of the state as "a lawful government of many families by means of a high and perpetual power" (Skinner, 1978:II/288).

Bodin saw the salvation of France in setting up such a sovereign national and central power. He belonged to the group of *politiques*, a group that desired the restoration of peace and order and that believed that the success of France demanded the suppression of political factions and religious controversies and the establishment of a strong monarchy depending on the unquestioned supremacy of the king. (The other members of this group were Du Bellay, Seruins, William Barclay, and Pierre Gregoire.) Bodin defined citizen as "free man, subject to the sovereign power of another within this context of the theory of sovereignty." Like Machiavelli before him and Hobbes after him, Bodin accepted absolutism in governmental affairs and framed the legalization of this absolutism grounded on the theory of sovereignty.

The philosophical basis of the absolutist nation-state had been evaluated by Hobbes. His theory of state was based on a rational feeling of self-preservation which led the human-being to set up a social contract. His political theory opened a new elan in the history of political science as the application of Cartesian method to political thought. He constructed an argument for absolute authority of the sovereign, claiming that the equal natural rights of man made the state of nature one of war. Natural law, which was a rule discovered by reason, led man to escape from the condition of war by establishing the state and the sovereign. After this establishment, the will of the sovereign became the only true law according to Hobbes. Absolutism around the centralization of nation-state found its philosophical and rational legalization with these ideas of Hobbes who was the founder of rational political philosophy and the modern idea of state.

So, the internal structure of the nation-state had been formed and legalized mainly by Machiavelli, Bodin, and Hobbes. The principles of the structure of the international system in which the nation-states became political units had been set up by Grotius, who used and acknowledged works of Conrad Braun, Ferdinand Vasques, Francisco Suarez, and Alberian Gentilis.

Conrad Braun tried to specify the principles of the international system, while Vasques claimed a composite law of nations governing the relations among independent states. Francisco Suarez developed a complete philosophical theory of international law. Gentilis, meanwhile, advanced the definition of the respective rights and duties of belligerent and neutral states, recognizing the territorial basis of sovereignty. He also discussed, in his work *De Legationibus* (1585), the rights and immunities of ambassadors and their relations to the states that sent and received them.

Grotius dealt mainly with three subjects: the law of nature, the law of nations and sovereignty. He claimed that "there might be some law among all or most states, and in fact there are agreed on by common consent which represent the advantage of all in general" like the internal laws of nation-states depend on the benefits of citizens. "Amongst all or most States, there might be, in fact there are, some laws, agreed on by common consent, which represent the advantage of all in general... and this is what is called the Law of Nations; if those laws be observed all nations will benefit, and aggressors who violate the laws of nature and nations break down the bulwarks of their future happiness and tranquility" (Bowle, 1961:298). He insisted that the justification for war is to win peace. The main contribution of Grotius was the definition of natural law of nations and setting up foundations for international law within a framework of sovereign nation-states.

The formation of nation-state system as a new socio-political inner structure of independent sovereign states and as a new international system was completed in the first half of the seventeenth century depending on these ideas. The Peace of Westphalia in 1648 declared the emergence of the European state system consisting of independent sovereign nation-states as a new elan in the political history of human beings.

This system of nation-state reached its peak in the nineteenth century through gaining an ideological characteristic as a philosophical, psychological, and social phenomenon, namely nationalism. It found its most sophisticated philosophical dimension in Hegel's personality whose philosophy attached the idea of the general will to the spirit of the nation, embodying itself in a national culture. This means the formation of a new unit together with its spirit: "that all the elements of a culture form a unit in which religion, philosophy, art, and morality mutually affect one another, that these several branches of culture all express the *spirit* —the internal intellectual endowment—of the people which creates them, and that the history of a people is the process in which it realizes and unfolds its unique contribution to the whole of human civilization" (Sabine & Thorson, 1973:573). His arguments that there could be no morality in the relations these self-contained units had with each other and that the individual was supposed to uphold and conform to rational political institutions and laws because of his presupposition that ideal morality was the union of the subjective (conscience) with the objective (law and tradition) marks the cornerstones of the continuity in the political philosophy of Western culture. As Snyder concludes, "just as Machiavelli in the early sixteenth century excluded morality from politics, so did Hegel in the early nineteenth century place nation-state above morality" (1968:43).

Hegel's conclusion on the history of civilization, that the national mind is a manifestation of the world-mind at a particular stage of its historical development, might be accepted as the foundation stone of the intellectual and imaginative development of nationalism as a secularized form of religion. Nationalism became a firmed secularized religion in its later process of development in the beginning of our age. Kelley describes this situation clearly: "Just as religions personify their gods, so does patriotism or nationalism tend to personify the idea of the nation to which it is directed.... The nation is pictured as possessing all the attributes of an ideal person."[5]

---

[5]Kohn (1949:21) uses an interesting simile between nationalistic struggles and religious crusades to underline the religious character of national feeling: "The

Thus, Hegel transformed Kant's famous "consciousness in itself" into a specific "state-consciousness" which assumes that there are universally valid moral laws but only a number of different systems of morality valid for different states. This phenomenon assumes a state-centered life as the ultimate materialization of national feeling and consciousness. Silvert's (1963:19) definition of nationalism as "the acceptance of the state as the impersonal and ultimate arbiter of human affairs" underlines its most significant characteristic. This state-centered and nation-oriented life as a modern phenomenon in Western civilization carries theoretical and imaginative elements originated from its *Weltanschauung* which contrasts absolutely with the Islamic idea of belief-oriented socio-political unity assuming a unitary aspect of life.

Islamic bicompartmentalization: *Dâr al-Islam* versus *Dâr al-Harb*

There is in contemporary literature and politics a veil of misperception related to Muslim political culture and its theological foundations. The oversimplification of facts for practical political reasons, the highly polarized categorizations, and the misuse of the literal meanings of some Islamic concepts are basic reasons for this misperception. For example, the imaginative interrelationships among *ummah*, *jihâd*, *Dâr al-Islam*, *Dâr al-Harb*, and Islamic state provide enough evidence for many scholars to present Islam as the most warlike religion (and sometime ideology) in history. Bernard Lewis' presentation about war and peace in Islam reflects such an approach: "According to Muslim teaching, *jihâd* is one of the basic commandments of the faith, an obligation imposed on all Muslims by God, through revelation.... The basis of the obligation of *jihâd* is the universality of the Muslim revelation. God's word and God's message are for all mankind; it is the duty of those who have accepted them to strive (*jahada*) unceasingly to convert or at least to subjugate those who have not. This obligation is without limit of time or space. It must continue until the whole world has either accepted the Islamic faith or submitted to the power of the Islamic state. Until that happens, the world is divided into two: *Dâr al-Islam* (the House of Islam, where Muslims rule) and *Dâr al-Harb* (the House of War, comprising the rest of the world). Between the two there is a morally, necessary, legally, religiously obligatory state of war, until the final and inevitable triumph of Islam over the unbelief. According to the law books, this state

---

German and Slav educated classes had, in the eighteenth century, willingly accepted French civilization; now the age of nationalism not only generated and deepened conflict but invested the struggle between nations with the halo of a semireligious crusade." Hayes' definition of nationalism as "the fusion of patriotism with nationality over all the other human loyalties" and Emerson's statement that "nationalism is no more than the assertion that this particular community is arranged against the rest of mankind" (Silvert, 1963:16-18) aim to show this characteristic of being a firmed secularized religion.

of war could be interrupted, when expedient, by an armistice or truce of limited duration. It could not be terminated by a peace, but only by a final victory" (Lewis, 1988:73).

The consciousness of fear and hostility by the non-Muslims in *Dâr al-Harb* against Islam is an inevitable consequence of such a presentation. Historical imaginations and attempts to justify Western colonialism gave rise to this gap of mutual understanding which sacrifices real facts for the surface appearances. As Peters (1979:4-5) describes, "The Islamic doctrine of *jihâd* has always appealed to Western imagination. The image of the dreadful Turk, clad in a long robe and brandishing his scimitar, ready to slaughter any infidel that might come his way and would refuse to be converted to the religion of Mahomet, has been a stereotype in Western literature for a long time. Nowadays this image has been replaced by that of the Arab 'terrorist' in battledress, armed with a Kalashnikov gun and prepared to murder in cold blood innocent Jewish and Christian women and children. The assumption underlying these stereotypes is that Moslems, often loosely called Arabs, are innately bloodthirsty and inimical towards persons of a different persuasion, and that owing to their religion, which allegedly preaches intolerance, fanaticism and continuous warfare against unbelievers. This view of Islam and Moslems, which developed in the Middle Ages, acquired new life and vigour in the era of European imperialism. Moslems were depicted as backward, fanatic and bellicose, in order to justify colonial expansion with the argument that it served the spread of civilization, which the French called *mission civilisatrice*. At the same time, this offered a convenient pretext for use of force against the indigenous population, for behind the outward appearance of submissiveness of the colonized Moslems, the colonizers saw the continuous danger of rebelliousness lurking, nourished by the idea of *jihâd* and waiting for an opportunity to manifest itself."

The methodological origin of this misperception is the selective matching of the political concepts and structures of two different paradigms. There is a concealed assumption behind these analyses which equates *Dâr al-Islam* to the nation-state of the contemporary international system. This assumption, together with the conception of *jihâd* as a continuous war, presents Islam as a potential threat to world peace similar to that caused by Nazism, which assumes a continuous war by a divinely selected nation against the rest of the world, or similar to socialist revolutionary dogmatism of Trotsky, who sought to transform class conflict into a universal and continuous revolution. We have to re-examine these judgements and equations by understanding the political concepts and structures within the internal consistency of each paradigm.

Ummah as the basis of socio-political unity

Von Grünebaum (1962a:50) asks a very crucial question in his article on the pluralistic diversification of the Muslim society: "Nations come and go. Empires rise and fall. But Islam persists and continues to include the nomads and the settlers, the builders of civilizations within Islam and those that destroy them. What then are the factors that keep together as one *ummah* those many people that consciously or not inclined to maintain their individuality while cultivating their tie with universal Islam as their most precious spiritual possession?"

Socio-political identification in Islamic political thought and practice is an extension of the belief in the unity of human responsibility and in the unity of life.

The basic dichotomy between believer (mu'min) and unbeliever (kâfir) as two different ontological/religious approaches and radically opposed categories can be defined as the choice between whether or not one wishes to accept this special responsibility on earth. This choice is also a choice of a way of life and a specific socio-political identity. Those who believe in the unity of Allâh and accept to be a member of Muslim socio-political society do not discard only their old ethnic identity but also all possible alternate identities. As Oda (1984:102-3) underlines, even if one is still physically determined by ethnicity (color of skin and language in the Qur'ânic phrase) it is no longer one's essential identity, which is rather as a Muslim who is equal before God with all other Muslims: "This indicates that believers must entirely change their mode of existence from the ethnic or tribal to the real Islamic mode of existence. These two modes of existence are never compatible." The Qur'ân clearly specifies this categoric differentiation of two parties belonging to alternative modes of existence and of social identity: "And if there is a party of you which believes in that wherewith I have been sent, and there is a party which believes not, then have patience until Allâh judge between us. He is the best of all who deal in judgement" (7:87).[6]

Ummah, as the Islamic mode of social existence, is the basis of socio-political unity in Islamic political thought and practice. Like other political key-concepts, it has been re-valuated after its usage within the Qur'ânic semantic field. Although Smith (1903:32) claims that its etymological origin is Hebrew ém, which means mother, through Arabic umm, Denny (1975:37) points out that there is nothing in the Qur'ânic usage of ummah to support this view. Ummah as a very significant key-concept has several meanings in the Qur'ân to indicate social groupings,[7] but it gained as a leitmotif a specific meaning to describe the religious-political unity of Muslims.

The concentration of verses including the term ummah in the third Makkan period (according to the Nöldeke chronology) and early Madînan period provides us significant clues regarding how the Qur'ânic revelation affected the socio-political imagination of Muslims at that time due to the fact that these periods mark

---

[6]This categoric differentiation is strengthened by such other Qur'ânic terms as hizb Allâh (party of Allâh) and hizb al-Shaytân (party of the devil). "The devil has engrossed them and so has caused them to forget remembrance of Allâh. They are the devil's party. Lo! is it not the devil's party who will be the losers? Lo! those who oppose Allâh and His Messenger, they will be among the lowest. Allâh has decreed: Lo! I verily shall conquer, I and my messenger. Lo! Allâh is strong, Almighty. You will not find folk who believe in Allâh and the Last Day loving those who oppose Allâh and His Messenger, even though they be their fathers or their sons or their brethren or their clan. As for such, He has written faith upon their hearts and has strengthened them with a Spirit from Him, and He will bring them into gardens underneath which rivers flow, wherein they will abide. They are Allâh's party. Lo! is not Allâh's party who are the successful?" (Qur'ân, 58:19-22).

[7]There are sixty-four instances of the term ummah in the Qur'ân, in both singular and plural forms. Forty-nine are in Makkan verses, while fifteen are in Madînan verses. Oda's (1984:95-96) classification of motifs for the term ummah in the Qur'ân provides a suitable framework to imagine the semantic field of this concept. A more detailed table from the perspective of chronology can be found in Denny (1975:46-47).

the most significant turning points in the formation of the first model of Islamic *ummah*. The term *ummah wasaṭah* as the ultimate form of this model has been used in the Madînan period when Islamic socio-political community has been formed in reality: "Thus We have appointed you a middle nation [*ummah wasaṭah*], that you may be witnesses against mankind, and that the messenger may be a witness against you. And We appointed the *qiblah* that you formerly observed only that We might know him who follows the messenger from him who turns on his heels. In truth it was a hard [test] save for those whom Allâh guided. But it was not Allâh's purpose that your faith should be in vain, for Allâh is full of pity, Merciful toward mankind" (Qur'ân, 2:143). This concept of *wasaṭ* (middle) does not mean ordinary, but balanced. On the contrary, according to the commentators, it is an extraordinary model in the sense of *khayr* (*khiyar 'adûlan* according to the *tafsîr* of Jalâlayn, 1982:29) and *fâḍilah* (*khiyar al-umam* or *afḍal* in *tafsîr* of Ibn Kathîr, 1986:I/190). Hence, Denny (1975:54-55) is absolutely right in concluding on this compound expression that "The *ummah wasaṭah* is a Madînan concept formulated by the Qur'ân when the concept of *ummah* as religious community reached its most developed stage. If in the past an *ummah* could have rejected its messengers (as in, e.g., 40:5, 27:83, and 29:18, all Makkan), the *ummah* concept in the Madînan period seems to have become more exclusively the term which applies to Muslims as the *ummah* par excellence, a concept and reality which possess an ontological status, constituted as it had been by the submission (*Islam*) of Muḥammad's people and at the same time born from the mercy (*raḥma*) of God in answer to the religious quest uttered in Abraham's prayer (2:127-9).... The *ummah wasaṭah* is witness to the rest of mankind, and Muḥammad is the witness to the Muslims of God's will: from God, to Muḥammad, to the *Ummah*, to the remainder of mankind proceed the Message and the Norm. It is not sufficient that a prophet alone should bear the entire message to mankind; rather, the believing community ingrains in itself the message by its obedience, expressed in rites such as the *ṣalât* and the orientation of the worshippers toward the *qiblah* at Makkah, as in 2:143. Religion in the Qur'ân is not essentially a matter of personal piety (although there is certainly much pertaining to individual religion); rather, the emphasis is on the communal aspects of religion. Muḥammad's fully matured spiritual life is unthinkable from the Muslims."

The idea of the responsibility of man gives a special responsibility to the Muslim political society, the *ummah*. The Qur'ânic definition of this socio-political community as *ummah al-muslimah* (Muslim community) rather than only as *ummah al-muslimîn* (community composed of Muslims) in 2:128,[8] implies that this socio-

---

[8] "Our Lord! And make us submissive unto Thee [*muslimah laka*] and of our seed a nation submissive unto Thee [*ummah muslimah laka*], and show us our ways of worship, and relent towards us. Lo! Thou, only Thou, are the Hearer, the Knower." Oda's clarification of the nuances in this verse shows the importance of socio-political unity as divinely responsible community in Islam: "The first part, 'make us two Muslims' is concerned with the individual decision of faith. Individual Muslims would establish a religious community according to the pattern by which religions are founded. This community would be called 'a religious community of Muslims,' or *ummah al-muslimîn* in Arabic. Abraham's prayer however, continues saying, 'make our descendents a community submissive to God.' The term *ummah al-muslimah* has more implications and significance than the earlier term *ummah al-muslimîn*. The *ummah al-muslimah* logically includes the

political unity has its importance as a totality performing its specific divine responsibility beyond its importance as being composed of individual Muslims. This mission of *ummah* specified by the Qur'ân as, "And hold fast, all of you together, to the cable of Allâh, and do not separate. And remember Allâh's favor unto you: how you were enemies and He made friendship between your hearts so that you became as brother by His grace... And there may spring from you an *ummah* [translated by Pickthall as 'nation,' by Yûsuf 'Ali (1983) as 'people,' and by Ismâ'il Fârûqî (1982) as 'society'] who invite to goodness, and enjoin right conduct and forbid indecency. Such are they who are successful" (3:103-04). The semantic fields of the expressions of *ummah al-muslimah* and *ummah wasaṭah* intersect in this verse from the perspective of divine responsibility. Another verse in the same *sûrah* defines the *sine qua non* of the best community (*khayr ummah*) as socio-political divine responsibility on the earth: "You are the best community that has been raised up for mankind. You enjoin right conduct and forbid indecency; and you believe in Allâh" (3:110).

The *ummah* is an open society for any human being who accepts this responsibility regardless of his origin, race, or color. Therefore, the compartmentalization into *ummah* and non-*ummah* is totally different from such dichotomies as the Semitic discrimination between Jew and Gentile, the Greek discrimination between barbarian and citizen, or modern nationalist hierarchical stratifications such as in Nazism which are beyond the control of human will. Such a responsibility is the basis of the identification and the political socialization process of a Muslim within a socio-political environment. This forms a logical, theoretical, and practical chain with the Qur'ânic verse, "the *ummah* of yours is one *ummah*" (21:92) and the belief in the unity of Allâh (*tawḥîd*). Belief in the unity of Allâh implies belief in the epistemological unity of truth which implies axiological unity of the divine responsibility of man and his life and socio-political unity of the *ummah* to realize the ideal lifestyle. The ethical qualities of this ideal lifestyle and *ummah* as the socio-political unity that aims to realize it has been described in the Qur'ân in details such as belief, honor, piety, justice, and righteousness.

The cause of being a member of Muslim community depends on some sort of "feeling," as Watt describes it within the framework of *ijma'*, rather than on concrete rules. Although there are some rules for membership in the Muslim community, such as *shahâdah*, *ṣalât*, and *zakât*; in fact "a man ceases to be a member if he does something which the general body of Muslims feel to be incompatible with membership" (Watt,1964:12). The area of compatibility with the membership of Muslim community embraces the ethical qualities consisting of a specific way of life originated from a comprehensive *Weltanschauung*. Thus, the *ummah* has been described based on an inter-connected approach from the perspective of ontologico-epistemologico-axiological base rather than from the perspective of an ethnic, linguistic, or territorial base, such as is the case with a nation-state. The personalistic character of Islamic law facilitates this characteristic of being beyond territory and physical limitations.

---

ummah al-muslimîn, but the latter would not necessarily be the *Ummah Muslimah*. The *Ummah Muslimah* signifies that in addition to each member's being a Muslim, and thus submissive to God, the community qua community must be submissive to God" (1984:105).

This metaphysical (in the sense of being beyond ethnic and territorial limitations) religious-political bond of the *ummah* is the base of the historical realization of the integration of political life in Islamic history. As Watt underlines, Islam had great success in integrating the political life of its adherents during the process of the formation of the *ummah* which, while it had a religious basis, was also a political body. "The success was not merely in forming such a body, but in managing to attach to it some of the valuable attitudes which, in the case of the pre-Islamic Arabs, had been attached to the tribe. One such attitude, arising from the feeling of brotherhood between the members of a tribe, led to a strong feeling of brotherhood among the members of the Islamic community, and this feeling contributed to the recognition of the equality of non-Arab and Arab within the community.... All this was a great achievement, and integrated the political life of the Muslims to a high degree, in that it formed a body politic in which were to be found very favorable conditions for the practice of the Islamic religion and the attainment of its end of salvation, that is, of a significance which transcended the historical process" (Watt, 1970:175).

Thus, the *principium individuationis* of the Islamic political way of thought that there should be a strong and direct link between ontological antecedents, axiological normativism and political unity, can not be accommodated to the *sine quo non* of Western tradition on socio-political unity, mentioned before. First of all, contrary to ethnic origin or place of birth, which could not be determined by the free will of the individual, as the criterion for citizenship in a secular political unity, Islamic political understanding presupposes a voluntary acceptance of a Muslim socio-political community through a socio-political identification dependent on the ontological approach. Second, unlike Christianity, in which "admission to the community is contingent not only on the desire of the would-be convert to join, but equally on the readiness of the community to accept him" (von Grünebaum, 1966:51) which in turn is contingent upon a demonstration of the candidate's knowledge of doctrine, scrutiny of his moral character, and finally the undertaking of several elaborate ritual steps, in Islam, a unilateral declaration before two witnesses to the unity of Allâh and the prophetic function of Muḥammad is enough to become a member of the *ummah* . As von Grünebaum (1962:44) stresses, "the community cannot and, in the Muslim view, ought not judge what is men's hearts: and it can and ought merely to observe the loyal adherence to those practices which symbolize in its eyes the loyal identification of the individual with the *ummah.*" The ease with which one is admitted to the community emphasizes for the individual the voluntariness of his participation and emphasizes for the socio-political community its openness.

From the perspective of attachment of socio-political unity to ontological/religious antecedents, it is almost impossible to translate *ummah* into any other language. It can be understood only within the conceptual structure of the all-inclusive Islamic framework which has been determined through the re-valuation of classical pre-Islamic Arabic terms by the Qur'ân within its semantic field end characteristic. As our etymological and semantic analysis shows, it can not be used correspondingly with nation, people, *Volk,* state, *etat,* or *status.* The Augustinian term *res publica* which was used for the Christian universal community as *res publica christiana* could not be a corresponding term for *ummah* because of its socio-political character. From the perspective of Augustinian terminology it carries the meanings both of *civitas* which was referring to state and of *res publica* . The Arabic terms of *sha'b* and *qawm* might be used to correspond to some usages of these Western concepts as nation, but they could not indicate the socio-political identification in the sense of the usage of *ummah* which denotes the universal Muslim political society constituted by *homo Islamicus* with a common ontological approach as a framework of *'aqâid* and with a common axiological normativeness as the basis of the comprehensive juridic scheme, *fiqh*. The socio-political orientation and identification of *ummah* could be evaluated only via this interesting link between *'aqâid* as a mode of belief and *fiqh* as a mode of life. The oneness of *ummah* depends on the common ontological approach of its members rather than on linguistic, geographic, cultural, or biological factors and is directly connected to the concept of Allâh and to the specific *imago mundi* originating from this belief in *tawhîd*.

The unity of the *ummah* has been strictly emphasized by Muslim political thinkers. The view—supported by almost all medieval jurists, including Abû Yûsuf, Mawârdî, Abû Ya'lâ, and Baghdâdî— that there should be only one caliph on the earth except in extraordinary cases aimed to preserve the universal unity of the socio-political community for the realization of the idea of best community mentioned in 3:110. In particular, the stimulus of Mawârdî's emphasis on the caliph's authority was based on this aim in an age when authority had been distributed to bureaucratic organs in the hands of military leaders.

This aim of the political unity of *ummah* was achieved in the early centuries of Islamic history. The rapid expansion of Islam had two significant historical consequences: the existence of Muslim populations under the control of non-Muslim states and the emergence of many Muslim states at the same time. These phenomena lay at the root of the conceptual, theoretical, and practical differentiation between *ummah*, *Dâr al-Islam*, and Muslim (or Islamic) state.

The existence of Muslim minorities in *Dâr al-Harb* necessitated a distinction between *ummah* and *Dâr al-Islam*. *Ummah* gained a broader meaning consisting of all individual Muslims, with a religious/spiritual bond continuing even in the absence of a common political authority. This metapolitical bond originated from a common *Selbstverständnis* of ontological consciousness creates a challenging power against the political bond of nation-state system. The tension between Muslim minorities and nation-states in contemporary politics originates from these alternative imaginations. Some nation-states, like Bulgaria and Thailand, have forced Muslims to accept non-Muslim names in an effort to demonstrate the supremacy of the nation-state and ultimate loyalty to it, but ummatic consciousness has continued to survive in spite of such oppressive measures. This phenomenon is an indication of the impact of *Weltanschauung* on political imagination. Again, the revival of ummatic consciousness in this century in spite of the absence of caliphate as the symbol of the political unity of *Dâr al-Islam* further demarcates *ummah* from *Dâr al-Islam*.

On the other hand, emergence of many Muslim states, in the sense of more than one centralized political authority, parallel to the expansion of Islam necessitated a demarcation between *Dâr al-Islam* and individual states. Even classical jurists had to acknowledge this reality. Al-Dabbûsî gives evidence of this when he states: "The distinguishing factor between the Muslim and non-Muslim territories is the difference of authority and administration. The same is true of the different principalities [*al-wilâyât al-mukhtalifah*] within Islamic territories [*Dâr al-Islam*] which are distinguished from one another [*mulûk al-Islam*] by the domination [*ghalabah*] and the execution of authority [*ijra' al-ahkâm*]" (Hamîdullah, 1987:151).

From this perspective of Muslim imagination, *Dâr al-Islam* denotes a world-system in the sense of a universal political system, while Muslim state (*al-dawlah*) denotes individual political authority. *Dâr al-Islam* implies a consistent world-system within which there is a common base of *Selbstverständnis*, a possibility for the realization of the divine responsibility, and a common axiological framework for the application of the prescriptivist legal system. It is in part an international system in its external relations. *Dâr al-Harb* is the counter-system for matters of international relations from this perspective. Therefore the analogy between this bicompartmentalization and internal conflicts of nation-state system and argumentations on *jihâd* based on this analogy is not correct. *Dâr al-Islam* could not be imagined like a nation-state which is in a continuous state of war for its expansion. Rather it is a *de facto* reality in the sense of judicial application and a consistent world-system in the sense of axiological prerequisites which shape political imagination and culture.

Islamic bicompartmentalization as the universal political system

The socio-political identification of *ummah* specifies a unique type of citizenship consisting of Muslims who decide to live together to perform their divine responsibility through the realization of a lifestyle originating from an axiological norm, together with non-Muslims (*dhimmis*) who accept the political sovereignty and patronage of the Muslim state as the realization of the political power of the *ummah* and have the autonomy to pursue their own lifestyles within a pluralistic legal structure. This divine responsibility of *ummah* has been transformed into a universal ideal of ordering people to act properly and preventing them from acting improperly (*al-amr bi al-ma'rûf wa al-nahy 'an al-munkar*). The ideal of the universalization of justice around this basic principle became a dynamic force for Islamic expansion.

The idea of political unity creates a bicompartmentalization of the universal political system between *Dâr al-Islam*, where the divine responsibility of man could be performed according to the rules of *fiqh*, and *Dâr al-Harb*, where Muslims do not have such an opportunity. Such a bicompartmentalization has not been determined either in the Qur'ân or in the *hadîths*. Rather, it was systematized by Muslim jurists during the development of *fiqh* and the enlargement of Muslim territories in order to specify the territories, dependent on the realization of political power, within which this juridic scheme could be applied. Al-Sarakhsî's judgement in *al-Mabsût* that "juristic punishments can not be applied in *Dâr al-Harb* [la tuqâmu al-hudûd fi Dâr al-Harb]"(Özel, 1982:71) marks the fundamental juristic criterion of this bicompartmentalization as well as the origin of and necessity for such a bicompartmentalization to specify the geographical boundaries within which the survival of a specific way of life and juristic scheme is possible. The meaning of this bicompartmentalization goes beyond its importance for military affairs. As will be shown, it does not mean that peaceful relationships can not be established with other communities and states.

Some scholars defined a third division within the world order, *Dâr al-'Ahd* (the House of Truce) or *Dâr al-Sulh* (the House of Covenant), to indicate those states that have peaceful agreements with an Islamic state from those that do not. But many Hanafî scholars insisted that there were only two divisions within the world order, because if the inhabitants of a territory had concluded a treaty of peace it became a part of *Dâr al-Islam*.

Dâr, which literally means country or place, has been applied to the Islamic juristic scheme together with its dimension of political authority and power. Ibn 'Âbidîn defines *dâr* in his *Radd al-Mukhtâr* as "the country under the government of a Muslim or non-Muslim" while al-Jassâs in *Mukhtaṣar al-Ṭaḥâwî* takes it to connote some attachment to political power and hegemony (Özel,1982:69).

As Khaddûrî (intr. ch. of Shaybânî, 1966:10) mentions, the Islamic conception of world order within a bicompartmental framework is a reflection of the basic assumption that only the members of the *ummah* are the subjects of the Islamic legal and ethical system while all other communities are the object of that system, although they are by no means denied certain advantages of the system when they come into contact with Islam. This subject/object relationship is consistent with the understanding of *ummah* as the political unity of Muslims. However, this difference is part of the legal framework rather than political, because caliph or imam is responsible for the well-being of all subjects, including non-Muslim communities.

Such a bicompartmentalization could not be regarded as a declaration of permanent war as some Orientalists argue, because according to many Muslim sects and jurists the normal and permanent state in international relations is the state of peace. The translation of *jihâd* as "holy war" in Western languages creates a misperception that Islam assumes a permanent war in its relations with other political units. *Jihâd*, as another very significant key-concept, has a more comprehensive meaning than the notion of war in Western languages. The Arabic terms corresponding to "war" are *ḥarb* and *qitâl*. The origin of *jihâd*, however, is *jahada* which means "to endeavor." Thus the meaning of *jihâd* is "exertion" or "the endeavor." The technical meaning of this term in Islamic thought, law, and practice is the act of exerting oneself in the way of Allâh to fulfill the divine responsibility. Its usage in the Qur'ân marks this meaning very clearly: "As for those who strive in Us, We surely guide them in Our paths, and lo! Allâh is with the good" (29:69). A war in the cause of Allâh is a specific type of *jihâd*, but *jihâd* does not mean merely an action during warfare. As Khaddûrî (intr. ch. of Shaybânî, 1966:15) clarifies, "The *jihâd*, in the broad sense of the term, did not necessarily call for violence or fighting."

Unlike some religions, Islam did not deny the reality of war. Rather, it specified the normative/juristic limitations of this reality.[9] Islam sets up a very sensitive

---

[9]Ḥamîdullah (1987:205-8) notes that classical Islamic sources forbid the following acts during war: (i) unnecessarily cruel and tortuous ways of killing; (ii) killing non-combatants (women, minors, servants, slaves and the like who have not joined in fighting, the blind, the disabled, very old, insane, non-combatant monks etc.); (iii) decapitating prisoners of war , (iv) mutilation of men or beasts; (v) treachery and perfidy; (vi) devastation, destruction of harvests, or unnecessarily cutting trees; (vii) slaughtering animals beyond what is necessary for food; (viii) excess and wickedness; (ix) adultery and fornication, even with captive women; (x) killing enemy hostages; (xi) severing the heads of fallen enemies; (xii) massacre after occupation; (xiii) killing parents, even if they are non-Muslims and in the enemy ranks, except in absolute self-defense; (xiv) killing peasants when they do not fight, (xv) killing traders, merchants, contractors, and the like if they do not

balance between its activist/dynamic element to universalize its normative way of thought and life, on the one hand, and the moral prerequisites during the process of this universalization, on the other. From this perspective, Islam accepts war in the way of Allâh as a natural means which will be used in cases of necessity, and it specifies the right conduct during war. Therefore it incites Muslims to make war against injustice and tyranny on the earth in order to universalize the norms of Islam, but it reminds Muslims of the priority of moral prerequisites even during that war. This characteristic originates from the early periods of Islamic history.

Ṭabarî's *Târîkh* reports an incident from the time of Abû Bakr that gives a very interesting example of this balance in Islam. "Abû Bakr went out [with the army] and he was walking, while Usâma [the leader of the army] rode. 'Abd al-Raḥmân ibn 'Awf was leading Abû Bakr's mount. Then Usâma said to him, 'Successor of God's Messenger, you will either mount, or I shall dismount.' He replied, 'By God you shall not dismount, and I will not mount. I must get my feet a little dusty in the path of God, for a raider [*ghazi*] with every step he takes has seven hundred merits credited to him and he is raised seven hundred degrees, while seven hundred sins are forgiven him!' .... Then he said: 'O ye people! Stand, while I give you ten words of advice, and learn them from me. Do not act treacherously; do not act disloyally; do not act neglectfully. Do not mutilate; do not kill little children or old men or women; do not cut off the heads of the palm-trees or burn them; do not cut down the fruit trees; do not slaughter a sheep or a cow or a camel except for food. You will pass by people who devote their lives in cloisters; leave them and their devotions alone. You will come upon people who bring you platters in which are various sorts of food; if you eat any of it, mention the name of God over it.... Go forth now in the name of God, and may He give you death by a wound or an epidemic!'" (1962:226-27; English version from Williams, 1971:262). Abû Bakr respected to the military commander of the army because of the high status of jihad in the Muslim conception of the purpose of life. Yet, he described the moral and behavioral principles of *jihad* to show that *jihad* does not mean to make war for the victory at any cost. Therefore, he did not incite the soldiers to get more booty from the war, but rather to welcome death in the path of Allâh in order to realize the basic Islamic norms.

Nevertheless, such a normative/juristic base does not mean that the principle of *jihâd* assumes a continuous process of warfare in the sense of psychological, political, and military relations. Hence, Khaddûrî's assertion (intr. ch. of Shaybânî, 1966:16) on this assumption of continuous war does not reflect the ideas of all Muslim scholars because, for example, Ibn Qudâmah reports in *al-Mughnî* that Abû Ḥanîfah insists on the argument that peace is more useful for Muslims than war in the process of the expansion of Islam (Abû Sulaymân, 1987:16, 19). The majority of the scholars (*jumhûr fuqahâ*) accept the priority of peace. Meanwhile, the historical reality does not confirm the assumption that Muslims assume a continuous state of war, for every Muslim state throughout Islamic history has signed treaties of peace with non-Muslim states.

---

take part in actual fighting; (xvi) burning a captured man or animal to death; (xvii) taking shelter behind enemy prisoners; (xviii) using poisonous arrows; and (xix) acts forbidden under general treaties so long as those treaties are in force.

A detailed analysis should underline as the basic characteristic that Islam offers a normative framework in international relations[10] to define legitimate actions/reactions against other political actors in the universal system. The basic key-terms of this normative framework are *musâwat* (equality), *'adâlah* (justice), *muqâbalah bi al-mithl* (retaliation), *ḥurriyah* (freedom), *ṣulh* (peace), *amân* (safe-conduct/security), and *wafâ bi al-'ahd (pacta sunt servanda)*. The most significant norm related to international relations is *musâwat* which implies that in the sufferings of this world Muslims and non-Muslims are equal and alike. Almost all Muslim scholars agree on this fundamental principle (Zaydân, 1967:130; Ḥamîdullah, 1987:75; Özel, 1984:38, 41).[11] This principle might be attached to the interpretations of *al-Raḥmân*, one of the holy names of Allâh, that this name embraces mercy of Allâh both for Muslims and non-Muslims on the earth.[12] Therefore, war aiming to suffer the world better than other nations could not be justified in Islamic theory.

The ontological equality of human beings before Allâh has been applied to the cases of international relations, especially through interpretation of the verse, "O mankind! We have created you male and female, and have made you nations and tribes that you may know one another. Lo! the noblest of you in the sight of Allâh is the best in conduct" (Qur'ân, 49:13).[13] The commentators mentioned several significant consequences of this verse. First, it specifies that the *raison d'etre* for the diversification of human being as nations is recognition of each other (*ta'âruf*) rather than competition. Another verse dictates the basis of legitimate competition because of the diversification as nations: "Had Allâh willed He could have made you one community. But that He may try you by that which He hath given to you. So vie one with another in good works [*khayrât*]" (Qur'ân, 5:48).

Second, 49:13 assumes peaceful relations (*ṣulḥ*) as the state of nature among human beings. This normative principle of *ṣulḥ* as the state of nature is supported by the verse, "Allâh forbids you only those who warred not against you on account of religion and drove you not from your homes, that you should show them kindness and deal justly with them. Lo! Allâh loves the just dealers" (60:8). Muslim scholars offer two arguments on the justification for war. Many , especially Hanafî scholars, argue that the justification for war is the attack of enemies against Muslims. For example, Dabbûsî asserts in *al-Asrâr* on this issue that the justification of lawfulness against *ahl al-kitâb* is their declaration of war against Muslims (Özel, 1982:51), and he connects this principle to the Islamic belief in the

---

[10]The term "international relations" should be used very carefully since Islamic political theory does not assume, at least in its classical theory, national unities as the actors of universal political system. "Interstate relations" might be more appropriate, but I prefer to use the former term because of its common usage as a classical branch of political theory.

[11]Ḥamîdullah (1987:75) quotes Dabbûsî's argument to underline this characteristic: "God has not made a difference between us and them with regard to the causes of worldly sufferings; for this world is not the Abode of Reward."

[12]See Yazir (1971:I/36).

[13]It should not be forgotten, however, that the nations (*shu'ub*) and tribes (*qabâ'ail*) mentioned in this verse are sub-groups in the hierarchy of social groupings compared to *ummah* as the ultimate religio-political unity, analyzed above.

natural innocence of human beings. Although others, especially Shâfi'î scholars, argue that the justification for war is the unbelievers' *kufr*, the majority accept this argument (Özel, 1982:55), which implies that war is temporary and comes of necessity. Almost all of them agree that war is permitted only to protect right and justice against the attacks of enemies and of tyrants. This approach has been supported by other principles, such as the fundamental rights of men in the sense of the right of life and freedom (*ḥurriyah*). Ibn Humâm in *Fatḥ al-Qadîr* and Ibn Taymiyyah in *al-Fatâwa al-Kubrâ* strictly underline that the natural position of the human being is *ḥurriyah*, while Ibn Qudâmah stresses the natural right of life in *al-Mughnî* (Özel, 1982:29). On the other hand, declaration of war is the ultimate recourse when agreement with the enemy becomes impossible.[14]

The denomination of non-Muslim states as *Dâr al-Ḥarb* does not mean that the natural and permanent relationship between Muslim and non-Muslim states is war. On the contrary, "brief spans of peace may be offered the inhabitants of the *Dâr al-Ḥarb*, whether by a peace treaty concluded between Muslims and non-Muslims or by an *amân*" (Khaddûrî, intr. ch. Shaybânî, 1966:18). According to Muslim scholars, *wafâ bi al-'ahd* is one of the basic norms in international relations unless the other side violates its treaties. *Muqâbalah bi al-mithl* (retaliation) is a counterpart of the principle of *'adâlah*, but it can not be applied to cases in which it is impossible to apply retaliation because of other norms of Islamic ethics. For example, even if an enemy assassinates hostages, Muslims can not react likewise.

The concept of Islamic state (*dawlah*): Historical transformation of the institutionalization of political power

The etymological and semantic transformation of the concept of *dawlah* provides significant clues for an elaborate analysis of the historical transformation of the institutionalization of political power. The root of this concept, *d-w-l*, means to change periodically, to alternate, to turn, to rotate, to change, to replace, to exchange, to be victorious over somebody, to substitute, and to handle alternately. Rosenthal (1965:2/177) argues that the etymological root of this concept may occur in Akkadian *dâlu* meaning "to wander around aimlessly" and Syriac *dâl* meaning "to

---

[14] Several hadiths related to the applications of the Prophet provided theoretical and practical foundations for the development of a specific law in the Islamic history on the conduct of war. For example, following *hadîth* from the Prophet related to his advice to the commander of the Muslim army specifies the rules of the negotiation before the war as well as ethical principles during the war: "Fight in the name of God and in 'the path of God' [truth]. Combat [only] those who disbelieve in God. Do not cheat or commit treachery, nor should you mutilate anyone or kill children. Whenever you meet your polytheist enemies, invite them [first] to adopt Islam. If they do so, accept it, and let them alone. You should then invite them to move from their territory to the territory of the emigres [Madînah]. If they do so, accept it and let them alone. Otherwise, they should be informed that they would be like the Muslim nomads [who take no part in the war] in that they are subject to God's order as [other] Muslims, but that they will receive no share in either *ghanima* or in the *fay*. If they refuse, then call upon them to pay the *jizya* (poll tax); if they do, accept it and leave them alone...." (Shaybânî,1966:76)

move, to stir." Nevertheless, it is evident that these ancient usages can not reflect the semantic richness of this Arabic concept.

Two Qur'ânic usages carry the meanings of handling alternately, following one another, exchanging between a group, passing around. The usage meaning "to follow one another" and "to alternate" can be seen in the verse, "These are vicissitudes [days] which We cause to follow one another for mankind [*tilkal ayyâmu nudâwiluhâ baynan nâs]*" (Qur'ân, 3:140). The usage meaning "to exchange among a group" can be seen in the expression "that it become not a commodity between the rich among you [*kay lâ yakûna dûlatan bayn al-aghniyâ minkum*]" (Qur'ân, 59:7). The traditions related to the death of Prophet in 'Aisha's house also reflect the meaning "turn of period": "*mâta Rasulullâh bayna sahriy wa nahriy wa fi dawlatiy*" (Ibn Hishâm, 1964:392).

The semantic transformation of the root *dwl* from its Qur'ânic usage to its contemporary one occurred in three stages. In the first stage, which gives the first indication of the political conceptualization of this root, the word was used to mean a change of political power or the victory of one dynasty over another. Expressions like *al-dawlah al-'abbâsiyyah* or *al-dawlah Abû Muslim* in *Tarîkh al-Tabarî* are examples of this first stage. The usage of Manzûr as *bi dawlatina* and *hadhihi dawlah* (Tabarî, 1965:7/469) reflects this semantic transformation in the direction of political conceptualization. Victory, power, change of dynasty, and the period of being in power are basic to this early usage. The usage of this concept both for the political structure and the change of that structure is also consistent with the traditional Muslim circular imagination of historical development.

At the second stage of the semantic transformation, the concept was used for continuity and for the ultimate political authority and structure rather than to mean political change. The description of the Ottoman state as "*devlet-i ebed müddet*" in the Ottoman political literature aims to show the perpetuity of political power, victory, and institution.

The last stage of this semantic transformation occurred after the political supremacy of the Western international system based on individual nation-states. The concept of *dawlah* has been used as the translation of "nation-state" in several Muslim languages during the last stage.

The historical evolution of *dawlah* in Islamic history has unique characteristics compared to the Western experience. There are basically two approaches related to the emergence of *dawlah* in Islamic history. The followers of the first approach argue that the organization of state came immediately after the *Hijrah* of the Prophet and that Madînan society carried all characteristics of the state structure. The second approach assumes that the authority of the Prophet was a religious authority rather than political authority and therefore Madînan society was based on a community structure rather than a state structure. These two different approaches are counterparts of two different understandings of state. The first view supposes that state is the universal concept for the institutionalization of political power, while the second view assumes a concept of state based on the modern nation-state and develops a comparative analysis on this foundation.

Analysis of this historical evolution from the perspective of the institutionalization of political power shows that a political society arose through a process starting from the *bay'ahs* in 'Aqabah. Madînan society under the leadership of the Prophet carried all functions of a political society and of the institutionalization of political power. However, this political structure was a reflection of a unique political imagination, mentality, and culture which was different from that in Western historical experience. Madînan society, which integrated theory and practice, political ideal and reality was absolutely different from the structures of the city-state, empire-state, and nation-state.

It differed from the ancient city-states because of a special type of membership based on belief which gave an equal ontologico-political status to each member and made society an open society for any human being, unlike the city-states, where political participation was a right of a privileged class of citizens. For example, only a third of the Athenian residents enjoyed political participation, and the differentiation between citizens, metics, and slaves was assumed as a natural hierarchy based on birth which, as a pre-destined ontological status, could not be eliminated . Moreover, Madînan society expanded to a very large geographical area within a short period unlike the historical characteristics of city-states.

Madînan political structure likewise contrasts with that of the Alexandrian and Roman empire-states. This is so both from the perspective of relations between the individual and society as well as from the perspective of relations between the political center and the periphery.

The philosophical foundations of the Hegelian nation-state were absolutely alien to Madînan political imagination because it is impossible to mention the existence of a transcendental and abstract understanding of state which is independent from the existence of the society and superior to it in this first political society in Islamic history. Institutionalization of power was assumed as a political instrument to realize the ethical and social ideals of the belief system. Hence, political mechanisms to control individuals and society on behalf of the state could not emerge and exist within the framework and environment of this political mentality.

The unique characteristics of the Madînan society were reflected both in the formation of the consciousness of the political membership and in the formation of the political leadership. The Madînan constitution defined a new political membership and ontologico-political status which destroyed traditional tribal membership in Arab society. The comprehensive leadership of the Prophet developed a new imagination of political power which was in contradiction with the tribal political structure of Arab society as well as with the individualized and limited forms of reciprocal authority in European feudalism. Therefore, the structuralization of political power could be completed and expanded parallel to the geographical expansion.

The fundamental problem of Muslims after the death of the Prophet was the formation of a new political leadership. The political leadership of the Prophet was based on a special knowledge and therefore could not be limited in the sense of the area of implementation. The transformation from this natural leadership to the system of caliphate was the cornerstone of the formation of the political mentality of Muslims as well as of the institutionalization of political power as *dawlah*. Starting with the caliphate of Abû Bakr, the areas of politics, state, and government were accepted as areas within the responsibility of the human being based on human capacity and reason. This model implementation specified the epistemological foundation of politics and the right of *ummah* as a political society to determine its political leadership through *shûrâ* and *bay'ah*.

Two events during the time of Abû Bakr accelerated the process of the institutionalization of political power, war against false prophets and war against the tribes who refused to pay *zakât*. War against false prophets guaranteed that there could not be any formation of authority after the death of the Prophet that was based on arguments from metaphysical epistemology. Thus, it has been proved that the authority of Abû Bakr based on a human consensus of *ummah* was superior to claims to personal metaphysical epistemological sources of authority. The war against the tribes who refused to pay *zakât* to the new leader demonstrated that the political authority of Abû Bakr was same as the essence and scope of the political authority of the Prophet in spite of the difference in epistemological foundation. Thus, the institutionalization of political power around a center was guaranteed in order to establish order, justice, and stability in the steadily expanding geographical area of the Islamic caliphate. The applications of the first four caliphs became axiomatic models for other theories of state in Islamic history.

The period starting with the Umayyads differs from this perspective. The understanding and structures of state in this period—except during the caliphate of 'Umar b. 'Abdul 'Azîz, who was called the second 'Umar—are not axiomatic models for the application in later periods. Rather they are historical realities which should be evaluated within their own frameworks. Some pre-Islamic political institutions were internalized during this period. The method of succession for the establishment of political authority was one of these internalized institutions. But this historical reality should not be over generalized, and it is not the case that Islamic political culture and institutionalization became merely a continuation of pre-Islamic Iranian or Byzantine traditions. Such an over generalization presumes that the formation of political authority is the only factor in socio-political institutionalization. The historical facts provide us enough evidence to demonstrate that formation of the political culture and institutionalization during this period was a more complex process which could not be explicated on the basis of oversimplified models. The history of political institutionalization is a combination of the formation of original institutions and re-interpretation of other political institutions based on Islamic norms. The relationship between judicial and executive organs of the state may be accepted as an original and unique reflection of political culture, while the institution of *wizârah* in Mawârdî's theory may be analyzed as an example of the re-interpretation of an internalized element.

On the other hand, the periods of caliphate based on succession from the Umayyads until the end of the Ottoman caliphate should not be oversimplified as an absolute category in spite of a common mentality-base and common procedural means for the formation of political authority. There was a very wide richness in political applications. It is impossible to argue that tribal centralization of political power in the hands of the family of Umayyads continued during the periods of the Abbasids. In particular, the Ottoman millet system carries very different characteristics in political culture and life. It is imperative to analyze state structures as the institutionalization of political power within the framework of judicial, economic, and social parameters.

Perhaps the most radical changes in the institutionalization of state in Islamic history came with the end of caliphate. This turning-point and the following stage of the imposition of the nation-state system in Muslim lands created an imaginative and structural confusion among the masses. The demarcation and internal consistency between *ummah*, *Dâr al-Islam*, and *dawlah* was lost while new political structures as nation-states populated by Muslims faced a comprehensive problem of political legitimacy. The challenge of the pioneers of the new structures of the nation-state system to the traditional political cultures and structures aimed to create a new understanding of state. State began to be visualized as a sovereign element within the international system instead of a political instrument for the ethico-legal ideals of the Islamic belief system. Thus, the imagination of *Dâr al-Islam* as an alternative world order was replaced by the imagination of being an element of the international system which was established by and based on the interests of the colonial powers.

Such a transformation was a real shock for Muslim masses, who before had always found *Lebensraum* for the realization of their ethico-legal ideals throughout the history. These conditions created a tension between Westernized elites who denied the ethico-legal ideals of the state and traditional culture as well as between international system which obliterated political *Lebensraum* for the realization of these ethico-legal ideals. The contemporary conception of the Islamic state emerged as an outcome of the defense mechanism of the Islamic culture. The failure, corruption, and oppressive methods of the political elites accelerated the process of the polarization toward the end of the century and the demands to create a *Lebensraum* for the reproduction of Islamic ethico-legal ideals based on a unique ontological, epistemological, and axiological *Weltanschauung* reached their peak.

CHAPTER 8

CONCLUDING COMPARATIVE REMARKS

The uniformist character of Western civilization is perhaps the most significant problem of our age. Despite superficial pluralistic slogans, pluralism in the sense of the survival of authentic cultures is today merely an excuse for Unesco to establish museums in restricted areas which do not have any relationship with real life. In his *A Study of History*, Toynbee argued (1939:IV/1-2) at the beginning of this century that no less than twenty-six civilizations had already died and been buried. Among these he included the Egyptian, the Andean, the Sinic, the Minoan, the Sumeric, the Mayan, the Judic, the Hittite, the Syriac, the Hellenic, the Babylonian, the Mexican, the Arabic, the Yucatec, the Spartan, and the Ottoman. He underlined that nine of the ten surviving civilizations—the Christian Near East, the Islamic, the Christian Russian, the Hindu, the Far Eastern Chinese, the Japanese, the Polynesian, the Eskimo and the Nomadic—were *in their last agonies* under the threat of either annihilation or assimilation by Western civilization. Toynbee's prediction has become a nightmare for authentic civilizations and cultures.

This agonizing situation became especially acute after the vertiginous developments in world communications. Very simple activities of human life—like drinking cola or wearing jeans—began to be interpreted as the victory of the universalization of the humanistic/democratic culture. In spite of its huge material and technological supremacy, Western civilization is itself in a state of crisis because of the erosion of its moral base due to a lack of normativity. The ethico-material, psycho-ontological, and environmental imbalances in current Western civilization, together with its military capacity for global destruction, have been transformed into a civilizational crisis all over the world.[1] Hence, unlike previous civilizational crises in history, this crisis is not a regional one. Rather, the crisis of Western civilization is as universalized as its lifestyle.

The coincidence of the death throes of authentic civilizations and the acute crisis in Western civilization led the leading figures of the civilizations that are under the threat of Western annihilation to search their own ways of life and thought. This is especially true of Muslim scholars and the Muslim masses, who inherited a really very impressive, consistent, and balanced civilizational experience. The all-inclusive Islamic *Weltanschauung*, which is absolutely alternative to the Western *Weltanschauung* rather than complementary, provides adequate theoretical and imaginative tools for such an attempt.

In the Western paradigm, the particularization in the ontological sphere creates a particularization of epistemological sources (revelation and reason) and of axiological consequences and spheres of life, which leads to an internal philosophical dynamism through internal conflicts at the expense of internal

---

[1]These imbalances and their relationships with the crisis in Western civilization are well explained by Mumford in *The Myth of the Machine* (1966), by Marcuse in *One Dimensional Man* (1972), by Roszak in *The Making of Counter-culture* (1971), by Toynbee in *The Present-Day Experiment in Western Civilization*, and by Camilleri in *Civilization in Crisis* (1976), to name a few.

consistency. This is the internal mechanism of the secularization of life and thought in the Western philosophical-social tradition. In contrast, the monotheistic foundation based on *tawḥíd* and its ontological reflections in the Islamic paradigm results in the idea of the unity of truth and the unity of life which provides a strong internal consistency within a holistic framework through harmonizing epistemology, eschatology, axiology and politics based on ontology. This internal consistency is the basic characteristic of the Islamic religio-cultural atmosphere which necessitates rejection of any type of particularization of ontology, epistemology, or axiology.

Therefore, every attempt at pyramidal institutional secularization in Muslim societies creates a strong theoretical response to protect the internal consistency through harmonizing ontology, epistemology, and axiology in a new balance. This is due to the contrast emerging from the reality of being an alternative *Weltanschauung* rather than from historical and institutional conflicts. The scholars and politicians who omit these fundamental differences will continue to be puzzled by the increasingly critical response of Muslim societies. This criticism parallels increases in modernization and Westernization because Islam offers an alternative political culture and alternative images supported by its consistent, holistic framework. Due to the reality that the Western challenge to Islamic civilization is not only a challenge of an alternative institutional and historical background but also a challenge of *Weltanschauung*, the oppressive institutional transformation strategies being exercised against Muslim societies can not overcome this irreconcilability. The very strong internal consistency of the Islamic theoretical framework provides always a potentiality to produce an alternative political culture, setting up a direct link between ontology and politics as long as the ontological approach around the belief in *tawḥíd* survives in the socio-political culture and images.

The irreconcilability of the philosophical and theoretical bases of Western and Islamic political theories, images, and cultures might be analyzed only within a well-defined framework of the interconnections among ontology, epistemology, axiology, and politics. The origins of the problem should be sought in the root-paradigms of two alternative *Weltanschauungs*. The originality of the Islamic paradigm is related to its theocentric ontology based on the belief of *tawḥíd* supported by the principle of *tanzíh*. The differentiations of ontological levels via ontological hierarchy and ontologically-defined epistemology are the cornerstones of the process from its *imago mundi* to the axiological foundations of political images and culture. The Western paradigm around proximity of ontological levels through a particularization of divinity supported by intrinsically polytheist and pantheist elements, is the philosophical origin of the secularization of life via rationalistic axiology. This is a specific character of the Western philosophical tradition based on epistemologically-defined ontology which has led to a relativized and subjectivized religion.

We have analyzed four significant political consequences of the philosophico-theological differences between the Islamic and Western paradigms: the way of justification of the socio-political system, the legitimation process for political authority, the alternative approaches to political power and pluralism, and the imagination of the universal political system.

The fundamental characteristic of the Islamic way of justification is its cosmologico-ontological orientation in the belief in the absolute unity and sovereignty of Allâh, as distinguished from realistic justification dependent upon the empiricist epistemology of the Western way of justification. This substantial difference has another two significant consequences. First, although this way of justification imposes an image of an ideal state with a substantive mission based on a meta-historical covenant, one of the original characteristics of the Islamic way of justification—in contrast to the Platonic ideal state and the Kantian and Hegelian ideal models—is the idea of a historical realization of this ideal state during the period of the Prophet and the first four caliphs. Therefore, some scholars differentiate this ideal period from the subsequent caliphate in the form of sultanate through the denomination "perfect caliphate" (e.g. Taftazânî, 1950:146). This not only becomes a model both for the process of justification and legitimacy in Islamic political thought throughout Islamic history, it also is a factor for the popularization of this way of justification by strengthening the hope among Muslim masses to re-establish it.

Second, the way of justification through theological transparency, around the belief of *tawḥîd* in Islam on a cosmologico-ontological sphere, accelerated the process of the popularization of belief by setting up a direct link between ontology and axiology via epistemological precision. This horizontal popularization of belief created an integration of ontological and political images even for the illiterate Muslim masses, without any need for a vertical religious organization such as Church in Christianity. This accelerated the process of popular justification of an Islamic polity within a framework of a strong internal consistency based on ontological hierarchy.

In contrast to this situation, both theology and mystery complexities around the proximity of ontological levels and the particularization of divinity in Christianity created a hermeneutical scattering among a theocratic elite within the organization of the Church and a depopularization of justification through a systematic ontological belief. This led to an epistemological softening between theology and philosophy, resulting in the secularization of knowledge and life. The process in the modern era cut the ambiguous line between ontological and political spheres in Christianity and formed a theoretical ground independent from belief for the justification of the political system.

The ontologico-cosmological imaginations are the determinant factors of the ways of justifications of the socio-political system. The nature-centered imagination of the modern version of the Western paradigm laid the foundation for the justifications from the perspective of the origins and aims of the state based on the theories of the state of nature and based on the utilitarian principles of the this-worldly happiness. The Qur'ânic semantic framework which constitutes an ontologico-political set of concepts constructs Muslim mind for the necessity of a socio-political order as a reflection of the cosmological order. The political difference of the ways of the justification is a counterpart of the imaginative difference between nature-centered mechanism and created cosmological order. Since Muslims presuppose a created cosmological order rather than a self-adjusting nature, the axiological link between ontological and political spheres is always dependent on the theocentric belief structure to justify the socio-political system, which is assumed to be an area of the responsibility of human beings as vicegerents of the Creator of the cosmological order. This coherence between ontological, axiological, and political imaginations provides a common ground among the different groups of the Islamic paradigm which could reproduce a consistent political culture throughout the centuries in spite of internal differences and external attacks. The support of the Ismâ'ilî groups in India for the preservation of the Sunnî caliphate in the first quarter of this century, the similar strategies of the Ṣûfî organizations and *salafî* movements to resist imposed Westernization policies throughout the colonial and neo-colonial periods, and the anti-Western characteristics of the Sunnî and Shî'ite movements to form independent socio-political entities for the fulfillment of the divine responsibility show this common ground.

The differences in the political legitimation process are epistemological and methodological facsimiles of this basic disparity of the Islamic and Western paradigms. A clear demarcation between epistemologico-axiological, prescriptivist and institutional/procedural dimensions of political legitimation displays the dilemma of the transfer of institutions as structural procedures by ignoring the living spirits of them which are outcomes of a set of epistemological and axiological presuppositions. The crisis of the political legitimacy in modern Muslim societies is evidence of this phenomenon.

The mechanism-based political legitimacy in Western tradition and its methodological counterparts assume that social mechanisms can produce their own values to legitimize their outcomes. There is no place in this way of political legitimation for eternal values, which precede the mechanisms and are perpetually independent from social structures. The subjectivized imagination of religion coincides with the relativity of norms which are subjects of natural institutions of social change. The mechanisms can produce the knowledge to legitimize political actions. Therefore, in democratic philosophy, political participation is itself an objective mechanism which can produce a knowledge, a value, and a law as epistemological, axiological, and prescriptivist dimensions of political legitimacy. So, secularization of law is an unavoidable consequence of the secularization of knowledge based on bicompartmentalization of divine and human sources of knowledge. This bicompartmentalization has been transformed into a coherent system of secular philosophy after the fusion of the divine and natural mechanisms.

The understanding of the ultimate epistemological authority and eternal values as outcomes of this epistemological authority in the Islamic paradigm contradicts this mechanism-based process of political legitimation. The mechanisms can not specify value-structure in Islam. Just the opposite. The validity of mechanisms can only be tested through the social realization of the values. Political participation as a mechanism can not produce values contradicting the eternal values, but it specifies administrative means of the procedural legitimacy as a subordinate of the epistemologico-axiological legitimacy. The transfer of the Western procedural means of political legitimation could not gain coherent and permanent status in the political culture of the Muslim world because of this contradiction. The ontologically impenetrable understanding of the mechanism-based legitimacy of the Western paradigm can not co-exist with the value-based legitimacy of the Islamic paradigm as an unavoidable consequence of the ontological transcendency. The structural similarities can not veil this dilemma. Therefore, Islamic traditions survived even under the oppressive pressures of secularist policies and could be revived and reproduced as an alternative value-system to Western paradigm in spite of the political, economic and social inabilities in the sense of the realization of these values as institutional and historical realities.

The struggle for survival as an alternative civilizational paradigm leads us to the question of pluralism. The horizontal segmentation of governed peoples into religious-cultural groups (like Jews, Orthodox Christians, Catholic Christians, etc.) in the form of the millet system and the rejection of the socio-economic pyramidal stratification of classes is the *principium individuationis* of Islamic political society. The rivalry between Islamic and Western political mentalities and structures proves that a religious-cultural pluralism of horizontal segmentation on sectorial bases cannot coexist with a socio-economic pluralism of pyramidal stratification.

A religious-cultural pluralism of horizontal segmentation on a sectorial base necessitates a specific economic mentality, eliminating the distinction between normative and positive economics which might be accepted as the axiological ground of the secularization of economics and the direction of positive economics through the regulations of normative economics originating from a comprehensive juridic scheme framed by *'aqâid*. It was, and is, almost impossible to realize a capitalist accumulation within such a norm of economic mentality (e.g., *zakât*, as a right of the poor over the rich, could not be meaningful for a rational *homo economicus*).

The survival of the lifestyles of several religious cultural groups within the territories of Muslim states could only be achieved in a socio-economic structure where economics has been accepted in the service of politics to establish social stability and justice. The Islamic economic assumption that everything needed should be produced and economic resources should be distributed justly, creating a horizontal sectorial differentiation, provided *Lebensraum* for the authentic local cultural lifestyles. Legal pluralism, guaranteeing and protecting the religious-cultural pluralism, gave the opportunity to minorities with the same socio-political identification based on the ontological approach to apply their authentic law to internal affairs.

Western socio-economic pluralism is completely opposed to this economic mentality. The universal uniformity of the contemporary Western lifestyle, which is destroying all multiplicities of authentic local cultures, is an ultimate consequence of the dependency of culture and politics on economics. The principal assumption of the Western economic mentality that everything produced should be consumed, in contrast to the Islamic assumption that everything needed should be produced, created a growth of necessities forming a culture of consumption which resulted in the internationalization of the Western lifestyle through the necessity of discovering ways to absorb the increasing production. The specific economic antecedent behind this socio-economic pluralism, which causes cultural monism, is the divorce of normative and positive economics and the assumption that resources should be distributed productively.

Thus Islamic religious-cultural pluralism based on ontologically justified political power resulted in legal pluralism because of the existence of authentic cultures. The law of the sovereign religio-political group, namely Islamic law, was not imposed on the other communities in the position of protected minorities. There have always been special laws, courts, and judges for the intra-communal affairs of these groups. This decentralization of law and plurality in the sense of judicial mechanisms, which have always been a theoretical principle and historical reality in Islam, are both an imaginative consequence and institutional guarantee of religious-cultural pluralism.

In contrast, standardization of law is a counterpart of standardization of lifestyle and of the monopoly of one cultural identity. From this perspective, universalization of the sovereignty of a specific community and monopolization of a specific lifestyle as a cultural standard are co-existent and interdependent phenomena which have their origins in socio-economic pluralism. But Muslims did not accept a customary action if it violated a most significant human value, such as the preservation of human life or preservation of family. For example the practice of offering up a beautiful girl to the god of the Nile in pre-Islamic Egypt, the widow's committing suicide by jumping on to the funeral pyre where the body of her husband was being burned in pre-Islamic India, and the consanguineous marriage in Khuvezvagdas law among the Zoroastrians in pre-Islamic Iran were prohibited after the conquest of these countries by Muslims.[2] Other elements of intra-communal law among the members of the pre-Islamic socio-political entities were preserved throughout the ages under the sovereignty of Muslim states.

This also resulted in institutional monism because of the substantive mission of the state to establish justice all over the world. At the same time, Western socio-economic pluralism, grounded on an ontologically impenetrable justification of political power, resulted in the uniformity of lifestyle protected by the monistic legal structure all over the world and institutional pluralism supported by the socio-economic pyramidal stratification within the societies.

Therefore, beyond institutional adaptations led by Westernized political elites, a "real" Westernization of a Muslim community could only be achieved through the establishment of a socio-economic functional differentiation. But such a functional differentiation could not be justified within an Islamic framework due to the principle that an Islamic political authority which is justified through ontological assumptions could not be identified with a socio-economic group in order to support it for the realization of capitalist accumulation, because of its substantive character, around the basic norms, which could not be accompanied by the pragmatic utilitarian approach. The direct control of the fundamental economic resources for a just distributive structure within a circular evolution can not produce a socio-economic pluralism. A socio-economic pluralism with a dynamic adventurous character aimed at the most productive distribution of economic resources leads to the destruction of the religious-cultural pluralism because of its uniformist tendencies. The destruction of Islamic religious-cultural pluralism and of tolerance for authentic cultures is the result of the universalization of Western cultural monism that is aimed at establishing only one lifestyle all over the world by the impact of a productive interpretation of economic development and of the culture of consumption accelerated by the help of the huge development of the system of telecommunication.

The question of whether or not Muslim societies will be transformed into a structure of socio-economic pluralism should be evaluated from this perspective of *Weltanschauung* rather than from the imposed institutional transformation strategies directed by Westernized political elites. Such institutional transformation attempts would produce counter attempts originating from the socio-political culture based on a strong and direct link between ontological and political spheres because of the difficulty of justifying the political power concentrated in imposed Western institutions (which assume an ontologically impenetrable justification of political power), creating a problem of a theoretical accommodation with the ontologically justified political power of the authentic political culture.

The demarcation between *ummah*, *Dâr al-Islam*, and *dawlah* should be clarified to understand the historical transformation of the Muslim imagination and reality related to the political power. These concepts are reflections of three different political spheres interconnected each other: *ummah* is a universal spiritual/political

---

[2]For details see H̲amîdullah (1981:29-30).

union; *Dâr al-Islam* is the politico-legal world order; *dawlah* is the institutionalization of political power. Therefore the existence of ummatic union has never formed a categorical segmentation such as in the case of Semite/Gentile, Aryan/non-Aryan, civilized/barbarian; while bicompartmentalization of the politico-legal order as *Dâr al-Islam* and *Dâr al-Harb* did not create a permanent war and monopolistic supremacy. Just the opposite. Unlike the modern international system it assumed the existence of an alternative world order instead of imposing its own order on other societies. The legal guarantee of *amn* for the non-Muslims in *Dâr al-Islam* created a stable and permanent *Lebensraum* for the co-existence and survival of the pluralistic entities. *Dawlah* is imagined as an instrument for the institutionalization of political power for the fulfillment of the mission of *ummah* and for security, welfare, and stability within *Dâr al-Islam*.

The demarcation between these levels was clear when Muslims could determine the parameters of the universal political system. Caliph as the successor of the Prophet was the universal leader of *ummah* including Muslims in *Dâr al-Harb*. When they faced any political problem, they asked support from the caliph as the representative of the political center. The caliphate was also the ultimate authority for stability and order in *Dâr al-Islam*. But this did not mean that all institutionalization of power was in the hands of the caliph. The emergence of many Muslim states in some historical periods because of the expansion of Islam or because of the political incapacity of the caliph made it clear that *Dâr al-Islam* is a politico-legal boundary beyond the power control of individual states. These individual states sometimes filled the political vacuum which arose as a result of the incapacity of the political center, as in the case of Salâhaddîn Ayyûbî's struggle against the Crusaders. Sometimes they asked approval from the caliph to legitimize their political power; as with the request of Seljukî sultan Tugrul's from the Abbasid caliph or Indian Muslim ruler's request from Ottoman caliph. However, none of them declared that *Dâr al-Islam* was limited within the geographical area controlled by their states.

This demarcation and political imagination was confused when Muslim states lost the power to be a determinant factor of the universal political system. The colonial and secularist political structures from the World War I to the end of World War II assumed the end of the traditional Islamic political culture. The formation of new nation-states after World War II complicated the existing political culture after this assumption. It destroyed the internal balance of the traditional political culture and institutionalization.

So, the imposition of the nation-state system in Muslim lands has shaken not only the traditional political structures but also political imagination and mentality because Muslims faced a new political unit as nation-state and a new universal political system composed of individual nation-states which were not reflecting the basic dimensions of the Islamic world-view. Muslim minorities in *Dâr al-Harb* as a part of the *ummah* encountered an identity crisis as citizens of a nation-state. Moreover, when they faced any suppression they could not find asylum such as in the case of the existence of caliphate. They have never enjoyed feeling of security under the collective security system because of the domination of Western powers in the process of decision-making. The internal conditions of the traditional lands of *Dâr al-Islam* were also criticized from the perspective of Islamicity of political systems due to the fact that many of these states were controlled by the secularized Western-oriented elites. These conditions created a tension between Muslim masses and international system and between Muslim imagination of politics based on an alternative *Weltanschauung* and political structures.

The concept of "Islamic state" became the focal point of this new era especially in the second half of this century to re-balance the internal consistency of the Islamic *Weltanschauung* and its practical reflections. There was not any necessity for the development of such a concept in traditional political culture based on tri-level spiritual/political formation of *ummah*, *Dâr al-Islam* and *dawlah* because it was illogical to mention an ontologically impenetrable political authority which was not justified by Islamic paradigmatic foundations. The leaders of Islamic communities such as Ikhwan al-Muslimîn or Jamâ'at-i-Islamî which were established in the post-caliphate era aimed at re-establishing the links between ontological and political images. The definitions of "the indispensable Islamic state as a pre-requisite of man's subservience to Allâh" (Zaydân, 1983:3) and "the universal and all-embracing Islamic state as an ideological state" (Mawdûdî, 1985:30-1) are the versions of modern rhetoric for this readjustment of the imaginative and theoretical connection between *Weltanschauung* and political culture. The widespread impact of Qutb's *Milestones* is a consequence of its significance to reinterpret Islamic concept of *tawhîd* as a foundation of social dynamism. 'Ali Shariatî's influence during the Iranian revolution originated from his impressive theory related to the historical dialectic determined by the Islamic theological and social imaginative connections against the tyrannical suppression. So, the socio-political dynamism in this era was directly influenced by the political rhetoric which aimed at establishing a new theoretical consistency between *Weltanschauung* and political ideals.

There is a new tendency in the Islamic polity after the challenge of globalization and collapse of the socialist regimes. Parallel to the revitalization of political tradition all over the world, this modern political rhetoric in Islamic political theory might be enriched with a process of the reinventing of the classical tradition. Meanwhile, in accordance with the challenge of the globalization against the nation-state system, the core issue for Islamic polity seems to be to reinterpret its political tradition and theory as an alternative world-system rather than merely as a program for the Islamization of individual nation-states. Proper understanding of the theoretical foundations for Islamic politics and of their paradigmatic reflections in Muslim history will therefore be crucial.

REFERENCES

'Abduh, M. (1966). *Risâlah al-Tawḥîd*. Trans. I. Musa'ad and K. Cragg as *The Theology of Unity*. London: Allen and Unwin.

'Ali 'Abdul (1982). "Tolerance in Islam." *Islamic Culture* 56:105-20.

Abdulbâqiy, M. F. (1984). *Al-Mu'jam al-Mufahras li Alfâẓ al-Qur'ân al-Karîm.* Istanbul: Al-Maktabah al-Islamiyyah.

Abû Dâwud (1981) *Sunan Abû Dâwud*, Istanbul: Çağrı.

Abû Ḥanîfah (1981a). "Fiqh al-Akbar." In *Imâm-i Azam'in Bes Eseri*. Ed. M. Öz. Arabic: 58-64, Turkish: 66- 72. Istanbul: Kalem Yay.

_____ (1981b). "Fiqh al-Absat." In *Imâm-i Azam'in Bes Eseri*. ed. M. Öz. Arabic: 35-55, Turkish: 41- 65. Istanbul: Kalem Yay.

Abû Sulaymân, 'A. (1987). *The Islamic Theory of International Relations*. Herndon, Virginia: International Institute of Islamic Thought.

Abû Ya'lâ b. al-Farrâ' (1983). *Al 'Aḥkâm al-Sulṭâniyyah*. Beirut: Dâr al-Kutub al-'Ilmîyyah.

Abû Yûsuf (1977) *Kitâb al-Kharâj* . 6. ed. Cairo: Salafiyyah.

Afnan, S. (1958). *Avicenna: His Life and Works*. London: Allen and Unwin.

Ahmed, M. (1971). "Key Political Concepts in the Qur'an." *Islamic Studies* 10:77-102.

Ahrens, K. (1930). "Christliches im Quran: Eine Nachlese." *Zeitschrift der Deutschen Morgenlandischen Gesellschaft* 82:15-68.

Allen, D. (1985). *Philosophy for Understanding Theology*. Atlanta: John Knox Press.

Anṣârî, M. A. (1963). "Miskawayh's Conception of Sa'âdah." *Islamic Studies* 2:317-335.

Arendt, H. (1958). "What was Authority." *Nomos* 1:84-97.

Aristotle, (1941). *The Basic Works*. Ed. Richard McKeon. New York: Random House.

_____ (1980). *The Nichomachean Ethics*, 2d ed. Trans. W. D. Ross. Oxford: Oxford University Press.

Arnaldez, R. (1965). "Falsafa." In *The Encyclopaedia of Islam* 2:769-75.

Arnold, T. W. (1965). *The Caliphate*. London: Routledge and Kegan Paul.

al-Ash'arî (1940). *al-Ibâna'an Usûl al-Diyânah*. Trans. Walter Klein. New Haven.

_____ (1953a). "Kitâb al-Luma'a fi al-Radd 'alâ Ahl al-Zaigh wa al-Bida'." Trans. R. J. McCarthy as "Highlights of the Polemic Against Deviators and Innovators" in *The Theology of al-Ash'arî*. Ed. R. J. McCarthy. Arabic: 1-83, English:1-115. Beyrouth: Imprimerie Catholique.

_____ (1953b). "Risâlat Istiḥsân al-Khawḍ fî 'Ilm al-Kalâm." Trans. R. J. McCarthy as "A Vindication of the Science of Kalâm." In *The Theology of al-Ash'arî*. Ed. R. J. McCarthy. Arabic: 87-97, English: 119-33. Beyrouth: Imperimerie Catholique.

_____ (1980). *Kitâb Maqâlât al-Islamiyyîn wa Ikhtilâf al-Muṣallîy*. Trans. H. Ritter as *Die Dogmatischen Lehren der Anhanger des Islam*. Wiebaden: Franz Steiner Verlag GMBH.

Augustine (1945). *The City of God*. Cambridge: Harvard University Press.

_____ (1961). *Confessions*. Trans. R. S. Pine-Coffin. Middlesex: Penguin Books.

Bachrach, B., and M. Baratz (1974). *Power and Poverty*. New York: Oxford University Press.

al-Baghdâdî (1935). *Al-Farq Bayna al-Firaq*. Trans. A. S. Halkin as *Muslim Schisms and Sects*. Tel Aviv: Palestine Publishing.

_____ (1981). *Kitâb Uṣûl al-Dîn*. Beirut: Dâr al-Âfâq al-Jadîdah.

Barker, E. (1927). *National Character and the Factors in Its Formation*. London: Harper and Brothers.

Barnes, H. E. (1965). *An Intellectual and Cultural History of the Western World*, 3 vols., 3d ed. New York: Dover Publications.

Bartley, W. W. (1964). *The Retreat to Commitment*. London.

Bartold, V. V. (1963). "Caliph and Sultan." Trans. N.S. Doniach in*Islamic Quarterly* 7:117-135.

Beard, C. (1927). *The Reformation of the Sixteenth Century in Its Relation to Modern Thought and Knowledge*, 2d ed. London: Constable.

Beck, L. J. (1965). *The Metaphysics of Descartes: A Study of the Meditations*. Oxford: Clarendon Press.

Becker, C. H. (1916). "Islampolitik." *Die Welt des Islams* 3:101-18.

Beetham, D. (1974). *Max Weber and the Theory of Modern Politics.* London: Allen and Unwin.

Bentham, J. (1843). *The Works of Jeremy Bentham.* Ed. J. Bowring. Edinburgh.

_____ (1965). *An Introduction to the Principles of Morals and Legislation,* 4th ed. New York: Hafner Publishing.

Berdyaev, N. (1960). *The Destiny of Man,* 2d ed. Trans. N. Duddington. New York: Harper and Row.

Berns, L. (1978). "Francis Bacon and the Conquest of Nature." *Interpretation* 7:1-27.

Bluntschli, J. K. (1892). *The Theory of State.* London: Clarendon.

Bogardus, E. (1955). *The Development of Social Thought.* London: Longman.

Bowle, J. (1961). *Western Political Thought.* London: University Paperback.

Bramsted, E. K., and K. J. Melhuish (1978). *Western Liberalism: A History from Locke to Croce,* 3 vols. New York: Longman.

Brawmann, M. M. (1972). *The Spiritual Background of Early Islam.* Leiden: E. J. Brill.

Brinton, C. (1963). *The Shaping of Modern Thought.* New Jersey: Prentice-Hall.

Broad, C. D. (1971). *Five Types of Ethical Theory,* 10th ed. London: Routledge and Kegan Paul.

Brümmer, V. (1981). *Theology and Philosophical Inquiry.* London: Macmillan.

Bryce, J. (1921). *Modern Democracies,* 2 vols. New York: Macmillan.

al-Bukhârî (1981). *Ṣaḥîḥ al-Bukhârî,* 8 vols. Istanbul: Çagri.

Bultmann, R. (1956). *Primitive Christianity in Its Historical Setting.* Trans. R. H. Fuller. New York: Meridian Books.

Burch, G. B. (1962). "The Place of Revelation in Philosophical Thought." *Review of Metaphysics* 15:396-409.

Burckhardt, J. (1981). *The Civilization of the Renaissance in Italy,* 2d ed. Oxford: Phaidon Press.

Burns, E. M. (1960). *Ideas in Conflict.* London: University Paperbacks.

Burrt, E. A. (1980). *The Metaphysical Foundations of Modern Science*, reprint from 2d ed. in 1932. New York: Routledge and Kegan Paul.

Campbell, T. D. (1971). *Adam Smith's Science of Morals*. New Jersey: Rowman and Littlefield.

Carlyle, R. W., and A. J. Carlyle (1950). *A History of Mediaeval Political Theory in the West*, 6 vols. Edinburgh: William Blavkwood and Sons.

Cartwright, D. (1959). "A Field Theoretical Conception of Power." In*Studies in Social Power* 183-220. Ed. D. Cartwright. Michigan: Michigan University Press.

Cassirer, E (1951). *The Philosophy of the Enlightenment*. Princeton: Princeton University Press.

_____ (1963). *The Individual and the Cosmos in Renaissance Philosophy*. Trans. Mario Domandi. New York: Barnes and Noble.

_____ (1979). *Symbol, Myth and Culture*. New Haven: Yale University Press.

Cohen, A. (1982). "On the Realities of the Millet System: Jerusalem in the Sixteenth Century." In *Christians and Jews in the Ottoman Empire* 2:7-18. Ed. B. Braude and B. Lews. New York: Holmes and Meier.

Cole, G. D. (1920). *Social Theory*. New York.

Collingwood, R. G. (1981). *The Idea of Nature*, 3d ed. Oxford: Oxford University Press.

Comte, A. (1858). *Cathecism of Positive Religion: Summary and Exposition of the Universal Religion*. Trans. R. Congreve. London: John Chapman.

Cornford, F. M. (1937). *Plato's Cosmology: The Timaeus of Plato*. New York: Harcourt, Brace and Company.

Craig, W. L. (1980). *The Cosmological Argument from Plato to Leibniz*. London: Macmillan.

Crone, P., and M. Hinds (1986). *God's Caliph: Religious Authority in the First Centuries of Islam* . Cambridge: Cambridge University Press.

D'entreves, A. P. (1963). "Legality and Legitimacy." *Review of Metaphysics* 16:687-703.

_____ (1967). *The Notion of State*. London: Oxford University Press.

Dacca, H. (1955). "The Shura." *Journal of the Pakistan Historical Society* 3:151-65.

Dahl, R. (1957). "The Concept of Power." *Behavioral Science* 2:201-02.

_____ (1967). *Pluralistic Democracy in United States: Conflict and Consent.* Chicago: Rand McNally.

Dante, A. (1963). "On Monarchy." In *Medieval Political Philosophy*, 418-436. Ed. R. Lerner and M. Mahdî. New York: Free Press.

De Boer, T. J. (1967). *The History of Philosophy in Islam.* Ed. E. R. Jones. New York: Dover Publications.

Dekmejian, R.H. (1985). *Islam in Revolution: Fundamentalism in the Arab World.* Syracuse: Syracuse University Press.

Denisoff, R. S. (1972). *Sociology: Theories in Conflict.* California: Wadsworth Publishing.

Denny, F. M. (1975). "The Meaning of Ummah in the Qur'an." *History of Religions* 15:34-70.

Descartes, R. (1927). *Selections.* Ed. Ralph Eaton. New York: Charles Scribner's Sons.

Dimont, M. (1962). *Jews, God and History.* New York: New American Library.

Doren, C. V. (1967). *The Idea of Progress.* New York.

Duning, W. A. (1916). *A History of Political Theories*, 3 vols. New York: Macmillan.

Durant, W. (1950). *The Age of Faith.* Vol. 4 of *The Story of Civilization.* New York: Simon and Schuster.

_____ (1961). *The Age of Reason Begins.* Vol. 7 of *The Story of Civilization.* New York: Simon and Schuster.

_____ (1972). *Caeser and Christ.* Vol. 3 of *The Story of Civilization.* New York: Simon and Schuster.

al-Ahwany (1963). "Al-Kindî." In *A History of Muslim Philosophy* 1:421-34. Ed. M. M. Sharîf. Wiesbaden: Otto Harrasowitz.

_____ (1963). "Ibn Rushd." In *A History of Muslim Philosophy* 1:540-64. Ed. M. M. Sharîf. Wiesbaden: Otto Harrasowitz.

Eliade, M. (1985). *A History of Religious Ideas.* Ed. A. Hiltebeitel and D. A.Cappadona. Chicago: University of Chicago Press.

Ellis, B. (1979). *Rational Belief Systems.* Oxford:Basil Blackwell.

Elser, K. (1893). *Die Lehre des Aristoteles über das Wirken Gottes.* Münster.

Fakhrî, M. (1983). *A History of Islamic Philosophy.* London: Longman.

Farber, M. (1967). *The Foundation of Phenomenology: Edmund Husserl and the Quest for a Rigorous Science of Philosophy.* Albany: SUNY Press.

Fârûqî, I. R. (1967). *Christian Ethics,* Montreal: McGill University Press.

_____ (1982). *Tawḥîd: Its Implications for Thought and Life.* Herndon, Virginia: International Institute of Islamic Thought.

Fazlurraḥmân (1963). "Ibn Sînâ." In *A History of Muslim Philosophy* 1:480-506. Ed. M. M. Sharîf. Wiesbaden: Otto Harrasowitz.

al-Fârâbî (1961). *Al-Fuṣûl al-Madanî.* Trans. D. M. Dunlop as *Aphorisms of the Statesman..* Cambridge: Cambridge University Press.

_____ (1964). *Kitâb al-Siyâsah al-Madaniyyah.* Ed. F. M. Najjâr. Beirut: Matbuat al-Katholikiyyah.

_____ (1969). *Kitâb Taḥṣîl al-Sa'âdah.* Trans. M. Mahdî as "The Attainment of Happiness" in *Al-Farabi's Philosophy of Plato and Aristotle,* 13-53. New York: Cornell University Press.

_____ (1983). *Kitâb Taḥṣîl al-Sa'âdah.* Ed. J. Yasin. Beirut: Dâr al-Andalus.

_____ (1985).*Kitâb Ârâ Ahl al-Madînat al-Fâḍilah.* Beirut: Dâr al-Machreq.

Feibleman, J. K. (1953). "History of Dyadic Ontology." *Review of Metaphysics* 6:351-67.

Feuerbach, L. (1957). *The Essence of Christianity.* Trans. G. Eliot. New York: Harper Torchbooks.

Figgis, J. (1914). *Churches in the Modern State.* London.

Flew, A. G. N. (1964). "Hobbes." In *A Critical History of Western Philosophy,* 153-69. Ed. D. S. O'Conner. London.

Frank, R. M. (1968). "The Kalâm: An Art of Contradiction-Making or Theological Science? Some Remarks on the Question." *Journal of the American Oriental Society* 88:295-309.

Frankfort, H. (1948). *Kingship and the Gods: A Study of Ancient Near Eastern Religion as the Integration of Society and Nature.* Chicago: University of Chicago Press.

Fraser, A. C. (1899). *Philosophy of Theism*, 2d ed. Edinburgh: William Blackwood and Sons.

Frazer, J. G. (1925). *The Golden Bough: A Study in Magic and Religion*. New York: Macmillan.

Friederich, C. J. (1941). *Constitutional Government and Democracy*. Boston: Little, Brown and Co.

_____ (1972). *Tradition and Authority*. New York: Praeger.

Fries, H. (1969). *Faith under Challange*. Trans. W. D. Seidensticker. London: Burns and Oates.

Galston, M. (1977). "A Re-Examination of al-Farabi's Neoplatonism." In *Journal of the History of Philosophy* 15:13-32.

Gätje, H. (1974). "Logisch-Semiologische Theorien bei Al-Gazzali." *Arabica* 21:151-82.

Gettell, R. G. (1959). *History of Political Thought*. London: Allen and Unwin.

al-Ghazzâlî (1910). *The Alchemy of Happiness*. Trans. C. Field. London: John Murray.

_____ (1916). *Faḍâiḥ al-Bâtịnniyyah wa Faḍâil al-Mustazhiriyyah*. Trans. I. Goldziher as *Streitschrift des Ghazali gegen die Batinijja-Sekte*. Leiden: E. J. Brill.

_____ (1924). *Mishkât al-Anwâr*. Trans. W. H. T. Gairdner as *The Niche for Lights*. London: Royal Asiatic Society.

_____ (1927). *Tahafot Al-Falâsifat*. Ed. M.Bouyges. Beyrouth: Imprimerie Catholique.

_____ (1933). *Ayyuha al-Walad*. Trans. G. H. Scherer as *O Youth*. Beirut: The American Press.

_____ (1971a). *Al-Maqsad al-Asnâ fi Sharh Ma'ânî Asmâ' Allâh al-Ḥusnâ*. Beirut: Dâr al-Machreq.

_____ (1971b). *Itikatta Iktisat*. Trans.O.Z.Soyyigit. Istanbul: Sönmez.

_____ (1983). *Al-Qisṭâs al-Mustaqîm*. Beirut: Dâr al-Mashriq.

_____ (1986a). "Fayṣal al-Tafriqah bayna al-Islam wa al-Zandaqah." In *Majmû'at Rasâil al-Imâm al-Ghazzâlî* 3:113-48. Beirut: Dâr al-Maktab al-'Ilmîyyah.

_____ (1986b). "Qawâid al-'Aqâid fi al-Tawḥîd." In *Majmû'at Rasâil al-Imâm al-Ghazzâlî* 2:123-29. Beirut: Dâr al-Maktab al-'Ilmîyyah.

_____ (n.d.) *Mi'yâr al-'Ilm.* Beirut: Dâr al-Andalus.

Gibson, J. (1931). *Locke's Theory of Knowledge and its Historical Relations.* Cambridge: Cambridge University Press.

Gierke, Otto von (1958). *Political Theories of the Middle Ages.* Trans. W. Maitland. Cambridge: Cambridge University Press.

Goitein, S. D. (1970).."Minority Selfrule and Government Control in Islam." *Studia Islamica* 31:101-17.

Goldziher, I. (1910). *Vorlesungen über den Islam.* Heidelberg: Carl Winters Universitätsbuchhandlung.

Grant, E. (1987). "Ways to Interpret the Terms 'Aristotelian' and 'Aristotelianism' in Medieval and Renaissance Natural Philosophy." *History of Religions* 25:335-58.

Grant, R. M. (1961). "Hellenistic Elements in I Corinthians." In *Early Christian Origins*: Ed. A. Wikgren. Chicago.

Green, V. H. H. (1967). *Renaissance and Reformation,* 3d reprint from 2d ed. London: Edward Arnold Publishers.

Grünebaum, V. G. E. (1946). *Medieval Islam: A Study in Cultural Orientation.* Chicago: University of Chicago Press.

_____ (1962a). "Pluralism in the Islamic World." *Islamic Studies* 1:37-59.

_____ (1962b). *Modern Islam: The Search for Cultural Identity.* Los Angeles: University of California Press.

_____ (1970). "The Sources of Islamic Civilization." *Der Islam* 46:1-55.

Guignebert, C. (1927). *Christianity: Past and Present.* New York.

Gümüshanevî (1984). "Jâmi al-Mutûn." In *Akaid Risâleleri* , 297-312. Ed. A. Nar. Istanbul: Selam.

Gurwitsch, A. (1966). *Studies in Phenomenology and Pschology.* Evanston: Northwestern University Press.

Hamilton, R. F. (1972). *Class and politics in the United States,* New York: Wiley.

Hamîduddîn, M. (1963). "Early Sufis: Doctrine." In *A History of Muslim Philosophy* 1:310-35. Ed. M. M. Sharîf. Wiesbaden: Otto Harrassowitz.

Hamîdullah, M. (1961). *Muslim Conduct of State*. Lahore: Sh. M. Ashraf.

_____ (1972). *Islam Peygamberi*, 2 vols. Istanbul: Irfan.

_____ (1980). "Tolerance in the Prophet's Deeds in Medina." In *Islam, Philosophy and Science: Four Public Lectures*. Paris: Unesco Press.

_____ (1987). *Majmû'ât al-Wathâiq al-Siyâsiyyah*. Beirut: Dâr al-Nafâis.

Hammond, R. (1947). *The Philosophy of Alfarabi and Its Influence on Medieval Thought*. New York: Hobson Book Press.

Harnack, A. (1965).*History of Dogma*, 7 vols. Trans. N. Buchanan. New York: Dover Publications.

Hassan, A. (1984). *The Doctrine of Ijmâ' in Islam*. Islamabad: Islamic Research Institute.

Hatch, E. (1957). *The Influence of Greek Ideas on Christianity*, New York: Harper.

Hegel, G. W. F. (1902).*Lectures on the Philosophy of History*. Trans. J.Sibree. New York: P. F. Collier and Son.

_____ (1968). *Lectures on the Philosophy of Religion together with a Work on the Proofs of the Existence of God*, 3 vols.; reprint from the first publication in 1895. Trans. E. B. Speirs and J. B. Sanderson. London: Routledge and Kegan Paul.

Heidegger, M. (1956). "The Way Back into the Ground of Metaphysics." In *Existentialism from Dostoevsky to Sartre*, 206-22. Ed. W. Kaufmann. New York: World Publishing Company.

Hitti, P. K. (1968). *Makers of Arab History* . New York: St. Martin's Press.

Hobbes, T. (n.d.). *Leviathan* . London: J. M. Dent andSons.

Hodgson, M. G. S. (1974). *The Venture of Islam: Conscience and History in a World Civilization*, 3 vols. Chicago: University of Chicago Press.

Hood, F. C. (1964). *The Divine Politics of Thomas Hobbes*. Oxford: Oxford University Press.

Horovitz, J. (1926). *Koranische Untersuchungen*. Berlin.

Horten, M. (1913). "Religion und Philosophie im Islam." *Der Islam* 4:1-4.

_____ (1973). "The System of Islamic Philosophy in General." Trans. J. Hager in *Islamic Studies* 12:1-36.

Horton, W. M. (1940). *God.* New York: Hazen Foundation.

Hourani, G. (1985). *Reason and Tradition in Islamic Ethics.* Cambridge: Cambridge University Press.

_____ (1976). *Averroes on the Harmony of Religion and Philosophy.* London: Gibb Memorial Trust.

Hsiao, C. K. (1927). *Political Pluralism.* London: Kegan Paul.

Humber, J. M. (1972). "Spinoza's Proof of God's Necessary Existence." *The Modern Schoolman* 49:221-33.

Hume, D. (1907a). "Concerning the Principles of Morals." In *Essays Moral, Political and Literary by David Hume,* 2 vols., 5th ed.; 169-289. Ed. T. H. Green and T. H. Grose. London: Longman, Green and Co.

_____ (1907b). "The Natural History of Religion." In *Essays Moral, Political and Literary by David Hume,* 2 vols., 5th ed.; 309-367. Ed. T. H. Green and T. H. Grose. London: Longman, Green and Co.

Husaini, W. A. (1980). *Islamic Environmental Systems Engineering.* London: Macmillan.

Husserl, E. (1900-01). *Logische Untersuchungen,* 2 vols. Halle A.S.: Max Niemeyer.

_____ (1954). *Die Krisis der Europäischen Wissenschaften und die Transzendentale Phänomenologie.* Ed. W. Biemel. The Hague.

Hyde, W. (1946). *Paganism to Christianity in the Roman Empire.* Philadelphia: University of Philadelphia Press.

Hye, M. A. (1963). "Ash'arism." In *A History of Muslim Philosophy* 1:220-44. Ed. M. M. Sharîf. Wiesbaden: Otto Harrasowitz.

Ibn al-Kalbî (1969). *Kitâb al-Aṣnâm.* Ed. Ahmad Zaki Pasha. Ankara.

Ibn 'Asâkir (1953). "Tabyîn Kadhib al-Muftarî fi mâ Nusiba ilâ al-Imâm Abû al-Ḥasan al-Ash'arî." With summary and translation in *The Theology of al-Ash'arî,* 145-205. Ed. R. J. McCarthy. Beyrouth: Imprimerie Catholique.

Ibn Ḥanbal (1982). *Musnad,* 6 vols. Istanbul: Çagri.

Ibn Kathîr (1986). *Tafsir al-Qur'ân al-Aẓîm,* 4 vols. Istanbul: Çagri.

Ibn Khaldûn (n.d). *The Muqaddimah: Kitâb al-'Ibar wa dîvân al-Mubtadâ wa al-Khabar fî Ayyâm al-'Arab wa al-'Ajam wa al-Barbar* , Dâr al-Fikr.

Ibn Manẓûr (n.d.). *Lisan al-Arab.* Cairo: Dâr al-Ma'arif.

Ibn Rushd (1938-51). *Tafsîr ma ba'd al-Ṭabî'ah: Great Commentary on Aristotle's Metaphysics,* 4 vols. Ed. M. Bouyges.

_____ (1958). *Talkhîṣ ma ba'd al-Ṭabî'ah.* Ed. Osman Amin. Cairo.

_____ (1964). *Kitab al-Kashf 'an Manahij al-Adillah,* Cairo: M.Qasim.

_____ (1973). *Faṣl al-Maqâl fi mâ bayna' al-Ḥikmati wa al-Sharî'ah min al-Ittisâl.* Ed. Elbir Nasri Nadir. Beirut: Dâr al-Mashriq.

_____ (1978). *Tahâfut al-Tahâfut.*Trans. S. Van Den Bergh as *The Incoherence of the Incoherence.* Cambridge: Cambridge University Press.

_____ (1966). *Commentary on Plato's Republic.* Trans. and ed. E. I. J. Rosenthal. Cambridge: Cambridge University Press.

Ibn Sînâ (1973). *Dânish Nâma-i 'Alâî (Ilahiyyât)* . Trans. P. Morewedge as *The Metaphysics of Avicenna.* New York: Columbia University Press.

Ibn Taymiyyah (1966). *Majmû'at al-Fatâwâ al-Kubrâ.* Cairo: Dâr al-Kutub al-Hadîthah.

_____ (1983). *Al-Risâlah al-Akmaliyyah.* Cairo: Matbûat al-Madanî.

_____ (1988a). *Kitâb al-Asmâ' wa al-Ṣifât.* Beirut: Dâr al-Kutub al-'Ilmîyyah.

_____ (1988b). *Al-Siyâsah al-Shar'iyyah* Beirut: Dâr al-Kutub al-'Ilmîyyah.

_____ (1988c). *Al-Khilâfah wa al-Mulk.* Zarqâ: Maktabah al-Manâr.

Ibn Ṭufayl (1905). *The Improvement of Human Reason Exhibited in the Life of Hayy Ibn Yakzan.* Trans. S. Ockley. Cairo: Al-Ma'âref Printing Office.

Inalcik, H. (1964). "The Nature of Traditional Society." In *Political Modernization in Japan and Turkey.* Ed. R. E. Ward and D. A. Rustow. Princeton: Princeton University Press.

Iqbâl, J. (1986). "The Concept of State in Islam." in *State Politics and Islam:,* 37-50. Ed. M. Ahmad. Indianapolis: American Trust Publications.

Iqbâl, M. (1934). *The Reconstruction of Religious Thought in Islam.* London: Oxford University Press.

al-Isfahani, R. (1921). *Al-Mufradât fi Gharâ'ib al-Qur'ân.* Cairo.

214   ALTERNATIVE PARADIGMS

Izmirli, I. H. (1981). *Yeni Ilm-i Kelâm*. Ankara: Umran Yayinlari.

Izutsu, T. (1966). *Ethico-religious Concepts in the Qur'ân*. Montreal: McGill University Press.

―――― (n.d.). *God and Man in the Qur'ân: A Semantical Analysis of Qur'anic Weltanschauung*. Trans. S.Ates as *Kur'an'da Allah ve Insan*. Ankara: Kevser.

al-'Îjî (1984). "Al-'Aqâid al-'Adudiyyah." In *Akaid Risâleleri*, Turkish: 187-93, Arabic: 437-40. Ed. A.Nar. Istanbul: Selam.

Jalâlayn, al-Imâmayn (1982). *Tafsîr al-Jalâlayn*. Beirut: Dâr al-Ma'arifah.

James, W. (1909a). *Pluralistic Universe*. London: Longman, Green and Co.

―――― (1909b). *The Meaning of Truth*. New York: Longman, Green and Co.

―――― (1916). *Pragmatism: A New Name For Some Old Ways of Thinking*. New York: Longman, Green and Co.

―――― (1929). *Selected Papers on Philosophy*, 5th ed. London: J. M. Dent and Sons.

al-Jâhiz (1969). *The Life and Works of al-Jâhiz*. Trans. and ed. C. Pellat. London: Routledge and Kegan Paul.

Jâmi, N. A. (1914). *Lawâ'ih*. Trans. E. H. Whinfield and M. M. Kazvini. London: Royal Asiatic Society.

Jenks, E. (1898). *Law and Politics in the Middle Ages*. New York.

Jonas, H. (1964). "Heidegger and Theology." *Review of Metaphysics* 18:207-34.

Jones, W. T. (1949). *Masters of Political Thought: Machiavelli to Bentham*, 2. vols. London: George G. Harrap and Co.

al-Juwainî (1968). "Shifâ al-Ghalîl fi Beyân mâ Waqa'a fi al-Tawrât wa al-Injîl min al-Tabdîl." In *Textes Apologetiques De Guwaini*, 38-83. Ed. M. Allard. Beyrouth: Dâr al- Machreq (Editeurs Imperimerie Catholique).

al-Kalabâdhî (1935). *Kitâb al-Ta'âruf li Madhhab Ahl al-Tasawwuf*. Trans. A. J. Arberry as *The Doctrine of the Sufis*. London: Cambridge University Press.

Kant, I. (1909a). "Fundamental Principles of the Metaphysic of Morals." In *Kant's Critique of Practical Reason and Other Works on the Theory of Ethics*, 1-84. Ed. and trans. T. K. Abbott. London: Longman, Green and Co.

_____ (1909b). "Critical Examination of Practical Reason." In *Kant's Critique of Practical Reason and Other Works on the Theory of Ethics*, 87-265. Ed. and trans. T. K. Abbott. London: Longman, Green and Co.

_____ (1910). *Critique of Pure Reason*. Trans. J. M. D. Meiklejohn. London: G. Bell and Sons.

Kelso, W. A. (1978). *American Democratic Theory*. Westport: Greenwood Press.

Khaddûrî, M. (1984). *The Islamic Conception of Justice*. Baltimore: Johns Hopkins University Press.

Khatîb, M. (1988). *Asmâ' Allâh al-Husnâ wa Sifâtuhu al-'Ulyâ*. Beirut: Mussasah al-Risâlah.

al-Khâzinî (1860) *Kitâb Mizân al-Hikmah*. Trans. C. N. Khanikoff as "Book of the Balance of Wisdom: An Arabic Work on the Water-Balance" in *Journal of the American Oriental Society* 6:1-128.

Kinalizâde, A. (n.d.) *Akhlâq-i 'Alâ'î*, 2 vols. Istanbul: Tercüman 1001 Temel Eser.

al-Kindî (1950a). "Al-Falsafah al-Ûlâ." In *Rasâil al-Kindî*, 91-162. Ed. M. A. Abû Rîdah. Cairo: Dâr al-Fikr al-'Arabî.

_____ (1950b). "Al-Fâ'il al-Haqq al-Awwal al-Tâm wa al-Fâ'il al-Nâqis allazî huwa bi al-Mejâz." In *Rasâil al-Kindî*, 180-85. Ed. M. A. Abû Rîdah. Cairo: Dâr al-Fikr al-'Arabî.

_____ (1950c). "Risâlah fi Wahdâniyyah Allâh wa Tanâhi Jirm al-'Âlam." In *Rasâil al-Kindî*, 199- 207. Ed. M. A. Abû Rîdah. Cairo: Dâr al-Fikr al-'Arabî.

_____ (1974).*Al-Falsafah al-Ûlâ*. Trans with commentary by Alfred L.Ivry as *Al-Kindî's Metaphysics: A Translation of Ya'qûb ibn Ishâq al-Kindî's Treatise "On First Philosophy."* Albany: SUNY Press.

King James' (Authorized) Version of the Holy Bible (1957). Philadelphia: A. J. Holman.

Klein, F. A. (1906). *The Religion of Islam*. Madras: S.P.C.K. Press.

Kohn, H. (1950). *The Twentieth Century: A Midway Account of the Western World*. London: Victor Gollancz.

_____ (1969). *The Idea of Nationalism* . New York: Macmillan.

Krieger, L. (1969). "Power and Responsibility: The Historical Assumptions." In*The Responsibility of Power*, 3-36. Ed. L. Krieger and F. Stern. New York: Doubleday.

Kuhn, T. (1970). *The Structure of Scientific Revolutions*. Chicago: University of Chicago Press.

Laing, G. J. (1963). *Survivals of the Roman Religion: Our Debt to Greece and Rome*. New York: Cooper Square.

Laistner, M. L. W. (1951). *Christianity and Pagan Culture in the Later Roman Empire*. Ithaca: Cornell University Press.

Lambton, A. (1954). "The Theory of Kingship in the Naṣîḥat al-Muluk." *Islamic Quarterly* 1:47-56.

_____ (1974)."Islamic Political Thought." In *The Legacy of Islam*, 2d ed. Ed. J. Schacht. Oxford: Clarendon Press.

_____ (1985). *State and Government in Medieval Islam*. Oxford: Oxford University Press.

al-Laqqânî (1984). "Jawhar al-Tawḥîd." In *Akaid Risâleleri:*, Turkish: 230-39, Arabic: 441-45. Ed. A. Nar. Istanbul: Selam.

Larson, M. A. (1959).*The Religion of the Occident*. New York: Philosophical Library.

Laski, H. J. (1921). *The Foundations of Sovereignty and Other Essays*. New York: Harcourt, Brace and Co.

_____ (1931). *An Introduction to Politics*. London.

Lasswell, H. D., and A. Kaplan (1950). *Power and Society*. New Haven.

Lauer, Q. (1982). *Hegel's Concept of God*. New York: SUNY Press.

Leaman, O. (1980). "Ibn Rushd on Happiness and Philosophy." *Islamic Studies* 52:167-81.

Lerner, R., and M. Mahdî (1963). *Medival Political Philosophy*. New York: The Free Press.

Lewis, B. (1984). *The Jews of Islam*. Princeton: Princeton University Press.

_____ (1988). *The Political Language of Islam*. Chicago: University of Chicago Press.

Lindbeck, G. A. (1948). "A Note on Aristotle's Discussion of God." In *Review of Metaphysics* 2:99-106.

Lindblom, C. E. (1977). *Politics and Market.* New York: Basic Books.

Locke, J. (1954). *Essays on the Law of Nature.* Ed. and trans. W. von Leyden. Oxford: Clarendon Press.

_____ (1965). *Two Treatises of Government* . Ed. P.Laslett. New York: New American Library.

Loewenstein, K. (1965). *Political Power and Governmental Process.* Chicago.

Macdonald, D. B. (1899). "The Life of al-Ghazzâlî, with Special Reference to His Religious Experiences and Opinions." *Journal of the American Oriental Society* 20:71-132.

_____ (1903). *Development of Muslim Theology, Jurisprudence and Constitutional Theory.* New York: Charles Scribner's Sons.

_____ (1909). *The Religious Attitude and Life in Islam.* Chicago: University of Chicago Press.

MacInerny, R. (1963). *A History of Western Philosophy.* Chicago: Henry Regnery.

Macpherson, C. B. (1962). *The Political Theory of Possesive Individualism: Hobbes to Locke.* Oxford: Clarendon Press.

Macquarrie, J. (1978). *Twentieth-Century Religious Thought: The Frontiers of Philosophy and Theology, 1900-1970,* 4th impression from 2d ed. London: SCM Press.

Madkour, I. (1963). "Al-Fârâbî." In *A History of Muslim Philosophy* 1:450-69. Ed. M. M. Sharîf. Wiesbaden: Otto Harrasowitz.

Magid, H. M. (1966). *English Political Pluralism.* New York: AMS Press.

Mahdî, M. (1972). "Islamic Philosophy in Contemporary Islamic Thought." In *God and Man in Contemporary Islamic Thought:,* 99-11. Ed. C. Malik. Beirut: American University Press.

Maimonides (1928). *The Guide for the Perplexed.* Trans. M. Friedlander. London.

Makari, V. (1976). "The Social Factor in Ibn Taymiyyah's Ethics." Philadelphia: Ph.D. dissertation, Temple University.

March, J. (1957). "Measurment Concepts in the Theory of Influence." *Journal of Politics* 19:222-26.

Marcus Aurelius (n.d.). *Thoughts* . Trans. Long. London: Frowde.

Mardin, S. (1983). *Din ve Ideoloji*. Istanbul: Iletisim.

_____ (1989). *Religion and Social Change in Modern Turkey: The Case of Bediüzzaman Said Nursi*. New York: SUNY Press.

Margoliouth, D. S. (1922). "The Sense of the Title of Khalîfah." In *A Volume of Oriental Studies Presented to E. G. Browne* . Ed. T. W. Arnold and R. A. Nicholson. Amsterdam: Philo Press.

Masûmî, M. S. H. (1963). "Ibn Bajjâh." In *A History of Muslim Philosophy* 1:506-26. Ed. M. M. Sharîf. Wiesbaden: Otto Harrasowitz.

al-Mawârdî (1973). *Al-Aḥkâm al-Sulṭânîyyah*. Cairo: Maktabah M. al-Ḥalabî.

_____ (1987). *Adab al-Dunyâ wa al-Dîn*. Beirut: Dâr al-Kutub al-'Ilmîyyah.

Mawdûdî, A. (1963). "Abû Ḥanîfah and Abû Yûsuf." In *A History of Muslim Philosophy* 1:674-704. Ed. M. M. Sharîf. Wiesbaden: Otto Harrasowitz.

_____ (1979). *Four Basic Quranic Terms*. Lahore: Islamic Publications.

_____ (1985). *Political Theory of Islam*. Lahore: Islamic Publications.

al-Mâturîdî (1981). *Kitâb al-Tawḥîd*. Trans. H. Erdogan. Istanbul: Hicret.

McCracken, D. J. (1950). *Thinking and Valuing*. London: Macmillan.

McGrade, A. S. (1974). *The Political Thought of William Ockham*. Cambridge: Cambridge University Press.

Merkl, P. H. (1972). *Political Continuity and Change*. New York: Harper and Row.

Mez, A. (1922). *Die Renaissance des Islams*. Heidelberg.

Mill, J. S. (1951). *Utilitarianism, Liberty and Representative Government*. New York: E. P. Dutton and Co.

Mills, C. W. (1959). *The Power Elite*. New York.

_____ (1974). *Power, Politics and People: The Collected Essays of C. W. Mills*. Ed. I. L. Horowitz. Oxford: Oxford University Press.

Mintz, S. (1969). *The Hunting of the Leviathan*. Cambridge: Cambridge University Press.

Missner, M. J. (1983). "Skepticism and Hobbes' Political Philosophy." *Journal of the History of Ideas* 44:407-27.

More, P. E. (1921).*The Religion of Plato*. Princeton:Princeton University Press

Morewedge, P. (1972). "Philosophical Analysis and Ibn Sina's 'Essence-Existence' Distinction." *Journal of the American Oriental Society* 92:425-35.

Morrall, J. (1958). *Political Thoughts in Mediavel Times*. London: Hutchinson.

al-Muḥâsibî (1974). *Kitâb al-'Ilm*. Trans. with commentary by L. Librande as "Islam and Conservation: The Theologian-Ascetic al-Muḥâsibî" in *Arabica* 30:125-46.

al-Muslim (1981). *Saḥîḥ al-Muslim*, 3 vols. Istanbul: Çagri.

Nasafî, A. (1962). "Kitâb Baḥr al-Kalâm fi 'Ilm al-Tawḥîd." In *A Reader on Islam*, 375-457. Ed. and trans. A. Jeffery. Gravenhage: Mouton and Co.

Nasr, S. H. (1964a). *Three Muslim Sages* . Cambridge: Harvard University Press.

_____ (1964b). *An Introduction to Islamic Cosmological Doctrines*. Cambridge: Belknap Press of Harvard University Press.

_____ (1972). "Sufism and the Integration of Man." In *God and Man in Contemporary Islamic Thought*, 144-51. Ed. C. Malik. Beirut: Centennial Publications.

Newton, I. (1803). *The Mathematical Principles of Natural Philosophy*. Trans. Andrew Motte. London: H. D. Symonds.

Nicholson, R. A. (1985). *A Literary History of the Arabs*. Cambridge: Cambridge University Press.

Nieuwenhuijze, V. C. A. O. (1985). *The Lifestyles of Islam: Recourse to Classicism Need of Realism*. Leiden: E. J. Brill.

Nisbet, R. (1962). *Community and Power*. New York: Oxford University Press.

Niẓâm al-Mulk (1987). *Siyâsetnâme*, 2d ed. Istanbul: Dergah.

Norris, R. A. (1965). *God and World in Early Christian Theology*. New York: Seabury Press.

O'Conner, D. S. (1964). *A Critical History of Western Civilization.* New York: The Free Press.

O'Leary, D. L. (1948). *How Greek Science Passed to the Arabs.* London: Routledge and Kegan Paul.

Obermann, J. (1921). *Der Philosophische und Religiöse Subjectivismus Ghazalis Ein Beitrag zum Problem der Religion.* Vienna: W. Braumüller Universitäts-Verlagsbuchhandlung Gesellschaft.

Oda, Y. (1984). "The Concept of the Ummah in the Qur'ân: An Elucidation of the Basic Nature of the Islamic Holy Community." *Oriens* 20:93-108.

Owens, J. (1963). *The Doctrine of Being in the Aristotelian "Metaphysics,"* 2d ed. Toronto: Pontifical Institute of Medieval Studies.

Özel, A. (1982). *Islam Hukukunda Milletlerarasi Münasebetler ve Ülke Kavrami.* Istanbul: Marifet.

Palmer, R. R., and J. Colton (1978). *A History of the Modern World.* New York: Knopf.

Parsons, T. (1958). "Authority, Legitimacy and Political Action." In *Authority* . Ed. C. J. Friederich. Cambridge.

_____ (1969). "On the Concept of Power." In *Political Power: A Reader in Theory and Research,* 251-85. Ed. R. Bell, D. Edwards, and H. Wagner. New York: The Free Press.

Passmore, J. (1972). *The Perfectibility of Man.* London: Duckworth.

Peters, F. E. (1968). *Aristotle and the Arabs: The Aristotelian Tradition in Islam.* New York: New York University Press.

Pipes, D. (1983). *In the Path of God: Islam and Political Power.* New York: Basic Books.

Plato (1917). *Five Dialogues.* Ed.E. Rhys. New York: J. M. Dent and Sons.

_____ (1937). *Dialogues,* 2 vols. Trans. B.Jowett. New York: Random House.

Polanyi, M. (1983).*Personal Knowledge: Towards a Post-Critical Philosophy.* London: Routledge and Kegan Paul.

Pollard, S. (1968). *The Idea of Progress: History and Society.* Middlesex: Penguin.

Polsby, N. (1971). *Community Power and Political Theory.* New Haven: Yale University Press.

Popper, K. R. (1959). *The Logic of Scientific Discovery.* Trans. by the author from *Logik der Forschung* (Vienna, 1934). London: Hutchinson.

Pringle-Pattison, S. A. (1920). *The Idea of God in the Light of Recent Philosophy.* New York: Oxford University Press.

al-Qâdî, W. (1988). "The Term 'Khalifa' in Early Exegetical Literature." *Die Welt des Islams* 28:392-411.

al-Qur'ân al-Karîm (1980). Trans. M. Y. Zayid. Beirut.

_____ (1983). Trans. and commentary by Yûsuf 'Ali. Brentwood: Amana Corp.

_____ (1986). 4th ed. Trans. H. H.Shâkir. New York: Mihrab Publisher and Book Distributor.

_____ (n.d.). Trans. M. M. Pickthall. London: Islamic Book Centre.

Qushayrî, A. (1986). *Sharḥ Asmâ Allâh al-Ḥusnâ.* Beirut: Dâr Azal.

Quṭb, S. (1978). *Milestones.* Bombay: Aarif.

_____ (n.d.). *Fi Ẓilâl al-Qur'ân.* Trans. M. E. Saraç, I. H. Sengüler, and B. Karliga as *Kuran' in Gölgesinde,* 16 vols. Istanbul: Hikmet.

Rand, E. K. (1928). *Founders of the Middle Ages.* New York: Dover Publications.

Raschid, M. S. (1981). *Iqbâl's Concept of God .* London: Kegan Paul International.

Raven, J. E. (1965).*Plato's Thought in the Making: A Study of the Development of His Metaphysics.* Cambridge: Cambridge University Press.

Râzî, F. (1978). "Kitâb al-Nafs wa al-Rûḥ." In *Al-Fikr al-Akhlâqî al-'Arabî,* 175-200. Ed. M. Fakhrî. Beirut: Al-Ahliyyah lil nashr wa al-tawzî'.

_____ (1984). *Lawami' al-Bayyinât Sharḥ Asmâ Allâh Ta'âlâ wa al-Ṣifât.* Beirut: Dâr al-Kitâb al-'Arabî.

Reese, W. L. (1980). *Dictionary of Philosophy and Religion.* New Jersey: Humanities Press.

Regan, R. J. (1986). *The Moral Dimensions of Politics.* Oxford: Oxford University Press.

Richards, D. A. J. (1971). *A Theory of Reasons for Action.* Oxford: Clarendon Press.

Riḍâ, Rashîd (1954). *Tafsîr al-Qur'ân al-Ḥakîm, Tafsîr al-Manâr.* Cairo.

_____ (1988). *Al-Khilâfah.* Cairo: Al-Zahrâ' al-I'lâm al-'Arabî.

Riesman, D. (1965). *The Lonely Crowd,* 13th reprint. New Haven: Yale University Press.

Riker, W. (1964). "Some Ambiguities in the Notion of Power." *American Political Science Review* 58:341-49.

Ringgren, H. (1951). "The Conception of Faith in the Qur'ân." *Oriens* 4:1- 20.

_____ (1962). "The Pure Religion." *Oriens* 15:93-96.

Roberts, D. (1960). *Existentialism and Religious Belief,* 3d ed. New York: Oxford University Press.

Robertson, J. M. (1914). *Short Story of the Free Thought,* 2 vols. London: G. P. Putnam's Sons.

Rogowski, R. (1974). *Rational Legitimacy: A Theory of Political Support.* Princeton: Princeton University Press.

Rosenthal, E. I. J. (1953). "The Place of Politics in the Philosophy of Ibn Rushd." *Bulletin of the School of Oriental and African Studies* 15:246-79.

_____ (1973). "The Role of the State in Islam: Theory and the Medieval Practice." *Der Islam* 30:1-29.

Rosenthal, F. (1970). *Knowledge Triumphant: The Concept of Knowledge in Medieval Islam.* Leiden: E. J. Brill.

Roszak, T. (1971). *The Making of a Counter Culture.* London: Faber and Faber.

Rousseau, J. J. (1948). *Emile.* Trans. B. Foxley. London: J. M. Dent and Sons.

Rubin, U. (1984). "Al-Ṣamad and the High God: An Interpretation of Sura CXII." *Der Islam* 61:197-217.

Russell, B. (1938). *Power: A New Social Analysis.* New York: W. W. Norton and Co.

_____ (1962). *History of Western Philosophy,* 8th ed. London: Allen and Unwin.

Sabine, G. H., and T. Thorson (1973). *A History of Political Thought,* 4th ed. Illinois: Dryden Press.

Santillana, D. De (1965). "Law and Society." In *The Legacy of Islam* , 8th reprint from 1st ed. in 1931, 284-311. London: Oxford University Press.

al-Sanûsî (1984). "'Aqâid al-Sughrâ." In *Akaid Risâleleri*, 198-203. Ed. A. Nar. Istanbul: Selam.

Sayre, W., and H. Kaufman (1970). *Governing New York City: Politics in the Metropolitan*. New York.

al-Sâbûnî, N. (1980). *Al-Bidâyah fi Usûl al-Dîn*. Trans. Bekir Topaloglu as *Maturidiyye Akaidi*. Ankara: Diyânet Yay.

Schact, J. (1964). *An Introduction to Islamic Law*. Oxford: Clarendon Press.

Schimmel, A. (1976). "Der Islam im Rahmen der Monotheistischen Weltreligionen." In *Islam und Abendland: Geschichte und Gegenwart*, 9-31. Ed. A. Mercier. Bern: Verlag Herbert Lang.

Schleiermacher, F. D. (1958). *Religion: Speeches to Its Cultural Despisers*. Trans. J. Oman. New York: Harper and Brothers.

Schrader, G. (1956). "Heidegger's Ontology of Human Existence." *Review of Metaphysics* 10:38-57.

Schumpeter, J. A. (1962). *Capitalism, Socialism and Democracy*. New York: Harper and Row.

Schuon, F. (1963). *Understanding Islam*. Trans. D. M. Matheson. London: Allen and Unwin.

Schwegler, A.(1871). *Handbook of the History of Philosophy*, 11th ed. Trans. J. H. Stirling. Edinburgh: Oliver and Boyd.

Seelye, K. C. (1920). *Moslem Schisms and Sects: Introduction and Translation of Al-Farq Bayn al-Firaq of Baghdâdî* New York: Columbia University Press.

al-Shahrastânî (1934). *Kitâb Nihâyat al-Iqdâm fi 'Ilm al-Kalâm*. Trans. A. Guillaume. London: Oxford University Press.

Shamsî, F. A. (1978). "Al-Kindî's Risâla fi Wahdâniyyah Allâh wa Tanâhî Jirm al-'Âlam." *Islamic Studies* 17:185-201.

Shapley, L. S., and Shubik (1969). "A Method for Evaluating the Distribution of Power in a Commitee System." In *Political Power: A Reader in Theory and Research:*, 209-14. Ed. R. Bell, D. Edwards, and H. Wagner. New York: The Free Press.

Sharîf, M. M. (1963-66). *A History of Muslim Philosophy*. Wiesbaden: Otto Harrasowitz.

———— (1965). "Muslim Political Theory and Institutions." In *Proceedings of the Third All-Pakistan Political Science Conference, 1962*. Karachi: International Press.

Sharwânî, H. Kh. (1977). *Studies in Muslim Political Thought and Administration*. Philadelphia: Porcupine Press.

Shaybânî (1966). *Siyar*. Trans. M. Khaddûrî as *The Islamic Law of Nations*. Baltimore: Johns Hopkins University Press.

Shâfi'î (1961). *Al-Risâlah*. Trans. M. Khaddûrî as *Islamic Jurisprudence*. Baltimore: Johns Hopkins University Press.

Shehadî, F. (1964). *Ghazzâlî's Unknowable God*. Leiden: E.J. Brill.

Sidgwick, H. (1929). *The Elements of Politics*. London: Macmillan.

Silvert, K. H. (1963). *Expectant Peoples: Nationalism and Development*. New York: Random House.

Simon, M. (1973). *Jewish Sects at the Time of Jesus*. Philadelphia: Fortress Press

Skinner, Q. (1978). *The Foundations of Modern Political Thought*, 2 vols. Cambridge: Cambridge University Press.

Smith, N. K. (1947). *Hume's Dialogues Concerning Natural Religion*, 2d ed. London: Thomas Nelson and Sons.

Smith, W. R. (1903). *Kinship and Marriage in Early Arabia*. Ed. S. A. Cook. London.

Snyder, L. (1968). *The New Nationalism*. New York: Cornell University Press.

Spinoza, B. (1930) *Selections*. Ed. J. Wild. London: Charles Scribner's Sons.

———— (1965a) "Tractatus Theologico-Politicus." In *The Political Works of Spinoza:*, 48-244. Ed.and trans. A. G. Wernham. Oxford: Clarendon.

———— (1965b) "Tractatus Politicus." In *The Political Works of Spinoza:*, 256-447. Ed.and trans. A. G. Wernham. Oxford: Clarendon .

Stahlin, W. (1961). *Pluralismus, Toleranze, Christenheit*. Nurnberg.

Strauss, L. (1959). *What is Political Philosophy and Other Studies*. Illinois: The Free Press.

———— (1961).*The Political Philosophy of Hobbes: Its Basis and Its Genesis*, 3d ed. Trans. E. M.Sinclair. Chicago: University of Chicago Press.

Ṭabarî (1962,1965) *Tarikh al-Tabarî*, v.3-7, Beirut: Dâr Sawaydân.

Taftazânî, S. (1950). *Sharḥ al-'Aqâid al-Nasafî*. Trans. E. E. Elder as *A Commentary on the Creed of Islam*. New York: Columbia University Press.

al-Taḥâwî (1987). *Uṣûl al-'Aqîdat al-Islamiyyah*. Beirut: Muessasat al-Risâlah.

Tanner, F. (1973). *The Mystery Teachings in World Religions*. Wheaton: Theosophical Publishing House.

Tarn, W. (1974). *Hellenistic Civilization*, reprinted from 3d ed. in 1952. Revised by G. T. Griffith. London: Edward Arnold.

Tawney, R. H. (1931). *Equality*. London: Allen and Unwin.

_____ (1950). *Religion and the Rise of Capitalism*. New York: New American Library.

Taylor, A. E. (1965). "The Ethical Doctrine of Hobbes." In *Hobbes' Studies*, 35-56. Ed. K. Brown. Cambridge:

Taylor, H. O. (1949). *The Mediaeval Mind: A History of the Development of Thought and Emotion in the Middle Ages*, 2 vols. Cambridge: Harvard University Press

_____ (1958). *The Emergence of Christian Culture in the West: The Classical Heritage of the Middle Ages*. New York: Harper and Brothers.

Tellenbach, G. (1970). *Church, State and Christian Society at the Time of the Investiture Contest*. Trans. R. F. Bennett. New York: Harper Torchbooks.

Tillich, P. (1967). *Systematic Theology*. Chicago:University of Chicago Press.

al-Tirmidhî (1981).*Sunan al-Tirmidhî*, 5 vols. Istanbul: Çagri.

Toll, C. (1976). "Arabische Wissenschaft und Hellenistisches Erbe." In *Islam und Abendland: Geschichte und Gegenwart:*, 31-59. Ed. A. Mercier. Bern: Verlag Herbert Lang.

Toynbee, A. (1939). *A Study of History*, 12 vols. New York: New York University Press.

Tritton, A. S. (1947). *Muslim Theology*. London: Royal Asiatic Society.

_____ (1965). "Reason and Revelation." In *Arabic and Islamic Studies in Honor of H. A. R. Gibb*, 617-630. Ed. G. Makdisî. Leiden: E. J. Brill.

Troeltsch, E. (1972). *The Absoluteness of Christianity*. London: SCM Press.

Truman, D. (1951). *The Governmental Process: Political Interests and Public Opinion.* New York: Knopf.

Ţûsî, N. (1964). *Akhlâq-i Nâşirî.* Trans. G. M. Wickens. London: Allen and Unwin.

Ullman, W. (1961). *Principles of Government and Politics in the Middle Ages.* London.

Valiuddîn, M. (1963). "Mu'tazilism." In *A History of Muslim Philosophy* 1:199-220. Ed. M. M. Sharîf. Wiesbaden: Otto Harrasowitz.

_____ (1974). "The Problem of the One and the Many: The Şûfî Approach." In *Islam and the Modern Age* 7:11-23.

Van Steenberghen, F. (1974). "The Problem of the Existence of God in Saint Thomas' Commentary on the Metaphysics of Aristotle." *Review of Metaphysics* 27:554-68. Trans. J. Wippel from Van Steenberghen, "Le probleme de l'existence de Dieu dans le commentaire de saint Thomas sur la Pysique d'Aristotle," *Sapientia (La Plata)* 26 (1971):163-72.

Vehbî, M. (1966). *Khulâşah al-Bayân fî Tafsîr al-Qur'ân,* 15 vols. Istanbul: Üçdal.

Viorst, M. (1965). *The Great Documents of Western Civilisation.* Philadelphia: Chilton Books.

Voll, J. O. (1982). *Islam: Continuity and Change in the Modern World.* Boulder: Westview.

Wagner, H. R. (1969). "The Concept of Power and the Study of Politics." In *Political Power: A Reader in Theory and Research,* 3-13. Ed. R. Bell, D. Edwards, and H. Wagner. New York: The Free Press.

Waldman, M. R. (1968). "The Development of the Concept of Kufr in the Qur'ân." *Journal of the American Oriental Society* 88:442-55.

Walker, J. (1956). *A Catalogue of the Arab-Byzantine and Post-Reform Umaiyad Coins.* London.

Walker, P. (1939). *An Outline of Man's History.* London.

Walzer, R. (1957). "New Studies on al-Kindi." *Oriens* 10:203-32.

_____ (1962). *Greek into Arabic: Essays on Islamic Philosophy.* Oxford: Bruno Cassirer.

Warrander, H. (1951). *The Political Philosophy of Hobbes.* Oxford.

Watkins, J. W. N. (1965). *Hobbes' System of Ideas.* London: Hutchinson.

Watt, W. M. (1964). "Conditions of Membership of the Islamic Community." *Studia Islamica* 21:5-12.

_____ (1968). *Islamic Political Thought.* Edinburgh: Edinburgh University Press.

_____ (1970). *Islam and the Integration of Society.* London: Routledge and Kegan Paul.

_____ (1972). *Islamic Philosophy and Theology* . Edinburgh: Edinburgh University Press.

_____ (1979). "The Qur'ân and Belief in a 'High God'." *Der Islam* 56:205-11.

_____ .(1988). *Islamic Fundamentalism and Modernity.* London: Routledge.

Weber, M. (1947). *The Theory of Social and Economic Organization.* New York.

_____ (1948). "Politics as a Vocation." In *From Max Weber: Essays in Sociology.* Ed. H. H. Gerth and W. Mills. New York: Routledge and Kegan Paul.

Weiss, J. (1959). *Earliest Christianity,* vol. 1. New York: Harper.

Wensinck, A. J. (1932). *The Muslim Creed: Its Genesis and Historical Development.* Cambridge: Cambridge University Press.

Whitehead, A. N. (1982). *Concept of Nature,* reprinted from paperback ed. in 1964. Cambridge: Cambridge University Press.

Williams, J. A. (1971). *Themes of Islamic Civilization.* Los Angeles: University of California Press.

Williams, M. (1980). "Coherence, Justification and Truth." *Review of Metaphysics* 34:243-73.

Willoughby, W. W. (1928). *An Examination of the Nature of the State.* New York: Macmillan.

Wolfson, H. A. (1934). *The Philosophy of Spinoza,* 2 vols. Cambridge: Harvard University Press.

_____ (1956). *The Philosophy of the Church Fathers.* Cambridge: Harvard University Press.

Wood, H. (1892). *God's Image in Man: Some Intuitive Perception of Truth,* 12th ed. Boston: Peters and Son.

Yazir, H. (1971). *Hak Dini Kur'an Dili*, 9 vols. Istanbul: Eser.

Yildirim, S. (1987). *Kur'an'da Ulûhiyyet.* Istanbul: Kayihan.

Zarkashî (1986). *Ma'nâ Lâ ilâha illa Allâh.* Beirut: Dâr al-Bashâir al-Islamiyyah.

Zaydân, A. (1963). *Aḥkâm Dhimmiyyîn wa al-Mustaminîn fi Dâr al-Islam.* Baghdad.

_____ (1983). *Role of the State and Individual in Islam.* Delhi: Hindustan Publications.

Zijdervald, A. (1927). *The Abstract Society: A Cultural Analysis of Our Time.* London.

INDEX